AMERICAN HISTORY
AND AMERICAN HISTORIANS

AMERICAN HISTORY AND AMERICAN HISTORIANS

A Review of Recent Contributions
to the Interpretation of the History of
the United States

BY

H. HALE BELLOT

*Commonwealth Fund Professor af American History
in the University of London*

UNIVERSITY OF LONDON
THE ATHLONE PRESS
1952

Published by
THE ATHLONE PRESS
at the Senate House, London, W.C.1

Distributed by Constable & Co. Ltd.
12 Orange Street, London W.C.2

Printed in Great Britain at
THE THANET PRESS
Margate

PREFACE

THIS is a book about other men's books and the history that is related in them. It first took shape as a course of lectures on 'Recent advances in the interpretation of American history' delivered, on the Watson Chair Foundation of the Sulgrave Manor Board, in the University of Birmingham in 1938. Since then, it has been much worked upon, but the work has also suffered much interruption. Its purpose is to answer the question what American history, as we now know it, is about. That history has been written anew by the last two generations of American historians ; and most of the American history that was published before 1910 has been out-moded. My endeavour has been to give some account of the new work and to indicate the conclusions that it points to. I have thus had two objects in view. The first has been the delineation of the characteristic features of American historiography, in so far as it has been concerned with the history of the United States, in the half century between 1890 and 1940 ; the second, a review of the successive chapters of the history of the United States in the light of this historical performance. But while I have kept both objects in mind throughout, both have not throughout been handled in the same way. In the first chapter I have sought to give an account of a particular phase of American historiography and in the bibliographical notes that occur throughout the book I have detailed the contributions that the new historiography has made to the several aspects of the history of the United States as I come to treat of them. In so doing I have included poor books as well as good, both because I have wanted to give a view of the extent to which particular topics have been discussed, and because for want of better one must make use of what one has. In the rest of the book I have addressed myself to a study of the events themselves. To the English reader, a number of the persons, institutions and places referred to in my preliminary survey of American historiography may be unfamiliar; and the plethora of new names will doubtless by some be found irksome. Yet, while the chapters that follow will not, I trust, be unintelligible if the first is passed over, they will lose something of their force. For it is the burden of my argument that the work done between 1890 and 1940 has radically altered our outlook ; and the significance of it will not be fully appreciated without an understanding of its place in the history of American historiography.

In offering this account I am aware that I have omitted almost entirely any allusion to historical biography. I did not set out consciously to do so ; and I yield to no man in my enjoyment of biographical literature. Neither do I hold any doctrinal opinions about the relation of biography to history, or intend to enter the lists of controversy set by Collingwood's assertion that biography is not properly history at all. I have merely, in practice, found myself turning only late and rarely to the lives of American statesmen or of American leaders in other walks of life. They do not tell me what, as a rule, I want to know. They may illuminate ; but they are not themselves comprehensive enough to satisfy. And I have written about what I have myself found useful.

My principal subject is the work and influence of the Middle Western school. There is at this time going on in the United States a lively discussion upon the nature of the historian's art ; and there are those who hold that the rise of this school denotes something more than the direction of the attention of the historian to a number of historical events that had hitherto been overlooked. It stood as well, it is argued, for a radical change in the character of historical writing. ' Historians ', said Henry Adams, ' undertake to arrange sequences— called stories, or histories—assuming in silence a relation of cause and effect. These assumptions, hidden in the depths of dusty libraries, have been astounding, but commonly unconscious and childlike ; so much so, that if any captious

critic were to drag them to light, historians would probably
reply, with one voice, that they had never supposed themselves
required to know what they were talking about.'[1] With
Turner, it has been said, came the first clear break with
the pure inductive method that proceeded without hypotheses
to the tabulation of the facts.[2] It is certainly the case that the
simultaneity of the innumerable events that fell within the
scope of Turner's interest made the mere establishment of
their order in a chronological sequence fruitless ; and the
new history was driven inescapably by the nature of its materials
to take a changed view of its task. But this change is a change
not restricted to the writers of American history ; it raises
philosophical as well as historical questions ; and I have been
content to describe the event within a limited field of American
historiography, without attempting to draw out its philosophical implications.

I do not pretend that what I have written will be easily read.
The history of a modern society is not an easy subject. It
deals with the emergence of problems of great complexity ;
and it cannot be understood without at least a nodding
acquaintance with a variety of technical matters.

The greater part of chapter I was first published in the
Transactions of the Royal Historical Society, and I have to
thank the Council for permission to reproduce it here. I am
likewise indebted to the editor of *History* for permission to
incorporate in chapter II an 'Historical Revision' on the mainland colonies in the eighteenth century contributed to that
journal in 1933. The list of works cited was made for me by
Miss Mary D. Wainwright, and I am also indebted to her for
the preparation of the material from which the maps were
drawn. The draughtsman was Mr. G. R. Versey of the department of Geography. I have to thank my colleague Professor

---

[1] *The Education of Henry Adams. An Autobiography.* (Massachusetts Historical Society :
Boston, 1918), p. 382.
[2] Cf. C. J. H. Randall, jr., & G. Haines IV, ' Controlling assumptions in the
practice of American historians ' in *Theory and Practice in Historical Study : a Report
of the Committee on Historiography.* Bulletin 54. (Social Science Research Council :
New York, 1946.)

ACKNOWLEDGEMENTS

I HAVE to record my thanks to the following for permission to make quotations from works published by them:—to the American Historical Association for passages from *The Diary and Correspondence of Salmon P. Chase,* the *Correspondence of Robert M. T. Hunter,* and the *Correspondence of Robert Toombs, Alexander H. Stephens and Howell Cobb,* and from *The Whig Party in the South* by A. C. Cole; to the American Antiquarian Society for a passage from their *Proceedings*; to D. Appleton-Century-Crofts Inc. for a passage from *A Constitutional History of the United States* by A. C. McLaughlin; to the Carnegie Institution of Washington for quotations from reports on *Judicial Cases concerning American Slavery and the Negro* edited by Helen T. Catterall; to the Columbia University Press for passages from *Reminiscences of an American Scholar* by J. W. Burgess; to the Connecticut Academy of Arts and Sciences for a quotation used by A. L. Bishop in his monograph on *The State Works of Pennsylvania*; to Constable & Co. for passages from *Charles W. Eliot, President of Harvard University* by H. James; to Dodd, Mead & Co., Inc., for a passage from *The Life of Daniel Coit Gilman* by F. Franklin; to Professor D. L. Dumond for passages from his book on *The Secession Movement, 1860–1861*; to Houghton Mifflin Co. for a passage from *Expansion and Conflict* by W. E. Dodd; to the Johns Hopkins University Press for passages from *Historical Scholarship in the United States, 1876–1901,* edited by W. S. Holt, and from O. Crenshaw, *The Slave States in the Presidential Election of 1860*; to the Macmillan Company for passages from *The Modern Corporation and Private Property* by A. A. Berle, jr., and G. C. Means; to the University of Michigan for a passage from the *History of the University of Michigan* by B. A. Hinsdale; to the Ohio State University Press for passages from *Western Influences on Political Parties to 1825* by H. C. Hockett; to Charles

Scribner's Sons for passages from Henry Adams' *History of the United States*; to the University of Wisconsin Press for passages from *The Early Writings of Frederick Jackson Turner*; to the State Historical Society for passages from the *Wisconsin Magazine of History*; and to the Yale University Press for a number of passages from *The Records of the Federal Convention* edited by Max Farrand.

H.H.B.

CONTENTS

MAPS

at the end

I

Some Aspects of the Recent History of American Historiography

Dᴜʀɪɴɢ the last seventy-five years, three influences have shaped American historiography. They have been the liberalization of the academic curriculum, the establishment of professional standards, and the adoption of a distinctively American in place of what had been an essentially European point of view. The process of liberalization and the establishment of professional standards affected, of course, the whole range of American historiography. The process of Americanization affected primarily the writing of the history of the mainland colonies and of the United States.

Despite the liberal example of the University of Virginia, the traditional method of education at American colleges was by a single required course in classics and mathematics, consisting in the main of recitation from textbooks. If he got beyond this, the student still took, not geology, but Hitchcock's *Geology*, not chemistry, but Silliman's *Chemistry*.[1] When Andrew Dixon White was at Yale in the early fifties, the study of history meant recitations from Putz's *Ancient History* and the Rev. John Lord's *Modern History of Europe*.[2] Sparks had delivered historical lectures which were the fruit of original research at Harvard between 1839 and 1849;[3] and Francis Lieber lectured upon

[1]W. P. Rogers, *Andrew D. White and the Modern University* (Ithaca, 1942), p. 39; *cf.* H. B. Adams, *The Study of History in American Colleges and Universities. Bureau of Education. Circular of Information No. 2, 1887* (Washington, 1887), p. 21; *The Autobiography of Andrew Dixon White* (2 vv., New York, 1905), i, 26–9, 289.
[2]White, *op. cit.*, i, 28.
[3]S. E. Morison (ed.), *The Development of Harvard University ... 1869–1909* (Cambridge, Mass., 1930), pp. 152–3.

political philosophy at South Carolina College, 1835–56, and at Columbia College from 1857 to 1876,[1] although the report which Burgess gives of his work at Columbia is that as a teacher he was a failure. But these were exceptions, and lectures, when they were delivered at all, consisted as a rule in little more than instruction in the prescribed text.[2] Academic education was essentially drill in the repetition of accepted truth. 'A product of the old order', writes the biographer of C. W. Eliot, 'once exclaimed to William James: "I can't understand your philosophy. When I studied philosophy, I could understand it. We used to commit it to memory." '[3]

The lead in the substitution of something richer and more varied for this anaemic curriculum was taken, in the third quarter of the century, by five men—H. P. Tappan and J. B. Angell, presidents of the University of Michigan from 1852 to 1863 and 1871 to 1909; Charles William Eliot, president of Harvard from 1869 to 1909; Andrew Dixon White, professor of history in the University of Michigan, 1857–68, and first president of Cornell, 1867–85; and Daniel Coit Gilman, first president of Johns Hopkins University, 1875–1901.

Influenced by what he knew of the German universities, Tappan had secured at the University of Michigan the establishment of an entirely unsectarian curriculum, and sought to provide a variety of courses and consequently, and of necessity, an option between them. 'It is proposed', ran the *Catalogue* during his administration, ' . . . at as early a date as practicable, to open courses of lectures for those who have graduated at this or other institutions. . . . These lectures, in accordance with the educational systems of Germany and France, will form the proper development of the University, in distinction from the College or Gymnasium now in operation.'[4] His endeavours and the work of J. B. Angell made, in the words of Andrew D. White, 'the real beginning of a university in the United States,

---

[1]Adams, *op. cit.*, pp. 66–7, 72; M. Curti, *Growth of American Thought* (1943), pp. 482–3.   [2]Adams, *op. cit.*, p. 21; *cf.* White, *op. cit.*, i, 255–6.
[3]H. James, *Charles W. Eliot, President of Harvard University, 1869–1909* (2 vv., 1930), i, 209.
[4]B. A. Hinsdale, *History of the University of Michigan* (Ann Arbor, 1906), p. 43b.

in the modern sense'.[1] Similarly impressed with the quantity and variety of instruction offered in the universities of continental Europe, C. W. Eliot, who became president of Harvard in 1869, set himself likewise to 'make the opportunities offered to students in all the departments richer and freer'.[2] One of the prime functions of the school, he thought, was to discover innate aptitude. It was the duty of the University to see that 'the natural bent and peculiar quality of every boy's mind should be sacredly regarded in his education; the division of mental labour', he went on, 'which is essential in civilized communities in order that knowledge may grow and society improve, demands this regard to the peculiar constitution of each mind, as much as does the happiness of the individual most nearly concerned.'[3] 'For the individual', he said in his inaugural address, 'concentration, and the highest development of his own peculiar faculty, is the only prudence. But for the State, it is variety, not uniformity, of intellectual product, which is needed.'[4] The instrument was multiplicity of courses and the elective system. Required courses were not at first altogether abandoned even for senior students, and their juniors were still more slowly relieved from them.[5] But enough freedom was secured to give scope to the teaching of men of original mind and to turn undergraduates from schoolboys reciting from textbooks into students such as went to lectures in a Continental university.[6] To the performance of this task of liberalization, an outstanding contribution was made by the work of Andrew Dixon White in Michigan and up-state New York— that 'extraordinary man', in the words of C. L. Becker, 'who probably had a greater influence on the history of higher

[1]*The Autobiography of Andrew Dixon White* (2 vv., New York, 1905), i, 292, *cf.* 272, 275–6; *The Reminiscences of James Burrill Angell* (1912), ch. x; H. M. Jones, *The Life of Moses Coit Tyler* (Ann Arbor, 1933), pp. 32, 161–2; H. B. Adams, *The Study of History in American Colleges and Universities. Bureau of Education. Circular of Information No. 2, 1887* (Washington, 1887), pp. 90–1; C. M. Perry, *Henry Philip Tappan* (Ann Arbor, 1933), ch. x.
[2]H. James, *Charles W. Eliot, President of Harvard, 1869–1909* (2 vv., 1930), i, 247, *cf.* 137–8.   [3]*Ibid.*, i, 169.
[4]S. E. Morison (ed.), *The Development of Harvard University . . . 1869–1909* (Cambridge, Mass., 1930), p. lxv.   [5]James, *op. cit.*, i, 259–60.
[6]*Ibid.*, i, 259, ii, 64–5, *cf.* 170–1; Morison, *op. cit.*, p. lxxii.

education in the United States in the nineteenth century than anyone else'.[1] A man of private means, White had lived in France, attending lectures at the Sorbonne and the Collège de France, and, devoting himself in particular to the study of the Revolution and Napoleon, had talked at the Invalides with veterans of Austerlitz and the Peninsular War. After a brief interlude as a diplomatic attaché in St. Petersburg, he matriculated at the University of Berlin, and there heard 'the lectures of Lepsius, on Egyptology; August Boeckh, on the History of Greece; Friedrich von Raumer, on the History of Italy; Hirsch, on Modern History in general; and Carl Ritter, on Physical Geography'; and he attended, without much understanding, the seminar of Ranke.[2] As professor of history at the University of Michigan from 1857 to 1868, reading the newly-appearing work of Buckle, Lecky, Draper, Darwin and Herbert Spencer, he lectured over the whole range of medieval and modern history. Using as his textbook for the 'junior' year Guizot's *History of Civilization in Europe*, he exacted from students of all grades wide collateral reading, and gave, as his highest duty, to the 'seniors' and to students from the law school, courses of lectures on such topics as 'German history from the revival of learning and the reformation to modern times' or 'the French Revolution',[3] enriching his teaching by the citation of original authorities and often by the exhibition of pieces from his own collection of original materials, particularly for the history of Revolutionary and Napoleonic France.[4] Appointed in 1867 as first president of Cornell University, though not relinquishing his lectures at Ann Arbor until 1868, White became the architect of the first modern American university that was both independent and untrammelled by tradition. The characteristic features of the institution which he designed were to be freedom from sectarian control and complete liberty of investigation; the development of scientific

[1]C. L. Becker, *Cornell University: Founders and Founding* (Ithaca, 1943), p. 213.
[2]White, *op. cit.*, i, 34–9.
[3]*Ibid.*, i, 42, 83–4, 257, 259–64; ii, 489–92, 506.
[4]Adams, *op. cit.*, pp. 98–100; *cf.* C. H. Andrews, 'These forty years', *Am. Hist. Rev.*, xxx (1925), 231–2.

and technical studies; 'the development, especially, of a well planned course in History and Political and Social Science adapted to the practical needs of men worthily ambitious in public affairs'; the more thorough presentation of the leading modern literatures; and the organization of these studies in equal and parallel courses of grouped subjects.[1] The department of history and political science was to be one 'where there should be something more than a mere glance over one or two superseded textbooks, where there should be large and hearty study and comparison of the views and methods of Guizot and Mill and Lieber and Woolsey and Bastiat and Carey and Maine and others'.[2] Lectures were generally used, and wide reading was required.[3] The primacy of classics and mathematics was thus denied, and free investigation spelt the overthrow of that school whose symbol was the textbook and whose chief distinction it was, in the words of Becker, 'to know and to enforce all of the right answers rather than to know or to ask any of the right questions'.[4]

To the work of Eliot at Harvard and White at Cornell, there was added in 1875 that of D. C. Gilman at Johns Hopkins. Gilman was at Yale with White, went to Europe with him in 1853 and to St. Petersburg as a fellow attaché in 1854, and spent the winter of 1854–5 in Berlin, taking during his travels a particular interest in technical and scientific institutions.[5] He was appointed to the presidency of Johns Hopkins in 1875 upon the independent but unanimous advice of Angell, Eliot and White.[6] The new university was designed as a postgraduate institution. That meant, at first, a university as distinct from a college; and in the event undergraduate work was not wholly omitted, and what was called graduate work did not involve original research. But the elective system was adopted in the shape of a choice between groups of related 'major' and 'minor' subjects;[7] and the distinctive principle of

[1]White, op. cit., i, 288, 300, 318, 341–2, 362–76; W. P. Rogers, Andrew D. White and the Modern University (Ithaca, 1942), pp. 96–8, 180.
[2]Adams, op. cit., p. 133. [3]Ibid., pp. 134–5. [4]Becker, op. cit., p. 17.
[5]F. Franklin, The Life of Daniel Coit Gilman (New York, 1910), pp. 15–35, 41.
[6]Ibid., pp. 193, 194–5, 325. [7]Ibid., pp. 188, 193, 195, 216, 225–7, 242.

the university from the start was the expectation of original investigation by the professoriate. 'The keynote of the German system,' writes Gilman's biographer, 'was also the keynote of Mr. Gilman's conception of the university that was to be; for he had in view the appointment of professors who had shown ability as investigators, whose duties as teachers would not be so burdensome as to interfere with the prosecution of their researches, whose students should be so advanced as to stimulate them to their best work, and the fruit of whose labors in the advancement of science and learning should be continually manifest in the shape of published results.'[1]

By the work of these men there was created in the United States the university in the modern sense, an institution where the single required course gave place to the pursuit of all branches of knowledge, and where free investigation was the aim. While, however, Tappan was in his day a philosopher of some repute, Angell, Eliot, White and Gilman were not themselves original investigators or scholars in any strict sense of that word. They were administrators of wide culture and liberal views, with a strong sense of social responsibility; and something happened to American historiography for which their work was indeed a preparation, but for which it was not by itself sufficient to account.

The porter of one of the Cambridge colleges is said to have remarked: 'The men who used to go in and out of this gate were gentlemen: now they are scholars.' By somewhere about the year 1910, something of that sort had happened to the writing of history in America. The editor of the correspondence of Herbert B. Adams has observed

in . . . Justin Winsor's *Narrative and Critical History of America* [8 vv., 1884–9], two of the thirty-four authors were professors of history and only eight others were university professors of other subjects. Of the entire number only one had received graduate training in history. In the American Nation Series, which appeared between 1904 and 1907, twenty-one of the

[1]Franklin, *op. cit.*, p. 196.

twenty-four authors were university professors, and all but two of them had done graduate work in history.[1]

It can indeed be said with some truth that very little American history that was written before 1900 is current to-day, though that little may be very important; and that after 1910 men of the elder school began to be outmoded, and if they did not altogether cease to produce, lost their importance. The characteristic works of the earlier period were the big narrative histories—James Schouler's five-volume *History of the United States under the Constitution* (1880–91), followed by volumes vi and vii (1899, 1913); Fiske's twelve volumes from *The Critical Period of American History* (1888) to *New France and New England* (1902); James Ford Rhodes' seven volumes on the *History of the United States from the Compromise of 1850* (1893–1906); and McMaster's eight-volume *History of the People of the United States from the Revolution to the Civil War* (1883–1913). Their counterpart in England was J. A. Doyle's five volumes on *The English in America* (1882–1907). All of these were begun between 1880 and 1894; and all were finished by 1913, save for supplementary and inferior volumes produced as after-thoughts.[2] None of the authors was in the full sense a trained historian. Schouler was a lawyer; Fiske, part philosopher, part sociologist, of great talent but of too vagrant an ambition to master anything, was only part historian and was disappointed of his hope of a chair of history at Harvard; Rhodes was an ironmaster; and J. B. McMaster, though for most of his career a professor of history in the University of Pennsylvania, a civil engineer by training, in so far as he can be said to have had any training at all, and, at the time of the publication of his first volume, a teacher of mathematics at Princeton. Since 1910, this kind of writing has almost ceased. Edward Channing's seven-volume *History of the United States* (1905–31) won only a contemporary reputation

[1] W. S. Holt (ed.), *Historical Scholarship in the United States, 1876–1901, as revealed in the Correspondence of Herbert B. Adams* (Baltimore, 1938), p. 9.
[2] J. Schouler, *History of the Reconstruction Period, 1865–1877* (New York, 1913); J. F. Rhodes, *History of the United States from Hayes to McKinley, 1877–1896* (New York, 1919), and *The McKinley and Roosevelt Administrations, 1897–1909* (New York, 1922); J. B. McMaster, *A History of the People of the United States during Lincoln's Administration* (1927).

which is not wearing well; and Channing was, indeed, a trained historian. Woodrow Wilson's five-volume *History of the American People* (1902) was a (very successful) work of popularization. To-day, only Mr. Oberholtzer has been so bold as to attempt anything of the kind in his five-volume *History of the United States since the Civil War* (1917–37). But this change is not to be attributed to White, and Eliot, and Gilman. It would, indeed, be truer to say that the great amateurs were their fellows and drew their strength from the same sources. White's own principal historical work was *A History of the Warfare of Science and Theology in Christendom* (1896). His aim as an educator was to produce good citizens and competent public servants, rather than scholarship. 'We ought to teach history', he said in 1878, 'in such a way that it can be applied to the immediate needs of our time. The period has hardly arrived for elegant and learned investigation on points of mere scholarly interest.'[1] It is to others, therefore, that there belongs the credit for the establishment of new professional standards, although their work was only made possible by what these notable university presidents had done.

As Tappan and Angell, Eliot, White and Gilman had been the leaders in the liberalization of the academic curriculum, C. K. Adams at Michigan, Moses Coit Tyler at Cornell, Henry Adams at Harvard, J. W. Burgess at Columbia, and Herbert B. Adams at Johns Hopkins were the leaders in the introduction of postgraduate training and the establishment of professional standards in American historiography. These men began their distinctive work between 1870 and 1882. When in 1871 J. W. Burgess looked for advanced courses in history, public law or political science, he could find none in the United States.[2] Ten years later, the new movement was well under way, and there were recognizable examples in America of what Burgess regarded as the characteristic features of the German system; 'the combination of studies at the election of the student, the

---

[1] Rogers, *op. cit.*, pp. 131–2; *cf.* pp. 158–60, 180.
[2] J. W. Burgess, *Reminiscences of an American Scholar. The Beginnings of Columbia University* (New York, 1934), p. 85.

giving of instruction by original lecture, and the exercise of the student in the seminarium'.[1] American academic terminology is, indeed, sometimes misleading; and it is necessary to be careful not to ante-date the appearance of the postgraduate seminar. The so-called 'graduate schools' were created by combining into a single course the last year or the last two years of undergraduate work for the bachelorship in arts with two further years of graduate work, and awarding to the successful a bachelorship or doctorate of philosophy.[2] In this scheme, the seminar began, in the senior year of the undergraduate course or in the graduate years only, as what we should now call an essay class, or at most as lectures upon the sources to classes of what we should describe as 'honours students'. Only in the course of time did this seminar grow into a research seminar in the strict sense.[3] Yet if original investigation and training in the methods of research were not in practice the first or the most obvious products of the newly-introduced education, they were nevertheless inherent in the ideals which it set before itself. Once the textbook had been dethroned and established truth exposed to examination, there was scope for original investigation; and that was the first and indispensable step in the advance.

The fugleman in the introduction of scientific historical training was C. K. Adams. Adams succeeded White as professor of history in the University of Michigan in 1868. A pupil of White's, he was a better scholar than his master; and his aims were more scientific. The year and a half in Germany and France which followed his promotion to the full professorship and which were spent in the study of history at Leipzig, Munich, Heidelberg, Berlin and Paris, gave him an insight into German methods; and he was less discursive than White and more interested in historical technique. On his return, he put on a bibliographical course on historians and historical books,[4] and he came back bent upon the introduction of the seminar

[1]Burgess, *op. cit.*, p. 366.   [2]Adams, *op. cit.*, pp. 76–7, 111–14.
[3]Adams, *op. cit.*, pp. 105–6, 110–11, 117 (Michigan); 156–7, 158–9 (Cornell); 171–4 (Johns Hopkins).   [4]Adams, *op. cit.*, p. 102.

method into the work at Michigan. The innovation first appeared in the report to the board for the year 1871-2. To begin with, what was done amounted to no more than the preparation of undergraduate theses and their discussion in class. But by 1882, and after the establishment of a School of Political Science of which Adams was the principal begetter,[1] the seminar had begun to grow into something like the place for graduate work which was its goal;[2] and in 1883 its facilities were substantially improved by the opening of a new library building and the foundation of a seminar library.[3] Two of the papers prepared in the seminar in 1882-3 were printed in the first volume of *Papers* issued by the American Historical Association in 1886.[4] But Adams left Michigan in 1885, to succeed White in the presidency of Cornell.

At Cornell, White had combined with the presidency of the University the deanship of the School of History and Political Science and a professorship of History; and it was natural, in these circumstances, that he himself should not have carried historical studies at Cornell to any stage more advanced than that to which he had carried them at Michigan.[5] But the appointment in 1881 of Moses Coit Tyler led to something more. Not only was it, save for Sparks' incumbency at Harvard between 1839 and 1849, the first appointment in the United States to what was in effect a chair of American History,[6] but it was also the appointment of a man who was himself an original investigator. Tyler was, no more than White, a trained

---

[1]C. F. Smith, *Charles Kendall Adams* (Madison, 1924), pp. 17-18; Adams, *op. cit.*, pp. 114-18.

[2]Smith, *op. cit.*, pp. 14-17; Adams, *op. cit.*, pp. 104-11; H. B. Adams, *Seminary Libraries and University Extension.* Johns Hopkins Univ. Studies, v, no. 11 (Baltimore, 1887), pp. 12-13; Holt, *op. cit.*, pp. 79-80; H. B. Adams, 'Methods of work in historical seminaries', *Am. Hist. Rev.*, x (1905), 521 n.; H. B. Adams, *Methods of Historical Study.* Johns Hopkins Univ. Studies, ii, nos. 1-2 (Baltimore, 1884), pp. 94-7.

[3]H. B. Adams, *The Study of History in American Colleges and Universities . . .* (Washington, 1887), pp. 121-3; Smith, *op. cit.*, p. 16; H. B. Adams, *Seminary Libraries . . .* (Baltimore, 1887), p. 13.

[4]G. W. Knight, 'History and management of federal land grants for education in the Northwest Territory'; Lucy M. Salmon, 'History of the appointing power of the President'.

[5]White, *op. cit.*, i, 381; Rogers, *op. cit.*, pp. 127-8, 133-40.

[6]Adams, *The Study of History . . .*, pp. 153-4; White, *op. cit.*, i, 383.

historian. But, holding since 1867 a chair of English Literature at the University of Michigan, where as a teacher he had become deeply imbued with the liberal doctrines of Angell and White,[1] he had published in 1878 his two-volume *History of American Literature, 1607–1765* and was to produce in 1897, in his two-volume *Literary History of the American Revolution*, one of the notable books published before 1900 which is still current and of which a photographic re-print has recently been issued.[2] Already stimulated by C. K. Adams to start a seminar in English Literature at Michigan,[3] Tyler used the same method in history at Cornell; and although his seminar appears not to have amounted in the main to what we should now ordinarily describe as such,[4] it had its own seminar library,[5] and when Adams came to Cornell in succession to White in 1885 and assumed, like his predecessor, a professorship of History, its activities were reinforced, and work of fully graduate standard was done, including the completion of one of the papers begun at Ann Arbor and destined to be published in the first volume of the *Papers* of the Association.[6]

Meanwhile, the first genuine postgraduate work had been done at Harvard under Henry Adams. Appointed assistant professor of History in 1870, Adams was the instrument which Eliot chose for the liberalization of historical studies at Harvard. A man of genius, but without formal training in historical research, while reforming the methods of teaching by requiring collateral reading and substituting discussion for recitations, he had no patience for the task of teaching undergraduates, whether by the old methods or the new,[7] and did his best work with a group of upper classmen and graduates whom he

---

[1]H. M. Jones, *The Life of Moses Coit Tyler* (Ann Arbor, 1933), pp. 160–8.
[2]M. C. Tyler, *The Literary History of the American Revolution, 1763–1783*, 2 vv. [Facsimile reprint] (Barnes & Noble: New York, 1941).
[3]Jones, *op. cit.*, p. 327, n. 74.   [4]Adams, *op. cit.*, pp. 156–7, 158–9.
[5]Adams, *op. cit.*, p. 162; *Seminary Libraries* . . . , pp 13–14.
[6]Lucy M. Salmon, *op. cit.*
[7]Morison (ed.), *The Development* . . . , pp. 154–5; H. B. Adams, *Seminary Libraries* . . . , pp. 14–15; *The Study of History* . . . , p. 358; J. T. Adams, *Henry Adams* (1933), chs. vii, viii; W. C. Ford (ed.), *Letters of Henry Adams, 1858–91* (1930), ch. vi; H. S. Commager, 'Henry Adams', in W. T. Hutchinson (ed.), *The Marcus W. Jernegan Essays in American Historiography* (Chicago, 1937).

gathered round him in 1874–6 for individual original work, among whom were numbered H. C. Lodge, H. O. Taylor and Edward Channing, and from whom came the first Harvard Ph.Ds. in History.[1] Yet, although Adams recognized his experiment in graduate work as a pedagogical success, he could find no satisfaction even here, and he resigned in 1877, writing 'Failure' at the head of the chapter in his autobiography in which the experience is related.[2] After this, although E. Emerton returned to Harvard from the seminars of Leipzig in 1876, and was appointed to a chair of Ecclesiastical History in 1882, A. B. Hart, who had been trained under von Holst in Freiburg, entered the department in 1883,[3] and Justin Winsor,[4] appointed librarian in 1877, placed at the service of these men a library adapted to the needs of scientific study and teaching; and although by 1886 the variety of opportunity offered for the study of history at Harvard rivalled that of a German university,[5] yet the graduate school at Harvard, by Eliot's own confession, did not thrive until it had been stimulated by the example of Johns Hopkins.[6]

Thus it was not until 1876 that what was to prove to be the enduring provision of postgraduate training in the methods of historical research was begun. This was the date of the appointments of J. W. Burgess to the professorship of History, Political Science and International Law at what was then Columbia College, and of Herbert B. Adams as a fellow of Johns Hopkins University, which opened its doors in that year.[7]

[1] G. B. Adams, 'Methods of work in historical seminars', *Am. Hist. Rev.*, x (1905), 521 n.; H. B. Adams, *Methods of Historical Study* . . . , pp. 87–8; J. L. Laughlin, 'Some recollections of Henry Adams', *Scribner's Magazine*, lxix (1921), 579–80.

[2] *The Education of Henry Adams. An Autobiography* (Massachusetts Hist. Soc., 1918), ch. xx.

[3] Morison, *op. cit.*, pp. 157, 158–9, and 'Albert Bushnell Hart, 1889–1939', *Mass. Hist. Soc. Proc.*, lxvi (1942), 434–8; *Am. Hist. Rev.*, xlix (1944), 192–4; W. C. Hill, 'Memoir of Albert Bushnell Hart', *New England Hist. & Gen. Reg.*, xcviii (1944), 2–5.

[4] E. Channing, 'Justin Winsor', *Am. Hist. Rev.*, iii (1898), 197–202.

[5] H. B. Adams, *The Study of History in American Colleges and Universities* . . . (Washington, 1887), pp. 41, 43–4; *Seminary Libraries* . . . pp. 14–16.

[6] F. Franklin, *The Life of Daniel Coit Gilman* (New York, 1910), p. 389, *cf*. Morison, *op. cit.*, pp. 162–3, 456; H. James, *Charles W. Eliot* . . . (1930), ii, 3–28.

[7] *Cf*. C. M. Andrews, 'These forty years', *Am. Hist. Rev.* xxx (1925), 234–5.

At Columbia, the order of events was different from that at Michigan, Cornell, or Harvard. The development of advanced studies preceded, instead of following, the liberalization of the undergraduate curriculum.

I found the institution to consist [Burgess wrote] of a small old-fashioned college, or rather school, for teaching Latin, Greek, and mathematics, and a little metaphysics, and a very little natural science, and called the School of Arts; a School of Mines for teaching a little more natural science and educating mining and civil engineers; and a School of Law of a quasi-proprietary nature, loosely connected with the college by a contract between the trustees of the college and Professor Theodore W. Dwight —the main provision of which regulated a division of the sum total of the fees between the college treasury and Professor Dwight and left the educational management and control of the school to the professor.[1]

Burgess came to this institution after a brief experience at Amherst, where the creation of a graduate school had been blocked by the obscurantism of the Faculty. A graduate of Amherst himself, he had been trained at Göttingen, Leipzig and Berlin, where he had studied under Waitz, Mommsen, Droysen, and Gneist, as well as some of the leading philosophers, jurists, and economists.[2] He was brought to Columbia by the foresight of the Trustees, and when he found insufficient scope in the School of Arts and that of Law as then constituted, and saw no prospect of their early reform, he was successful in 1880 in persuading the Trustees to found a Faculty and School of Political Science, the character of which he was himself to shape. Visiting Paris in that year to survey the organization of the newly-founded *École libre des sciences politiques*, he devised a programme of studies in history, economics, public law and political philosophy extending over three years and leading, upon the presentation of a thesis, to the degree of Ph.D.[3]

The first principle of the system of education which the Faculty of Political Science followed in all its work [he records] was free

[1]J. W. Burgess, *Reminiscences of an American Scholar* . . . (New York, 1934), p. 161; *cf.* A. Nevins, *Hamilton Fish* . . . (New York, 1936), pp. 96–9.
[2]Burgess, *op. cit.*, pp. 99, 102–4, 107–9, 121–31.
[3]Burgess, *op. cit.*, pp. 187–92, Adams, *The Study of History* . . ., pp. 75–82; *A History of Columbia University, 1754–1904* (New York, 1904), pp. 223–9.

and untrammelled individual research and complete freedom of instruction in imparting the results of such research. Their attitude towards what was considered established truth was one of question, if not of distrust, as being something produced by the thought of man and, therefore, at best only an approximation to truth, and needing continuous re-examination and readjustment under purer light and changing conditions. The progressive development of truth, instead of the monotonous maintenance of so-called established truth, was our principle.[1]

The method was that in which Burgess had been trained, and included a bibliographical seminar on the German model[2] and the conduct of research seminars by the professors;[3] and a special room was set aside in the library for a library of history and political science.[4] Starting in this spirit with four colleagues in 1880, Burgess built within a decade a truly scientific and creative school with the characteristic features of the German system.[5] The library resources which were essential to its work were gathered together by Melvil Dewey, who became librarian at Columbia in 1882.[6] The outward marks of its progress were the foundation of the Academy of Political Science in 1882;[7] the printing of theses, begun in 1884[8] and growing into the 'Columbia University Studies', the first of which was published in 1891; and the foundation of the *Political Science Quarterly* in 1886. The school, essentially a law school in the eighties, was in full flower in the nineties, and its graduates, as Burgess recalled with just pride, were being summoned to fill the chairs of history, economics, sociology, constitutional, administrative, and international law, political science and philosophy throughout the land.[9] Under the stimulus of its example, Columbia College grew between 1888 and 1891 into a real university.[10]

[1]Burgess, *op. cit.*, p. 203.   [2]Adams, *op. cit.*, pp. 82–3.   [3]Burgess, *op. cit.*, p. 198.
[4]Adams, *op. cit.*, pp. 82–4; *Seminary Libraries* . . . , pp. 17–18.
[5]Burgess, *op. cit.*, p. 366; Adams, *The Study of History* . . . , pp. 82–3; *A History of Columbia University, 1754–1904* (New York, 1904), pp. 267–78.
[6]Burgess, *op. cit.*, pp. 217–18.
[7]Adams, *op. cit.*, pp. 85–6; Burgess, *op. cit.*, p. 201.   [8]Adams, *op. cit.*, pp. 84–5.
[9]Burgess, *op. cit.*, p. 244; *cf. A Bibliography of the Faculty of Political Science of Columbia University, 1880–1930* (New York, 1931).
[10]Burgess, *op. cit.*, pp. 231–9; *A History of Columbia University, 1754–1904* (New York, 1904), pp. 230–8.

Herbert B. Adams had, like Burgess, been fully trained in the German universities; and these two men were the first really competently equipped historical scholars to reach responsible positions in the American academic world. Appointed at the age of twenty-six, and on the recommendation of Bluntschli, to a fellowship without teaching responsibilities at Johns Hopkins in 1876, Adams gave voluntary classes from the start, was promoted to the rank of associate in 1878 and taught his first regular classes in 1878–9, was placed in charge of the Historical Seminary in 1881, became an associate professor and master of his own department in 1883, and was promoted to full professor in 1891, remaining at Johns Hopkins until shortly before his death in 1901. When the University opened in 1876, an Historical Seminary had been established under the direction of Austin Scott, who came once a week from Washington, where he was employed as an assistant to Bancroft.[1] This seminar Adams made the principal instrument of his endeavours, and its products began to appear in 1882 in the shape of the 'Johns Hopkins University Studies'. Adams' own direct contributions to scholarship ceased in 1883, and he devoted himself thenceforth to the training of his students, to the promotion of higher education in the United States at large, and in particular to measures designed to raise the level of historical scholarship.[2] What these multifarious activities meant to American historians is vividly illustrated by his published correspondence.[3]

Adams had been in Germany from 1874 to 1876. He went first to Heidelberg, where he heard Ihne on Roman history, Kuno Fischer on German literature and philosophy, and Treitschke on politics. The winter semester of 1874–5 was spent in Berlin, where he heard E. Curtius on Greek art and archaeology, Grimm on early Christian and Italian art, Lepsius

---

[1] W. S. Holt (ed.), *Historical Scholarship in the United States, 1876–1901* . . . . . (Baltimore, 1938), pp. 13–14; *Herbert B. Adams. Tributes of Friends* (Baltimore, 1902), pp. 13–17, 32–3.
[2] J. A. Woodburn, 'Promotion of historical study in America following the Civil War', *Illinois Hist. Soc. Journal*, xv (1923), 452–3.
[3] Holt, *op. cit.*

on Egyptology, Zeller on Greek philosophy, Droysen on the
French Revolution, and Treitschke again, who had moved to
Berlin in that year. He returned to Heidelberg in 1875, and
worked under Bluntschli, taking his Ph.D. in the Faculty of
Political Science, with Bluntschli and Knies as his examiners.
During the last year at Heidelberg, he attended the historical
seminar of Erdmannsdörffer.[1] He found the seminar which
was conducted by Scott at Johns Hopkins little more than a
class, its employment consisting in the preparation of weekly
reports on topics arising out of Scott's work for Bancroft and
assigned for investigation; and it was conducted with the aid
of a few original sources gathered together on a table in the
library of the Maryland Historical Society.[2] In 1881, Adams
transformed this into a full graduate seminar,[3] the numbers,
which in Scott's seminar had begun at 6 or 8, rising by 1887
to 25.[4] It met at first in a lecture room at the Peabody Institute
containing a substantial library, but in 1883 was provided
with its own seminary library in the University. To the furnishing and arrangement of this, and of similar rooms in other
universities, Adams attached the greatest importance. It was an
Institute of Historical Research in little,[5] and its creation was
a step in advance of anything that Henry Adams had done
at Harvard or Burgess had yet done at Columbia. The Johns
Hopkins seminar was the first fully organized and fully equipped
historical seminar in the United States.

In each centre of activity—Michigan, Cornell, Harvard,
Columbia, Johns Hopkins—the aim, it will be seen, and in a
large measure the means adopted to achieve it, were similar—
enquiry instead of authority, lectures and wide reading in place
of recitations from a textbook, some acquaintance with the
sources of history for all and genuine research for a few; ample
libraries, reserved collections, open access, and the seminar
room; and the publication of results in journals and mono-

---

[1]*Herbert B. Adams. Tributes of Friends . . .*, pp. 12–13.
[2]Adams, *op. cit.*, pp. 171–3.
[3]*Cf.* R. S. Baker, *Woodrow Wilson. Life and Letters* (8 vv., 1927–39), i, 176–9.
[4]Adams, *op. cit.*, pp. 172, 194, 238–9.
[5]*Ibid.*, pp. 177–93.

graphic series. The influence of all this was rapid and far-reaching; and the part played in it by Johns Hopkins was astonishing. It was indeed a remarkable institution that, starting with 89 students in 1876,[1] could produce in History, James Franklin Jameson (1882), Woodrow Wilson (1886), Charles M. Andrews (1889) and C. H. Haskins and F. J. Turner (1890), besides a number more of historians of only lesser rank,[2] while from other departments in the faculty came such men as Josiah Royce (1878), Thorstein B. Veblen (1881–2), John Dewey (1889), and J. H. Hollander (1894). There were very few historical pies baked in the United States between 1876 and 1901 in which Herbert B. Adams did not have a finger; and in the baking of most of them his part was a large one. Johns Hopkins men carried the ideas of the school all over the States, and Adams kept in close touch with them. He was one of the founders of the American Historical Association in 1884,[3] and its first secretary. The origins of the *American Historical Review* (1895) are to be sought at Harvard and Cornell,[4] but Adams had a large share in its conduct. The 'Johns Hopkins University Studies' were a model for similar series, and carried the influence of Johns Hopkins far afield.[5]

> There is talk [Bryce wrote to Adams from Boston in 1883] of establishing an historical seminary like yours. They have got a capital law school, indeed when I see that, and when I see your organization for historical and Staatswissenschaftlich studies I blush for the motherland which with all her vast endowments has nothing so satisfactory.[6]

The cumulative effect of this new academic activity was that by 1910 the 'gentlemen' writing history for 'gentlemen' had been effectively put out of business.

But the new school was essentially European in origin and

[1] D. C. Gilman, *The Johns Hopkins University (1876–1891)*. Johns Hopkins Univ. Studies, ix, nos. 3–4 (Baltimore, 1891), pp. 66, 72.

[2] *Cf.* 'Bibliography of history, politics, and economics, 1876–1901', in *Herbert B. Adams. Tributes of Friends* (Baltimore, 1902).

[3] J. F. Jameson, 'The American Historical Association, 1884–1909', *Am. Hist. Rev.*, xv (1910), 1–20; 'Early days of the American Historical Association, 1884–1895,' *Am. Hist. Rev.*, xl (1935), 1–9; Jones, *op. cit.*, pp. 218–20.

[4] Morison, *op. cit.*, p. 157; Jones, *op. cit.*, pp. 265–6.

[5] *Cf.* Holt, *op. cit.*, pp. 65–6.   [6] *Ibid.*, p. 71.

outlook.[1] Henry Adams' seminar produced a volume of *Essays in Anglo-Saxon Law*;[2] and Adams' own bitter and scornful volumes on the *History of the United States* during the administrations of Jefferson and Madison were a study of high politics in the European tradition, and dealt very largely with foreign relations. Burgess was a political scientist rather than a historian; and, a Southern Unionist who had fought in the Civil War on the Northern side, had been ripe to be deeply influenced in his thinking by what he had found in Germany. His master was von Gneist,[3] and his conception of the function of history was that it was the chief preparation for the study of the legal and political sciences.[4] The Johns Hopkins school under the leadership of Herbert B. Adams was equally Germanic. Adams was himself primarily a teacher of European and medieval history.[5] The spring from which the historical interests of a lifetime flowed was an episode which occurred in Heidelberg, in Erdmannsdörffer's seminar on Otto of Freising;[6] and under the influence of Henry Adams, Herbert B. Adams made the study of Germanic origins the foundation of the work at the new university.[7] The 'whole tenor of our researches at the J.H.U.', he wrote, 'is to show the continuity of English institutions in America'.[8] The first number of the 'Johns Hopkins University Studies' was *An Introduction to American Institutional History* by Freeman; and other early contributions to the series written by Adams himself were *The Germanic Origin of New England Towns* and *Saxon Tithingmen in America*. When it was proposed, in 1890, to promote Adams and confer upon him the title of Professor of American History, he replied to the President, 'I have no ambition to be known as Professor of American History. At least five-sixths of my three years' course of lectures to graduates and *all* of my undergraduate classes are in the

---

[1]*Cf.* E. Saveth, 'Race and nationalism in American historiography: the late nineteenth century', *Pol. Sci. Quart.*, liv (1939), 421–41.

[2]Little, Brown & Co., Boston: Macmillan & Co., London, 1876; Adams, *Methods of Historical Study* . . . , p. 88.

[3]Burgess, *op. cit.*, p. 131.   [4]Adams, *The Study of History* . . . , p. 236.

[5]Holt, *op. cit.*, pp. 13, 145–6.   [6]Adams, *Methods of Historical Study* . . . , pp. 66–7.

[7]Adams, *op. cit.*, p. 101; *cf.* W. C. Ford, *Letters of Henry Adams* (1930), pp. 235–7.

[8]Holt, *op. cit.*, p. 55; *cf.* Adams, *Methods* . . . , pp. 14–15; Baker, *op. cit.*, i, 174.

European field. I do not object to the phrase "Institutional History", for that describes very happily the nature of my university work in class and seminary. As "Professor of Institutional History" I could have a fair field for comparative studies in Church and State . . . without being regarded as an American provincial.'[1]

This European domination led to a revolt; and it came from within the gates of the citadel itself. By 1923, it was necessary for Haskins to argue that 'while American history is our first business, it is not our sole business';[2] so far had the revolt been carried. The leader was Frederick Jackson Turner.[3]

Turner became a fellow of Johns Hopkins in 1888, returning in 1889 as assistant professor to the University of Wisconsin, where he had previously been an instructor. He proceeded to his Ph.D. at Johns Hopkins in 1890, the subject of his thesis being 'The character and influence of the Indian trade' in Wisconsin.[4] At Johns Hopkins, he was intimate with Woodrow Wilson, five years his senior, and at that date a special lecturer at the University.[5] Wilson himself had been restive as a student under Adams, finding his lectures thin and being oppressed by the insistent concentration upon institutional history.[6] In reviewing in *The Dial*, in 1889, Roosevelt's *Winning of the West*, Turner wrote:

> America's historians have for the most part, like the wise men of old, come from the East; and as a result our history has been written from the point of view of the Atlantic coast . . . But the American occupation of the Mississippi basin has not found its historian. General United States history should be built upon the fact that the centre of gravity of the nation has passed across the mountains into this great region. To give to our history the new proportions which this fact makes necessary, must be the work of the younger generation of students.[7]

In 1893, he read before the American Historical Association

---

[1]Holt, *op. cit.*, pp. 145–6.   [2]*Am. Hist. Rev.*, xxviii (1923), 215.
[3]For a list of 'References on the life and work of Frederick Jackson Turner' see *The Early Writings of Frederick Jackson Turner* (Madison, 1938), pp. 269–72.
[4]Johns Hopkins Univ. Studies, ix, nos. 11–12 (Baltimore, 1891), reprinted in *Early Writings* . . . (1938).
[5]*Early Writings* . . . , pp. 21, 24; R. S. Baker, *Woodrow Wilson. Life and Letters* (8 vv., 1927–39), ii, 124–5.
[6]Holt, *op. cit.*, p. 90, n. 1; Baker, *op. cit.*, i, 178–80.   [7]*Early Writings*, p. 22.

a paper entitled 'The significance of the frontier in American history'.[1] He had read it to Woodrow Wilson before its delivery and found in him one who shared his discontent with the neglect of this subject and the excessive importance attached to the 'expansion of New England'.[2] His essay was, in fact, notice that the leadership in the writing of American history had, for the time, passed to the Middle West.

Let it be said at once, however, that it is not intended to suggest that, even in the field of American history itself, notable, most notable, historical work was not done in the East. In the nineties there came from Columbia G. L. Beer's *Commercial Policy of England toward the American Colonies*, published in 1893 when the author was only twenty years of age;[3] and W. A. Dunning's *Essays on the Civil War and Reconstruction* (1897). Burgess had been joined in 1890 by H. L. Osgood,[4] whom he had started upon his career at Amherst, and who, after a year in Berlin and an interval of school teaching, had spent fifteen months in London, where in consequence of some articles on socialism contributed to the *Political Science Quarterly* he became acquainted with members of the Fabian Society. The work of Beer was one of the firstfruits of the teaching of these two men. It was to be followed, after 1900, by a long series of monographic studies, in the same field, issuing from Columbia and culminating in Osgood's own *American Colonies in the Seventeenth Century* (3 vv., 1904–7) and *American Colonies in the Eighteenth Century* (4 vv., 1924), based throughout upon the records and laying new and massive foundations for the study of the colonial period. Dunning[5] was also an early pupil of Burgess, taking

[1]Am. Hist. Assoc., *Annual Report, 1893* (Washington, 1894); State Historical Society of Wisconsin, *Proceedings*, xli (Madison, 1894); *The Frontier in American History* (New York, 1920).   [2]Baker, *op. cit.*, ii, 125.
[3]*George Louis Beer, a Tribute* (New York, 1924); A. P. Scott, 'George Louis Beer', in W. T. Hutchinson (ed.), *The Marcus W. Jernegan Essays in American Historiography* (Chicago, 1937), pp. 313–22.
[4]D. R. Fox, *Herbert Levi Osgood. An American Scholar* (New York, 1924); E. C. O. Beatty, 'Herbert Levi Osgood', in W. T. Hutchinson, *op. cit.*, pp. 271–93; W. R. Shepherd, 'An historian of the thirteen colonies', *Col. Univ. Quart.*, xxi (1919), 79–81; H. F. Coppock, 'Herbert Levi Osgood', *Miss. Valley Hist. Rev.*, xix (1932–3).
[5]*Truth in History and Other Essays by William A. Dunning. With an Introduction by J. G. de Roulhac Hamilton* (New York, 1937).

his Ph.D. in 1885 and being appointed to the staff in 1886; and his *Essays*, than which nothing more penetrating has yet been written about the civil war and reconstruction, were likewise followed during the next twenty-five years by a whole series of 'Columbia Studies' on the period of reconstruction. No less stimulating were two volumes by C. A. Beard, a Columbian Ph.D. of 1904, on *An Economic Interpretation of the Constitution* (1913) and *Economic Origins of Jeffersonian Democracy* (1915), which opened a new chapter in the study of the political ideas of that period. With the emphasis of the later work of Osgood falling upon the eighteenth century, the appointment of C. M. Andrews to Yale in 1910 gave the lead in work upon the history of the American colonies in the seventeenth century to that university.[1] At the same time, it was in the East that there was elaborated that technical apparatus which the new school of history required. An immense influence was exercised by the multifarious activities of the American Historical Association, and by the *American Historical Review*, of which J. Franklin Jameson was editor from 1895 to 1901 and from 1905 to 1927. Close relations were established between students of history wherever at work throughout a continental area; and the force of organized historical opinion was brought to bear upon the preservation and publication of historical records and the elevation of the standards of historical writing.[2] From the Department of Historical Research of the Carnegie Institution under A. C. McLaughlin (1903–5) and J. Franklin Jameson (1905–28)[3] came a long series of guides to materials for American history to be found in foreign archives, followed in

---

[1]L. H. Gipson, *Charles McLean Andrews and the Re-Orientation of the Study of American Colonial History. Circular no. 112. Studies in the Humanities, no. 17* (The Institute of Research, Lehigh Univ., Bethlehem, Pa., 1935); L. W. Labaree, 'Charles McLean Andrews, historian', *William & Mary Quart.*, 3rd ser., i (1944), 3–14; G. W. Pierson & L. W. Labaree, 'Charles McLean Andrews, a bibliography', *ibid.*, 15–26.

[2]F. J. Jameson, 'Early days of the American Historical Association, 1884–1895', *Am. Hist. Rev.*, xl (1935), 1–9; 'The American Historical Association, 1884–1909', *Am. Hist. Rev.*, xv (1910), 1–20; *Historical Scholarship in America . . . A Report by the Committee of the American Historical Association . . .* (New York, 1932), pp. 6–9; G. W. Prothero, 'The American Historical Association'. The Historical Association, *Leaflet 27* (Jan. 1912).

[3]*Am. Hist. Rev.*, xliii (1938), 243–52.

later years by important documentary publications; and the annual bibliography of *Writings on American History* was started by that Institution with the year 1903, and has been continuously issued by one body or another since 1906. As custodian of the Library of Congress from 1899 to 1939, Herbert Putnam created for historians a scientific instrument of research of the first quality. The profession was supplied with a standard secondary authority by the issue, under the general editorship of A. B. Hart of Harvard, of the *American Nation* in 26 volumes between 1904 and 1907; and from Harvard came in 1912 that indispensable handbook of all students of American history, the *Guide to the Study and Reading of American History*, based upon an earlier work of 1896.[1]

Yet it remains true that the most distinctive feature of American historiography in the generation after 1890 was the work of the Middle Western school. The thesis presented in Turner's essay was that down to his own day American history had been in a large degree the history of the colonization of the Great West, and that the existence of an area of free land, its continuous recession, and the advance of American settlement westward explained American development. There had been a constant return to primitive conditions on a continuously advancing frontier. 'This perennial rebirth, this fluidity of American life, this expansion westward with its new opportunities, its continuous touch with the simplicity of primitive society, furnish the forces dominating American character.'[2] The true point of view, therefore, 'is not the Atlantic coast, it is the Great West'. 'Too exclusive attention', he wrote, with an eye on Johns Hopkins, 'has been paid by institutional students to the Germanic origins, too little to the American factors.' Each successive frontier had left behind it its characteristic influence. 'The advance of the frontier has meant a steady movement away from the influence of Europe, a steady growth of independence on American lines. And to study this advance, . . . is to study the really American part of our

---

[1] E. Channing, A. B. Hart and F. J. Turner, *Guide to the Study and Reading of American History* (Ginn & Co., 1912).   [2] *Early Writings . . .*, p. 187.

history.'[1] To this argument, there are, it will be observed, two branches; and there has been a tendency, encouraged by Turner himself, to lay the greater stress upon that which has the lesser validity. That which was indisputable was that the true point of view for the understanding of American history was the West; that the fundamental fact of American history down to the year 1890 was the settlement of a continent. That which was more doubtful was the contention that that which is characteristically American derives overwhelmingly from a specialized frontier psychology and institutional frontier peculiarities which are the product of frontier conditions. And so much ink has been spilled in controversy about the sub-sidiary argument, that there is some danger of Turner's contribution to the development of American historiography getting out of focus. The important feature is that the centre of interest shifted from federal politics to the history of states and minor localities; from European origins to American environment and American experience; from constitutional forms to the vital forces that call these organs into life.

> Every day [wrote Henry Adams in 1890, referring to the year 1806] a million men went to their work, every evening they came home with some work accomplished; but the result was matter for a census rather than for history. The acres brought into cultivation, the cattle bred, the houses built, proved no doubt that human beings, like ants and bees, could indefinitely multiply their numbers, and could lay up stores of food; but these statistics offered no evidence that the human being, any more than the ant and bee, was conscious of a higher destiny, or was even mechanically developing into a more efficient animal.[2]

And these matters therefore had no place in the *History of the United States*. What Adams was thus ready to pass by was precisely what Turner set out to study. Turner himself never, indeed, wrote a big book. It would scarcely be unjust to say that he never finished a book at all, for even about those volumes that were not in form collections of separate papers

---

[1]*Early Writings . . .*, pp. 188–9.
[2]H. Adams, *History of the United States of America During the Second Administration of Thomas Jefferson* (2 vv., New York, 1890), i, 212.

there was something fragmentary and incomplete. Yet between 1893 and his death in 1938, no one exercised so far-reaching an influence upon the study and writing of American history as he did.

Second only to Turner in the creation of the Middle Western school was C. W. Alvord.[1] An easterner by origin, with two years in Berlin and a brief period in Chicago, Alvord began by teaching history and mathematics at the preparatory school of the University of Illinois, and was appointed an instructor in History at the University itself in 1901. It was characteristic of what was going on in the American historical world that he taught European history, with the Italian renaissance as the main field of his interest. In 1905, he was sent by the Illinois State Historical Society to examine an early French document in one of the Illinois towns of the Mississippi valley settled by the French in the eighteenth century, and there discovered what remained of the archives of the French and Virginian administration of the Illinois country from 1720 to 1790. From that day he became the architect of an Illinois school of American history that quickly took the lead in the Middle West. Performing immense labours in the promotion of historical activities in the State of Illinois and in the Mississippi valley at large, to which I shall presently return, his own principal contribution was his two-volume *The Mississippi Valley in British Politics. A Study of the Trade, Land Speculation, and Experiments in Imperialism culminating in the American Revolution*, published in 1917. The book satisfied both the canon of Osgood and Beer, in that it was a study of British policy and not a study of the results in ignorance of the policy from which they flowed, and the canon of Turner, in that the explanation was sought in the history of westward expansion; and Alvord thus set the problem in a new light and saw further into it than anyone had seen before.

The fruit of this alliance of scientific method with a western

[1]S. J. Buck, 'Clarence Walworth Alvord, historian', *Miss. Valley Hist. Rev.*, xv (1929), 309-20; M. Dargan, jr., 'Clarence Walworth Alvord', in W. T. Hutchinson (ed.), *The Marcus W. Jernegan Essays in American Historiography* (Chicago, 1937), pp. 323-38.

outlook, towards which the first steps were thus taken in Wisconsin and Illinois, was the appearance in one after another of the universities of the upper Mississippi valley of teachers and writers whose work could be grouped under the name of a Middle Western School. Their books came thick from the presses from 1910 onwards.

But the growth of this school was not confined to the universities. There were two other centres of activity—the State historical societies and the State departments of archives and history.[1] Writing to Herbert B. Adams from Brown University in 1890, Franklin Jameson said:

> I consider the hope of good historical writing in the future to rest with the teachers, now that the instruction of graduates has reached such an extension as to make 'Schools', personal followings, and the learning of the trade possible. The historical societies I consider of little account intellectually, except as trustees of material and as possible furtherers of publication.[2]

In the fifty years which have elapsed since that letter was written, the history of the societies has been a history of infiltration by the trained historian; but infiltration has, with some notable exceptions, been much slower in the East than in the West. In the Mississippi valley, indeed, infiltration is sometimes not the right word at all, for the trained historian has been in control from the start.

The eastern societies were many of them of venerable antiquity. The oldest of them was the Massachusetts Historical Society, founded in 1791. It was followed by the New York Historical Society, 1804; the American Antiquarian Society, 1812; the Rhode Island Historical Society, 1822; the Maine Historical Society and the New Hampshire Historical Society, 1823; the Historical Society of Pennsylvania, 1824; the Connecticut Historical Society, 1825; and the Virginia Historical Society, 1831. Such societies were privately endowed and often

---

[1] J. P. Boyd, 'State and local historical societies in the United States', *Am. Hist. Rev.*, xl (1935), 10–37; E. B. Greene, 'Our pioneer historical societies', *Indiana Hist. Soc. Publication*, x, no. 2 (1931); C. Crittenden and D. Godard (eds.), *Historical Societies in the United States and Canada. A Handbook*. The Am. Assoc. for State and Local History (Washington, 1944).   [2] Holt, *op. cit.*, p. 128.

exclusive. They had strong antiquarian and genealogical
interests. Their attention was concentrated upon the colonial,
revolutionary, and at latest the early constitutional periods.
They had fostered historical interest when history had been
neglected by the universities; but they had contributed, and
most of them have yet contributed, very little to the study of
the history of the United States in the nineteenth century.

> In five years' work in Washington [wrote Franklin Jameson in
> 1910], so circumstanced that I am likely to know of historical
> researches undertaken in national archives or library, I have
> hardly known an instance in which the publishing authorities
> of any eastern historical society have set on foot any serious
> researches in these great and rich repositories. Seldom indeed
> do they touch the period since 1783.[1]

Their publications consisted of annual reports, transactions,
and 'collections' of documentary but often also of secondary
material. They contributed little to historical journalism.
The genealogical societies produced the *New England Historical
and Genealogical Register* (1874+), and the *New York Genealogical
and Biographical Record* (1870+). But the only journals of
long standing that have been issued by the older historical
societies are the *Pennsylvania Magazine of History and Biography*
(1877+) and the *Virginia Magazine of History and Biography*
(1893+).

The history of the societies founded in the states of the Mississippi valley has been very different.[2] They have commonly
received state support; their work has been more or less sys-
tematically correlated with that of the State Departments of
Archives and History upon the one hand and with the popularization of historical knowledge upon the other; and they

[1] J. F. Jameson, 'The present state of historical writing in America', *Proceedings
of the Am. Antiq. Soc.*, n. s., xx (1911), 413–14.
[2] A. H. Shearer, 'State Historical Societies', *New York State Historical Assoc.
Quart. Journ.*, iii (1922), in *Proceedings of the New York State Hist. Assoc.*, xx, 195–204;
E. B. Greene, 'Report of conference on the work of state and local historical
societies', *Am. Hist. Assoc. Rept.* (*1907*), p. i; (*1908*), pp. 49–64; S. K. Stevens,
'Organization and aid for local history in the United States', *Pennsylvania History*,
vii (1940), 79–88; S. J. Buck, 'The progress and possibilities of Mississippi valley
history', *Miss. Valley Hist. Rev.*, x (1924), 5–20.

have been closely associated with the historical departments
of the state universities. The details of their organization have
varied from state to state, depending largely upon the geographical distribution of the state capital, the university,
and the society itself. Indiana, Iowa, Michigan, Wisconsin,
Illinois, and Minnesota have been the most vigorous in the
promotion and organization of historical work. The oldest
surviving historical societies in the Mississippi valley are the
Indiana Historical Society (1830) and the Ohio Archaeological
and Historical Society (1831). The first destined to become state
historical societies were those of Wisconsin and Minnesota,
established in 1846 and 1849. But these early historical societies
of the Mississippi valley were very much like their eastern
fellows. They were largely under the control of journalists and
retired politicians; their interests were antiquarian and
anecdotal; their meetings were opportunities for the display
of rhetorical elegance: the first annual address of the President
of the State Historical Society of Wisconsin, delivered in the
presence of the judges of the Supreme Court and the Board of
Regents, 'elaborated in its researches and felicitous in its style',
was approvingly described as 'classical in its tone and pervaded
throughout with a spirit of accuracy and of beauty.'[1] Their
publications, though bearing such titles as 'collections', were,
in fact, for the most part devoted to reminiscences, biographical
sketches, obituaries, and proceedings. The landmarks in the
establishment of a new order are the co-operation of Turner
with Thwaites at the Wisconsin State Historical Society, which
began in 1888; the association of Alvord with the work of the
Illinois State Historical Library in 1905; the founding of the
Mississippi Valley Historical Association in 1907 and of the
Mississippi Valley Historical Review in 1914;[2] the appointment
of the Michigan Historical Commission in 1913, when it took
over the collections and the publishing activities of the Pioneer
and Historical Society of Michigan; the re-organization of the

---

[1]L. P. Kellog, 'The services and collections of Lyman Copeland Draper',
Wisconsin Mag. of Hist., v (1922), 246; *Collections of the State Hist. Soc. of Wisconsin*,
i (reprint, 1903), p. xxxix.
[2]*Bull. Instit. Hist. Res.*, ii (1924), 31–6.

Minnesota Historical Society in 1915, when it was made an organ of the state; and the organization of a Department of History and Archives of the Indiana State Library in 1914, and of the Indiana Historical Survey of the Indiana Historical Commission in 1916.

Ohio has been embarrassed by the vigour of the sects which have thriven within it, and its divisions have no doubt been largely due to its geographical position and the history of its settlement, which made it the uncongenial meeting place of streams of population drawn from very diverse sources. Neither of its two rival societies, the Historical and Philosophical Society of Ohio (Cincinnati) and the Ohio State Archaeo-logical and Historical Society (Columbus), was able to dominate the state;[1] and the latter, the more active of the two, laid emphasis upon archaeology rather than history. Only within quite recent years have there been signs of successful organiza-tion under the leadership of the University. In Indiana and Iowa, geography has also presented difficulties; and Iowa was embarrassed by the removal of the capital from Iowa City to Des Moines in 1857 and the establishment of the State Depart-ment of History there in 1882. But the two states are con-spicuous for the careful co-ordination, in rather different com-binations in each, of the activities of the university, concerned with research; the State Department, concerned with the collection, and the historical society concerned with the publica-tion, of historical materials: and in both states much attention has been given to the historical education of the general public.[2]

[1] W. H. Siebert, 'The future of the Ohio Valley Historical Association', *Ohio Hist. Teachers' Journ.*, xix (1920), 183–9; *Miss. Valley Hist. Rev.*, i (1915), 61; ii (1916), 104; C. E. Carter, 'Some notes on Ohio historiography', *Ohio Arch. & Hist. Pubs.*, xxviii (1919), 185 ; F. P. Weisenberger, 'A half century of the writing of history in Ohio', *ibid.*, xliv (1935), 326–52; L. Shephard, 'The Historical and Philosophical Society of Ohio', *Ohio State Archaeol. & Hist. Quart.*, liv (1945), 89–95; E. J. Benton, 'The Western Reserve Historical Society', *ibid.*, 96–103.
[2] *Miss. Valley Hist. Rev.*, i (1915), 241–2, 333; J. A. Woodburn, 'The Indiana Historical Society, a hundred years', *Indiana Hist. Soc. Pub.*, x (1930), 5–6; B. F. Shambaugh, 'A brief history of the State Historical Society of Iowa', *Iowa Journal of Hist. & Politics*, i (1903), 139–52; B. F. Shambaugh, 'The Iowa school of research historians', *Miss Valley Hist. Assoc. Proc.*, iv (1910–1), 152 ; L. B. Schmidt, 'The activities of the State Historical Society of Iowa', *Hist. Teachers' Mag.*, vi (1915), 75–81.

In Michigan, the re-organization was principally due to C. H. van Tyne, professor of History in the University of Michigan: and by 1923 the *Collections* had become a scientific documentary series; the University was issuing a series of monographic studies of state history; and the Commission was active in the collection of historical materials and the stimulation of public interest in historical matters.[1] But the lead in the establishment of a new order came from Wisconsin, Illinois and Minnesota.

The state of Wisconsin has the oldest and richest tradition in historical scholarship of the Mississippi valley. The founder of this was Lyman Copeland Draper.[2] Born in 1815 and in the main self-educated, he began as a boy to collect materials for the history of the trans-Alleghany pioneers, and before he was twenty-five had entered into a correspondence, which was to continue throughout his life, with prominent pioneers or their descendants. To this he began in 1840 to add personal interviews, to secure which he travelled for nearly a quarter of a century, and at intervals thereafter, up and down the backwoods of New York, Ohio, Kentucky, Virginia and Tennessee. In the course of these travels he collected a mass of original manuscript material going back as far as the year 1756. To the collection of this, he presently added that of newspapers. On the re-organization in 1854 of the State Historical Society of Wisconsin, founded in 1846, Draper was, through the influence of his friend Judge Larrabee, appointed its secretary. At the outset of his administration, the Society's library contained fifty volumes. By the date of his retirement in 1886, it had grown to over 118,000 volumes, and contained, as well, a large collection of pamphlets and manuscripts, to which, after his death in 1891, were added

[1]G. N. Fuller, 'Historical work in Michigan', *Mich. Hist. Mag.*, vii (1923), 232–47; *Am. Hist. Rev.*, xxxv (1930), 941; G. N. Fuller, 'The Michigan Historical Commission', *Michigan Historical Commission, Bulletin No.* 1 (1913).
[2]R. G. Thwaites, *The State Historical Society of Wisconsin* (Madison, 1898); P. L. Johnson, 'The founding of the State Historical Society of Wisconsin', *Wisconsin Mag. of Hist.*, xxvi (1942–3), 72–8; R. G. Thwaites, 'Lyman Copeland Draper', in *Collections of the State Hist. Soc. of Wisconsin*, i (Reprint, 1903), pp. ix–xxix; L. P. Kellog, 'The services and collections of Lyman Copeland Craper', *Wisconsin Mag. of Hist.*, v (1922), 244–63.

the Draper manuscripts themselves. Draper's own writings were fragmentary. His chief work as an historian was the editing and publication of the *Wisconsin Historical Collections*, the first volume of which appeared in 1855, for the first ten of which he was responsible, and in the preparation of which he was a pioneer in making available the original materials for the history of the frontier. In 1887, Draper was succeeded by R. G. Thwaites,[1] who held office until 1913. A prodigious worker, Thwaites wrote some fifteen historical works, and edited and published something like 168 volumes. But he was pre-eminently an organizer. He separated the *Proceedings* from the *Collections*, making the latter purely documentary publications; and above all he strengthened the connection between the Society and the university, securing the association of State Historical Society and university library in a single building on the university campus, offering new facilities and greater freedom of work in the Society's collections, and admitting Turner, as a young instructor, to hold a seminar in the library. When the Society was newly housed in 1901 in a building after Thwaites' own plan, the library became, in Turner's words, 'one of America's greatest historical workshops'.[2] 'Draper', Turner concluded, 'was the founder; Thwaites was the great historical editor and modernizer, the builder of a new type of state historical society.'[3] In 1914, Alvord read to the Mississippi Valley Historical Association a 'Critical analysis of the work of Reuben Gold Thwaites' which is a model of discriminating eulogy. He praised him as a man of business and an editor; the first to supply the Middle West on a generous scale with a collection of printed sources; the first to unite the state historical agency and the university department so that they gave each other mutual assistance; the maker of the Society in its modern shape and a great

---

[1] *Miss. Valley Hist. Rev.*, i (1915), 158–9; F. J. Turner, *Reuben Gold Thwaites: A Memorial Address* (Madison, 1914); C. W. Alvord, 'A critical analysis of the work of Reuben Gold Thwaites', *Miss. Valley Hist. Assoc. Proc.*, vii (1914), 321–33.

[2] Turner, *op. cit.*, pp. 27–8; J. Schafer, 'Cooperation between state universities and state historical societies', *Tenn. Hist. Mag.*, vii (1921–2), 69–73.

[3] Turner, *op. cit.*, p. 58.

popularizer of scientific history; not a great writer of history; but one whose services to historical study in the West had been of the first order.[1] Thwaites was succeeded as Superintendent in 1914 by M. M. Quaife, who began the publication of the *Wisconsin Magazine of History* in 1917; and he, in turn, by Joseph Schafer in 1920.[2] Schafer, a pupil of Turner's, who returned to Wisconsin after twenty years at the University of Oregon, wrote during his period of office, a *History of Agriculture in Wisconsin* and three volumes of a history of the settlement of the state,[3] which lay the foundations for the history of Wisconsin more securely than they have been laid for any other Middle Western state, and are both a model of what should be done elsewhere and full of interest for students of primitive settlements of which no such records have survived as are available to the historian of the nineteenth century.

What Alvord admired in Wisconsin he himself achieved in Illinois. The Illinois State Historical Society, founded in 1899, was a private organization, though receiving support from the state to the extent of the publication of its *Transactions* by the State Historical Library; it had a large membership; and it was mainly occupied with the popularization of history. Alvord turned, therefore, to the State Historical Library, founded in 1889, for an ally with the university in the promotion of the scientific study of the history of the state of Illinois. He himself became the editor of the Library's *Illinois Historical Collections*[4] in 1904, and produced, between then and 1919, volumes 2 to 15 of the series. He procured in 1911 the appointment by the legislature of a commission to make plans for a state education building to house the Historical Library, the society, the department of education and allied interests. With the assistance of a report on the 'Public archives and historical interests of the state of Illinois', prepared for the Commission by Dr. Leland

---

[1]Alvord, *loc. cit.*

[2]*Joseph Schafer, Student of Agriculture* (State Historical Society of Wisconsin, Madison, 1942).

[3]*Four Wisconsin Counties* (1927); *The Wisconsin Lead Region* (1932); *The Winnebago-Horicon Basin* (1937). The State Hist. Soc. of Wisc., Madison.

[4]T. C. Pease, 'The Illinois Historical Collections', *Ill. Hist. Soc. Trans.* (1922), pp. 66–8.

in 1913, he further secured inclusion in the plan of provision for a public archive.[1] The building at Springfield was finally completed in 1923. At the same time as he was doing this, Alvord created in the University of Illinois at Urbana an organization, formally established in 1915 as a permanent department under the name of the Illinois Historical Survey, for the scientific study of state history.[2] 'No books', he wrote in 1908, 'have been printed on the West previous to the Revolution that will not be completely superseded by the work of real research.'[3] The *Illinois Historical Collections* under his hand became the model for the publications of state agencies in the historical field; and the creation of a public archive in association with State Historical Library and State Historical Society added a new element to the equipment of the Middle West.

In 1914, Dr. S. J. Buck, who had worked under Alvord in Illinois, became Superintendent of the Minnesota Historical Society, and carried to that state the lessons learnt in Illinois and Wisconsin. An act of the legislature in 1915, assuring the erection of a new building for the Society at St. Paul, provided also for the care in that building of the state archives;[4] and the Society became one of the most highly organized in the Middle West and closely associated with the work of the University of Minnesota.[5] The publication of *Minnesota History* began in 1915.

While, however, activities similar, if on a less magnificent scale, spread in Missouri, Kansas and Nebraska, for long they made very little progress below the mouth of the Ohio river.[6] Higher education could not thrive in the ruin left in the South by the Civil War; the universities lagged behind those of the

[1] *Miss. Valley Hist. Rev.*, i (1915), 58–9; vii (1921), 127.
[2] *Ibid.*, i (1915), 59, 65; ii (1916), 75; *cf. Miss. Valley Hist. Assoc. Proc.*, i (1909), 98–110.
[3] *Miss. Valley Hist. Assoc. Proc.*, i (1909), 108.
[4] *Miss. Valley Hist. Rev.*, i (1915), 240.
[5] *Cf.* S. J. Buck, 'The Minnesota Historical Society', *Mich. Hist. Mag.*, iv (1920), 688–716; Mary W. Berthel & H. D. Cater, 'The Minnesota Historical Society; highlights of a century', *Minn. Hist.*, xxx (1949), 293–330.
[6] 'Annals of the Missouri Historical Society', *Bulletin of the Missouri Hist. Soc.*, iv (1947), 31-41; K. Mechem, 'The Historical Society, after seventy-five years', *Kansas Hist. Quart.*, xix (1951), 74-80.

North, and the local historical societies remained in the hands of the unskilled.[1] The states of the lower Mississippi valley show, in consequence, some of the most conspicuous blanks in the American historical map. Very little scientific work has yet been done upon the history of Kentucky. We know something about the history of the settlement of Tennessee and Alabama and about the early history of political parties in those areas, but next to nothing about the settlement of Arkansas, Mississippi, or Louisiana after the French and Spanish period. Only very lately have the departments of history in the universities entered the field of state history, and little more has yet been achieved by them than the improvement of the state historical journals, sometimes, as in Louisiana, by the university securing control of the existing journal; sometimes by the organization of a new society and the launching of a new journal, as in the case of the East Tennessee Historical Society, with its *Publications*.[2] The most important of such early advances as were made were the work, not of the universities or of the state historical societies, but of State Departments of Archives and History. Attention was called by the American Historical Association during the late nineties to the general neglect of state archives; in 1899, a Public Archives Commission was appointed by the Association; and between 1900 and 1913, reports were published on the archives of thirty-five of the states. The result was the adoption in many states of legislation aiming at reform. In some, the care of the records was entrusted to the office of the Secretary of State; in some, it was handed over to the state historical society or the state library; in others, there was established a new department of archives and history. Two of these last were to become the principal influences in the promotion of the more scientific study of history in the lower Mississippi valley. They were the Alabama Department of Archives and History (1901), and the

[1] *Miss. Valley Hist. Rev.*, i (1915), 333, 400–4.
[2] W. R. Jillson, 'A sketch and bibliography of the Kentucky State Historical Society, 1836–1943', *Register of the Kentucky St. Hist. Soc.*, xli (1943), 179–230; W. Chandler, 'A century of the Tennessee Historical Society . . .', *Tenn. Hist. Quart.*, ix (1950), 3–9.

Mississippi Department of Archives and History (1902). A History Commission, with similar functions, was established in Arkansas in 1905.[1] In Alabama and Mississippi this action had been preceded by the appointment of History Commissions to report on materials for the history of the states. Under the chairmanship of T. M. Owen, an outstanding southern historian and later first permanent president of the Mississippi Valley Historical Association,[2] a valuable *Report* on the materials for the history of Alabama was published in 1901. The chairman of the Mississippi Commission was F. L. Riley, professor in the University of Mississippi, secretary and re-organizer of the Mississippi Historical Society, and a graduate of H. B. Adams' seminar at Johns Hopkins;[3] and that Commission also produced a valuable report.[4] Owen was appointed the first State Archivist of Alabama, and did work of much distinction; but he died prematurely in 1920.[5] Dunbar Rowland,[6] appointed first Archivist of the state of Mississippi, put in order a great mass of archival material, made important additions to the collection, and supervised for the Mississippi Historical Society the issue of a series of *Publications*. But the soil was too thin for the labours of these men to become as fruitful as they should have been; and the promise of fifty years ago is still unfulfilled, although notable work has been done in Virginia and North Carolina.

To the work of the historians of the Mississippi valley there has to be added that of the historians of the great plains and

---

[1] T. C. Blegen, 'A Report on the public archives'. The State Hist. Soc. of Wisc., *Bull. of Information*, no. 94 (1918), pp. 30–62; *Miss. Valley Hist. Rev.*, i (1915), 404, 405; ii (1916), 534–5.

[2] *Miss. Valley Hist. Assoc. Proc.*, i (1909), 98.

[3] *Am. Hist. Rev.*, xxxv (1930), 432; *Herbert B. Adams. Tributes of Friends* (Baltimore, 1902), *s.v.*; C. S. Sydnor, 'Historical activities in Mississippi in the nineteenth century', *Journ. Southern History*, iii (1937), 139–60; F. L. Riley, 'The work of the Mississippi Historical Society, 1898–1908', *Miss. Hist. Soc. Pub.*, x (1909), 34–45.

[4] *Report of the Alabama History Commission to the Governor of Alabama, December 1, 1900. Publications of the Alabama Hist. Soc. Miscellaneous Collections* vol. i (Montgomery, 1901); *Report of the Mississippi Historical Commission. Publications of the Mississippi Hist. Soc.* vol. v (Oxford, Miss., 1902); W. D. McCain, 'History and program of the Mississippi State Department of Archives and History', *Am. Archivist*, xiii (1950), 27–34.

[5] *Am. Hist. Rev.* xxv (1920), 562.   [6] *Miss. Valley Hist. Rev.*, xxiv (1938), 609.

the mountain states. The structure of historical activities in the West and Southwest is that of the Middle West rather than of the lower Mississippi valley. The universities of the Middle Border stand upon the edges of the northern plains, and the lead in the Southwest has been taken by the Universities of Texas and Oklahoma; and much of the history of the cattle country and of the sod-house frontier has been filled in. But the tide of scientific enquiry has not yet covered the mountain states, the history of the mining frontier is not yet written, and the work of the state historical societies at Bismarck and Pierre, at Cheyenne, Helena and Boise is only in its beginnings. The most notable contribution to the understanding of the West has been Professor **W. P. Webb's** *The Great Plains* (1931).[1] But although much that is true of the valley does not hold for the plains, the work done in this field has been an enlargement and elaboration of that of the Middle Western school rather than, in a wider point of view, any radical revision of it.

These multifarious activities, academic and other, have, for the most part since 1900, resulted in the foundation of a host of new journals and the publication of a whole library of monographic literature, which has put a quite new complexion upon American history, so that the *American Nation* (1904–7), summing up the older learning, has become a bourn beyond which, save in the search for documentary material or biographical detail, the student of to-day need seldom travel. The result was also to isolate and to atomize American history.[2] The student turned inward, to the almost complete neglect of the external world; and, within the boundaries of the United States, devoted himself more and more to the history of some particular aspect or region. But there are signs that the disease carried within itself its own remedy. Two features will at once attract the attention of the observer of the American historical

---

[1] *Cf. An Appraisal of Walter Prescott Webb's 'The Great Plains' . . . Critiques of Research in the Social Sciences*, iii. Bulletin 46. Social Science Research Council (1940); and more profitably, J. W. Caughey, 'A criticism of the critique of Webb's *The Great Plains*', *Miss. Valley Hist. Rev.*, xxvii (1940–1), 442–4.

[2] *Cf.* C. J. Hayes, 'The American frontier—frontier of what ?', *Am. Hist. Rev.*, li (1946), 199–216.

scene to-day; and they have an organic connection with one
another. They are the cultivation of social history,[1] and the
growing interest in the history of the American mind. Their
relation consists in the fact that, on the one hand, if social
history is to be more than the collection of *bric-à-brac* overlooked by previous historians, it must become a history of
popular psychology, and that, on the other, the study of the
history of the American mind looks like becoming the study,
not merely of the highest intellectual achievements of that
mind, but also of its more ordinary operations. In this con-
vergence of interests may perhaps be found the idea that will
reduce to intelligible order the disparate studies of to-day.
But there is also a large re-integration in progress. The South-
western and Californian school, of which the leader is Professor
H. E. Bolton, working in an area in which the social foundations are Spanish, finds itself driven to make of American history
more than the history of the United States.[2] At the same time,
the students of immigration, of whom M. L. Hansen was the
most notable,[3] working in the heart of the Middle West itself,
reached a similar conclusion. It became clear that the force
which uprooted the German peasant of the Palatinate or the
Irish peasant of Munster was the same as that which set the
farmer of Vermont in motion for the industrial towns of Massachusetts or the new lands of the Mississippi valley; and a call
has come for a study of the Atlantic basin which shall be quick
to discover a Vermont in Ulster or in the Argentine a Middle
Border, and ready to look even at the slave trade itself as a
chapter in such a story. If this happens, a new significance
will be given to American diplomatic history. American diplomatic history is a subject which has attracted many workers
during the last forty years, and the equipment gathered together in Washington for its study can be equalled in few
capitals of the world. But, while in the Latin American field,
where the problems have long been brooded upon, work of

---

[1] W. E. Lingelbach (ed.), *Approaches to American Social History* (1937).

[2] H. E. Bolton, *Wider Horizons of American History* (1939).

[3] *The Immigrant in American History* (Cambridge, Mass., 1940); *The Atlantic Migration, 1607–1860* (Cambridge, Mass., 1941).

great interest has been done, much of the other output has been immature and jejune. A publication of the Department of Commerce, *The United States in the World Economy*,[1] shows what the history of American foreign relations might be; and if it were to develop in that way, it would become one of the most powerful instruments of re-integration. It would also become one of the most difficult of historical pursuits.

BIBLIOGRAPHICAL NOTE

i. To the early history of American historiography the best introduction is J. F. Jameson, *The History of Historical Writing in America* (Houghton & Mifflin: Boston, 1891). This is continued in J. S. Bassett, *The Middle Group of American Historians* (Macmillan: New York, 1917). The most valuable general surveys of the growth of the modern school are:—W. A. Dunning, 'A generation of American historiography', *Annual Report of the American Historical Association . . . 1917*, pp. 345–54 (Govt. Printing Office: Washington, D.C., 1920); J. F. Jameson, J. B. McMaster and E. Channing, 'The present state of historical writing in America', *Proceedings of the American Antiquarian Society*, n.s. xx, pp. 408–34 (Worcester, Mass., 1911); E. Emerton and S. E. Morison, 'History 1838–1929', in S. E. Morison (ed.), *The Development of Harvard University . . . 1869–1929*, pp. 150–77 (Harvard Univ. Press: Cambridge, Mass., 1930); C. J. H. Hayes, 'History', in D. R. Fox (ed.), *A Quarter Century of Learning, 1904–29* (Columbia Univ. Press: New York, 1931); C. M. Andrews, 'These forty years', *American Historical Review*, xxx, pp. 225–50 (1924–5); A. M. Schlesinger (ed.), *Historical Scholarship in America* (Ray Long & Richard R. Smith, Inc.; New York, 1932); J. H. Randall, jr., & G. Haines IV, 'Controlling assumptions in the practice of American historians', in *Theory and Practice in Historical Study: a Report of the Committee on Historiography* (Social Science Research Council: New York, 1946).

ii. For the lives and critical estimates of the narrative historians, see W. T. Hutchinson (ed.), *The Marcus W. Jernegan Essays in American Historiography* (Univ. of Chicago Press: Chicago, 1937), for Schouler, Wilson, McMaster, Fiske, Rhodes, and Channing;

[1]Govt. Printing Office, Washington, D.C., 1943; H.M.S.O., 1944.

J. L. Whitney, *Justin Winsor* (Press of C. Hamilton: Worcester, Mass., 1898); J. S. Clarke, *Life and Letters of John Fiske* (Houghton & Mifflin: Boston, 1917); E. F. Goldman, *John Bach McMaster, American Historian* (Univ. of Pennsylvania Press: Philadelphia, 1943); M. A. de W. Howe, *James Ford Rhodes* (Appleton: New York, 1929); S. E. Morison, 'Edward Channing' in *Massachusetts Hist. Soc. Proceedings*, lxiv, pp. 250–84 (Boston, 1932); and E. D. Ross, 'Oberholtzer's "History of the United States since the Civil War" ', *Mississippi Valley Historical Rev.*, xxiv, pp. 341–50 (1937–8).

iii. On the lives of the pioneers in the organization of scientific historical work in the United States, see *The Autobiography of Andrew Dickson White*, 2 vv. (Century Co.: New York, 1905); C. F. Smith, *Charles Kendall Adams* (Univ. of Wisconsin: Madison, Wisc., 1924); *Herbert B. Adams, Tributes of Friends*, Johns Hopkins Univ. Studies, xx, extra no. (Johns Hopkins Press: Baltimore, 1902); J. M. Vincent, 'Herbert B. Adams', in H. W. Odum (ed.), *American Masters of Social Science* (Henry Holt: New York, 1927); H. M. Jones, *The Life of Moses Coit Tyler* (Univ. of Michigan Press: Ann Arbor, Mich., 1933); J. T. Adams, *Henry Adams* (A. & C. Boni: New York, 1933); *The Education of Henry Adams—an Autobiography* (Massachusetts Hist. Soc., 1918); H. D. Cater (ed.), *Henry Adams and His Friends* (Houghton, Mifflin: Boston, 1947); and W. C. Hill, 'Memoir of Albert Bushnell Hart', *New England Hist. & Genealogical Register*, xcviii, pp. 2–5 (1944).

iv. On the founders of the new school, see for the literature relating to F. J. Turner, the list of 'References on the life and work of Frederick Jackson Turner' in F. Mood (ed.), *The Early Writings of Frederick Jackson Turner* (Univ. of Wisconsin: Madison, Wisc., 1938). Of the writings there listed the most valuable are C. L. Becker, 'Frederick Jackson Turner', in H. W. Odum (ed.), *American Masters of Social Science* (Henry Holt: New York, 1927); J. Schafer, 'The author of the "frontier hypothesis" ', *Wisconsin Mag. of History*, xv, pp. 86–103 (1931–2); Louise P. Kellog, 'The passing of a great teacher—Frederick Jackson Turner', *Historical Outlook*, xxiii, pp. 270–2 (1932); M. E. Curti, 'The section and the frontier in American history—the methodological concepts of Frederick Jackson Turner', in S. A. Rice (ed.), *Methods in Social Science* (Univ. of Chicago Press: Chicago, 1931); and A. Craven, 'Frederick Jackson Turner', in W. T. Hutchinson (ed.), *The Marcus W. Jernegan Essays in American Historiography* (Univ. of Chicago Press: Chicago, 1937). For others among the leaders, see D. R. Fox,

Herbert Levi Osgood. An American Scholar (Columbia Univ. Press: New York, 1924); H. F. Coppock, 'Herbert Levi Osgood', *Mississippi Valley Hist. Rev.*, xix, pp. 394–403 (1932–3); E. C. O. Beatty, 'Herbert Levi Osgood', in W. T. Hutchinson (ed.), *op. cit.*; J. G. de Roulhac Hamilton (ed.), *Truth in History and Other Essays by William A. Dunning* (Columbia Univ. Press: New York, 1937); C. E. Merriam 'William Archibald Dunning', in H. W. Odum (ed.), *op. cit.*; *George Louis Beer, a Tribute* (Macmillan: New York, 1924); A. P. Scott, 'George Louis Beer', in W. T. Hutchinson (ed.), *op. cit.*; 'John Franklin Jameson', *Am. Hist. Rev.*, xliii, pp. 243–52 (1937–8); L. W. Labaree, 'Charles McLean Andrews, historian', *William & Mary Quart.*, 3rd ser., i (1944), 3–14; G. W. Pierson & L. W. Labaree, 'Charles McLean Andrews, a bibliography', *ibid.*, 15–26; M. Blinkoff, *The Influence of Charles A. Beard upon American Historiography*. Monographs in History no. 4 (Univ. of Buffalo, N.Y., 1936); S. J. Buck, 'Clarence Walworth Alvord', *Mississippi Valley Hist. Rev.*, xv, pp. 309–20 (1929); M. Dargan, jr., 'Clarence Walworth Alvord', in W. T. Hutchinson (ed.), *op. cit.*; and *Joseph Schafer, Student of Agriculture* (State Hist. Soc. of Wisconsin: Madison, Wisc., 1942).

v. On the early history of the historical societies there is a work by L. W. Dunlap, *American Historical Societies, 1790–1860* (priv. ptd.; Madison, Wisc., 1944). On their later development see A. H. Shearer, 'State Historical Societies', *New York State Historical Assoc. Quart. Journal*, iii, pp. 195–204 (1922); D. R. Fox, 'State history', *Political Science Quarterly*, xxxvi, pp. 572–85 (1921); E. B. Greene, 'Our pioneer Historical Societies', *Indiana Historical Soc. Pubs.*, x, no. 2 (1931); J. P. Boyd, 'State and local Historical Societies in the United States', *Am. Hist. Rev.*, xl, pp. 10–37 (1934–5); C. Crittenden & Doris Godard, *Historical Societies in the United States and Canada: a Handbook* (Amer. Assoc. for State and Local History: Washington, D.C., 1944).

vi. For the history of historiography in the South, see E. M. Coulter, 'What the South has done about its history', *Journal of Southern History*, ii, pp. 3–28 (1936); F. M. Green, 'Writing and research in Southern history', *Proc. S. Carolina Hist. Assoc., 1942*, pp. 3–17 (Columbia, S.C., 1942); W. H. Stephenson, 'A half century of Southern historical scholarship', *ibid.*, xi, pp. 3–32 (1945), 'Herbert B. Adams and Southern historical scholarship at the Johns Hopkins University', *Maryland Hist. Mag.*, xlii, pp. 1–20 (1947), 'John Spencer Bassett as a historian of the South', *North Carolina Hist. Rev.*, xxv, pp. 289–317 (1948), and 'William P. Trent as a

been mainly by way of elaboration. Yet this work had its
shortcomings. It confined itself too closely to the development
of governmental institutions and public policy. It took too little
account of what the governed were meanwhile doing. It took,
in particular, too little notice of what was going on in the back
lands, and it was too little assisted by economic analysis of the
problems of investment and trade. There was everything to be
said for taking one step at a time. But that implied that further
steps would have to be taken later. And in two directions, in
subsequent years, has the outlook been enlarged. The revolt
of Turner and his followers led to a new study of the influence
of the frontier upon the history of the mainland colonies in
the eighteenth century; and the unhappy experience of the
twentieth century has awakened us to the deep and far-
reaching effects in international relations of the pressure
exercised by creditors upon debtors, and has given a new significance to the history of colonial currency and the exchanges.

The service performed by the Columbia school, and the first
step taken to deepen our understanding of colonial politics
during this period, was the study of the records of central
and colonial government; and the key to the subject was discovered in the history of the legislatures, both colonial and
imperial. The most obvious feature in the development of
colonial administration in England during the eighteenth
century was a steady increase in parliamentary interference,
of which the outward sign was a tendency to substitute acts of
parliament for orders in council as instruments for the regulation of colonial affairs, and of which the cause was in part a
growth of interest in the colonies among the manufacturing
and commercial classes and the increase of the influence of
those classes in parliament, and in part the conflict with France
and the growing appreciation of the importance in that conflict
of the colonial field. But this phenomenon was not in itself so
important as another change by which it was accompanied.
The two houses not only became more active in colonial affairs
as they became more interested and more powerful; they also,
as they arrogated to themselves more and more effectively the

exercise of the sovereign authority of the crown in parliament, asserted more and more confidently that this authority knew no bounds. And an imperial control of colonial affairs which yearly became, not merely more active but less restrained, was certain sooner or later to present the colonists with issues of quite fundamental importance.

At the same time that this change was going on at home, on the American continent an equally decisive development was taking place, and one to which all the more important colonial conflicts are related. Prompted by much the same parliamentary ideals, involved in contests with the executive closely parallel to those which were fought out at home, pursuing their endeavours to resolve particular difficulties and satisfy particular grievances, the several colonial legislatures began also to set up claims to unlimited authority, and to desire on the one hand to free themselves from superior control and on the other to subordinate to themselves executive and judiciary. But whereas the wielders of the authority of the crown in parliament at Westminster had only to contend with the vague and vulnerable doctrine of the common law and right reason, and with such limits to absolutism as the courts might seek to impose in response to the petition of individuals aggrieved by their arbitrary acts, the colonial legislatures found subtracted from their jurisdiction such matters as the crown might act upon whether in council or in parliament and were shackled with what was in effect a written constitution in the shape of charter or governor's instructions, with the review of their acts by the king in council, with the requirement that colonial legislation should not be repugnant to the laws of England, and with the activities of colonial judges in many ways less responsive to legislative influence than their brethren at home. There ensued in consequence a number of often petty quarrels, varying much in their individual particulars from place to place and from time to time, and not completely and still less methodically exemplified in any one colony, and yet all reducible to one general pattern.

The problem before the colonial legislatures was twofold.

They had first to make themselves supreme in the colony, and then to secure the freedom of their authority from any external control. To achieve the first of these purposes they pursued a relentless war upon the independence of the executive and the judiciary. In their attack upon the executive they sought to capture the control both of finance and administration. Prompted not so much by abstract theory as by the desire to prevent the waste and misapplication of public funds, the lower houses laid claim to an initiative in financial legislation similar to that enjoyed by the house of commons, and sought to evade executive control of the expenditure of such funds as they had granted by a variety of devices, the more easily employed by reason of the shift of the dependence of colonial governments from regular revenue to legislative grants. They had recourse to the practice of specific appropriations. They substituted for the system of lodging public moneys with the receiver-general and their expenditure on warrants drawn by the governor in council, that of lodging them in the hands of a treasurer appointed by and responsible to the assembly itself, setting a committee of the assembly to examine the accounts and restraining the governor from making payments without its authorization. At the same time, the legislature sought to establish a like supremacy in the sphere of administration by making the officials dependent upon itself, either securing to itself their appointment or requiring by legislative command their obedience if they were appointed by others, and enforcing its authority by an attack upon such independent sources of revenue as fees, substituting in their stead salaries paid by itself; or where it was unsuccessful in the realization of this plan, delegating to legislative committees what were essentially executive functions and thus carrying out itself what it would not entrust to officials insufficiently under its control. In this setting the notorious disputes about the salaries of the governors have their place as symptoms of legislative encroachment, though their importance has probably been a good deal exaggerated. And as the executive, so also the judiciary suffered attack. Here the aim of the legislatures was first to oppose the non-statutory courts, especially those of chancery and admiralty, and secondly to render the statutory courts more responsive to the movements of public opinion by substituting judicial salaries for remuneration by fees, by putting the judicial officers of the assembly in the place of appointed magistrates, by removing the courts from urban centres to rural areas, or varying the distribution of powers between general and local tribunals and extending the jurisdiction of inferior courts. And, paradoxically, it is to be observed that, in consequence, the tenure of judges during pleasure, the badge of their servility at home, became in the colonies the condition of their independence. The clamour for the grant of tenure during good behaviour was but legislative ambition in disguise, and the power of royal dismissal of magistrates dependent upon the legislature for bread-and-butter became essential to the preservation of the integrity of the bench. The full meaning of this legislative purpose was revealed when from time to time the legislature directly invaded the province of the judiciary and substituted legislative fiat for judicial process. At the same time there was upon the one hand a tendency to revert to earlier conceptions of the source of political power and to regard the authority of the colonial legislature not as deriving from the royal writ but as resulting spontaneously from the act of free association; while, on the other, there arose a demand for the enlargement of the electorate, which in one aspect was a demand for a fuller representation of the western and poorer counties.

To constitute the legislature—and that meant to an ever-increasing degree a single popular chamber—the supreme authority in the colony was not, however, in itself sufficient without the removal of external control. To substantiate their claims to be equivalent to parliament and above the law, the colonial legislatures must free themselves from imperial interference; and this they sought to achieve in three ways. They tried to constrain the chief executive to obedience rather to legislative acts than to royal instructions. They resorted to resolves instead of acts or to temporary legislation which would expire before it could be passed upon by the king in council. And they attacked judicial review by means of the restraint of appeals to the king in council and such a modification of the character of the colonial judiciary as to render the judges no longer guardians of a law beyond the reach of the colonial legislatures.

Had this constitutional development been unilateral there would have been much to be said for its imperial opponents. The part had no title to legislate for the whole. The concession of the claim of numerous and unconnected legislatures to pass upon matters of common concern could only result in a medley of discordant pronouncements that was no acceptable alternative to a coherent system; to replace a common law by a conflict of laws would be a retrograde movement. And it could plausibly be argued that it was desirable to restrain colonial legislatures from the arbitrary invasion of the rights of minorities, religious, racial, economic or what not, and to give these minorities a protection from injustice that no mere majority could override. But the trouble was that the development of novel claims to absolutism was not all on one side. The imperial case was itself vitiated by the doctrine of parliamentary omnipotence. The issue was not simply one between a supreme law and a sovereign which claimed the right to do whatsoever seemed to it to be good in its own eyes. It was only partly that. Imperial policy, which in one point of view stood for the preservation of a higher law against the assaults of popular fiat, in another merely opposed fiat to fiat. If many resented its interference because it required from the would-be sovereign people of the colony an obedience incompatible with their claim to self-sufficiency, to others it appeared as arbitrary power which on its own side knew no limits. And nowhere was it more dangerous than in religion. In parliamentary omnipotence the episcopalians would find their most efficient instrument. What the situation was tending to was, as Thomson Mason put it in 1774, the erection in respect to each of the colonies of 'two supreme legislatures'.[1]

[1]*Virginia Gazette*, 14 July, 1774. *Cit.* A. M. Schlesinger, *The Colonial Merchants and the American Revolution, 1763–1776* (New York, 1917), p. 368.

Such a constitutional development made the preservation of a large measure of common interest all the more important. Distinct and equal powers without an operating centre—and that was what it was coming to—can only successfully remain members of a single political system if their circumstances are so similar that they will be led to identical or at least reconcilable decisions on all the more important matters of common concern. And it was just this identity of interest that became more and more lacking as the century advanced. On the one hand, British commercial and industrial interests became ever more active and more exigent; upon the other, the colonists entered upon tasks the nature and needs of which were but very imperfectly appreciated at home. And if they were little understood at the time, historians also have been slow to appreciate them since. It was precisely these topics that the Columbia school itself overlooked, although the first steps in their elucidation were taken by G. L. Beer.

Beer set himself to discover the springs of British commercial policy and to look upon its effects in the mainland colonies in the light of its larger intentions. The result was to substitute, for the traditional picture of the almost malicious enforcement of an obsolete, oppressive, and irrational system of trade at the expense of the colonies, a picture of imperial statesmanship very greatly dissatisfied with the experience of the Seven Years' War and in particular with the insufficiency of the colonial contribution to its military operations and the persistent colonial trading with the enemy in defiance of the navigation laws, and turning under the spur of these discontents to reforms in a system which was generally accepted and accepted in particular by the colonies because on the whole it served their interests.[1] But Beer's work was incomplete. It was intended to be, and it remained, essentially a study of a particular aspect of governmental policy and of the execution of that policy; and it was unfinished. After a preliminary sketch of *The Commercial Policy of England toward the American Colonies*, written at

[1] *Cf.* L. W. Labaree, *Royal Government in America* (New Haven, Conn., 1930), p. 121.

the age of twenty and published in 1893, Beer produced a more intensive study of *British Colonial Policy, 1754–1765*, and then turned back to the sixteenth century to work out exhaustively from the records the gradual evolution of that policy from its earliest beginnings. This work he had only carried down to the year 1688 when he was interrupted by the war of 1917. The three volumes on *The Origins of the British Colonial System, 1578–1660* (1908) and *The Old Colonial System, 1660–1754, Part I, The Establishment of the System, 1660–1688*, 2 vv. (1912) laid massive foundations, although the gap between 1688 and 1754 was never filled. But the whole ground had still not been covered, even in the years that had been dealt with.

The challenge to the Germanic and institutional outlook of Johns Hopkins contained in Turner's essay of 1893 on 'The significance of the frontier in American history' was a challenge also to the work of the Columbia school. It called attention to that problem of the western lands which had figured too little in the work of either Osgood or Beer. But it did not bear fruit until their work was almost done. The importance of the western lands in the history of the mainland colonies in the eighteenth century was first fully demonstrated in Alvord's two volumes on *The Mississippi Valley in British Politics*, published in 1917. Their most notable precursors had been G. H. Alden, *New Governments West of the Alleghanies before 1780* (1897), R. L. Schuyler, *The Transition in Illinois from British to American Government* (1909), and C. E. Carter's *Great Britain and the Illinois Country, 1703–1774* (1910). What was to prove to be a seminal work appeared at an unpropitious time; the book was a difficult book; there were the mistakes in it that are not to be avoided in a pioneer work cutting a path through unexplored country; and it was only rather slowly that its importance was appreciated.

The subject of the back lands is one of great difficulty, and it is not surprising that the historian has been slow to master it. In the complicated, obscure, and ever shifting rivalry of interests, imperfectly reported and but partially understood, that revolved about the disposal of the back lands were mingled far-reaching problems of politics, law, and economics; while the divergent aims of imperial and provincial policy, the rivalry of colony with colony, and the conflict between tidewater and back country within each colony, permitted of a variety of permutations and combinations making argument inconsistent and rendering it easy to mistake accident for principle.

The problems created by a western advance were forced upon the attention of contemporary authority by two agencies that continued in operation throughout the long progress of the frontier across the continent. The backwoodsmen, the moving frontier of settlement itself, pressed upon the hunting grounds of the Indian; and the more vigorous and progressive among the business minds, denied an outlet in the development of colonial manufactures, addressed themselves to the employment of their growing capital in Indian trade and operations in real estate, and enlisted in their enterprise the support of powerful mercantile interests at home. Between these two groups of settlers and speculators there were elements both of common interest and latent hostility. The plans of the monied men to promote Indian trade and frontier settlement were themselves not without their inherent contradictions; and the idea of profitable traffic in land conflicted with the settler's doctrine that man was entitled to such gifts of nature as he could appropriate and that such value as the land possessed arose from the activity of those who occupied and developed it. But both groups alike desired the extinction of Indian title in areas beyond the bounds of established civilization.

The elucidation of the history of the back country has been, in the main, the work of that Middle Western school of history that took its rise in Wisconsin, Illinois, and Michigan. The problem in all its essential features was there at the opening of the eighteenth century.[1] The story of its development falls into two parts, corresponding to the division of responsibility for Indian affairs between the Northern and Southern Depart-

[1]See map 1 and C. W. Alvord, *The Illinois Country, 1673–1818* (Chicago, Ill., 1922), p. 35.

5

ments in 1755. The subject of the first chapter in both is the history of the fur trade and of the effect of the growth of that trade upon the Indians. In the north, the first white penetration of the upper Mississippi valley was effected by the French *coureurs de bois* moving out of the valley of the St. Lawrence at the beginning of the seventeenth century; and it led to the discovery by Jolliet and Marquette of the upper waters of the Mississippi river by way of the Fox-Wisconsin portage in 1673. That this advance should have taken so wide a sweep to the west was due to the circumstances of Indian history. The effect upon the Indian of the white man's readiness to buy furs was to revolutionize his way of life.[1] He ceased to be self-sufficient. Neglecting his crops, discovering new wants, substituting above all fire-arms for his native weapons, he gave himself over to hunting and became the purveyor of a single export and wholly dependent upon the traders. The forest economy was thus thrown out of balance and forest society set in flux. Able to kill more animals more quickly than before and having a motive to do so, the frontier tribe discovered the need and possessed the means to extend its hunting grounds at the expense of those who were both geographically and socially its more backward neighbours. The first Indians to be so stimulated and so equipped were the Iroquois and the Neutrals, supplied by the Dutch at Albany; and it was their attacks upon the Hurons and Algonquins in the middle of the seventeenth century that checked French penetration south of the Lakes, deflected the line of French advance to the northwest, and led to the penetration of Wisconsin between 1654 and 1682. The result was that the area between the Great Lakes and the Ohio became for a hundred years the scene of conflict, first between the Iroquois, serving the English traders, and the Western Indians, backed by the French, and then between the French and English themselves. Defeated in Wisconsin in 1654, the Iroquois, seeking a fresh supply of furs, renewed their attacks during the last quarter of the seventeenth century; and there

[1] *Cf.* W. W. Folwell, *A History of Minnesota*, 4 vv. (Saint Paul, Minn., 1921–30), i, 85–6.

ensued a series of Indian wars to which between 1689 and 1701 the French and English also became parties. The result was a set-back for the Iroquois and the reversal in the eighteenth century of the drift of settlement that under the fury of their attack had thinned the population of the Illinois country in the seventeenth.[1] The successful establishment of French military and trading posts at Detroit and in the Illinois at the turn of the century encouraged a reverse movement of the Indians from northwest to southeast; and the failure of the French finally to subdue the Indians of Wisconsin, culminating in the Fox War of 1728–38, led to the transfer of the principal French trade routes to the Illinois country. But this reverse flow met a northwesterly movement into the Illinois country, of Indians retreating from south and east before the expansion of English settlement; and the effective French penetration of the Ohio valley did not occur until the English were already pressing down the western slopes of the Alleghany mountains.

The somewhat similar history of the back lands of the South has also been written in the main by the same school of historians. But the work was undertaken later, and is not complete. The deepest penetration of the back lands by English traders before 1700 was that effected by those who went out from the Carolinas, developing the contacts first made with the Cherokees by the Virginians in the last quarter of the seventeenth century.[2] Their advance was a challenge not only to Spain but also to the French, and stimulated the establishment of the latter on the Gulf of Mexico at the turn of the century. The result, before a generation had passed, was the blocking of the open way round the southern end of the Appalachian mountains. There followed forty years of complex forest diplomacy. In this the Creek Confederation played in the south a part somewhat similar to that played in the north by the Iroquois. Opportunity lay in the rivalry of the white men. The French, established in the Mississippi valley and relying upon the resent-

---

[1]For a contrary opinion see T. Bodley, *Our First Great West* (Louisville, Ky., 1938), p. 8.
[2]C. W. Alvord & L. Bidgood, *The First Explorations of the Trans-Allegheny Region by the Virginians, 1650–1674* (Cleveland, O., 1912), pp. 91–2.

ment that would be caused by the restless thrust of British
settlement, looked to the Indians as an instrument with which
to drive the British back to the sea; and they found their
chances improved by the consolidation of the tribes in the confederation after the Yamasee War of 1715–16. The British,
sensing their danger, strengthened their hold upon the coast,
substituting royal for proprietary government in South
Carolina in 1721 and founding the colony of Georgia in 1732;
but also, while adhering to a policy of territorial expansion
and putting it indeed into immediate effect in Georgia, sought
to allay antagonism and to offset French influence by the promotion of trade and by mediation in the quarrels of the tribes.
In these circumstances, the Indian towns became the scene of
the anxious negotiations of rival colonial authorities. In these,
the opportunities of the French lay in the unwillingness of the
more favourably placed tribes to allow the far Indians direct
contact with the traders and in the quarrels of the more favourably placed among themselves; and the British were embarrassed by the hostility between the Six Nations upon the one
hand and Cherokees, Creeks, and Catawbas upon the other,
and after 1748, when peace was made between the Cherokees
and the Six Nations, by the use of Cherokee country by the
latter as a base for raids upon the Catawbas. Yet on balance
British policy in the south achieved its aim, and the battle
with the French was fought out farther north. But that still left
the deeper conflicts of the frontier unresolved. Colonial government had nowhere been wholly successful in the regulation of
Indian trade or the removal of its abuses; and the thrust of
white settlement was unremitting.

   The first British penetration of the Mississippi valley was
effected by the New York fur traders moving up the Mohawk
towards the Great Lakes and by the Carolina traders advancing round the southern end of the Appalachians, to whom
reference has already been made. The penetration in the north
was halted by the readiness of the Albany traders to find their
profit in supplying English goods to the French, by the strength
of the Iroquois which enabled them to defend their profits as

middlemen by refusing to admit the establishment of direct contacts with the far Indians of the fur-bearing country, and by the building of forts by the French at Detroit in 1701 and Niagara in 1727. That in the south had, by the end of the first quarter of the century, been successfully blocked by the French establishment in Louisiana. But in the course of the southern conflict the problem of the western lands had emerged in its familiar shape. The penetration of the West by British traders had been recognized by London as necessary to the effective competition with Spain and France for the control of the interior. That recognition carried with it the need for the formulation of an imperial Indian policy; it caused the planting of back settlements to be regarded with favour; but it raised issues that divided the merchants, supported by powerful interests in London and looking to the uncontrolled exploitation of the Indian trade, from the tidewater planters, anxious for peace upon the frontier; and it gave rise in South Carolina to the subsidiary dispute whether the regulation of Indian trade, if regulation there were to be, should fall to the governor or to the commons' house. But when in the middle of the eighteenth century, the tide of settlement washed up against the eastern foothills of the dividing mountains, the natural avenues round the ends of the range to north and south were no longer open and the line of least resistance led over the Wilderness trail from Pennsylvania and from the headwaters of the Potomac to those of the Monongahela, whence the settlers moved down to occupy the lands between the Ohio and the Tennessee that had divided the northern and southern Indian confederations and had lain a no-man's-land between them.

The question that their advance raised was whether penetration into the Indian country should, on grounds of public policy, be encouraged or restrained, and if it were to be allowed, whether, by whom, and upon what principles it should be regulated; how, if regulation there were to be, the expenses of regulation should be met; and whether, indeed, the western lands were to be a source of revenue or to be treated as a means of promoting settlement and expanding markets. These problems became a matter of practical politics with the formation of the Ohio Company in 1747. Their solution became urgent after 1763. But that solution, as has been indicated, affected a great variety of conflicting interests; its consideration at Westminster was bedevilled by the vicissitudes of English politics during the critical years between 1763 and 1770; and the problem itself did not stand still while ministers and their officials tried to make up their minds what to do about it.

Broadly stated, the issue was whether individuals, acting alone or in partnership, could be allowed to acquire land direct from the Indians and the frontier be thus left to advance without public control, when such invasions of Indian territory were certain to contain a large admixture of force or fraud and were likely to bring down upon the community foreign or Indian war; and when such proceedings were certain, sooner or later, to raise matters of public interest and require public intervention if only for the determination of disputed titles: or whether title could be acquired only by the crown, in which case the conveyance might be so effected as to do justice to the Indian or at least not drive him to desperation, and the land acquired be made a source of public profit and granted upon such terms as would, by a system of quit rents, retain a public title and render the use of the land amenable to public control. And if the answer were, as it must be, that a wholly unregulated advance could not be tolerated, then the further question arose whether an Indian policy could be worked out by the individual colonies, lacking as they did any effective means of coöperation, or whether there must not be established an imperial system. And if that, in turn, were conceded, then it would further fall to be determined whether, if the West were not abandoned, but the gradual extinction of Indian title sought by treaty, the costs of the necessary Indian department and military establishment could be met by the collection of a colonial revenue derived in whole or in part from quit rents levied upon the lands acquired and disposed of.

Faced with these issues, there were men both in the colonies

and at home who preferred to leave the Indian in the possession of his hunting grounds. To the established interests of the
tidewater and the piedmont western expansion meant additional trouble and expense, the decline of land values, the loss
of labour, and in the long run competition in their markets
and a shift in the centre of gravity threatening them with a loss
of their political power. To the minds of some at home it looked
like an invasion of legally vested rights, whether of the
Indians or of the holders of colonial charters, and bore a sinister
resemblance to the evil tendencies of imperial policy in India;
while it could plausibly be argued that it was economically
unsound, since interior colonies would be incapable of profitable trade with England, must of necessity develop their own
manufactures, would be detrimental to the interests of the fur
trade, and would draw population from the mother country
as well as from the tidewater. And yet if opposition such as this
was as futile as to forbid the tide to flow, there was still much
division among those who accepted a forward policy; and there
were competing interests ready to exploit this. There were rival
land companies; and only in a short view were the aims of
Indian trade and interior settlement compatible. The unauthorized settlers upon the frontier had little relish for enquiries into their title and less for a demand for quit rents or
any procedure that would bring the risk of sale over their
heads to legitimate purchasers. The colonies with claims
to western lands were as much opposed to imperial interference
as those without them welcomed it. The Pennsylvania traders
were jealous of the interest in territory within their beat beyond the mountains newly shown by some of the leading figures
in Virginia; and the rival claims to jurisdiction advanced by the
two states invited the public support of private competitors and
the exploitation both of the jealousy of Northern and Southern
Indian departments in the Debatable Land and of the conflict
of jurisdiction between crown and colony. In such circumstances diversities of legal opinion were readily exploited;
and, as occasion served, the same parties argued with an equal
show of conviction that Indian cessions could be made to the

crown alone, that the crown could act only as the agent of the colony, and that good title could be acquired directly from the Indians by the individual purchaser.

In the event, the inherent difficulties of the problem and the disturbed state of English politics frustrated any satisfactory solution. A tentative and hesitating approach was made towards a comprehensive plan for the establishment of a temporary boundary to immediate settlement and the imperial management of the problems that lay beyond it. It looked to the imperial supervision of Indian relations and the regulation of Indian trade upon which they so largely depended; the orderly extinction of the Indian title to lands coveted by the white man, with a view to the eventual erection of new colonies; the maintenance of the military establishment and Indian department necessary to the execution of such a policy, and the levy of colonial taxation to meet the cost; and the diversion, for the time being, of the pressure of emigration to Nova Scotia and Florida. But the plan was never fully worked out; it was too expensive; and there were too many interests opposed to it for its adoption to be feasible without steadier and more masterful insistence than any statesman or connection could bring to bear during those distracted years. It dwindled, consequently, to an immature scheme to turn control over to the colonies under some general imperial supervision, the costs being met out of the proceeds of quit rents and requisitions; and it came finally to the mere obstruction of unregulated western expansion without the substitution of any effective alternative, and to a levy of colonial taxation for the maintenance of a military establishment that would only have been acceptable to colonial opinion if it had been employed upon the frontier.

Consequently the debate about the western lands resulted in no simple alignment of political forces. Though they had from time to time their allies in the east, the actual settlers upon the back lands felt a steady discontent with the policies both of the provincial capitals and of Westminster. Williamsburg could champion their cause when their enemy was the Pennsylvania traders organized in an alien land company; and even on occasion support them against speculators who were citizens of the colony of Virginia itself. But in general the interests of tidewater, and therefore of colonial legislatures, and of the back country were divergent. Yet the greater sympathy with western expansion shown at Westminster was, on the other hand, more than offset in the minds of frontiersmen by an undue squeamishness about the treatment of Indians and a pedantic regard for the niceties of the law of real property; and there can be no doubt that royal government earned little merit in their eyes. The stand of the powerful forces enlisted in the land companies was on the contrary less consistent. Franklin saw in a central colonial administration of the western lands a better prospect for the pursuit of the interests of the Pennsylvania traders than in reliance upon any effective resistance to Virginian claims by the Quaker majority in Philadelphia; and the Pennsylvania traders sought later in London rather than Philadelphia the promotion of the interests of the Indiana Company, and found there powerful mercantile and political support. Just so, the Company when in 1776, upon the disappearance of the prospects of the Vandalia Company in which it had temporarily been merged, it was met with a condemnation of individual purchases from the Indian by the Virginia Convention, saw its only hopes in the transfer of jurisdiction over the back country, not to the several states but to the Continental Congress, where business interests were powerfully represented. But that did not mean that there was an alliance between the land companies and the centre whether that centre lay in Westminster or in the capital of a colonial confederation. If the Ohio Company, finding little comfort at Williamsburg, appealed like the Pennsylvanians to Westminster, its domestic rivals, the Greenbrier and Loyal Companies, received local support; and when the influence of the Ohio Company itself was ousted at Westminster by that of the more powerful Walpole Company, it in turn became the champion of the claims of the colony. Save for the actual settlers upon the frontier, therefore, the differences were thus differences of opportunity and tactics rather than differences of policy between those abroad and those at home. Progressive was pitted against conservative, imperialist against the more cautious and the more careful, the ineluctable trend of events against the arguments of the law. There were westerners in the east; and the colonies were as much divided on the matter within and between themselves as the mother country was divided from them.

The cross-currents were thus many, and the chart is complicated. There were men at home alive to the possibilities of the frontier; and the selfish interests of the tidewater stretched here and there back across the Atlantic. Indeed the student of American history has from the start, if he is to avoid falling into confusion, to beware of the belief that men can be classed according to the sovereign authority to which they look. They are rather to be divided according to their interests and to their ideas about the proper nature and scope of that authority wherever it may reside. Nationalism and legislative absolutism can be predicated of a variety of political bodies situated in a variety of places: the conflicting interests of settler, trader, and speculator, of back country and seaboard, of private enterprise and public control, of settlement and revenue may be served now by one and now by another political authority. The most durable feature in this case is the disregard by the tidewater of the interests of the frontier; and although Westminster was in some respects a further 'east', the expansionists sometimes fared better there than in the provincial capitals. It cannot be said simply, therefore, that the failure of Westminster to deal decisively and successfully with the problem of the western lands is to be added to the list of colonial grievances. Yet the general drift is clear. A new question was in process of shaping itself, and it received no satisfying answer. In consequence there was bred a discontent compounded of impatience both with the restraining hand of Westminster, where only the negative elements of a western policy survived the negligent attention and divided aims of English politicians, and with the narrow selfishness of the tidewater interests that controlled the provincial governments. There had indeed begun that march across a continent that was to have so large a share in the transformation, during the coming century, of the life of the whole Atlantic seaboard, and that called for an altogether new instrument of government to control it.

The problem of the western lands was thus closely associated with two deep-seated causes of dissension, neither of which has yet received sufficiently penetrating analysis. They are the conflict of interest between tidewater and back country within the several colonial societies, and the relentless pressure of a continued passive balance of trade upon the economy of a debtor community. In relation to the first, public land policy was a crucial matter. While the Indian danger had been close, the back settlements had been a welcome screen for the inhabitants of the coastal areas. But that danger by the middle of the eighteenth century had become more remote; and it was the early part of that century that witnessed the arrival of the first great wave of immigration that was without loyalty to England or was actively hostile towards it, the immigration of Germans and Scotch-Irish. These elements sought the frontier; they needed land and credit; they had unfamiliar notions; and finding their interests neglected and themselves inadequately represented in the colonial legislatures, they developed unwelcome political ambitions. As little satisfied with the policy that prevailed at the provincial capitals as any colonist with the policy of Westminster, they came to threaten a revolt within a revolt. The defence of colonial rights was the defence of the rights of a limited class and a restricted region. It found its own radical critics in the unenfranchized classes of the towns and in the western counties. There is a by-play interfused with the classical quarrel with crown and parliament. The effect of the insistence by Turner and Alvord upon the importance of the frontier was to call attention to this. That insistence has not substantially modified the conclusions of Osgood and his followers in their own field, but it sets those conclusions against a wider background. It has given a new significance to a good deal that was previously familiar without being fully understood ; and there is still much to be done to draw out its full implications in this early period.

In relation to the problem of the external balance of payments, it was a matter of some moment that the land companies were frustrated. They were the most advanced form of business structure that had developed in the colonies. They were the head of a vigorous flow pushing to find an outlet. It had been dammed back when it sought this in other directions. There was danger in the persistent obstruction of so powerful a force. The direction of attention to the deflationary influence exercised upon the colonial economy by the pressure of imperial policy is more recent than the direction of attention to the problem of western lands. Beer was familiar with the pressure put upon the colonial debtor by his English creditor and with the imperial veto, at the behest of that creditor, of the measures of relief to which the debtor had recourse. But it was no part of his business to examine the influence of that policy upon the internal economy of the colonies. No subject recurs with greater regularity in the journal of the Commissioners for Trade and Plantations during the eighteenth century than that of paper money. But it has as yet received little detailed treatment. Its early history has been dealt with in monographic studies by C. J. Bullock, A. M. Davis, and C. P. Nettels;[1] and the broad outlines of the later phases of the problem have been sketched in the study of *The Roots of American Civilization* by the last of these writers. But the deeper implications have hardly been considered.

Engaged in an ever-growing volume of business, always owing large sums to British houses, lacking a mint and dependent upon a variety of foreign coins, the colonists suffered normally from a confusion of the colonial exchanges and a difficulty in making sterling remittances. From their embarrassments they sought relief in paper money and stay laws, only to meet the steady opposition of imperial authority to any impairment of the rights of creditors; and the conflict of interest between debtor and creditor in the shape of disputes about a paper currency became in the eighteenth century a constantly recurring theme of colonial politics. The Board of Trade and

[1] See p. 72 below.

the English merchants were willing to concur in the emission of bills sufficient to serve the needs of the colonists for a circulating medium. But they insisted upon this being accompanied by provisions to prevent depreciation, and they set their face against the constitution of paper a legal tender in payment of debt or taxes. The effect was to leave scope for differences of opinion between debtors and creditors as to what was in fact sufficient to meet colonial needs and whether the currency had appreciated or was being inflated. This situation, instead of being alleviated in the course of time, was greatly exacerbated by that development of British economic policy which became marked after the close of the Seven Years' War. As the interest shifted from the tropical to the northern colonies, and colonies came more and more to be valued as markets rather than as sources of the supply of exotic commodities, the pressure upon the continental colonies was steadily increased to constrain them to buy more than they sold, and the financial embarrassments which they had always experienced were aggravated. By a persistent endeavour to stifle colonial manufactures, by the veto of colonial restraints upon the importation of slaves, by the more efficient check of illicit trade and particularly by the interruption of the trade with the foreign West Indies, and by colonial taxation, the creditors made the already hard lot of the debtors harder still. They imposed upon them a growing adverse balance of visible trade and an increasing difficulty in buying those sterling bills which were needed to fill the gap. The imperial parliament and the colonial legislatures became the representatives in large measure of rival economic interests; and the straitened debtor was called upon to make those adjustments required to restore equilibrium, the burden of which might more justly have fallen upon the broader shoulders of the creditor. Add such a divergence of interest to the claims to the possession of distinct and equal powers knowing no higher law than their own will, and you have a formula that will comprehend most of the events relating to the mainland colonies that occurred between 1700 and 1775.

BIBLIOGRAPHICAL NOTE

i. When in 1900 Osgood was invited to contribute a volume on the mainland colonies in the eighteenth century to the series entitled *The American Nation*, edited by A. B. Hart, he declined on the ground that our knowledge of the period was not then ripe for summary,[1] and although there was ultimately included in the series a valuable study by E. B. Greene, entitled *Provincial America, 1696–1740*, Osgood was in the main fully justified. In 1900, almost all the necessary preliminary work on the history of particular colonies or of particular problems had yet to be done; and none of the attempts to generalize made between 1900 and 1924 was really satisfactory. Of these attempts much the most valuable was the volume by E. B. Greene (1905) to which reference has just been made. But even Greene was constrained to deal very much less fully with the years 1714–42 than with those which went before; and in the next volume in the series, *France in America, 1497–1763*, by R. G. Thwaites, the history of the domestic affairs of the colonies and of their constitutional relations with the home government from 1742 to 1763 was almost wholly neglected in favour of the older and more familiar topics of discovery and war. The chapter by J. A. Doyle in volume vii (1903) of the *Cambridge Modern History* on 'The English Colonies, 1700–1763' was no more than a brief descriptive sketch based upon the older authorities; and while that author's volume on *The Colonies under the House of Hanover* (1907) was in the range of its interest a notable advance upon the work of Thwaites, it was derived almost exclusively, save for the history of Georgia, from printed sources, and made but little use of such of the modern monographic studies as had by that date been published by American scholars. It treated generously the history of religion and of learning. It recognized, clearly and fully, the importance of English parliamentary development in the eighteenth century to the history of colonial government. But it barely carried the study of constitutional changes in the colonies themselves beyond a discussion of the problems of fees and governors' salaries, and it was far from being a definitive study. E. Channing's *History of the United States*, volume ii, *A Century of Colonial History, 1660–1760* (1908), treated the period on a slightly more liberal scale than Greene, and contained a rather more continuous narrative of the domestic history of the several colonies. But, like its predecessors, it becomes much slighter after it passes the year 1714, and it added little of substance to what was to be found in earlier works, was so partisan as sometimes to be quite

[1] D. R. Fox, *Herbert Levi Osgood* (New York, 1924).

misleading;[1] and it was on the whole a far less satisfactory volume than Doyle's. The sections relating to the eighteenth century in the volumes by C. M. Andrews, *The Colonial Period* (1912), and C. L. Becker, *Beginnings of the American People* ('Riverside History of the United States', volume i, 1915), were written by scholars who were themselves authorities upon this period; but, while drawing upon the new work and full of suggestive remarks, they were written upon too small a scale to admit of that detailed exposition and argument that was needed. And it was still possible for Andrews to complain in 1914 of the neglect and misinterpretation of the years 1700–50, and for J. T. Adams as late as 1922 to speak of the eighteenth century as the unexplored region of New England history.[2] All this was changed by the work of Osgood and of Turner and that of their disciples.

ii. For the political and constitutional history of the colonies, and for the history of the imperial administration of their affairs, the standard authority is now H. L. Osgood, *The American Colonies in the Eighteenth Century*, 4 vv. (Columbia Univ. Press: New York, 1924). To this work there may usefully be added five books of very different scale and purpose that are nevertheless of a general character—C. M. Andrews, *The Colonial Background of the American Revolution* (Yale Univ. Press: New Haven, Conn., 1924; 2nd ed. revised, 1931), J. T. Adams, *Provincial Society, 1690–1763*, being vol. iii of 'A History of American Life', edited by A. M. Schlesinger and D. R. Fox (Macmillan: New York, 1927), M. W. Jernegan, *The American Colonies, 1492–1750* (Longmans, 1929), Käthe Spiegel, *Kulturgeschichtliche Grundlagen der Amerikanischen Revolution* (Oldenbourg: Munich & Berlin, 1931), and C. P. Nettels, *The Roots of American Civilization. A History of American Colonial Life* (F. S. Crofts: New York, 1938). The work of Osgood himself has been developed in a number of monographs dealing with the several histories of particular colonies or with particular aspects of colonial life common to all the colonies, many of which were the work of his own pupils, namely:—

(a) J. B. Brebner, *New England's Outpost; Acadia before the Conquest of Canada*. Col. Univ. Studies, 293 (Columbia Univ. Press: New York, 1927); J. T. Adams, *Revolutionary New England, 1691–1776* (Atlantic Monthly Press: Boston, 1923); W. B. Weeden, *Economic*

---

[1] Compare, e.g., the accounts of the New York governorship of Lord Bellomont in Channing, ii, 303–6 and Osgood, *The American Colonies in the Eighteenth Century*, i, 272–86.

[2] *Am. Hist. Rev.*, xx (1915), pp. 43–7; xxviii (1923), pp. 673–81; *cf.* J. T. Adams, 'Opportunities for research in the eighteenth century', *Ann. Rept. of the Am. Hist. Assoc. for the year 1922*, i, 325 (Washington, 1926).

and Social History of New England, 1620–1789, 2 vv. (Houghton Mifflin: New York, 1890); W. H. Fry, *New Hampshire as a Royal Province.* Col. Univ. Studies, 79 (Columbia Univ. Press: New York, 1908); A. B. Hart (ed.), *Commonwealth History of Massachusetts*, vol. ii, *1689–1775* (States History Co.: New York, 1928); Susan M. Reed, *Church and State in Massachusetts, 1691–1740.* Univ. of Illinois Studies in the Social Sciences, iii. no. 4 (Urbana, Ill., 1914); H. R. Spencer, *Constitutional Conflict in Provincial Massachusetts* (Fred J. Heer: Columbus, O., 1905); E. Kimball, *The Public Life of Joseph Dudley . . . 1660–1715.* Harvard Hist. Studies, xv (Harvard Univ. Press: Cambridge, Mass., 1911); G. A. Wood, *William Shirley, Governor of Massachusetts, 1741–1756.* Col. Univ. Studies, 209 (Columbia Univ. Press: New York, 1920); W. B. Weeden, *Early Rhode Island. A Social History of the People* (Grafton Press: New York, 1910); Edith A. Bailey, *Influences toward Radicalism in Connecticut, 1754–1775.* Smith College Studies in History, v, no. 4 (Northampton, Mass., 1920); O. Zeichner, *Connecticut's Years of Controversy, 1750–1776* (Univ. of N. Carolina Press: Chapel Hill, N.C. 1949); M. B. Jones, *Vermont in the Making* (Harvard Univ. Press: Cambridge, Mass., 1939); C. Williamson, *Vermont in Quandary, 1763–1825* (Vermont Hist. Soc.: Montpelier, Vt., 1949); C. W. Spencer, *Phases of Royal Government in New York, 1691–1719* (Fred J. Heer: Columbus, O., 1905); C. L. Becker, *The History of Political Parties in the Province of New York, 1760–1776.* Univ. of Wisconsin Bulletin No. 286 (Madison, Wisc., 1909); A. E. Peterson, *New York as an Eighteenth Century Municipality prior to 1731.* Col. Univ. Studies, 177 (Columbia Univ. Press: New York, 1917); G. W. Edwards, *New York as an Eighteenth Century Municipality, 1731–1776.* Col. Univ. Studies, 178 (Columbia Univ. Press: New York, 1917); Alice M. Keys, *Cadwalader Colden, a Representative Eighteenth Century Official* (Columbia Univ. Press: New York, 1906); E. P. Tanner, *The Province of New Jersey, 1664–1738.* Col. Univ. Studies, 80 (Columbia Univ. Press: New York, 1908); E. J. Fisher, *New Jersey as a Royal Province, 1738 to 1776.* Col. Univ. Studies, 107 (Columbia Univ. Press: New York, 1911); D. L. Kemmerer, *Path to Freedom; the Struggle for Self-government in Colonial New Jersey, 1703–1776* (Princeton Univ. Press: Princeton, N.J., 1940); W. R. Shepherd, *History of Proprietary Government in Pennsylvania.* Col. Univ. Studies, 16 (Columbia Univ. Press: New York, 1896); W. T. Root, *The Relations of Pennsylvania with the British Government, 1696–1765.* Pubs. of the Univ. of Pennsylvania. History (Univ. of Pennsylvania Press: Philadelphia, 1912); C. H. Lincoln, *The Revolutionary Movement in Pennsylvania, 1760–1776* (Appleton: New York, 1901); N. D. Mereness, *Maryland as a Proprietary Province* (Macmillan: New York, 1901); C. P. Gould, *The*

Land System in Maryland, 1720–1765. Johns Hopkins Univ. Studies, xxxi, no. 1, and *Money and Transportation in Maryland, 1720–1765, ibid.* xxxiii, no. 1 (Johns Hopkins Press: Baltimore, Md., 1913, 1915); P. S. Flippin, *The Royal Government in Virginia, 1624–1775.* Col. Univ. Studies, 194 (Columbia Univ. Press: New York, 1919); E. I. Miller, *The Legislature of the Province of Virginia.* Col. Univ. Studies, 76 (Columbia Univ. Press: New York, 1907); P. S. Flippin, *The Financial Administration of the Colony of Virginia.* Johns Hopkins Univ. Studies, xxxiii, no. 2 (Johns Hopkins Press: Baltimore, Md., 1915); L. Dodson, *Alexander Spotswood, Governor of Colonial Virginia, 1710–1722* (Univ. of Pennsylvania Press: Philadelphia, 1932); C. L. Raper, *North Carolina; a Study in English Colonial Government* (Macmillan: New York, 1904); R. D. W. Connor, *The Colonial and Revolutionary Periods, 1584 to 1783,* being vol. i of the 'History of North Carolina' edited by R. D. W. Connor (The Lewis Publishing Company: Chicago & New York, 1919); W. R. Smith, *South Carolina as a Royal Province, 1719–1776* (Macmillan: New York, 1903); E. McCrady, *The History of South Carolina under the Proprietary Government, 1670–1719* (Macmillan: New York, 1897) and *The History of South Carolina under Royal Government, 1719–1776* (Macmillan: New York, 1899); R. L. Meriwether, *The Expansion of South Carolina, 1729–1765* (Southern Publishers: Kingsport, Tenn., 1940); W. A. Schaper, 'Sectionalism and representation in South Carolina'. *Annual Report of the American Historical Association for the Year 1900,* vol. i (Govt. Printing Office: Washington, D.C., 1901); J. R. McCain, *Georgia as a Proprietary Province* (R. G. Badger: Boston, 1917); P. S. Flippin, 'Royal Government in Georgia, 1752–1776'. *Georgia Hist. Quart.,* viii–x (1924–6), xii–xiii (1928–9); J. E. Callaway, *The Early Settlement of Georgia* (Univ. of Georgia Press: Athens, Ga., 1948); C. L. Mowat, *East Florida as a British Province, 1763–1784* (Univ. of California Press: Berkeley, Calif., 1943); C. Johnson, *British West Florida, 1763–1783.* Yale Hist. Pubs., xlii (Yale Univ. Press: New Haven, Conn., 1943); C. N. Howard, *The British Development of West Florida, 1763–1769* (Univ. of California Press: Berkeley, Calif., 1947).

(b) A. B. Keith, *Constitutional History of the first British Empire* (Clarendon Press: Oxford, 1930); E. B. Greene, *The Provincial Governor in the English Colonies of North America.* Harvard Hist. Studies, vii (Longmans, Green: New York, 1898); L. W. Labaree, *Royal Government in America.* Yale Hist. Pubs., Studies, vi (Yale Univ. Press: New Haven, Conn., 1930); O. M. Dickerson, *American Colonial Government, 1696–1765* (Arthur H. Clark: Cleveland, O., 1912); A. H. Basye, *The Lords Commissioners of Trade and Planta-tions . . . 1748–1782.* Yale Hist. Pubs., xiv (Yale Univ. Press:

New Haven, Conn., 1925); Margaret M. Spector, *The American Department of British Government, 1768–1782.* Col. Univ. Studies, 466 (Columbia Univ. Press: New York, 1940); R. B. Morris, *Studies in the History of American Law with Special Reference to the 17th and 18th Centuries.* Col. Univ. Studies, 316 (Columbia Univ. Press: New York, 1930); E. B. Russell, *The Review of American Colonial Legislation by the King in Council.* Col. Univ. Studies, 155 (Columbia Univ. Press: New York, 1915); J. H. Smith, *Appeals to the Privy Council from the American Plantations* (Columbia Univ. Press: New York, 1950); J. F. Burns, *Controversies between Royal Governors and their Assemblies in the Northern American Colonies* (priv. ptd., Wright & Potter Printing Co.; Boston, 1923); E. I. McCormac, *Colonial Opposition to Imperial Authority during the French and Indian War.* Univ. of California Pubs. in History, i (Univ. of California Press: Berkeley, Calif., 1911); C. F. Bishop, *History of Elections in the American Colonies.* Col. Univ. Studies, 8 (Columbia Univ. Press: New York, 1893); A. E. McKinley, *The Suffrage Franchise in the Thirteen English Colonies.* Pubs. of the Univ. of Pennsylvania. Series in History, no. 2 (Ginn: Boston, 1905); Mary P. Clarke, *Parliamentary Privilege in the American Colonies.* Yale Hist. Pubs., xliv (Yale Univ. Press; New Haven, Conn., 1943); A. L. Cross, *The Anglican Episcopate and the American Colonies.* Harvard Hist. Studies, ix (Longmans, Green: New York, 1902); B. W. Bond, jr., *The Quit-rent System in the American Colonies.* Yale Hist. Pubs., vi (Yale Univ. Press: New Haven, Conn., 1919). The series of Columbia University Studies also contains a volume by G. A. Washburne on *Imperial Control of the Administration of Justice in the Thirteen American Colonies, 1684–1776,* no. 238 (Columbia Univ. Press: New York, 1923), but it hardly deserves inclusion in this list.

(c) G. L. Beer, *The Commercial Policy of England toward the American Colonies.* Col. Univ. Studies, 9 (Columbia Univ. Press: New York, 1893); W. J. Ashley, *Surveys, Historic and Economic* (Longmans, 1900); G. B. Hertz, *The Old Colonial System.* Pubs. of the Univ. of Manchester. Hist. Ser. iii (Manchester, 1905); Kate Hotblack, *Chatham's Colonial Policy* (Routledge, 1917); G. L. Beer, *British Colonial Policy, 1754–1765* (Macmillan: New York, 1907); A. A. Giesecke, *American Commercial Legislation before 1789* (Appleton: New York, 1910); E. R. Johnson *et al.*, *History of Domestic and Foreign Commerce of the United States,* vol. i (Carnegie Institution: Washington, D.C., 1915); Helen J. Crump, *Colonial Admiralty Jurisdiction in the Seventeenth Century* (Longmans, 1931); Elizabeth E. Hoon, *The Organization of the English Customs System, 1696–1786* (Appleton-Century: New York, 1938); V. S. Clark, *History of Manufactures in the United States, 1607–1860* (Carnegie Institution of Washington: Washington, D.C., 1916; revd. ed. 1929); Eleanor L. Lord, *Industrial*

Experiments in the British Colonies of North America. Johns Hopkins Univ. Studies. Extra vol. xvii (Johns Hopkins Press: Baltimore, Md., 1898); A. C. Bining, *British Regulation of the Colonial Iron Industry* (Univ. of Pennsylvania Press: Philadelphia, 1933); M. W. Jernegan, *Laboring and Dependent Classes in Colonial America, 1607–1783* (Univ. of Chicago Press: Chicago, 1931); A. E. Smith, *Colonists in Bondage; White Servitude and Convict Labor in America, 1607–1776* (Univ. of N. Carolina Press: Chapel Hill, N.C., 1947); S. McKee, jr., *Labor in Colonial New York, 1664–1776.* Col. Univ. Studies, 410 (Columbia Univ. Press, New York, 1935); R. G. Albion, *Forests and Sea Power; the Timber Problem of the Royal Navy, 1652–1862.* Harvard Econ. Studies, xxix (Harvard Univ. Press: Cambridge, Mass., 1926); A. L. Cross, *Eighteenth Century Documents relating to the Royal Forest, the Sheriffs and Smuggling.* Univ. of Michigan Pubs. in Hist. & Pol. Sci., vii (William Clements Library: Ann Arbor, Mich. 1928); R. G. Lounsbury, *The British Fishery at Newfoundland, 1634–1763.* Yale Hist. Pubs., xxvii (Yale Univ. Press: New Haven, Conn., 1934).

iii. To this elucidation by the Columbia school of the history of the established settlements, the influence of F. J. Turner led the Middle Western school to add the elucidation of the history of the back country. In this field the classical work is C. W. Alvord's *The Mississippi Valley in British Politics,* 2 vv. (Arthur H. Clark: Cleveland, O., 1917), which both broke new ground and linked the activities in the backwoods with the politics of Westminster.

(a) Upon the history of colonial population and its movements, which is fundamental to any understanding of the advance of the frontier, see *A Century of Population Growth . . . 1790–1900.* Bureau of the Census (Govt. Printing Office: Washington, D.C., 1909); *Statistical Atlas.* Twelfth Census of the United States taken in the year 1900 (United States Census Office: Washington, D.C., 1903); E. B. Greene & Virginia D. Harrington, *American Population before the Federal Census of 1790* (Columbia Univ. Press: New York, 1932); Stella H. Sutherland, *Population Distribution in Colonial America* (Columbia Univ. Press: New York, 1936); A. B. Faust, *The German Element in the United States,* 2 vv. (Houghton, Mifflin: New York, 1909; revd. ed., 1927); W. A. Knittle, *Early Eighteenth Century Palatine Emigration* (Dorrance: Philadelphia, 1937); C. A. Hanna, *The Scotch-Irish . . .* 2 vv. (Putnam's: New York, 1902); W. F. Dunaway, *The Scotch-Irish of Colonial Pennsylvania* (Univ. of N. Carolina Press: Chapel Hill, N.C., 1944).

(b) On the early history of the Mississippi valley east of the river and for the history of the advance of settlement into it, see generally

H. E. Chambers, *Mississippi Valley Beginnings. An Outline of the early History of the earlier West* (Putnam's: New York, 1922), as well as, for maps, the older volumes by J. Winsor, *The Mississippi Basin. The Struggle between England and France, 1697–1793* (Houghton, Mifflin: Boston, 1895) and *The Westward Movement. The Colonies and the Republic West of the Alleghanies, 1763–1798* (Houghton, Mifflin: Boston, 1897). For the northern area, see Louise P. Kellog, *The French Régime in Wisconsin and the Northwest.* Wisconsin Hist. Ser., i (State Hist. Soc. of Wisconsin: Madison, Wisc., 1925); C. W. Alvord, *The Illinois Country, 1673–1818*, being vol. i of 'The Centennial History of Illinois' (Illinois Centennial Commission: Springfield, Ill., 1920); C. A. Hanna, *The Wilderness Trail*, 2 vv. (Putnam's: New York, 1911), a general account of the penetration of the Ohio valley by the Pennsylvania traders; F. W. Halsey, *The Old New York Frontier, 1614–1800* (Scribner's: New York, 1901); Ruth L. Higgins, *Expansion in New York, with especial reference to the Eighteenth Century* (Ohio State Univ.: Columbus, O., 1931); D. M. Ellis, *Landlords and Farmers in the Hudson-Mohawk Region, 1700–1850* (Cornell Univ. Press: Ithaca, N.Y., 1946); C. H. McIlwain (ed.), *An Abridgement of the Indian Affairs . . .* Harvard Hist. Studies, xxi (Harvard Univ. Press: Cambridge, Mass., 1915); G. A. Cribbs, *The Frontier Policy of Pennsylvania* (the author: Pittsburg, Pa., 1919); *Report of the Commission to locate the Sites of the Frontier Forts of Pennsylvania*, 2 vv. (W. S. Ray: State Printer: Harrisburg, Pa., 1916): J. S. Walton, *Conrad Weiser and the Indian Policy of Colonial Pennsylvania* (G. W. Jacobs: Philadelphia, 1900); Mary C. Darlington, *History of Colonel Henry Bouquet and the Western Frontiers of Pennsylvania, 1747–1764* (priv. ptd.: Pittsburg, Pa., 1920); S. J. & Elizabeth H. Buck, *The Planting of Civilization in Western Pennsylvania* (Univ. of Pittsburg Press: Pittsburg, Pa., 1939); F. Parkman, *The Conspiracy of Pontiac and the Indian War after the Conquest of Canada*, 2 vv. (Little & Brown; Boston, 1851); H. H. Peckham, *Pontiac and the Indian Uprising* (Princeton Univ. Press: Princeton, N.J., 1947).

The history of the Southern area has been less fully explored. A valuable general sketch was provided by H. E. Bolton's introduction to his edition of *Arredondo's Historical Proof of Spain's Title to Georgia* (Univ. of California Press: Berkeley, Calif., 1925), separately issued as H. E. Bolton & Mary Ross, *The Debatable Land, a Sketch of the Anglo-Spanish Contest for the Georgia Country* (1925). The standard authorities are V. W. Crane, *The Southern Frontier, 1670–1732* (Duke Univ. Press: Durham, N.C., 1928), and J. R. Alden, *John Stuart and the Southern Colonial Frontier; a Study of Indian Relations, War, Trade and Land Problems in the Southern Wilderness, 1754–1775* (Univ. of Michigan Press: Ann Arbor, Mich., 1944). But these leave a gap that is only in part filled by T. Bodley, *History of Kentucky before the Louisiana Purchase in 1803* (S. J. Clarke Publ. Co.: Chicago, 1928) and S. C. Williams, *Dawn of Tennessee Valley and Tennessee History* (Watauga Press: Johnson City, Tenn., 1937). There is a more general sketch in E. Dick, *The Dixie Frontier; a Social History of the Southern Frontier* (Knopf: New York, 1948). Particular aspects of the subject are dealt with in C. W. Alvord & L. Bidgood, *The First Explorations of the Trans-Allegheny Region by the Virginians, 1650–1674* (Arthur H. Clark Co.: Cleveland, O., 1912); L. K. Koontz, *The Virginia Frontier, 1754–63.* Johns Hopkins Univ. Studies, xliii, no. 2 (Johns Hopkins Press: Baltimore, Md., 1925); F. B. Kegley, *Kegley's Virginia Frontier; the Beginning of the Southwest; the Roanoke of Colonial Days, 1740–1783* (Southwest Virginia Hist. Soc.: Roanoke, Va., 1938); J. G. Johnson, *The Colonial Southeast, 1732–1763; an International Contest for Territorial and Economic Control.* Univ. of Colorado Studies, xix, no. 3 (Boulder, Colo., 1932); J. P. Corry, *Indian Affairs in Georgia, 1732–1756* (George S. Ferguson: Philadelphia, 1937); Helen L. Shaw, *British Administration of the Southern Indians, 1756–1783* (Lancaster Press: Lancaster, Pa., 1931); and R. B. Truett, *Trade and Travel around the Southern Appalachians before 1830* (Univ. of N. Carolina Press: Chapel Hill, N.C., 1935). J. T. Lanning, *The Diplomatic History of Georgia—a Study of the Epoch of Jenkins' Ear* (Univ. of N. Carolina Press: Chapel Hill, N.C., 1936) is based upon a wide range of manuscript sources, but is a very ill executed work and so badly written as to be sometimes unintelligible and always troublesome to understand.

The wealth of documentary material relating to the obscure events of the back country that has survived is astonishing, and modern scholars have been able, not only to write a very full account of the doings of very humble persons in very remote places, but also to render intelligible the forces that were at work. An illustration of how vivid and how clear the story can be made is afforded by a remarkable series of biographies covering the frontier from north to south, A. Pound, *Johnson of the Mohawks* (Macmillan: New York, 1930); P. A. W. Wallace, *Conrad Weiser, 1696–1760* (Univ. of Pennsylvania Press: Philadelphia, 1945); A. T. Volwiler, *George Croghan and the Westward Movement, 1741–1782* (Arthur H. Clark Co.: Cleveland, O., 1926); M. Savelle, *George Morgan, Colony Builder* (Columbia Univ. Press: New York, 1932); S. E. Slick, *William Trent and the West* (Archives Publ. Co. of Pennsylvania: Harrisburg, Pa., 1947); and J. W. Caughey, *McGillivray of the Creeks* (Univ. of Oklahoma Press: Norman, Okla., 1938).

(c) The vexed and perplexing history of the western lands is still difficult to master. It calls for the talents of an historian who is also a conveyancing lawyer; and for all that Alvord did for it, it still awaits its Maitland. The clearest introduction to the subject will be found in T. Bodley, *Our First Great West*. Filson Club Publications no. 36 (John P. Morton: Louisville, K., 1938), although that work must be read with discrimination;[1] and an indispensable handbook is C. C. Royce, *Indian Land Cessions in the United States*. Eighteenth Annual Report of the Bureau of American Ethnology . . . 1896–97, pt. 2 (Govt. Printing Office: Washington, D.C., 1899). The foundations were laid in the work of Alvord already frequently referred to (*cf.* p. 68). To it should be added, G. H. Alden, *New Governments West of the Alleghanies before 1780*. Univ. of Wisconsin Bulletin, Hist. Ser. ii, no. 1 (Madison, Wisc., 1897); C. E. Carter, *Great Britain and the Illinois Country* (American Hist. Assoc.: Washington, D.C., 1910); R. L. Schuyler, *The Transition in Illinois from British to American Government* (Columbia Univ. Press: New York, 1909); W. R. Riddell, *Michigan under British Rule; Law and Law Courts, 1760–1796* (Michigan Hist. Commission: Lansing, Mich., 1926); N. V. Russell, *The British Régime in Michigan . . . 1760–1796* (Carleton College: Northfield, Minn., 1939); Louise P. Kellogg, *The British Régime in Wisconsin and the Northwest* (State Hist. Soc. of Wisconsin: Madison, Wisc., 1935); L. K. Koontz, *Robert Dinwiddie; his Career in American Colonial Government and Westward Expansion* (Arthur H. Clark Co.: Glendale, Calif., 1941); and J. A. James, *The Life of George Rogers Clark* (Univ. of Chicago Press: Chicago, 1928).

On the fur trade, see W. E. Stevens, *The Northwest Fur Trade, 1763–1800*. Univ. of Illinois Studies in the Social Sciences, xiv, no. 3 (Urbana, Ill., 1926); Ida A. Johnson, *The Michigan Fur Trade*. Michigan Hist. Pubs., Univ. Ser., v (Michigan Hist. Commission: Lansing, Mich., 1919); I. Lippincott, *A Century and a Half of Fur Trade at St. Louis*. Washington Univ. Studies, iii (St. Louis, Mo., 1916). On the land companies, see T. P. Abernethy, *Western Lands and the American Revolution* (Appleton-Century: New York, 1937), *cf.* p. 100 *infra*; S. Livermore, *Early American Land Companies; their Influence on Corporate Development* (Commonwealth Fund: New York, 1939); F. Harrison, *Virginia Land Grants, a Study of Conveyancing in relation to Colonial Politics* (priv. ptd., The Old Dominion Press: Richmond, Va., 1925); K. P. Bailey, *The Ohio Company of Virginia and the Westward Movement, 1748–1792* (Arthur H. Clark Co.: Glendale, Calif., 1939); G. E. Lewis, *The Indiana Company, 1763–1798: a Study in Eighteenth Century Frontier Land Speculation and Business Venture* (Arthur H. Clark Co.: Glendale, Calif., 1941).

[1] *Cf. Am. Hist. Rev.*, xlv (1940), 165–6; *Mississippi Valley Hist. Rev.*, xxv (1938–9), 400–1.

commerce, western lands, and imperial defence that was in many respects reasonable and enlightened, but was also greatly embarrassed by the political confusion of the years 1763–75 and tended insensibly to the formation of a new and revolutionary conception of the nature of the authority of the crown in parliament. By it, also, the development of the mainland colonies in the eighteenth century has, in many respects for the first time, been made clear, revealing a trend in constitutional development and the emergence of a new factor in the settlement of the back country, which, upon that side of the ocean, produced a constitutional situation and a play of new social and economic forces very difficult to reconcile with the policy of Westminster and very little understood there. And there has at least been thrown out the suggestion, to put it no higher, that the whole situation was profoundly exacerbated by peculiar currency and exchange conditions. The picture presented, therefore, is that of the pursuit of a plan for imperial reform which involves the extension of the scope of parliamentary activity and the advance of claims to parliamentary omnipotence, meeting a colonial situation in which there is both a parallel development in the several colonies tending to the emergence of just such claims to legislative absolutism on the part of the colonial assemblies as the fresher minds at home were making for the authority of the crown in parliament at Westminster, and a radical agitation for the transfer of the effective exercise of that legislative authority to bodies at once more popular and less friendly to the imperial connection than those returned on the existing franchise and with the existing distribution of representation. Given the fulfilment of these tendencies, the adoption of an imperial policy viable throughout the empire would come to depend upon one imperial and numerous colonial legislatures, each claiming to be bound by no law but its own will, reaching spontaneously, on matters of common policy, a common conclusion. It was the less to be expected that this would occur when the two groups were steadily drifting apart in economic interest, future ambitions, social structure, and intellectual habits.

And when the exercise of the wisest statesmanship was thus required, the condition of English politics not only precluded the steady pursuit of any one policy, but greatly interfered even with the proper study of the problem. In consequence, such measures as were adopted intensified the discontents of the up-country radicals without winning the allegiance of more than a fraction of the propertied classes. The powerful body of colonial opinion opposed to the claims of the colonial radicals and to the establishment of the despotic authority of the colonial legislatures, but with no use for new-fangled notions of unlimited parliamentary authority at Westminster, was alienated when imperial policy damaged it in its pocket and offended its ideas of constitutional law. It is possible that the constitutional development of the imperial and colonial legislatures was such as to preclude the survival of the imperial system in any case, and that this was merely a constitutional expression of a divergence of economic interest that made it inevitable that the two parties should go upon their separate ways. But it is arguable that it was erroneous political and constitutional doctrines that were at fault. And it is conceivable that the trouble arose from no more than technical errors in the organization of trade, banking, and currency.

G. L. Beer's study of *British Colonial Policy, 1754–1765* (1907) revealed an imperial administration driven by the experience of the Seven Years' War to address itself to the problems of imperial defence and commercial regulation. Upon the first of these further light was shed by Alvord's examination of the problem of the western lands; to the understanding of the second much was added by the study of the history of the colonial merchants, most notably in C. L. Becker's *The History of Political Parties in the Province of New York, 1760–1776* (1909), and Professor A. M. Schlesinger's *The Colonial Merchants and the American Revolution* (1918).

The military experience of the Seven Years' War had been unsatisfactory. While the colonies were traditionally regarded as entitled to defence in return for obedience and the whole burden of naval operations during war and of the protection of trade during peace was borne by the mother country, the apportionment of duties in military matters was less clear. The colony was expected to provide for local defence, receiving aid in the shape of arms, ammunition, and the wherewithal to make the necessary presents to the Indians. The service of colonial troops outside the limits of the colony was voluntary; and imperial troops were garrisoned in those places that were peculiarly exposed. But this system was felt to be unsatisfactory even before the war; and it worked very badly during it. As large a force as possible was levied in the colonies, on account of the difficulty of raising troops in England and in order to save the cost of transport, the crown furnishing arms, ammunition, tents, provisions and artillery; and the greater part of the moneys spent by the colonies in levying, clothing, feeding and paying the provincial troops was subsequently refunded by parliamentary grant. But the consequence of the system was that the burden of service was inequitably distributed among the several colonies, and that military operations were hampered by deficiences both in the numbers of troops voted and those actually raised, by their lateness in assembling, and by disputes about their terms of service. When the war ended with a great extension of territory, including immense unsettled areas, the burdens of military administration were increased. The colonies failed to establish any efficient control of the abuses of the Indian trade or of the trespasses of the white settler upon the hunting grounds of the tribes; and the home government was presented with the need to maintain an imperial Indian department and garrisoned posts in the West which reinforced the case for military reorganization. The conclusions reached, when that problem was faced, were that a considerable force must be maintained in the colonies both to forestall any attempt upon the part of France to recover her lost possessions and to police the unsettled areas; that the colonies, on the evidence of the war, were unlikely to be either willing or able to maintain such a force; that it must take the form of a body of imperial troops; and that the expense of its provision should be met from colonial taxation.

This military policy, with its financial implications, might have been successfully carried through if it had won and retained the support of the business community; and it was not inconceivable that it should have done so. The more alert minds in that body were deeply interested in the exploitation of the West, and were in time and under another leadership to turn away from the sea and its mercantile ventures to the building of new communities in the Mississippi valley. But military reorganization was accompanied by commercial reorganization; and in the confusion of English politics the larger ends of military reorganization itself were lost sight of.

The old colonial system operated, on the whole, not unfairly to the colonies. They suffered a variety of restraints upon their economic life. Colonial manufactures were restricted. European goods required by the colonies must be shipped from England. The export of enumerated articles, notably naval stores, tobacco, and, with certain exceptions, rice, from the colonies was restricted to home ports; and obstacles were placed in the way of the importation even there of colonial cereals and meat. Colonial vessels exporting non-enumerated commodities to continental Europe had thus to go to England for return cargoes; and colonial purchases of molasses, sugar, or rum were confined to the British West Indies. But British manufactures were, on the whole, superior to foreign and would have been preferred in any case; England was the natural entrepôt for trade going out from Europe to the colonies; and the greater part of the English import duty was refunded on re-shipment to America, so that continental goods actually sold more cheaply in the colonies than in England itself; and bounties upon naval stores, a monopoly of the home market for tobacco and rice, a drawback of duties on the re-export of these commodities to the continent, and the protection afforded to American shipping were a fair return for such disabilities as were suffered. But the enjoyment of much does not exorcise the desire for more; and the merchants of the middle and New England colonies were, moreover, in fact hard put to it to find the means of paying for what they imported, and were only

able to do so at all by their trade in the non-enumerated articles
to foreign ports in Europe and the West Indies. While, therefore, the system was on the whole effective, particularly in
securing the restriction of the colonial trade to British and
colonial shipping and the shipment of the enumerated commodities to British ports, any further restriction of the trade
with foreign ports would render the adjustment of the balance
between colonial imports and exports impracticable except
by measures of restriction from which the colonists were precluded. Therefrom there arose a conflict of colonial and imperial interest; and there followed, after the war, the adoption
of measures bitterly resented by the colonists.

Unhappily the interruption of the supply of Canada and
the French West Indies was during the Seven Years' War a
matter of great military importance. Canada in a large measure
drew what it needed from Cape Breton; the French colonies at
Cape Breton and in the West Indies drew upon the continental
colonies and Ireland. If these supplies could be cut off, the
French West Indies would suffer a scarcity, French operations
on the St. Lawrence and the Ohio would be hampered, the
French would find it difficult to re-fit men-of-war or to organize
privateering, and the economic life of the English colonies
would be protected from serious derangement by the demands
of the military. But the trade offered great temptations. The
demand for provisions in the French West Indies was keen,
and the disposal of supplies of sugar, rum, and molasses was
difficult when export to France was cut off. Intercourse was
effected under the guise of flags of truce for the exchange of
prisoners of war, and by way of the Dutch West Indies or
Spanish colonial ports; and it was maintained upon a substantial scale in spite of the best efforts of the authorities to
break it up. The result was the plentiful supply of the enemy's
islands, together with a stringency in the continental colonies
that impeded the conduct of military operations, a rise in the
price of French products, and their export to United Kingdom
markets in competition with the products of British colonies
without the offset of the duties provided by the Molasses Act

of 1733. The effect was substantially to relieve what had been
the increasing pressure of colonial indebtedness to the mother
country. There was an influx of coin into the continental
colonies for the pay and provisioning of the troops. The French
paid high cash prices for the foodstuffs they needed and could
obtain by the illicit trade. There was an increased demand for
agricultural products. In consequence, domestic prices rose.
The country debtor was sensibly relieved; and the remission
of sterling by the merchant became easier. Money became
available for investment in land and in stocks of trading goods.

The very reasonable decision to adopt measures to remedy
the defects of the commercial system revealed by the war and,
if necessary, to promote the further development of that system
involved, therefore, much more than a provision for the future
against an unpatriotic disregard of public interest in the pursuit
of private gain. The economic consequence of the conclusion
of peace was the recurrence, with increased force, of the
financial difficulties of the colonists. The currency was con-
tracted. There was a fall in the demand for merchandise and
for agricultural products, and a further decline in trade as a
result of the loss of the illicit traffic with the French colonies
and of the trade developed with Havana and the French
islands captured during the war but restored at the peace.
Prices fell, and the relation of debtor and creditor was once
again disturbed to the disadvantage of the former and to the
embarrassment in particular of those who had incurred obligations during the period of inflation in order to speculate in land
or to lay in stocks of trading goods. Thus there was revived,
in an aggravated shape, the condition that was developing
before 1756. The internal debtors found it increasingly difficult
to meet their obligations; and the planter and merchant owing
money to British houses found it increasingly difficult to make
sterling remittances.

What this counted for in the history of the Revolution has
been shown by the works of Becker and Professor Schlesinger.
Without any deliberate intention, the measures adopted at
Westminster produced, in these circumstances, very real dis-

tress among the commercial classes in the colonies. The restriction of the West India trade of New England, New York, and Philadelphia by the Sugar Act of 1764 resulted in something like a commercial crisis. Further serious embarrassment was caused by the Stamp Act to business that was already depressed; and the depression was deepened by the measures of 1767. In particular, the difficulty of making sterling remittances was aggravated by the requirement of payment in gold, silver or sterling bills of the stamp duties and the Townshend duties; and the distress caused by this was spread in 1764 by the extension to other colonies of the prohibition of a paper currency imposed upon New England in 1751. In this way very formidable forces were recruited to a political agitation that might never have become dangerous without them. The boycotts of 1764–6 and 1767–70 were the work of the merchants and planters, and were economic in motive. They were directed, and the first of them successfully directed, to the exercise of pressure in matters peculiarly interesting to these classes; and they had the incidental advantages of enabling the merchants to dispose profitably of old stock, of facilitating the recovery from customers of debts that had been long outstanding, and of easing the demand for sterling. The most conspicuous grievances of the merchants and planters were allayed by the repeals of 1766 and 1770; and the general economic situation was relieved by the improvement of the trade balance in the years 1770–3, and by the increase in the supply of currency assisted by the exemption from the act of 1764 granted to New York in 1770 and by the act of 1773 permitting colonial paper to be made a legal tender for provincial duties and taxes. The boycott resumed in 1767 collapsed after 1770, when its ends had been substantially gained. But rein had been given to a political dispute in which fundamental constitutional issues had been raised.

The investigations of Osgood and other students of the constitutional history of the mainland colonies in the eighteenth century have shown how grave those constitutional issues had become and how radical were the oppositions to which they

were leading. They were formulated in their most uncompromising shape in the Declaratory Act of 1766 and by the
retention of the duty on tea in 1770 for the express purpose of
asserting the authority of parliament.

Imperial control had a dual aspect. It stood, in the first
place, for the limitation of the legislative authority of the colonies
by the enforcement of a higher law. This was directed to the
prevention of the commission of injustice and the arbitrary
invasion of personal liberties by the colonial legislatures, and
to the regulation of matters of common concern and the avoid-
ance of that anarchy which would result if the discordant pronouncements of unconnected legislatures were allowed to
prevail. Its function in the latter respect was to prevent the
growth, within the imperial sphere, of that conflict of laws
relating to persons, property, and legal procedure which in the
international sphere it is the function of private international
law to reconcile, and to preserve a public law that should
safeguard the interests of the whole from sacrifice to the interests of its several parts. Its instruments were judicial review,
disallowance, and imperial legislation. By the delivery of judgment in the privy council against a party relying upon a
colonial act which was held to be unconstitutional, a limit was
set to the authority of the colonial legislature and it was rendered
subject to the control of a fundamental law. By the disallowance, by the king in council, of colonial legislation a like subordination was enforced. That which encroached upon the
prerogatives or interests of the crown, which invaded ecclesiastical rights, conflicted with English law, or was inconsistent
with the commercial policy of the imperial government, that
which injured the interests of another colony or was an invasion
of the rights of private property or personal liberty was liable
to such disallowance. And where the general interest was not
sufficiently served by the law as it stood, the overriding authority
of imperial legislation was there to fill the gap. But imperial
control had also a second and very different aspect. There was
developing at Westminster a parliamentary absolutism which
itself was not subject to judicial review, was in effect uncon-

7

trolled by a veto, was legally unchecked by any other legislative authority unless it were the treaty-making power of the crown, and was becoming less and less ready to admit that its legislative power was limited by any higher law, constitutional or international. And that authority laid claim to as full power of legislation in the colonies as it possessed in the United Kingdom.

To this duality at Westminster a similar duality in the colonies was opposed. By some, parliamentary claims to absolutism were resisted as such. By these persons the idea that parliamentary enactment was not open to question and could override, without dispute, custom, generally accepted legal maxims, and public or private rights was rejected. Even the claim that within parliament the decision of the majority was binding was disputed, since the ultimate sanction of law lay in assent. There perdured in their minds, that is to say, a conception of parliament as a conference of estates involving the regard of the constituency as a natural and spontaneous growth and of parliament as a meeting of a number of these distinct and natural groups, as opposed to the conception that all individuals were members of one state and might for electoral convenience be divided into districts of homogeneous population. There followed the view that parliament was competent to bind all in that which concerned all, but was not competent to bind an estate, without its assent, in that which peculiarly affected it and affected others but slightly or not at all, and in particular was not competent to tax without the assent—not indeed of all taxpayers—but of some at least of those who would share the burden. By others in the colonies, however, a very different view was held. By them, to the absolutism of parliament was opposed the absolutism of the colonial legislature. They accepted, without question, the prevalence of the will of the majority and the unfettered authority of the legislature. But they argued that the sovereign authority of the people of the several colonies was exercised in the colonial assemblies; that the fiat of such authority ought not to be frustrated by judicial review or disallowance in the privy council;

and that the colonies being separate and independent interests
were either not subject to parliament at all or were subject
only in matters of common concern. Such a theory had its
historical weaknesses. Although from time to time there had
been colonial opposition to the exercise of the authority of
parliament, the generally accepted rule was that the common
law and acts in affirmance thereof antecedent to settlement,
together with all subsequent acts in which the colonies were
particularly mentioned, were of force in the colonies. But if
it was historically weak, the theory was also logically cogent.
Parliament was unsympathetic to colonial needs because its
members had no experience of colonial conditions. Its acts
were damaging to colonial interests not so much from intention
as from ignorance. It had no conception of the significance of
westward expansion and no real understanding of what that
involved; and though not of set purpose, it denied the means
of escape from the pressure of a steady deflation and an adverse
balance of trade, by insistence upon a system which precluded
the development of colonial manufactures and required the
colonists to make large purchases in England. It was in fact
true that the colonies were distinct groups with their own
interests and not merely numerical divisions of the population
of a homogeneous state. There was much to be said, therefore,
for the argument that they should not be bound, in matters
peculiarly affecting them, without their assent, and that such
an assent could not be given by the vote of a house of commons in which their peculiar point of view was not represented.
There would indeed, had parliamentary reform by then been
achieved and representation in the imperial parliament
granted to the colonies, have been almost as much to say for
the argument that still they would not have been bound by a
decision carried by a majority to which they were in united
opposition. And the historical invalidity of the colonial case
was not quite so conclusive as it looked at first sight. The
authority of the crown in parliament which was to operate in
the colonies in the future was not the authority that had
operated there in the past. As the effective exercise of sove-

reignty passed from the crown itself to the house of commons it became at once more active, more parochial, and less impartial. The crown could at least take an imperial point of view, though it was no doubt subject to the pressure of interested parties. The house was an interested party itself.

The two schools of colonial thought are illustrated by the arguments of James Otis and Patrick Henry. Pleading before the superior court of Massachusetts in 1761, against writs of assistance issued by the court of exchequer to officials authorizing them to search for uncustomed goods, valid for an indefinite time and requiring no return, Otis contended that 'no act of parliament can establish such a writ', for 'an act against the constitution is void; an act against natural equity is void'; and this doctrine is set forth in his pamphlet *The Rights of the British Colonies asserted and proved*, published in Boston in 1764. The opposite doctrine was upheld by Patrick Henry in the Parsons' Cause in 1763. In 1758, the legislature of Virginia, following a precedent of 1755, passed an act for the relief of debtors. That act made salaries that were payable in tobacco payable, also, at the option of the payer, in currency at the rate of 2d. a pound. The clergy and certain officers were affected. They found themselves in receipt of paper useless for transactions beyond the limits of the colony and so depreciated within it that at the market price a pound of tobacco was worth 6d.; and they appealed to the privy council and secured the disallowance of the act in 1759. On a suit for recovery in 1763, Henry argued that the act was good law because one of utility and because it was authenticated by the only authority that could give force to laws, 'the authority of a legal representative, of a council, and of a kind and benevolent and patriotic governor'. Patrick Henry, that is to say, upheld that very doctrine of legislative absolutism that James Otis denied. Its character was not altered by predicating it of a governor in assembly instead of the crown in parliament.

This picture of the issues raised by the disputes between the colonies and the mother country is, of course, a rationalization after the event. The argument as it developed was a confused and blundering pursuit of only fitfully apprehended ideas. Positions at one time adopted had subsequently to be abandoned; and many were content to stop short in the endeavour to reach a stand that was impregnable. Clarification of thought came gradually, and it was never complete. Intellectual confusion had its political advantages, even its political necessity. Few can afford in a time of peril to be too nice about the logic of their allies. Yet the fundamental division in the colonial mind and the coherence of each school within itself are nevertheless there; and they can by after-comers be disengaged from the turmoil of events; and unless indeed this disentanglement is effected, subsequent history can hardly be understood.

If the older view of the American Revolution is compared with that revealed by the later work, it will be seen that what has been brought out is the variety and complexity of the scene, but that there has all the same been discovered in it an intelligible pattern. The older version of the story is that mutual discontents grew out of the experience, upon the one hand, by the imperial government during the Seven Years' War, of the excessive and exasperating particularism of the several colonies, making it difficult to secure co-ordinated military effort and leading to the embarrassments of an extensive smuggling trade with the French West Indies; and the experience, upon the other, by the colonies, of the grave disadvantages resulting from the operation of the navigation laws and a mercantilist system. This resulted in the recourse by Great Britain to a strict enforcement of the navigation laws and the permanent establishment in America of a portion of the regular army, partly in order to make good the insufficiencies of the colonial military system and partly in order to meet enlarged imperial responsibilities. This in turn required the levy of colonial taxation to meet at least part of the expense; and that produced a constitutional dispute over the relation of taxation to representation, which is commonly represented as a popular revolt against a corrupt and unrepresentative house of commons, with an implication that, had the Reform Bill of 1832 been carried a couple of generations earlier, all would have been well. In the newer view, the mercantile system is no longer regarded as having been a conscious political device but is seen rather as an historical rationalization of a number of haphazard decisions. Colonial policy appears as a search for imperial economic self-sufficiency which, while it demanded sacrifices, distributed burdens and advantages not inequitably between mother country and colonies. The stricter enforcement of the laws of trade after 1763 is seen, not as the pedantic enforcement of an obsolete, oppressive and irrational system, but as an administrative measure designed to meet particular shortcomings. The emphasis is shifted from commercial regulation to defence, as the prime concern of British statesmanship in the colonial field after 1763; and the problem of defence is seen to be linked with that of the western lands. But at the same time, the commercial oppression that the colonists suffered, it is now realized, was far-reaching. It was not merely that they were denied opportunity for economic activity in which they would have liked to engage. The urge to extend their foreign trade and multiply their home manufactures had its source in something more than the growing enterprise of a young and vigorous people impatient of the restraints imposed by the system of their elders. It was generated by the pressure put upon them to buy more than they could pay for. Set in this light, the ministerial measures of 1763 to 1774 take on a new aspect. They cease to wear the air of an arbitrary and wanton attack upon colonial liberties, and assume the drab colour of a failure, in the face of a baffling and urgent problem calling for solution during a period of exceptional political confusion, to avoid the only too familiar faults of imperfect information, piecemeal concessions to private interest, compromise and delay. The political conflict which this failure brought to a head had been long maturing. But upon the colonial side there were two distinguishable elements. One was impatience with the unpopularity and excessively English character of the imperial authority, and the desire to transfer the exercise of sovereignty in the government of the colonies from the crown in a parliament elected on a very limited franchise and lacking in colonial representation, to a colonial and more popular assembly. The other was a translation from theology into the language of politics of a deep-rooted conception of a rule of law binding upon sovereign as well as subject, resulting in a highly conservative opposition to legislative absolutism, whether it was threatened at Westminster or in the colonial capitals, and the offer, as a barrier to arbitrary government by an imperial parliament, of the doctrine that no distinct group can be bound without the assent at least of like persons and that there are in any case fundamental rights that no sovereign can touch. While some, that is to say, sought to enthrone, as the supreme authority, the majority of the electorate, and that electorate a colonial electorate, others were bent upon the limitation of the sovereign authority wherever it might reside, whether in the crown in an eighteenth century parliament or in a popular legislature imperial or colonial. Thus from one point of view the fault of the imperial government was, not that it was sixty years behind the times, but that it was an innovating body, setting up new-fangled claims and breaking in upon established and fundamental rights; and the substantial planters and merchants, spurred to political thought by economic inconvenience, found themselves ranked with the radical politicians of the seaports and the back country. Unless this feature of the Revolution is understood, the Constitution is hardly comprehensible.

II. The Constitution

The development of the present view of the origins and character of the Constitution formed in the Philadelphia Convention of 1787 began with O. G. Libby's study of the *Geographical Distribution of the Vote of the Thirteen States on the Federal Constitution, 1787–8* (1894), and was continued in the work of Beard, McLaughlin and Schuyler, aided by the documentary publications of W. C. Ford, Fitzpatrick, Farrand and Burnett.

The progress in understanding achieved by this work derived in the main from regarding the Constitution as a product of particular historical circumstances rather than of abstract reasoning, and from seeking its origins in colonial experience rather than in a literary ancestry. The most challenging ideas were those put forward by Beard in his *Economic Interpretation of the Constitution of the United States* (1913) and *Economic Origins of Jeffersonian Democracy* (1917). These books, indeed, created a pother which threatened for a time to obscure the issue. Beard showed that the bulk of the members of the Constitutional Convention and of the supporters of the Constitution during the campaign for ratification belonged to a creditor class. The investigation of their personal financial interests appeared to some to cast a reflection upon their moral integrity; and the debate was in danger of going off into one about human motives, while the historically more important corollary was forgotten. This corollary was that the Constitutional Convention represented effectively only one of the two economic interests that were in conflict in the United States between 1783 and 1787, that the adoption of the Constitution by the ratifying conventions was a victory of creditor over debtor, and that the American constitution is not, and was not intended to be, a democratic instrument in the sense that it meant to instal the principle of the absolute authority of the majority. And that branch of the thesis was of fundamental importance. Unless it is rightly understood, the interpretation of subsequent American history is inextricably confused. Once it is appreciated, it forces the resolution of the idea of democracy into two distinct concepts—the enthronement of King Numbers, and government by persuasion.

Following up the earlier work of Libby on the geographical distribution of the vote of the thirteen states on the federal Constitution of 1787–8, the thesis advanced by Beard was that the opposition to the adoption came in the main from the small farmers who were, in general, debtors by the nature of their calling, and who, where they were frontier settlers, were in particular burdened with debts, incurred in the purchase of their farms, due to monied men who had speculated in western lands. These small farmers were reinforced by the holders of property confiscated from the loyalists and retained in violation of the treaty of 1783, and by persons owing pre-war debts to subjects of Great Britain, due for payment under the treaty but repudiated by the state legislatures. To these groups there were incongruously added the large landowners of the Hudson river valley, able under the Articles to shift the burden of taxation from land to imports, and afraid of the transfer, under a Constitution which forbade the levy by states of duties upon imports, of the weight of state taxes to their own landed property. Support for the Constitution came, on the other hand, from the southern slave-owning planters, anxious for strong government; and from the monied interests throughout the country. Those interests were hampered under the Articles by obstacles placed in the way of business by the lack of protection for manufactures, the discriminations imposed with impunity by foreign powers upon American shipping, and the instability of the monetary system. They saw their interests attacked in the state legislature by the passage of paper money and stay laws designed to reduce the value of debts by the depreciation of the currency and to postpone their payment. They were the holders of state and continental securities the value of which would be enhanced by adoption of the new constitution; and they were speculators in western lands, often by the purchase at depreciated rates of land script issued to the Revolutionary soldiers, the value of which would rise with the establishment of a central government capable of dealing with the Indians and of securing an orderly settlement of the frontier. Of these business men, two groups were pre-eminently active under the Articles in promoting a reform. They were those working for the provision of a revenue sufficient to discharge both the principal and interest of the public debt— and the holders of this security are calculated to have gained at least $40,000,000 by adoption—; and those working for legislation advantageous to shipping, manufactures, and western land interests. The two were, moreover, clearly, often one and the same.

There was some danger that Beard's books would feed the superstition that it is more sordid to pursue the interests of a

creditor than those of a debtor; and it is easy to divert the
argument to a profitless debate upon the depravity of man as a
political animal, in which it is difficult to make much progress.
But the great value of the works was their demonstration of the
unpopular character of the Constitution as originally devised,
of its embodiment of one rather than the other of the two
elements present in the Revolution, of the idea, namely, that
distinct groups with peculiar interests should not be overridden
by the mere superiority in numbers of other persons and that
there were fundamental rights no sovereign could invade,
rather than the idea that the people should rule. Such an
approach was to prove most fruitful. It was much more than a
demonstration of the play of economic motives; and it set the
pattern for the work of a generation.

It is clear from a large body of monographic work on the
history of the several states summarized in Professor Allan
Nevins' book on *The American States during and after the Revolution* (1924), that one immediate effect of the Revolution was the
establishment of a legislative absolutism within the several
states threatening a despotism that would be worse than that
of Westminster in so far as it was nearer home and more
popular and therefore more plausible. But it is also clear, upon
the other hand, that the relations between the states approached
a condition of anarchy and almost reached on occasion that of
open war. And it is equally clear from the records of the Continental Congress and the correspondence of its members that
legislative absolutism at the centre, which might in certain
circumstances prevail under the Articles, was unworkable in a
country embracing such profoundly different geographical
areas and such deeply divided interests; and that unless the
theoretical powers of an absolute Congress were rendered in-
effective by the practice of parliamentary manoeuvre, the
result would be defiance and secession.

The result of war and revolution, as is so often the case, was
to accelerate the pace rather than to alter the direction in
which events were moving. The constitutional reorganization
effected in the several states was the fulfilment of the aims of

the colonial reformers. It spelt the enthronement of the authority of the lower houses of the several legislatures; and in most states the exercise of this authority passed into the hands of more radical politicians than had commonly been powerful during the colonial period. 'Our chief danger', said McHenry in the Federal Convention, 'arises from the democratic parts of our constitutions. It is a maxim which I hold incontrovertible, that the powers of government exercised by the people swallows up the other branches. None of the constitutions have provided sufficient checks against the democracy. The feeble Senate of Virginia is a phantom. Maryland has a more powerful senate, but the late distractions in that State, have discovered that it is not powerful enough. The check established in the constitution of New York and Massachusetts is yet a stronger barrier against democracy, but they all seem insufficient.'[1] This establishment of the uncontrolled rule of the majority resulted from the lack of independent standing of the executive and judiciary under the new state constitutions; the lack, within the state legislatures, of the exercise of any effective check upon the lower by an upper chamber; and the absence of any imperial authority to which appeal might be made for the redress of grievances. There developed much legal instability, produced by incoherent legislation, the successive and inconsequent fiats of mutable assemblies: and there was a widespread attack upon individual and minority rights in the shape of invasions of personal liberty and attacks, in particular, upon the rights of property by the making of depreciated paper a legal tender and the closing of the courts to creditors or by other similar measures impeding the collection of debts. All this was thrown into vivid relief by the outbreak of Shays' rebellion in Massachusetts in 1786; and Gouverneur Morris could say in the Federal Convention in the following year that he 'concurred in thinking the public liberty in greater danger from Legislative usurpations than from any other source', and that 'Legislative tyranny [was] the great danger to be appre-

[1] M. Farrand (ed.), *The Records of the Federal Convention of 1787*, 3 vv. (New Haven, Conn., 1911), i, 26-7.

hended.'[1] At the same time, the pursuit of a purpose common to all the states was near to frustration by the operation of thirteen independent sovereignties barely removed by the adoption of the Articles from being in what Luther Martin described as 'a state of nature towards each other'.[2] The operations of Congress were embarrassed by the failure of the several states to take the measures necessary for the execution of the treaties it had entered into; by the pursuit by the several states of uncoördinated commercial policies, which deprived it of an essential diplomatic weapon; and by the maintenance of independent relations with, and independent policies towards, the Indians. Within the Union itself, actual conflict between the states was threatened. They were guilty of unfriendly acts towards one another, such as the taxation of a neighbouring state lacking convenient ports by the levy of duty upon goods shipped to it through their own, or the invasion by the paper-money legislation of one state of the rights of the citizens of another; while individual states levied troops without the consent of Congress, and concluded regional agreements one with another.

Those who were disturbed by this state of affairs were doubtless divided among themselves. They embraced both those who had no quarrel with legislative absolutism except when its exercise fell into the wrong hands, who saw in a strengthened federal authority only the means of obstructing legislation unfriendly to their interest, and who were ready to accept for convenience doctrines to which they felt no intellectual loyalty; and those who, by force of whatever combination of circumstance and logic, were opposed upon principle to legislative absolutism wherever it showed itself. But those two could combine, as they had combined in the Revolution, for the common purpose of setting limits to the new claims of the state legislatures; and while the opponents upon principle of legislative absolutism in the states were the last to wish to establish

---

[1] M. Farrand (ed.), *The Records of the Federal Convention of 1787*, 3 vv. (New Haven, 1911), ii, 76, 551.
[2] *Ibid.*, i, 324, *cf.* 437.

it at the centre, their allies, whatever upon principle they may
have been ready to accept, were driven by experience to the
same conclusion. What had happened under the Articles, which
provided for decisions in some cases with the approval of nine
states and in others with that of a bare majority of seven,
showed that the Confederation embraced areas too profoundly divided to submit to 'the Iron Hand of voting'.[1] And
there is a sense in which it is true that the inefficiency of the
Continental Congress was a mark of political maturity. Government by a single-chamber and unchecked legislature instinc-
tively provoked, as the only alternative to the break-up of the
Confederation, recourse to parliamentary devices the most
effective of which was to stay away and prevent the assembly
of a quorum, in order that unacceptable decisions might not
be reached.

Against this background the work of the Constitutional
Convention can be more accurately judged than it has been
before. The task of the Convention was to establish a rule of
law beyond the reach of transient majorities and to end the
prospect of armed conflict between the states. This it was
sought to do by the erection of a federal system and the division
of sovereign authority between the federation and its com-
ponent parts, precluding the latter from independent action
in certain matters of common interest and constraining them
to recognize a comity of states, rendering their citizens subject
to a dual allegiance, and submitting both the parts and the
whole to the overriding rule of a fundamental law embodied
in a written constitution. This system not only set limits to the
sovereign authority of the several states in their dealings with
their own citizens, binding them in such dealings to the observance of certain fundamental rules. It was also careful, in fetter-
ing the authority of the states, to avoid the establishment of a
new despotism at the centre. 'If a faction', wrote Madison subsequently in *The Federalist*, 'consists of less than a majority,
relief is supplied by the republican principle, which enables

[1]E. C. Burnett (ed.), *Letters of Members of the Continental Congress*, 8 vv. (1921–
36), vii, 378.

the majority to defeat its sinister views by regular vote. It may clog the administration, it may convulse the society; but it will be unable to execute and mask its violence under the form of the Constitution. When a majority is included in a faction, the form of popular government, on the other hand, enables it to sacrifice to its ruling passion or interest both the public good and the rights of other citizens. To secure the public good and private rights against the danger of such a faction, and at the same time to preserve the spirit and the form of popular government, is then the great object to which our enquiries are directed.'[1] It was for this reason that there were repeated in the federal sphere the limitations of sovereignty imposed upon the states. The federal sovereign, like the sovereign state, was controlled by a law that it could neither ignore nor override. Moreover even within these limits, every care was taken to prevent, in the federal sphere, that prevalence of the occasional will over the permanent reason which had been so troublesome within the states and of which the inconvenience had there been rendered so obvious by the fall of power into the 'wrong' hands. The federal legislature was deliberately so constituted as to impede the facile translation of transient opinion into legislation. It made a virtue of legislative incompetence. The two houses were chosen by different electorates and in part at different times; and the provisions for the election of the president were different again. The independence of legislative, executive and judiciary was sought to be secured in order that each might exercise a check upon the others. The fixed term of the legislature, its control of its own returns, and the exclusion of office-holders from its body; the fixity of tenure and of salary of the executive; and the security of tenure during good behaviour and the fixed salaries of the judges, were so many devices to reinforce the independence of these several branches by the variation of the sources from which they derived their authority, and to give strength to legislative participation in executive business and judicial appointments, to the exercise of the veto and to judicial review. And the whole

[1] *The Federalist*, no. 10. P. L. Ford (ed.) (New York, 1898), p. 59.

was clinched by placing the amendment of this constitution beyond the reach of ordinary legislative competence and requiring a long-drawn-out process calculated to secure peculiar interests from assaults prompted by the whim of a moment, and to insure that that only was adopted which in the long run recommended itself as just to a reason which had taken account of more than the immediate occasion.

The most critical problem faced and overcome by the Convention in the erection of this system was that of representation. 'The two extremes before us', said Madison, 'are a perfect separation & a perfect incorporation, of the 13 States. In the first case they would be independent nations subject to no law, but the law of nations. In the last, they would be mere counties of one entire republic, subject to one common law:'[1] 'those on one side,' it was repeated, 'considering the States as districts of people composing one political Society; those on the other considering them as so many political societies.'[2] Said the former, 'State attachments, and State importance have been the bane of this Country';[3] 'there can be no cure for this evil but in doing away States altogether and uniting them all into one great Society';[4] 'no amendment of the confederation, leaving the States in possession of their Sovereignty could possibly answer the purpose';[5] 'we must resort therefore to a national legislation over individuals';[6] 'the Genl. Gov! is not an assemblage of States, but of individuals for certain political purposes—it is not meant for the States, but for the individuals composing them; the *individuals* therefore not the *States*, ought to be represented in it'.[7] It followed that representation must be proportional; 'equal numbers of people ought to have an equal n.° of representatives, and different numbers of people different numbers of representatives';[8] and it was necessary either that the whole population of the United States be regrouped for electoral purposes in 'districts of individuals',[9]

---

[1]M. Farrand, *The Records of the Federal Convention of 1787*, 3 vv. (New Haven, 1911), i, p. 449, *cf.* 177.
[2]*Ibid.*, p. 461.   [3]*Ibid.*, p. 530.   [4]*Ibid.*, p. 202.
          [5]*Ibid.*, p. 283.   [6]*Ibid.*, p. 256.
     [7]*Ibid.*, p. 406.   [8]*Ibid.*, p. 179.   [9]*Ibid.*, p. 450.

'that a map of the U.S. be spread out, that all the existing boundaries be erased, and that a new partition of the whole be made into 13 equal parts',[1] or that some states must count for more than others. But the small states feared for the sacrifice of their particular interests; there must be 'to each sovereign State an equal vote';[2] 'power is given to the few to save them from being destroyed by the many';[3] 'a distinct and equal vote' was therefore required 'for the purpose of defending themselves in the general Councils'.[4] To this the large states and the nationalists replied that they saw the general interest being sacrificed to the particular, a majority of states recording votes inimical to the interests of a majority of the people; 'unequal numbers of Constituents w^d be represented by equal numbers of votes';[5] 'seven States will control six: seven States, according-to the estimates that had been used, composed 24/90 of the whole people. It would be in the power then of less than 1/3 to overrule 2/3 whenever a question should happen to divide the States in that manner';[6] 'the Majority of States might . . . injure the majority of people'.[7] The contest, as Hamilton said, was 'a contest for power'.[8] 'If', observed Franklin, 'a proportional representation takes place, the small States contend that their liberties will be in danger. If an equality of votes is to be put in its place, the large States say their money will be in danger'.[9] The solution was found, after much tough argument, in a compromise that gave equal representation in the senate and proportional representation in the house, so that in the one states and in the other individuals prevailed; and in a further compromise that conceded the measurement of proportion by wealth as well as by numbers, though only that wealth which was wealth in slaves, so that it was asked with much logical force 'why . . . sh^d the blacks, who were property in the South, be in the rule of representation more than the cattle & horses of the North'.[10]

[1]Farrand, *op. cit.*, p. 177.   [2]*Ibid.*, pp. 176–7.   [3]*Ibid.*, p. 484.
[4]*Ibid.*, p. 355.   [5]*Ibid.*, p. 579.
[6]*Ibid.*, pp. 482–3.
[7]*Ibid.*, p. 486.   [8]*Ibid.*, p. 466.
[9]*Ibid.*, p. 488.   [10]*Ibid.*, p. 201.

This conflict and its solution went to the roots of the problem of sovereignty. Limited in any case by a rule of law, sovereignty for better security was also to be divided. The union was to be neither a league of independent states, nor a consolidated government of a group of subordinate provinces. The states survived and spoke as states in the senate; but their citizens were also citizens of the union and were individually represented in the house. It was denied that 'there must be one supreme power, and one only',[1] or that 'two Sovereignties can not co-exist within the same limits'.[2] 'The United States', observed Mason, 'will have a qualified sovereignty only. The individual States will retain a part of the Sovereignty'.[3] 'The U.S.', added Ellsworth, 'are sovereign on one side of the line dividing the jurisdictions—the States on the other—each ought to have power to defend their respective Sovereignties'.[4] 'The preservation of the States in a certain degree of agency', as Dickinson had foreseen, would 'produce that collision between the different authorities which should be wished for in order to check each other.'[5]

The dominant purpose is to protect rights by limiting authority, to preclude the rebirth of that imperial absolutism which had threatened at Westminster, in the shape of a popular absolutism in the United States. Two principles are clung to. The first is that sovereign authority, even when vested in the people, is still subject to a rule of law. The second, that when you have to deal, not with 'one homogeneous mass, in which everything that affects a part will affect in the same manner the whole',[6] not with a unit divided into 'districts of individuals',[7] but with distinct interests having a local habitation, then, that which peculiarly affects the part should receive the assent of that part and is not made valid by the overriding vote of other parts not at all, or not comparably, affected. It is this which explains the too numerous devices to check and to balance. It is this anxiety to secure the prevalence of the

---

[1] Farrand, *op. cit.*, p. 34. [2] *Ibid.*, p. 287. [3] *Ibid.*, ii, 347.
[4] *Ibid.*, p. 349. [5] *Ibid.*, i, 153. [6] *Ibid.*, p. 422.
[7] *Ibid.*, p. 450.

8

supreme law and permanent reason, to this sensitive care for
the protection of the consciously separate group, whether it be
an economic interest or a geographical area, from arbitrary
government by an alien majority, that the recent writers on
American constitutional history point as the characteristic of
the party that prevailed in 1789. And this conclusion has
been reached, not by the analytical study of political theories,
but by the illumination of the familiar texts by a fuller knowledge of the circumstances in which they had their origin. The
study of the constitutional history of the colonies, of the course
of events in the several states upon the establishment of independence, and of the social standing of the makers of the
Constitution and of the party that carried the ratifying conventions has established distinctions where before the separate
notions were confused in a glow of undifferentiated democracy.
There is revealed something very different from that which it
fell to the lot of Bryce to study nearly a century later, when
what struck his attention was the 'experiment in the rule of the
multitude', 'the sovereignty of the masses'.[1] That was not the
aim of the fathers, though it was in the minds of many of their
contemporaries. The settlement of a continent and a civil war
lay between.

From this investigation of the situation in the United States
during the years immediately following the establishment of
independence two fresh lines of study take their rise. On the
one hand lies a search into the remoter origins of the Constitution which carries those who pursue it back to the middle ages;
and it becomes necessary to examine the part played by the
colonial clergy as transmitters of the ideas which lay in the minds
of the politicians. On the other hand, the call is clear for a new
study of the revolt against the creditors. Its starting point is
Beard's examination of the *Economic Origins of Jeffersonian
Democracy* (1915). It has recently been much advanced by Professor Jensen's study of *The Articles of Confederation* (1940),
though there is now some risk that the Constitution, deprived
of the reputation of being a supreme embodiment of the

[1] James Bryce, *The American Commonwealth*, 3 vv. (1888), i, 1, 5.

principles of democracy, may come to be regarded in the eyes
of a school whose attention is fixed upon what Samuel Adams
called 'free internal Government'[1] as no more than a reactionary
plot to frustrate the achievement of the Revolution. It must
proceed by a more critical investigation of Jefferson himself
and of French influences. It involves the continuation into the
post-revolutionary years of the study of the social and political
history of the several states. And it is there caught up in the
larger subject of the settlement of the Mississippi valley and the
reaction of that event upon the seaboard communities.

BIBLIOGRAPHICAL NOTE

THE REVOLUTION

For a guide to the now voluminous literature upon the course
of the American Revolution the reader should go in the first instance
to S. M. Pargellis & D. J. Medley, *Bibliography of British History,
1717–1789* (Clarendon Press: Oxford, 1951). The point to be made
here is that the work done during the last generation upon what
came before the Revolution and what followed after has put the
Revolution itself in a new light.

The account of the American Revolution given by W. E. H.
Lecky in his *History of England in the Eighteenth Century*, 8 vv. (Longmans, 1878–90), now most easily accessible in the fourth of the
'English' volumes of the cabinet edition (Longmans, 1902), has not
in its main structure been radically altered, and the standard works
of the forty years that followed did not add materially to it save in
so far as they took account of the writings of G. L. Beer. Sir G. O.
Trevelyan's six volumes, *The American Revolution*, vol. i, pts. 1, 2
(in 2 vols.) & 3, 4 vols. in all (Longmans 1899–1907; new ed. 4 vv.,
1905–12), and *George III and C. J. Fox*, 2 vv. (Longmans, 1912–14,
new ed., 2 vv. being vols. v–vi of *The American Revolution*, 1916, 1915)
were a delightfully vivid picture of events, but added nothing to our
understanding of the Revolution. The two volumes in the 'American
Nation', G. E. Howard, *Preliminaries of the Revolution, 1763–1775*
and C. H. Van Tyne, *The American Revolution, 1776–1783* (Harper
& Bros.: New York, 1905), the third volume of E. Channing,
A History of the United States. The American Revolution, 1761–1789
(Macmillan: New York, 1912), and C. H. Van Tyne, *The Causes
of the War of Independence* and *The War of Independence. American Phase*
(Constable, 1922, 1929) followed what had become the conven-

[1] M. Jensen, *The Articles of Confederation* (Madison, Wisc., 1940), p. 110, n. 7.

tional pattern; and of this phase in the historiography of the Revolution, H. E. Egerton, *The Causes and Character of the American Revolution* (Clarendon Press: Oxford, 1923) was an authoritative summary.

The new light came from the definition of the constitutional issues by the work of Osgood and his followers, Beer's examination of colonial policy that was part of that work, the new study of the problem of the western lands, the revelation by Becker, Schlesinger and others of the nature of the financial difficulties of merchants and planters, and the fresh examination of the Constitution that was accompanied by and contributed greatly to a more critical appreciation of the ideas of the Revolution itself.

i. For particulars of the work of Osgood and the Columbia school, see pp. 64–8 above; for the projection of this work into the Revolutionary period, see paragraph i, p. 103 below.

ii. The development of a crisis in the handling of the problem of the West has been traced by four British scholars, V. Coffin, *The Province of Quebec and the Early American Revolution*. Bulletin of the Univ. of Wisconsin, i, no. 3 (Madison, Wisc., 1896); R. Coupland, *The Quebec Act* (Clarendon Press: Oxford, 1925); Chester Martin, *Empire and Commonwealth* (Clarendon Press: Oxford, 1929); and G. S. Graham, *British Policy and Canada, 1774–1791* (Longmans, 1930). For the handling of the Indians by the new authority, see W. H. Mohr, *Federal Indian Relations, 1774–1788* (Univ. of Pennsylvania Press: Philadelphia, 1933). The more particular question of the influence of the land companies is dealt with in T. P. Abernethy, *Western Lands and the American Revolution* (Appleton-Century: New York, 1937), a difficult book, because dealing with a difficult subject, and not a final treatment of it, but a book to be read and re-read and thought about. Of particular aspects of this subject there are special studies in H. B. Adams, *Maryland's Influence upon Land Cessions to the United States*. Johns Hopkins Univ. Studies, iii, no. 1 (N. Murray: Baltimore, 1885), and J. A. Barrett, *Evolution of the Ordinance of 1787*. Univ. of Nebraska Seminary Papers (Putnam's: New York, 1891), and in the histories of the several land companies listed above, on page 71.

iii. Attention was first called to the political effect of the strain caused by the persistent passive balance of trade in C. L. Becker, *The History of Political Parties in the Province of New York, 1760–1776*. Bulletin of the Univ. of Wisconsin, no. 286 (Madison, Wisc., 1909). The subject was treated in detail in A. M. Schlesinger,

The Colonial Merchants and the American Revolution. Col. Univ. Studies, 182 (Columbia Univ. Press: New York, 1918); and there is to be added to this a group of more specialized studies, W. S. McClellan, *Smuggling in the American Colonies at the Outbreak of the Revolution, with special reference to the West Indies Trade* (Moffat, Yard: New York, 1912); C. M. Andrews, *The Boston Merchants and the Non-Importation Movement* (Wilson: Cambridge, Mass., 1917); G. H. Guttridge (ed.), *The American Correspondence of a Bristol Merchant, 1766–1776. Letters of Richard Champion.* Univ. of California Pubs. in History, xxii, no. 1 (Univ. of California Press: Berkeley, Calif., 1934); A. S. Williamson, *Credit Relations between Colonial and English Merchants in the Eighteenth Century.* Univ. of Iowa Studies in the Social Sciences, x, no. 2 (Iowa City, Ia., 1932); R. A. East, *Business Enterprise in the American Revolutionary Era.* Col. Univ. Studies, 439 (Columbia Univ. Press: New York, 1938); W. T. Baxter, *The House of Hancock; Business in Boston, 1724–1775.* Harvard Studies in Business History, x (Harvard Univ. Press: Cambridge, Mass., 1945); Virginia D. Harrington, *The New York Merchant on the Eve of the Revolution.* Col. Univ. Studies, 404 (Columbia Univ. Press: New York, 1935); F. N. Mason (ed.), *John Norton & Sons . . . , being the Papers from their Counting House for the Years 1750 to 1795* (Dietz Press: Richmond, Va., 1937); C. C. Crittenden, *The Commerce of North Carolina, 1763–1789.* Yale Hist. Pubs., xxix (Yale Univ. Press: New Haven, Conn., 1936); Leila Sellers, *Charleston Business on the Eve of the American Revolution* (Univ. of N. Carolina Press: Chapel Hill, N.C., 1934).

iv. The more critical appreciation of the ideas of the American Revolution draws its strength from the work of the last forty years on the constitutional history of the several states and of the Union, of which some particulars are given below, pp. 105–6. The outstanding works, in which the new influences do not make themselves fully felt until the twenties, are H. Friedenwald, *The Declaration of Independence; an Interpretation and Analysis* (Macmillan: New York, 1904); J. H. Hazelton, *The Declaration of Independence, its History* (Dodd: New York, 1906); Correa M. Walsh, *The Political Science of John Adams* (Putnam's: New York, 1915); C. L. Becker, *The Declaration of Independence* (Harcourt, Brace: New York, 1922); R. G. Adams, *Political Ideas of the American Revolution* (Trinity College Press: Durham, N.C., 1922); C. H. McIlwain, *The American Revolution* (Macmillan: New York, 1923); C. F. Mullett, *Colonial Claims to Home Rule, 1764–1775.* Univ. of Missouri Studies, ii, no. 4 (Univ. of Missouri: Columbia, Mo., 1927); R. L. Schuyler, *Parliament and the British Empire* (Columbia Univ. Press: New York, 1929); A. B. Keith, *The Constitutional History of the First British Empire*

(Clarendon Press: Oxford, 1930); B. F. Wright, jr., *American Interpretations of Natural Law* (Harvard Univ. Press: Cambridge, Mass., 1931); C. L. Becker, *The Heavenly City of the Eighteenth Century Philosophers* (Yale Univ. Press: New Haven, Conn., 1932); C. F. Mullet, *Fundamental Law and the American Revolution, 1760–1776.* Col. Univ. Studies, 385 (Columbia Univ. Press: New York, 1933); R. T. E. Latham, 'The law and the commonwealth', in W. K. Hancock, *Survey of British Commonwealth Affairs,* vol. i (Oxford Univ. Press, 1937); G. H. Guttridge, *English Whiggism and the American Revolution.* Univ. of California Pubs. in History, xxviii (Univ. of California Press: Berkeley, Calif., 1942). To these may be added, as casting light from a rather different angle, F. J. Hinkhouse, *The Preliminaries of the American Revolution as seen in the English Press, 1763–1775.* Col. Univ. Studies, 276 (Columbia Univ. Press: New York, 1926); Dora M. Clark, *British Opinion and the American Revolution.* Yale Hist. Pubs., xx (Yale Univ. Press: New Haven, Conn., 1930); and P. Davidson, *Propaganda and the American Revolution* (Univ. of N. Carolina Press: Chapel Hill, N.C., 1941).

The wider subject of the intellectual changes that occurred in the mainland colonies in the eighteenth century and that affected the foundations of political thought has not yet been successfully attacked. The classical authority is M. C. Tyler, *History of American Literature, 1607–1765,* 2 vv. (Putnam's: New York, 1878), and *Literary History of the American Revolution, 1763–1783,* 2 vv. (Putnam's: New York, 1897. Facsimile edition, Barnes & Noble: New York, 1941). Nothing comparable has been written by later generations. V. L. Parrington, *Main Currents in American Thought,* vol. i, 'The Colonial Mind, 1620–1800' (Harcourt, Brace: New York, 1927) is more soberly judged now than when it was published. It was a gallant foray; but it was vitiated by a loose use of terms that employed 'democracy' to cover alike the liberal and the egalitarian, so that it ceased to have any precision and came to mean little more than 'a good life for everybody'[1]; and much of the volume was mere declamation. Some general sense of the change of the climate of opinion that came with the decline in theology and the rise in its place of law and politics as the common subject of discussion can be got from J. F. Jameson, *The American Revolution considered as a Social Movement* (Princeton Univ. Press: Princeton, N.J., 1926); Käthe Spiegel, *Kulturgeschichtliche Grundlagen der Amerikanischen Revolution* (Oldenbourg: Munich & Berlin, 1931); and two volumes in 'The History of American Life', J. T. Adams, *Provincial Society, 1690–1763,* and E. B. Greene, *The Revolutionary Generation, 1763–1790* (Macmillan: New York, 1927, 1946). And there are a few more

[1] M. Curti, *The Growth of American Thought* (New York, 1943), p. 479.

specialized studies, notably Alice M. Baldwin, *The New England Clergy and the American Revolution* (Duke Univ. Press: Durham, N.C., 1928), a book that missed its way, for what is of most interest is, not that many clergy became mere politicians, but the extent to which politics continued to be influenced by ideas that were in origin theological; C. H. Maxson, *The Great Awakening in the Middle Colonies* (Univ. of Chicago Press: Chicago, Ill., 1920); and W. M. Gewehr, *The Great Awakening in Virginia, 1740–1790* (Duke Univ. Press: Durham, N.C., 1930).

v. In no work on a large scale have the new conclusions been satisfactorily gathered up. But they will be found in varying measure in smaller and introductory volumes and in essays in interpretation, notably, J. A. Woodburn, *Causes of the American Revolution*. Johns Hopkins Univ. Studies, x, no. 12 (Johns Hopkins Press: Baltimore, Md., 1892); T. C. Smith, *The Wars between England and America*. 'Home Univ. Library' (Williams & Norgate, 1914); C. L. Becker, *The Eve of the Revolution*, 'Chronicles of America', vol. xi (Yale Univ. Press: New Haven, Conn., 1918); A. M. Schlesinger, *New Viewpoints in American History* (Macmillan: New York, 1922); E. B. Greene, *The Foundations of American Nationality* (American Book Company: New York, 1922); C. H. Van Tyne, *England and America, Rivals in the American Revolution* (Cambridge Univ. Press, 1927); R. Coupland, *The American Revolution and the British Empire* (Longmans, 1930); L. J. Davitt, *A Re-Study of the Movement toward American Independence, 1760–1778* (Catholic Univ. of America: Washington, D.C., 1929); R. B. Morris (ed.), *The Era of the American Revolution. Studies inscribed to Evarts Boutell Greene* (Columbia Univ. Press: New York, 1939); C. P. Nettels, *The Roots of American Civilization* (Crofts: New York, 1938), and J. C. Miller, *Origins of the American Revolution* (Little, Brown: Boston, 1943).

THE CONSTITUTION

i. The revival of the prestige of the Supreme Court, from the low level to which it fell during the years of civil war and reconstruction, has been a remarkable and not easily understood feature of recent American history, and it is quite insufficiently explained by the growing anxiety of property for shelter within the defences of the law. It has found its reflection in American historiography and has had a great influence upon the recent study of the history of the Constitution. The new work had a precursor in O. G. Libby,

Geographical Distribution of the Vote of the Thirteen States on the Federal Constitution, 1787–8. Bulletin of the Univ. of Wisconsin, i, no. 1 (Madison, Wisc., 1894), but begins effectively with two publications of 1912, drawing their immediate sustenance from contemporary politics, but having roots that went deeper; A. C. McLaughlin, *The Courts, the Constitution and Parties* (Univ. of Chicago Press: Chicago, 1912), and C. A. Beard, *The Supreme Court and the Constitution* (Macmillan: New York, 1912). It was continued in M. Farrand, *The Framing of the Constitution of the United States* (Yale Univ. Press: New Haven, Conn., 1913); C. A. Beard, *An Economic Interpretation of the Constitution of the United States* (Macmillan: New York, 1913; re-issue, with new introduction, 1935) and *Economic Origins of Jeffersonian Democracy* (Macmillan: New York, 1915); R. L. Schuyler, *The Constitution of the United States; an Historical Survey of its Formation* (Macmillan: New York, 1923); C. Warren, *The Making of the Constitution* (Little, Brown: Boston, 1928); A. C. McLaughlin, *The Foundations of American Constitutionalism* (New York Univ. Press: New York, 1932), and *A Constitutional History of the United States* (Appleton-Century: New York, 1935), the ripe fruit of a lifetime and the culmination of this chapter in historiography. The temper changes perceptibly in C. Read (ed.), *The Constitution Reconsidered* (Columbia Univ. Press: New York, 1938): the old certainties have gone, and scepticism prevails. M. Jensen, *The Articles of Confederation; an Interpretation of the Social-Constitutional History of the American Revolution, 1774–1781* (Univ. of Wisconsin Press: Madison, Wisc., 1940) is a defence of the single-chamber legislative absolutism that the establishment of the Constitution overthrew. It has been followed by a study of *The New Nation. A History of the United States during the Confederation, 1781–1789* (Knopf: New York, 1950).

This work of interpretation was accompanied by a group of important documentary publications, W. C. Ford *et al., Journals of the Continental Congress,* 34 vv. (Govt. Printing Office: Washington, D.C., 1904–37); M. Farrand (ed.), *The Records of the Federal Convention of 1787,* 3 vv. (Yale Univ. Press: New Haven, Conn., 1911; revd. ed., 4 vv., 1937); E. C. Burnett (ed.), *Letters of Members of the Continental Congress,* 8 vv. (Carnegie Institution of Washington: Washington, D.C., 1921–36).

Upon the new government, see J. Hart, *The American Presidency in Action, 1789; a Study in Constitutional History* (Macmillan: New York, 1948); L. D. White, *The Federalists; a Study in Administrative History* (Macmillan: New York, 1948); L. D. Baldwin, *Whiskey Rebels; the Story of a Frontier Uprising* (Univ. of Pittsburgh Press: Pittsburgh, 1939).

ii. To this fuller understanding of the history of the Constitution an important contribution was made by the study of Revolutionary history of the several States. This work was summarized in 1924 in A. Nevins, *The American States during and after the Revolution* (Macmillan: New York, 1924). The principal monographs are Margaret B. Macmillan, *The War Governors in the American Revolution*. Col. Univ. Studies, 503 (Columbia Univ. Press: New York, 1943); W. A. Robinson, *Jeffersonian Democracy in New England*. Yale Hist. Pubs., iii (Yale Univ. Press: New Haven, Conn. 1916); R. F. Upton, *Revolutionary New Hampshire* (Dartmouth College; Hanover, N.H., 1936); H. A. Cushing, *History of the Transition from Provincial to Commonwealth Government in Massachusetts*. Col. Univ. Studies, 17 (Columbia Univ. Press: New York, 1896); S. B. Harding, *The Contest over the Ratification of the Federal Constitution in the State of Massachusetts*. Harvard Hist. Studies, ii (Harvard Univ. Press: Cambridge, Mass., 1896); A. E. Morse, *The Federalist Party in Massachusetts to the Year 1800* (The University Library: Princeton, N.J., 1909); F. G. Bates, *Rhode Island and the Formation of the Union* ([Columbia Univ.]: New York, 1898); R. J. Purcell, *Connecticut in Transition, 1775–1818* (American Hist. Assoc.: Washington, D.C., 1918); W. C. Abbott, *New York in the American Revolution* (Scribner's: New York, 1929); E. W. Spaulding, *New York in the Critical Period, 1783–1789* (Columbia Univ. Press: New York, 1932); O. T. Barck, jr., *New York City during the War for Independence*. Col. Univ. Studies, 357 (Columbia Univ. Press: New York, 1931); T. J. Wertenbaker, *Father Knickerbocker Rebels; New York City during the Revolution* (Scribner's: New York, 1948); C. E. Miner, *The Ratification of the Federal Constitution by the State of New York*. Col. Univ. Studies, 214 (Columbia Univ. Press: New York, 1921); C. R. Erdman, jr., *The New Jersey Constitution of 1776* (Princeton Univ. Press: Princeton, N.J., 1929); L. Lundin, *Cockpit of the Revolution. The War for Independence in New Jersey* (Princeton Univ. Press: Princeton, N.J., 1940); R. P. McCormick, *Experiment in Independence; New Jersey in the Critical Period, 1781–1789*. Rutgers Studies in History, no. 6 (Rutgers Univ. Press: New Brunswick, N.J., 1950); J. P. Selsam, *The Pennsylvania Constitution of 1776* (Univ. of Pennsylvania Press: Philadelphia, 1936); B. A. Konkle, *George Bryan and the Constitution of Pennsylvania* (W. J. Campbell: Philadelphia, 1922); R. J. Ferguson, *Early Western Pennsylvania Politics* (Univ. of Pittsburgh Press: Pittsburgh, Pa., 1938); R. L. Brunhouse, *The Counter-Revolution in Pennsylvania, 1776–1790* (Pennsylvania Historical Commission: Harrisburg, Pa., 1942); J. B. McMaster & F. D. Stone (eds.), *Pennsylvania and the Federal Constitution, 1787–1788* (The Historical Society of Pennsylvania. Inquirer Printing & Publishing Co.:

Lancaster, Pa., 1888); H. M. Tinkcom, *The Republicans and Federalists in Pennsylvania, 1790–1801* (Pennsylvania Historical and Museum Commission: Harrisburg, Pa., 1950); B. W. Bond, jr., *State Government in Maryland, 1777–1781* (Johns Hopkins Press: Baltimore, Md., 1905); C. A. Barker, *The Background of the Revolution in Maryland* (Yale Univ. Press: New Haven, Conn., 1940); P. A. Crowl, *Maryland during and after the Revolution; a Political and Economic Study.* Johns Hopkins Univ. Studies, lxi, no. 1 (Johns Hopkins Press: Baltimore, Md., 1943); H. J. Eckenrode, *The Revolution in Virginia* (Houghton, Mifflin: New York, 1916); J. M. Leake, *The Virginia Committee System and the American Revolution.* Johns Hopkins Univ. Studies, xxxv, no. 1 (Johns Hopkins Press: Baltimore, Md., 1917); C. R. Lingley, *The Transition in Virginia from Colony to Commonwealth.* Col. Univ. Studies, 96 (Columbia Univ. Press: New York, 1910); F. H. Hart, *The Valley of Virginia in the American Revolution, 1763–1789* (Univ. of N. Carolina Press: Chapel Hill, N.C., 1942); E. W. Sikes, *The Transition of North Carolina from a Colony.* Johns Hopkins Univ. Studies, xvi, 10–1 (Johns Hopkins Press: Baltimore, Md., 1898); Louise I. Trenholme, *The Ratification of the Federal Constitution in North Carolina.* Col. Univ. Studies, 363 (Columbia Univ. Press: New York, 1932); D. H. Gilpatrick, *Jeffersonian Democracy in North Carolina, 1789–1816.* Col. Univ. Studies, 344 (Columbia Univ. Press: New York, 1931); J. H. Wolfe, *Jeffersonian Democracy in South Carolina.* James Sprunt Studies in Hist. & Pol. Sci., xxiv, 1 (Univ. of N. Carolina Press: Chapel Hill, N.C., 1940); B. Barrs, *East Florida in the American Revolution* (Guild Press: Jacksonville, Fla., 1932).

iii. Upon the subject of French influence in the United States, see H. M. Jones, *America and French Culture, 1750–1848* (Univ. of N. Carolina Press: Chapel Hill, N.C., 1927); B. Faÿ, *L'esprit révolutionnaire en France et aux États-Unis à la fin du xviiiᵉ siècle* (Champion: Paris, 1925); O. Vossler, *Die Amerikanischen Revolutionsideale in ihrem Verhältnis zu dem Europaischen* (Oldenbourg: Munich & Berlin, 1929); A. Lasseray, *Les français sous les treize étoiles, 1775–1783* (Protat Frères: Macon, 1935); Kathryn Sullivan, *Maryland and France, 1774–1789* (Univ. of Pennsylvania Press: Philadelphia, 1936); W. d'Ormesson, *La première mission officielle de la France aux États-Unis, Conrad-Alexandre Gérard, 1778–1779* (Champion: Paris, 1924); G. Chinard, *Jefferson et les idéologues* (Johns Hopkins Univ. Press: Baltimore, Md., 1925); H. Knust, *Montesquieu und die Verfassungen der Vereinigten Staaten von Amerika* (Oldenbourg: Munich & Berlin, 1922); Frances S. Childs, *French Refugee Life in the United States, 1790–1800* (Institut Français de Washington: Washington, D.C., 1940);

C. D. Hazen, *Contemporary American Opinion of the French Revolution.*
Johns Hopkins Univ. Studies. Extra vol. xvi (Johns Hopkins Press:
Baltimore, Md., 1897); E. P. Link, *Democratic Republican Societies,*
1790–1800 (Columbia Univ. Press: New York, 1942); and M. Min-
nigerode, *Jefferson Friend of France, 1793; the Career of Edmond Charles
Genêt* . . . (*1763–1834*) (Putnam's: New York, 1928).

IV

The Settlement of the Mississippi Valley

WHEN in 1894 F. J. Turner sent to some of the older scholars off-prints of his paper on 'The significance of the Frontier in American history', one of them replied thanking him for his 'curious and interesting contribution' and another observed that he must be a 'very provincial man'.[1] What they had had put before them, but had failed to appreciate, was the first demonstration that the cardinal factor in the transformation of the United States of 1787 into the United States of 1861 was the settlement of the Mississippi valley. That thesis is now so generally accepted as to make it difficult to recover the older point of view. But it is only the work of the Middle Western school, beginning with Turner's paper, that has brought this about.

The Mississippi valley fills an area of over a million and a quarter square miles, and is twice the size of the Denmark, Holland, Belgium, France, Germany, Czechoslovakia and Italy of 1939. It contained in 1790 about 130,046 white persons[2], a number substantially less than that of the population of the city of Coventry in 1938 (167,083). By 1940 there had been erected within it twenty states of the Union containing a population of just on sixty-four million. In 1860 its population had already grown to over fourteen and a half million.

By 1783, the obstacles that had embarrassed the exploitation

[1]J. Schafer, 'The author of the "frontier hypothesis" ', *Wisconsin Mag. of Hist.*, xv (1931), pp. 96–7.
[2]*Annual Report of the American Historical Association for the Year 1931*, vol. i (Washington, D.C., 1932), pp. 397, 398–408.

of the West between 1763 and 1775 had disappeared, in so far as the experience of war had taught the necessity of colonial co-operation and had weakened inter-colonial jealousies and to the extent that the expansionists were now relieved of the opposition that had shown itself in Westminster. Those who had refused to accept the penetration of the West because of their mistrust of the foundation of interior colonies or their tenderness for the rights of the Indians could no longer interfere. Gone, too, was the drag of those who, while willing to foster a well-regulated western advance, were not willing to meet the cost of its administration out of English revenues and failed to provide it out of colonial. Yet the road was by no means alto-gether clear. If in the seats of authority there was now a wider acceptance of the idea of western expansion, there were still those who insisted that the advance must be orderly, that it must therefore be centrally controlled, that orderliness and control would be costly, and that western lands must be made a source, not now of imperial, but of federal revenue. More-over, the Indian had still to be reckoned with; and because of the Indian, the settlement of the Mississippi took, at the out-set, a direction and assumed a character that was in a short span to undergo a radical change.

The two natural lines of advance into the Valley led, the one through the broken hills at the southern end of the Appalachian mountains, and the other up the valleys of the Hudson and the Mohawk in the north (maps 2 and 5). But these were still blocked by the Indians, to the south by the power of the Cherokees and the Creeks; to the north by the Iroquois, from 1763 to 1775 recent allies in war whose rights must needs be respected and enjoying from 1783 to 1794 support from the British retention of the northwestern posts. And it was not until the defeat of the northwest Indians in 1810-1 and of the British alliance with the Indians in 1813, and until Jackson's defeat of the Creeks in 1814, that these natural avenues were opened. During the early national, as during the colonial period, there-fore, the principal part in the settlement of the West was played by Pennsylvania, Maryland, Virginia, and North Carolina. The

route from New England through up-state New York, of which
the Genesee Road and Great Western Turnpike became parts,
running from Albany to the headwaters of the Allegheny at
Olean Point was of minor importance. Population advanced, in
the main, southwest from the principal ports of arrival, moving
along the valleys running parallel with the mountains through
the up-country of the middle and southern states and filtering
through the gaps in the hills made by the headwaters of the
streams flowing into the Atlantic or the Mississippi. It thus approached the Old Northwest from the south. The most convenient lines from the more populous areas and the ports of New
York, Philadelphia and Baltimore were the path from Philadelphia to Pittsburgh that became the Lancaster pike, and the
Potomac-Pittsburgh path that became the National Road to Fort
Cumberland and Wheeling, whence the journey was continued
by flat-boat or keel-boat down the Ohio river. But these routes
were hampered by the labour of the return up-stream and by
exposure to attacks from the Shawnees from the north bank of
the Ohio. Great importance therefore was acquired by the
Cumberland routes, used both by settlers from Virginia and
North Carolina and by those from the northeast deflected by
the difficulties of the Ohio. These paths ran from Philadelphia
up the Shenandoah, or from Richmond through the Blue Ridge,
to the New River, Fort Chissel, and the Holston, and thence
by the Wilderness Road through the Cumberland Gap or
south to Knoxville, into what was to become Kentucky and
Tennessee. They were supplemented by two other routes of
less importance and rather later development, the trail from the
headwaters of the James river to the Great Kanawha and a
road from the confluence of the Holston and the Clinch to the
valley of the Cumberland and Nashville.

The course of this settlement had a radical effect upon its
character. Expansion became a function, not of the northeast,
but of the southwest. It was effected by the population of the
up-country of the southern states or by immigrants entering
middle or southern ports and adapting themselves to the habits
of the southern frontier. It was essentially the now unimpeded

and reinforced advance of the backwoodsmen of the colonial era, of people living in log cabins, disliking near neighbours, cultivating but little land, and almost entirely self-sufficing; keeping to the woodlands partly as a matter of habit, partly because heavy timber was thought to mean richer soil, and partly because settlement on prairie land required a capital expenditure for the provision of wood and water of which the settlers were incapable. It was the migration of a people whose descendents were found unchanged by Cecil Sharp in the Appalachian mountains in 1917, singing the English folk songs in an earlier form than had survived in the mother country,[1] and who were observed by Mrs. Trollope in Ohio in 1828;[2] a people who bred an Abraham Lincoln in Kentucky in 1809,[3] and who chose the heavy timber in Wisconsin in the forties and fifties, still contented with the produce of the forest and a small clearing in the woods;[4] a humble, isolated, self-reliant stock, reinforcing the agrarian, up-country, radical opinions of the South against the commercial, capitalist, creditor interests of the cities of the northern and middle states.

In these circumstances it is not surprising that the northeast should have regarded the growth of the West with some alarm. The traditional antipathy of tidewater to back country grew to a larger dimension. The anxieties that delayed the re-distribution of seats within the several states and the grant of a due measure of representation to the back country took a wider range. The commercial and creditor interests saw themselves threatened at the national centre, if the new communities created in the West were to be incorporated in the Union as states, with a consequent shift of the weight of numbers into the columns of their political opponents and jeopardy to their puritan way of life.

[1] A. H. Fox Strangways, *Cecil Sharp* (1933), pp. 142–77.
[2] Frances Trollope, *Domestic Manners of the Americans*, ed. M. Sadleir (Routledge, 1927), pp. 41–3; *cf.* J. Schafer (ed.), *Intimate Letters of Carl Schurz, 1841–1869* (Madison, Wisc., 1928), p. 123.
[3] A. J. Beveridge, *Abraham Lincoln, 1809–1858*, 2 vv. (1928), i, ch. i.
[4] J. Schafer, *Wisconsin Domesday. Town Studies*, vol. i (Madison, Wisc., 1924), pp. 12b, 40–4.

In succession to the first phase in the history of the west there followed in the eighteen-twenties a quite revolutionary change, the nature and extent of which it took contemporaries something like a generation to realize; and in order fully to understand it the historian has had to address himself to the study of the history of transportation and of alterations in the course and character of migrant and immigrant.

The first effective picture of this process of settlement was presented in chapters i–viii of the volume on *The Rise of the New West, 1819–1829*, contributed by Turner in 1906 to the series entitled 'The American Nation'. But these chapters were a conspicuous and significant deviation from the chosen path of that series, and those which follow them in Turner's own volume and return to the beaten track lack Turner's characteristic qualities and are a baffled and inconsequent assembly of conventional political information. The effect of the settlement of the Mississippi valley upon the national history had not then been worked out by the historians.

The picture of North America before the coming of the white man as a 'pathless wilderness' is a myth.[1] The continent in its primitive state was already threaded with the countless tracks of beast and man, many of them of great length and habitual use. But even when path became turnpike and pack train gave place to wagon, the carriage of goods by land over the immense distances separating the far-flung settlements taxed to the utmost the available resources. From the beginning, therefore, water transport played a great part in the history of white penetration; and for the movement of bulk freight the road system was, broadly speaking, little more than a series of links between navigable waters. Upon the first phase in the settlement of the west the thousand miles of the Ohio river and the further waterways provided by its tributaries thus had a decisive influence; and the energies of the enterprising were bent to the improvement of this river system and the establishment of con-

[1] *Cf.* A. B. Hulbert, *Soil: Its Influence on the History of the United States* (New Haven, 1930), ch. v.; B. W. Bond, *The Foundations of Ohio* (Columbus, O., 1941), pp. 29–31.

nections with it.[1] Apart from improvements to the navigation
of the Ohio itself, there were two principal heads of activity.
Efforts were directed to the development of connections between the Ohio and the Atlantic seaboard; and other efforts
to the linkage with the Ohio system of the traffic of the upper
Northwest and the Great Lakes.[2]

In the east, three were projects of principal importance,
and in two of these Washington himself was a leader. The
Potomac river was regularly used by the servants of the Ohio
Company once it had been linked to the Ohio valley by
Cresap's path of 1750, converted by Forbes into the road from
Wills Creek to the Red Stone on the Monongahela in 1753-4;
as early as the seventeen-sixties schemes for its improvement were
mooted; and in 1772 an act of the Virginia legislature established a company to open the navigation of the river. The
jealousy of Maryland and the Revolutionary war delayed
matters; but the scheme was revived in 1783, and by 1802 work
had been completed as far as the Great Falls. But the physical
difficulties were formidable and the resources of Virginia and
Maryland insufficient. The company was driven to seek public
assistance in 1819, and was eventually absorbed in a more far-
reaching endeavour that was more broadly based, the Chesapeake and Ohio Canal Company of 1828, formed to construct
a canal from the Chesapeake to the Ohio in preference to
further expenditure upon improvements to the Potomac itself,
and successful in 1850 in carrying the canal from Georgetown
to Cumberland. Meanwhile, however, rival projects were
started both to the south and to the north. That to the south
was an endeavour to establish a connection between the James
and the Great Kanawha, and its history took a course somewhat similar to that of the Chesapeake and Ohio canal.
Founded in 1785, the James River and Kanawha Company
built a canal round the falls at Richmond and carried the
improvement of the river from Lynchburg to Crow's Ferry,
improving as well the main bed below Lynchburg and its

[1] C. H. Ambler, *History of Transportation in the Ohio Valley* (Glendale, Calif., 1932),
pp. 394-7.   [2] See map 3.

9

branches. Financially the venture proved to be one of the most successful internal improvements carried out to that date. But it had its critics, who complained both of the insufficiency of the services of the company upon the stretch of water with which it had dealt and its failure to reach more distant object-ives. The company was accordingly bought out in 1820 and made an agency of the state of Virginia; and under this direc-tion some progress was achieved, between 1820 and 1828, with the improvement and extension of the canal above Richmond, the building of a canal across the Blue Ridge, the improvement of the Great Kanawha itself, and the completion of a turnpike between the two waters. Further expenditure was then checked by sectional jealousy within the state, and in 1835 private enterprise was called in again when a second James River and Kanawha company was formed. By 1851 the canal had been carried to Buchanan, and in 1854 the tidewater connec-tion was completed. During the decade between 1850 and 1860 the company was at the height of its activities, operating the Richmond dock and tidewater connection, the canal from Richmond to Buchanan, the Kanawha turnpike, and the Kanawha River Improvement. The northern rival of the Potomac route was the development of transportation between Pennsylvania and the West. The work was impeded by physical obstacles, bedevilled by politics, embarrassed by gross corrup-tion and waste, and in any case undertaken too late. Begun as a state enterprise in 1826, a through route was built between Philadelphia and Pittsburgh by 1834, to be sold in 1857 at the buyer's price to the Pennsylvania Railroad Company. The motives of the promoters are clearly expressed in a memorial presented to the legislature in 1825.

. . . henceforward the intercourse between the East and the West is to be carried on by means of inland navigation. This is decided by what is already done. No State, therefore, can expect to participate largely or beneficially in this interesting intercourse, unless she offer such a channel of communication. The cheap-ness and expedition of transportation by water are so far beyond those of every other mode of conveyance within our reach, as to put competition entirely out of the question. This single fact your Memorialists believe to be of sufficient weight to render all argument superfluous, unless we are disposed to give up the well-earned reputation of Philadelphia, and to suffer her to fall back from her established character and standing.[1]

Neither cheapness nor expedition, however, were practicable upon a route that rose at its summit to 2,322 feet above mean tide or by a system of mixed canal and railroad transportation that necessitated four transhipments. Moreover, in order to secure sufficient political support to undertake the main task, innumerable unconnected projects were embraced, not for their economic viability, but in the name of political fairness or as a mere political trade. The moral strength of the state proved unequal to the temptations offered by so extensive a system of state works. And by the time the through route was completed, the traffic of the back country had, in fact, for more than eight years been accustomed to move eastwards by way of the Erie Canal; and the era of the railroads had begun. But Philadelphia had also been concerned not only with the building of the main line through the mountains to Pittsburgh, but also to divert traffic that might otherwise go by way of the lower Susquehanna to Chesapeake Bay and Baltimore, and to secure the traffic from the northeastern districts of Pennsylvania and from up-state New York. To these ends, obstruction was offered to the improvement of the navigation of the lower Susquehanna until after the construction of the Chesapeake and Delaware Canal in 1829; and an attempt to tap the traffic from the northeast, pursued until 1824 by the building of turnpikes, was continued by the construction of the Schuylkill Navigation in 1825 and of the Union Canal linking Reading on the Schuylkill with Middletown on the Susquehanna between 1821 and 1827.[2]

[1]Memorial to the Legislature. United States Gazette, 11 February, 1825, *cit.* A. L. Bishop, *The State Works of Pennsylvania.* Connecticut Academy of Arts and Sciences, *Transactions* xiii, 263.

[2]C. Bacon-Foster, *Early Chapters in the Development of the Potomac Route to the West* (Washington, D.C., 1912); G. W. Ward, *The Early Development of the Chesapeake and Ohio Canal Project* (Baltimore, 1909); W. S. Sanderlin, *The Great National Project: a History of the Chesapeake and Ohio Canal* (Baltimore, 1946); W. F. Dunaway, *History of the James River and Kanawha Company* (New York, 1922); A. L. Bishop, *The State Works of Pennsylvania* (New Haven, 1907); J. W. Livingood, *The Philadelphia, Baltimore Trade Rivalry, 1750–1860* (Harrisburg, 1947).

While these endeavours were being made to facilitate traffic between the eastern and southern tributaries of the Ohio and the Atlantic seaboard, in the Old Northwest, on the other flank of the Ohio system, the extension of navigable water was sought in order to bring the outer reaches into touch with the river. In Ohio, there grew up during the years 1816 to 1822 an agitation for the building of a canal or canals to reach Lake Erie. In the eighteenth century the Wabash had become the main line of communication between Canada and Louisiana, and although the principal portage shifted further east after the establishment of American independence, interest in the Wabash route was revived in Indiana by the experience of the war of 1812. Further west, in Illinois, a suggestion to use the old Illinois route to provide through communication from the Lakes to New Orleans was made as early as 1810. In each case the aim was in the first place to establish connection with the Ohio river.

In 1822, Ohio undertook the construction of the Ohio and Erie canal from Cleveland to Portsmouth along the Mus-kingum-Scioto route, and of the Miami Canal from Dayton to Cincinnati; and the work was completed by 1833. In the same year of 1822, provision was made by the legislatures of Indiana and Illinois for improvements at the Grand Rapids of the Wabash; and in 1823 a proposal to build a canal connecting the Wabash and the Maumee was considered by them. But it was not until 1827 that Indiana mustered sufficient resources, with the aid of a federal land grant, to undertake extensive operations. In 1829 an agreement was entered into with Ohio for the building of the section within that state. Work was begun in 1832, and the first section was opened in 1835. In 1836 a larger scheme was launched for the extension of the canal to Terre Haute and thence to the White River, and for the construction of a Central Canal from Peru to Evansville; and the work was completed as far as Lafayette in 1843, and ultimately carried to Evansville in 1853. In 1845, when the Miami Extension Canal had been built by Ohio, a junction between the Ohio system and that of Lake Erie and the

Wabash was effected, and in 1849 the canals were combined as the Miami and Erie. In Illinois, deficient resources led to similar delays, and before a start was fairly made, the competing claims of railroads arose to confuse the debate. But the construction of a canal to connect the Illinois river with Lake Michigan was at last begun in 1836, and after encountering many difficulties was ultimately completed in 1848. To the same system belongs also the Pennsylvania-Erie Canal of 1834.[1]

Upon this system the introduction of railroads had at first no decisive effect. The use of steam locomotion created no expectation of any radical change in the modes of transportation. A new source of power was to be employed, but a new direction of traffic was not looked for. The steam wagon, like the steam boat, travelled upon a public highway. Rails were an improvement of the road surface; and steam power turned out to be greater than horse power. But the first railroads were still toll roads, the builder supplying only the road and the motive power.[2] They were an improvement of, and might provide an extension to, the links between water systems. They were not at first expected to supersede them. In 1838, railroads where available were substituted as the post routes of the federal government;[3] and by the forties they were generally accepted as superior to turnpike, river and canal for the transport of passengers and light freight. But it was to be long before they were to provide through freight for the shipment of bulky commodities over great distances.

If subsequent events are for the moment put out of mind, the picture that remains is that of a West centred upon the Ohio

[1]C. C. Huntington & C. P. McClelland, *History of the Ohio Canals* (Columbus, O., 1905); E. L. Bogart, *Internal Improvements and State Debt in Ohio* (New York, 1924); E. J. Benton, *The Wabash Trade Route* (Baltimore, 1903); J. W. Putnam, *The Illinois and Michigan Canal* (Chicago, 1918).

[2]I. L. Sharfman, *The Interstate Commerce Commission*, 4 vv. in 5 (New York, 1931–7), i, 120; W. F. Gephart, *Transportation and Industrial Development in the Middle West* (New York, 1909), p. 159; L. H. Haney, *The Congressional History of Railways to 1850* (Madison, Wisc., 1908), pp. 43–4, 82, 87; E. C. Kirkland, *Men, Cities, and Transportation. A Study of New England History, 1820–1900*, 2 vv. (Cambridge, Mass., 1948), i, 104, 116.

[3]L. H. Haney, *op. cit.*, pp. 72–3.

valley, with Philadelphia, Baltimore, and Richmond as its metropolitan cities. To the fully satisfactory functioning of its economic system there were indeed serious obstacles. The normal imbalance of its trade with the principal sources of its supply was aggravated by the fact that its returns were made in commodities of great bulk which had to travel up-stream as well as across the mountains. But there was an alternative outlet by way of the Mississippi and New Orleans, and there was the promise of the growth of a triangular traffic.[1] The outlook of the war hawks of 1812 was not as landlocked as it has sometimes been represented to have been. Shipbuilding developed in the yards of the Monongahela; the ships of Ohio ports began to deliver the products of the West in southern markets, carrying thence the products of the South to Atlantic ports, where ship and cargo were sold to meet the debts due to exporters to the Valley; and in 1803 there arrived at Liverpool the first vessel cleared from the western waters.[2] Yet the system remained highly vulnerable. As late as 1850 there were still breaks in the continuity of water transportation between Buchanan and the Great Kanawha, between Cumberland and the Ohio, and between Hollidaysburg and Johnstown; and advantage was taken of this with revolutionary effect by the state of New York.

Following upon early efforts made between 1792 and 1808 to improve the navigations of the Mohawk and to provide links with the Susquehanna system upon the one hand and the Great Lakes by way of the Oneida and Oswego upon the other, surveys were made between 1808 and 1817 for a through canal from Lake Erie to the Hudson river; and between 4 July, 1817, and 26 October, 1825, the Erie Canal was

---

[1] A. P. Whitaker, *The Spanish-American Frontier, 1783–1795* (New York, 1927), pp. 28–9; and *The Mississippi Question, 1795–1803* (New York, 1934), pp. 13–14, 16–17; J. A. Robertson, *Louisiana under the Rule of Spain, France, and the United States, 1785–1807.* 2 vv. (Cleveland, O., 1911), i, 220; C. H. Ambler, *History of Transportation in the Ohio Valley* (Glendale, Calif., 1932), pp. 94–5; H. C. Hubbart, *The Older Middle West, 1840–1880* (New York, 1936), pp. 75–6; R. C. Downes, *Frontier Ohio, 1788–1803* (Columbus, O., 1935), pp. 101–21.

[2] Ambler, *op. cit.*, pp. 97–8; W. F. Gephart, *Transportation and Industrial Development in the Middle West* (New York, 1909), p. 94.

built.[1] By 1830 the tolls collected on the traffic exceeded a million dollars a year; and in 1834 the legislature of New York authorized the enlargement of the canal. And this was accompanied between 1818 and 1826 by the development of a steamboat service upon the Lakes. Down to 1859 the traffic was sufficient to employ both the New Orleans and Erie route to capacity, and no serious effect was exerted upon the Ohio route until the building of the trunk railroads, but the tide was on the turn.[2]

But what New York had done became decisive when, within six years of the opening of the Erie Canal, there began the first migration of population on a large scale from New England to the Mississippi valley and the first stage in the great nineteenth century immigration from Europe which lasted from 1830 to 1860 and reached its climax in the years 1847–54. New England had already made a contribution to the peopling of western Pennsylvania and up-state New York in the closing years of the eighteenth century and the opening years of the nineteenth; the settlement effected by the Ohio Land Company at Marietta in 1787 was a New England settlement; and the settlement of northeastern Ohio by New Englanders had begun in 1796. Yet the latter were but New England contributions to the occupation of the Ohio valley. After 1814, the movement gathered new force and took a new direction. With the removal of the Indian danger that resulted from the war of 1812, and with the growth of traffic by way of the Erie Canal and the Great Lakes, there began the settlement of the upper counties of the Old Northwest and of the lower counties of the Lake peninsulas that were to become the states of Michigan and Wisconsin. By 1840, the vacant lands of Ohio had been occupied. Following a substantial movement of New Englanders into Indiana Territory between 1829 and 1830, there began

---

[1]H. W. Hill, *An Historical Review of Waterways and Canal Construction in New York State* (Buffalo, 1908); F. H. Severance (ed.), *Canal Enlargement in New York State. Papers on the barge canal campaign and related topics* (Buffalo, 1909); [F. H. Severance], *The Holland Land Co. and Canal Construction in Western New York* (Buffalo, 1910).

[2]W. F. Gephart, *Transportation and Industrial Development in the Middle West* (New York, 1909), pp. 119, 183, 197.

in 1830 the great New England migration to what were to
become the states of Indiana and Illinois. The settlement of
Michigan was first stimulated upon any scale by the opening
of the Erie Canal and the development of steamboat traffic
in the West, but thereafter proceeded rapidly and was effected
predominantly by emigrants from New England and New
York. Wisconsin was virtually unsettled in 1826, but there
started in that year an immigration from the south attracted
to the lead region round Galena; and settlement was greatly
accelerated after the Black Hawk war of 1834, when the occupation of the lake shore was begun by settlers coming from
the east. Into this northeastern stream flowed the migration
from Europe. Interrupted by war for a couple of generations,
the flow was resumed after 1815, and between 1830 and 1860,
in the first of its nineteenth century stages, it came chiefly from
Wales, the Scottish Highlands, Ireland, Holland, Belgium,
the upper Rhine, Norway and Sweden.[1] Both religious dissent
and political discontent had a part in setting the emigrants in
motion. But the economic distress of the agrarian population
of northwestern Europe counted for more. Of the Welsh and
Highland Scottish migrations we have less detailed knowledge
than of the others. In part this is due to a shortcoming of
British historiography; in part, though Welshmen would
gather in neighbourhoods,[2] to the greater difficulty of tracing
the footsteps of immigrants who were not linguistically clearly
distinguishable from those among whom they settled, and who
in some degree, if for that reason only, acted individually
rather than in communities; the frequent presence upon the
frontier of the Scotch-Irish settlers of the back country of Pennsylvania and Virginia before the War of Independence distort-
ing the evidence afforded by distinctively Scottish personal
names. Of the Irish migration there has been more study.
There had been an exodus from Ireland to America throughout
the eighteenth century, but W. F. Adams concluded that

[1]M. L. Hansen, *The Atlantic Migration, 1607–1860* (Cambridge, Mass., 1941).
[2]*Cf.*, *e.g.*, J. Schafer, *Wisconsin Domesday Book. Town Studies*, vol. i (Madison,
Wisc., 1924), pp. 23–6.

between 1725 and 1812 it never exceeded 6,000 a year and only reached that figure exceptionally.[1] A new emigration set in after 1815, and it reached the figure of 20,000 a year in 1818. It was at first an emigration chiefly of farmers, city shopkeepers, and artisans, and not of the agricultural proletariat; and it came chiefly from Ulster. It was not until 1819–23 that the emigration of the really poor began, and it was then drawn from the south. By 1840, unskilled labour and the poorer catholic and native elements were preponderant, and Cork had super-seded Belfast as the principal port of departure. Numbers rose to 65,000 in 1831 and 1832, and to 77,000 in 1845. By that year, it is calculated[2] that Ireland had in the previous thirty years contributed to the population of the United States a million permanent immigrants. It was the largest single immigration, and made up 44 per cent of the foreign born in 1850;[3] and the way was thus prepared for the great emigration of 1847–1857. But while the Irish labourer often found employment in the building of canals and railroads, Ireland, particularly after the shift of the principal point of departure from Ulster to Munster, did not at this period contribute large numbers to the settle-ment of the Mississippi valley. Four-fifths of the Irish im-migrants in 1850 were still in the northeastern states.[4] A much larger contribution was made to the population of the frontier by the Scandinavians and the Germans. A trickle of emigration from Norway to the United States began about 1825 and was prompted in the first instance by the intolerance shown towards the Quakers of Stavanger[5]; but an exodus upon any consider-able scale did not begin until 1837, reaching a peak in 1847. It was stimulated by a combination of pietist opposition to the rationalized theology of the Lutheran church and of the political and economic discontent of the *bønder*, reinforced after 1845 by the dislike of compulsory military service. By 1915, the number of emigrants had reached a total equal to

[1]W. F. Adams, *Ireland and Irish Emigration to the New World from 1815 to the Famine* (New Haven, Conn., 1932), pp. 69–70.
[2]*Ibid.*, p. 335.   [3]*Ibid.*, p. 352.   [4]*Ibid.*, pp. 351–2.
[5]T. C. Blegen, *Norwegian Migration to America* (Northfield, Minn., 1931), pp. 30–50.

four-fifths of the population of Norway in 1801, a proportion only exceeded by Ireland.[1] The first settlement was made in up-state New York. In the thirties and forties the Norwegians went in the main to Illinois, Missouri and Wisconsin, but also made the first beginnings of Norwegian settlements in Iowa and Texas.[2] The heaviest Swedish emigration belongs to a later period, but Swedish emigration to Wisconsin began in 1841, and extended in that decade and the next to other states in the Old Northwest and the Middle Border, particularly into Minnesota, as well as into Pennsylvania, New York, and Texas, before it was checked by an economic revival in Sweden in 1855 and the depression of 1857 in the United States.[3] Like the Irish immigration, it began by being middle class but became predominantly an emigration of a redundant agricultural proletariat. But unlike the Irish emigration it remained essentially a movement in search of land. The emigration from Germany was at once the largest, numerically, of the continental emigrations, the most persistently diverse in social origin and in geographical destination, and the most complex in its political influence. Already before the Revolution the German states had made one of the two most important contributions of alien influence to the social structure of the colonies, the other being the North Irish. In the nineteenth century the movement started afresh under the impulse of the political discontents of 1817 to 1835 and 1848 to 1854, and of the economic distresses of the peasantry. It began, on a large scale, as an emigration from the upper Rhineland, and, because that was its source, travelled at first back along the road taken by the imports of cotton that went to the mills of Alsace, crossing France to Rouen and Havre, and entering the United States by way of New Orleans.[4] In consequence there grew up German settlements in Texas and Missouri, and the city of St. Louis became a centre of German influence. But these Germans did not come to work in factories, nor were they tolerant of

[1] *Ibid.*, pp. 19–20, 22.   [2] *Ibid.*, pp. 53–6, 61–4, 129–30, 151–3, 177–89.
[3] F. E. Janson, *The Background of Swedish Immigration, 1840–1930* (Chicago, Ill., 1931).
[4] M. L. Hansen, *The Atlantic Migration, 1607–1860* (Cambridge, Mass., 1941).

slavery; and, like the Scandinavians, they settled mainly in the Old Northwest and the Middle Border. And they included at all times, and particularly after 1848, a number of highly educated men, the so-called Latin farmers, who took at once an active part in American politics.

The effect of these events, crowded as a decisive proportion of them were into little more than the second quarter of the century, was to put an entirely new complexion upon the growth of the West, though so radical a change effected in so brief a time was not easily or at once apprehended. The prospect that the settlement of the interior was to be a reinforcement of the up-country South vanished, and a quite new prospect opened. The settlement of the Mississippi valley now followed a new route, was pursued by a different kind of settler, and was to have quite different social and economic consequences. It is true that the older strain in the migratory stock did not at once shake off familiar habits of mind. It is the case that the few notices that we have of Irish emigration to the West before 1817 are all of settlements in Kentucky;[1] that Germans like the pietist Rapp and his followers went to southern Kentucky in 1815; and that Englishmen like Flower and Birkbeck and the Owens, between 1818 and 1824, still sought the Ohio valley. But the great bulk of the immigration in the generation between 1820 and 1850 took another course. Many of the Irish arrived by way of Canada; the normal route for the New Englanders was from their own back counties through up-state New York; and emigrants from up-state New York itself could hardly do anything but approach the Ohio states from the north downwards. The Scandinavians came almost entirely to northern ports, and travelled west by the Erie canal and the Lakes; the Welsh and Scots appear very largely to have done the same; and if the earlier nineteenth-century German immigration often entered the States by way of New Orleans, it did not stay in the lower Mississippi valley, or even move up the Ohio, but went further north. The effect was

---

[1]W. F. Adams, *Ireland and Irish Emigration to the New World from 1815 to the Famine* (New Haven, Conn., 1932), p. 108.

that settlement no longer spread from the southern and western
faces of the Old Northwest, up-stream along the rivers flowing
into the Ohio, but through the upper counties of Ohio, Indiana,
and Illinois from the Lake front downwards,[1] and intoMichigan
and Wisconsin. The watershed between the Great Lakes and
the Ohio is low; and the traffic along the canals and river
improvements of the Old Northwest designed to serve the
Ohio system could easily be made to flow the other way.[2]
Chicago and St. Louis took the place of Pittsburgh and Cincinnati as the great collecting and distributing centres. Moreover, though still keeping to the river valleys and the woodlands, and not, until the coming of the railroads after 1850,
moving out into the prairies of Illinois, into northwestern Wisconsin, or into the trans-Mississippi area of the Middle Border,
the settlers were now no self-sufficient backwoodsmen. Often
travelling in organized companies and establishing town
settlements, the migration was a migration of farmers looking
to a market for the disposal of their surplus agricultural production and expecting to buy their capital and consumer goods
from the East. Everywhere, unless it were in the small clearing
of some traditional backwoodsman come up from the Ohio
valley, location was determined by accessibility. Want of a
means of transport nullified the virtues of good soil. The
strange phenomenon of the forties and fifties, when men and
women crossed hundreds of weary miles of what in time were
to become bonanza farms, in order to reach the Far West, is
explained by the uselessness of that land without navigable
rivers until the railroads crossed it.[3] And the revolution in the
settlement of the Mississippi valley was completed when, be-

[1] E. J. Benton, *The Wabash Trade Route* (Baltimore, Md., 1903), pp. 97–8, 106–7;
F. Merk, *Economic History of Wisconsin* (Madison, Wisc., 1916), p. 273; W. F.
Adams, *Ireland and Irish Emigration to the New World from 1815 to the Famine* (New
Haven, Conn., 1932), pp. 87–102.
[2] H. C. Hubbart, *The Older Middle West, 1840–1880* (New York, 1936), pp. 73–4;
A. C. Cole, *The Era of the Civil War, 1848–1870* (Chicago, 1922), pp. 5, 29–30, 33,
52; E. J. Benton, *op. cit.*, pp. 42, 105–6; J. W. Putnam, *The Illinois and Michigan
Canal* (Chicago, Ill., 1918), pp. 102–4; C. H. Ambler, *History of Transportation in
the Ohio Valley* (Glendale, Calif., 1932), p. 143; F. Merk, *op. cit.*, pp. 224–5, 288,
357–8.
[3] F. Merk, *Economic History of Wisconsin* (Madison, Wisc., 1916), ch. x.

tween 1835 and 1860, the navigable waters and the port of New Orleans gave place, as the transportation system of the Old Northwest, to railroads leading from the interior of Wisconsin, Michigan, Iowa and Illinois to the Lake cities, delivering freight to be forwarded by the eastern trunk lines or by Lake traffic to Montreal or Buffalo and by the Erie Canal to New York.

Here, then, was something very different from what any but the most perspicacious[1] in the Northeast had foreseen, and something much more grateful. It contained the germs of an economic and political alliance between North and West upon the basis of a diversion of the energies of the North Atlantic states from arduous agriculture and no longer opulent commerce to industry and finance, and the creation of a transportation and monetary system capable of effecting the exchange of eastern manufactures for the agricultural surplus of the West. It resulted in the building of an industrial and financial structure designed to serve a protected and ever-expanding domestic market, and the organization of American agriculture for the production of an exportable surplus of staple crops; and by virtue of the heavy drafts upon Europe for population, shipping, and capital, the production of such a surplus could be carried far beyond the consumptive capacity of the American market without the necessity of depriving American industry of its protection by high rates of duty upon imports. But to recognize all this required the most irksome intellectual and political adjustments and the most radical changes in business habits; and they were made reluctantly. By nothing is this better illustrated than by the history of United States public land policy; and a knowledge of that history, determining as it did the manner in which title to land was obtained, is indispensable to a firm understanding of the social and political affairs of the Western states.

The determination of United States public land policy involved the solution of technical problems of great complexity. Its history is the history of what at various periods that policy

[1] *Cf.* E. S. Brown, *Constitutional History of the Louisiana Purchase* (Berkeley, Calif., 1920), pp. 145–6.

had as its aim and of how effectively that aim was achieved. The political task was to decide when, to what classes of persons, and upon what terms title in the public lands should pass; the technical task, to see that plots were accurately delimited and a sound title to them conveyed to those to whom public policy pointed as the desirable owners.

Two clearly distinguished methods of acquiring title to public lands had grown up during the colonial period. In the South, the method was that of indiscriminate location. By this method, sale was made to the purchaser, not of a particular plot, but of a warrant for a stated acreage. This warrant the purchaser himself proceeded to locate at his own discretion upon the unsold public lands. What he chose was then surveyed by the public surveyor or his deputy, a certificate issued, and, after public notice and failing a counter-claim within the prescribed period, a formal grant made by the issue of a patent. A patent issued to Adam Hoops in 1765 is an example of what resulted, the grant in this case being made by the Proprietaries of the Province of Pennsylvania. It runs, in part, as follows:

> Whereas . . . a warrant was issued . . . requiring the Surveyor General to accept into his office the . . . survey made . . . for the said Adam Hoops and make return thereof into our Secretary's office in order to confirmation to him, the said Adam Hoops, on his paying to our use the purchase money . . . , and whereas . . . the Surveyor General hath made return of the said resurvey[1] of the said Land, which is therein described as follows (that is to say), Beginning at a Post, standing by Letort Spring, thence by the Hon'ble Proprietaries Surveyed Lands south seventy-five Degrees and a half East one hundred and fifty-four perches to a marked Black Oak, North forty Degrees East fifty perches to a post, South seventy-three degrees East twenty-one perches to a marked Black Oak, North forty-nine degrees East one hundred and twenty-nine perches to a marked Black Oak, and South one degree East one hundred and ninety perches to a post, thence by Wm. Graham's Land South Eighty-Six degrees West three hundred and forty-one perches to a Post, standing by Letort Spring aforesaid, Thence down the same, on the several Courses thereof, one hundred and fifty-six perches to the place of Begin-

---

[1] Adam Hoops having had the lands twice surveyed.

ning, containing Two hundred and thirty-two acres and one hundred and eleven perches of Land and allowance of six Acres P'r cent. for Road, &ca. . . . We . . . Do . . . grant . . . unto the said Adam Hoops . . . the said . . . Land.[1]

It is obvious not only that this procedure would easily lead to overlapping claims and conflicting titles, but also that it was an extravagant way of disposing of a public asset. No system would prevent the choicer lands from going first. But indiscriminate location gave the greatest possible opportunity to the settler to select only the best, and reduced to a minimum the marketability of what was left in the interstices between one patent and another. In New England the procedure was more orderly. There, preliminary survey and lay out into compact tiers of territory divided into townships sub-divided into tracts preceded the sale of townships as units and by auction. The land could still be culled over. But the purchaser could have no doubt about the location of what he had bought; if he got his stakes wrong, he could easily be put right[2]; and what was left over was, if ever it became eligible, a plot of regular dimensions and marketable shape.

The lands of the Mississippi were, for much the greater part, federal lands, since, with it is true substantial reservations, the states had ceded their western lands to the federal government in 1784 and areas subsequently added to American territory were acquired directly by the federal authority from foreign powers. From 1785 to 1820 these lands were disposed of in accordance with a policy inherited from the colonial period. Its object was orderly settlement and the collection of revenue from land sales. To that end there was adopted in the Northwest Land Ordinance of 1785 and the Land Act of 1796 the New England method of prior survey. The extinction of Indian title and the systematic division into townships of six miles square subdivided into lots of one mile square was to precede actual settlement, and the townships were to be offered

[1]*Pennsylvania Archives*. Third Series, vol. ix (Harrisburg, Pa., 1896), pp. 531–3.
[2]*Cf.*, *e.g.*, J. Schafer, *Wisconsin Domesday Book. Town Studies*, vol. i (Madison, Wisc., 1924), p. 88c.

for sale, alternately by whole townships or in lots, at $1.00 an acre, raised in 1796 to $2.00. But neat plans are easier made than executed; exceptions had already been created by history; and on occasion principle was sacrificed to expediency.[1] The state cessions were encumbered with guarantees of the confirmation of previous sales and grants and of the titles of the French inhabitants of the Illinois country. Virginia reserved the grants made to George Rogers Clark and title to lands promised to Virginian troops if her own lands could not satisfy them; Connecticut retained a western reserve out of which to reimburse the sufferers from raids during the Revolutionary war; Congress itself set aside reserves to satisfy the holders of military bounty warrants; large sales were made to private companies on modified terms, which resulted in the withdrawal of land from public auction and the substitution, over large areas, of corporate for public ownership. There were, moreover, still lands on sale within the boundaries of the original states, in western New York, western Pennsylvania, Virginia, Georgia, and other areas. In consequence, much settlement on the frontier that took place before 1810 was settlement on lands outside the federal land system or on federal lands exploited by speculative land companies; and much of the rest of it was mere irregular squatting on federal lands by persons without legal title, reinforced by innocent purchasers of plots marketed by the bankrupt Scioto Company before its own title had been completed or by Symmes beyond the limits of his patent.[2] The westward moving population that was not thus satisfied went to lands in Kentucky and Tennessee that had never been included in the public land system, to lands in Tennessee included in that system but taken up under the laws of North Carolina, or to lands claimed under foreign titles. The attempt to promote orderly settlement by sales in large tracts at a relatively high minimum price was thus unsuccessful; and there emerged in the earliest years what were to prove

[1] See map 4.
[2] P. J. Treat, *The National Land System, 1785–1820* (New York, 1910), pp. 58–9, 60–3, 107, 373–8; for map, see B. H. Hibbard, *A History of the Public Land Policies* (New York, 1924), p. 53.

to be the most stubborn and intractable problems connected with the disposal of the public domain.

The first of these problems was the selection of that unit and those terms of sale that would be the most effective, and this in fact raised the whole question of what the aim of public land policy was to be. The second was to ensure to a settler upon unsurveyed land, or upon surveyed land not yet proclaimed for sale, an opportunity to buy in due course at the minimum price and obtain security against the loss of his improvements to an out-bidder at auction. The third was to deal with the elusive but pervasive land speculator. An ever-present feature of the frontier, and of every kidney, he ranged from the actual farmer who sold land improved by his own labour; through the settler who deliberately entered more than he intended to cultivate, reckoning to cover by the re-sale of what he did not need the initial cost of what he kept; to the man who never intended any cultivation at all and sought a wholly unearned increment: and in all shapes except the first he aroused bitter resentment. Yet avoided though he perhaps usually was by the native settler,[1] he had nevertheless, when not merely a professional shark, a function to perform as an agent to the foreign immigrant; and he could in his own eyes appear a wholly innocent investor and as such found himself in company of the utmost respectability. But it was not for his advantage that public policy was ostensibly devised; and when that policy seemed to favour him unduly, a remedy was called for. To these problems the answer was sought successively in systems of credit, pre-emption, graduation, and finally free grant. But it took a couple of generations to move from the first to the last; and it cost a revolution in individual mental habits and sectional outlook.

The credit system, begun in 1800 and terminated in 1820, was a compromise that was the source of much embarrassment. A system of deferred payments for public lands incorporated in the act of 1800, it was compounded of an assumption that

---

[1] *Cf., e.g.*, J. Schafer, *Wisconsin Domesday Book. Town Studies*, vol. i (Madison, Wisc., 1924), p. 11a–b.

the public domain must be made a source of revenue, a desire upon the part of the East to prevent a fall in eastern land values or a rise in eastern wages, and a need to do something to meet the discontents of the West. But, designed as a means of promoting sales to actual settlers without a reduction of price, it in fact stimulated speculative entries by these settlers of lands in excess of those they intended to retain, and led to much loose finance, to much distress among debtors, and to constant pressure for the adoption of measures for their relief; while it failed to divert those bent upon the choicer lands from entering areas not yet proclaimed for sale or where no survey at all had yet been made or, indeed, even the Indian title extinguished, and yet left their holdings invalid and their future unprovided for. When, therefore, the great migration by the Erie canal and the Lakes began, neither the squatter nor the speculator had been successfully dealt with; and indeed the high cost of public lands actually encouraged them both. This cost was set by the minimum acreage offered at public auction and the price per acre. The area had been gradually reduced from the section of 640 acres of 1785 to the half-quarter section of 80 acres of 1820; and the price per acre had come down from the $2.00 of 1796 to $1.25 in 1820. But these figures were still too high for the humbler settler, who was likely to have exhausted his resources in meeting the cost of transportation, of his cabin and his stock, and of his first year's supplies and his first crude improvements. There grew up, therefore, in the West, a demand for cheaper lands or for virtually free lands, and for protection for the squatter; and this, in its turn, brought into issue the whole policy of western settlement. In retrospect, the picture presented is that of a public mind bringing itself reluctantly to the acceptance of a new political fact. The situation was confused and offered ample scope for manoeuvre; and it took a generation to force the party leaders to face its realities.

The North Atlantic states, anxious to keep up the price of western lands, yet apprehensive lest the accumulated proceeds of public land sales should jeopardize the maintenance of the protective tariff that by many was only tolerated as a necessary

means of raising federal revenue, sought either to limit sales
for a time to lands already in the market, or, if that were impracticable, then at one and the same time to block a reduction
in price and preserve the tariff by distributing the proceeds of
sales among the states in proportion to their population, with
the incidental advantage of ensuring the larger share of those
proceeds to the older and more populous areas. In opposition
to this stood the South Atlantic states, ill served by a protective
tariff and still looking to a political alliance with the Old Northwest; and they found their opportunity in the events of 1828,
when there was enacted a steep increase of tariff rates and
when there was defeated a graduation bill, first introduced in
1824 by Benton, the leading representative of the West, which
provided for the reduction step by step of the price of public
lands that had failed, after a specified number of years had
passed, to find a purchaser. But the political coöperation that
ensued between South and West in opposition to distribution
belonged to the past and had within it the seeds of dissolution.
Some relief to actual settlers was afforded by acts of limited
application granting rights of pre-emption.[1] But in the debates
of 1832 the West voted for the tariff and the South opposed a
reduction in the price of lands and the grant of rights of pre-
emption; in 1833, the South showed a readiness to accept distribution itself as the price of a compromise upon the tariff;
and in 1836-7 the measure was supported upon its merits by
Calhoun, anxious as he was to find means of financing the construction of a railroad to link the South with the West and
ready to adopt this way provided the necessary constitutional
amendment were carried. While the cordiality of the co-
operation between South and West cooled, moreover, the co-
operation of North and West began. Neither political party
in the North could any longer afford to neglect the growing
political power of the West. Van Buren, finding support in the
West for his monetary policy and urged on by pressure from
eastern labour for the adoption of a more liberal land policy,

[1] B. H. Hibbard, *A History of the Public Land Policies* (New York, 1924), pp. 151-8;
R. M. Robbins, *Our Landed Heritage* (Princeton, 1942), p. 50.

declared himself in his Annual Message of 5 December, 1837, in favour of the early settlement of the public domain, graduation, sale in limited quantities and to those only who would themselves develop the land, and the grant of the right of pre-emption. In the election of 1840, the Whig nomination of Harrison was a bid for Western support, though care was taken to make no precise promises on public land policy; and during the Whig administration of 1844–5, Clay became the reluctant author of the first far-reaching enactment into law of Western plans for the disposal of the public domain. The readjustment of the tariff was due in 1842, and a new factor had been introduced into the situation by a financial panic in 1837 that had brought to insolvency a number of the more heavily indebted states. A bill was accordingly introduced by Clay in 1841 providing for distribution, as a means at once of preserving high tariff rates, protecting the creditors of the states, and bringing relief to debtors, but including also the grant to settlers of the right to purchase before the date of public auction the land upon which they had squatted. Upon the motion of the Southern Whigs the bill was amended so as to provide for the suspension of distribution if a rate of duty should be imposed in excess of 20 per cent and in violation of the compromise of 1833; and the bill passed in that form. In 1842, customs revenue fell to an extent requiring such an increase above 20 per cent; the political situation in Washington after the death of Harrison and the succession of Tyler to the presidency precluded a repudiation of the bargain embodied in the Southern amendment; and it became necessary to sacrifice distribution to a moderate increase in the rates of duty. Thus from the manoeuvre of parties and of sections within parties the West profited. But the lines were yet far from being clearly drawn. The South still had hopes of the West: the West was not yet ardent in support of the tariff: the Northeast was no more willing than the South to concede the full demands of the settlers. The West, indeed, was still little more than a make-weight in the rivalries of the established parties of the Atlantic seaboard. It got what it could by exploiting its opportunities;

but it was off with the old love without being entirely on with the new.

The Pre-emption Act of 1841 did not satisfy the settlers. It applied only to surveyed land proclaimed for sale. Unless they were protected by the extra-legal activities of a Claim Association that intimidated outside bidders, it gave no more to the settler than the privilege, in order to prevent his claim from being sold over his head, of making payment before auction, at the minimum price; and that was a thing he often found it difficult to do. And it left open the possibility that extensive purchases of unsettled lands would still be made by speculators, to the detriment both of settlers embarrassed by the survival in their midst of undeveloped land held for a rise and of newcomers driven to go farther into the wilderness than would otherwise have been necessary. The West, therefore, continued to press for a reduction in the price of left-over lands. But it also reached at last the logical conclusion that had been inherent in the plans for credit, pre-emption, and graduation, and began to ask outright for donations to actual settlers. In so doing it was in fact proposing, not a reform in the mechanics of land settlement, but a radical alteration in the objects of public land policy. The public domain was to be treated, not as a source of revenue, but as a means of promoting settlement. The first notable proclamation of this policy had occurred in Andrew Jackson's message to Congress of 4 December, 1832. The first ventures looking towards its enactment into law were launched in Congress in the years 1844–6.[1] But they were not to be successful until after the outbreak of the Civil War. So radical a change of policy was not feasible in slack water. The tide must first run strongly. And the alliance of North and West was not complete when control of the federal government fell into the hands of the South in 1853; and, as it developed, its purpose was confused by the adoption of a policy of land grants in aid of railroad construction and by the too late enactment of graduation.

[1] G. M. Stephenson, *Political History of the Public Lands, 1840–1862* (Boston, 1917), pp. 114–17.

The first grant to railroads distinct from grants of rights of way, was made in 1833 in the shape of the authorization of the use by a railroad of lands granted to the Illinois and Michigan Canal; the first direct grant was that made in 1841 to the Mississippi & Alabama of a percentage of the net proceeds of sales of public lands; the first extensive direct grants of the lands themselves were those made to the Illinois Central, the Mobile & Chicago, and the Mobile & Ohio in 1850.[1] This use of the public domain to stimulate railroad construction was wished for by many western settlers in order to make markets more accessible to them and to produce a rise in the value of their holdings. The grants were also looked upon with favour by eastern capital. That they were so favoured showed finally and conclusively that eastern capital had come to understand what the West had to offer to it. But the grants also complicated the situation. They turned the western railroads, in the first instance, into land companies; and they put immense tracts of land upon the market; they afforded the settler a new opportunity to buy land outside the public land system; and they created a railroad interest opposed to the donation to settlers of homesteads upon the public domain now likely to undermine the value of railroad holdings. At the same time, the Graduation Act, so long the ambition of the West, when it came in 1854, seemed to many reformers a measure of doubtful merit. Providing for a reduction in the price of public lands proportioned to the number of years that had elapsed since they were first proclaimed for sale, it was carried in a period of Southern dominance because the policy found favour in the Southwest. There, the owners of large plantations practising a soil-exhausting economy were glad to buy at low prices the less productive land as their older lands wore out. But in the upper Mississippi valley the advantages of graduation had now come to look more doubtful. The settler who had bought good land at the full government price looked with some jealousy upon sales to newcomers at cheaper rates; cheap entry upon

[1] L. H. Haney, *The Congressional History of Railways to 1850* (Madison, Wisc., 1908), pp. 186, 194, 197-8.

poor land was not the boon to a poor man that free entry upon better land would be; and there was some risk that graduation would encourage late entry, postponed for a fall, or purely speculative purchases looking, not to the development of the land, but to the unearned increment to be reaped on re-sale. It was not until 1852 that a homestead bill passed the House of Representatives; and it was blocked by Southern influence in the Senate and the presidency from that date until 1860. It was a plank in the Republican platform of that year, and was made an issue by the Republicans in the campaign. It was only enacted into law in 1862, after the withdrawal of the Southern states. It provided that a head of a family or a person of twenty-one years or over, being a citizen or having filed a declaration of an intention to become one, should be entitled to 160 acres of unappropriated public domain on which he should have filed a pre-emption claim, or which at the time of application was subject to pre-emption, provided he should settle upon the land and cultivate it, in return for the payment of a $10.00 fee for a patent at the end of five years.

This history of transportation, of internal migration and foreign immigration, and of the way in which title to land was obtained, is a necessary foundation of any understanding of the course of events in the Mississippi valley; and in the course of events in the valley lies the explanation of the re-alignment of the sections in the nation at large. Upon this history alone can state history be soundly built; and only when state history has been duly studied will national history become fully comprehensible. People, land, and the manner of their conjunction are the core of Middle Western and Southwestern history; and the history of the Middle West and of the Southwest is in this period at the roots of the history of the United States.

The most securely based of the state histories is that of the state of Wisconsin; and this is due to the work of Joseph Schafer. A student at Wisconsin under Turner, Haskins, and Ely, Schafer returned to Madison in 1920 after twenty years at the

University of Oregon, to spend a further twenty years as
Superintendent of the State Historical Society of Wisconsin.
He at once launched a scheme for what he called a *Wisconsin
Domesday Book*.[1] He proposed to compile a record of the original
grantees of Wisconsin lands and of all subsequent changes in
ownership, supplemented by such information about the
individual owners as could be collected from the census,
county archives, town, school, and church records, the records
of fraternal societies, business houses, and factories, letters,
diaries, farm account books, and the local press. 'Early civilization in Wisconsin', he wrote, 'as in other western states, results
primarily from the interaction of two forces; an agricultural
population of several distinct origins and characters and a body
of land which was at first almost free but which varied widely
in natural fertility and in the ease with which it could be sub-
dued to the uses of the farmer. The social historian needs to
know in detail . . . the conditions under which the several
classes of land were occupied and the types of settlers who
occupied them. He needs to know both how the settlers dealt
with the land under varying circumstances and how the land
reacted upon the settlers economically and socially.'[2] Plat
books listing all land areas were available for most of Wisconsin for 1915 and for 1870, but nothing similar existed for
the pioneer period. Schafer proposed to prepare such an atlas
for 1860. The original surveyors' township plats showing the
natural features of the land and its subdivision down to one-
fourth of a quarter section, i.e., to areas of 40 acres, survived,
together with the surveyors' field notes containing descriptions
of the land. The Land Office tract books recorded the sale of
this land in forty-acre lots or multiples thereof. But there was
much speculation in western lands, and it did not follow that
the buyer from the Land Office, first opened in Wisconsin in
1834, was the pioneer settler. This deficiency in the record
Schafer proposed to make good by means of local enquiry

[1]*Wisconsin Mag. of History*, iv (1921), 61–74; *cf.* 'The microscopic method applied
to history', *Minnesota Hist. Bul.*, iv (1922), 3–20, and 'The Wisconsin Domesday
Book; a method of research for agricultural historians', *Agricultural History*, xiv
(1940), 23–32.   [2]*Ibid.*, 63.

through the schools and other agencies, while the original settlers or their immediate descendants were still alive. 'Ask', he wrote, 'an octogenarian who has resided continuously in section 6, township 7, range 1 W since 1853: "When did J. Allen Barber sell the southeast quarter of the southeast quarter of this section to L. Felton?" and the answer, while perhaps definite in form, would be of little or no value. Ask him if L. Felton (to whom that particular tract entered by Barber in 1853 was patented in 1877) was the first actual settler upon it who made a farm of it, and the answer if definite would be practically conclusive. The date of Felton's purchase from Barber can be ascertained from the record either locally or at the county seat. That would give the approximate date of his settlement there.'[1] Schafer failed, in the event, to secure the financial assistance necessary to execute so large a project, and the first volume of the survey,[2] appearing in 1924 and covering twenty-three of the 2,000 townships of Wisconsin, had no successor. Yet Schafer left a *History of Agriculture in Wisconsin* and three volumes of a regional history of the state[3] which, though the fruits of less exhaustive research than he had wished, lay the foundation for the history of Wisconsin more securely than they have been laid for any other Middle Western state.

The first settlements in Wisconsin, then under the government of Michigan Territory, occurred between 1819 and 1836 in the lead region in the southwest corner of the state. The settlers were predominently English-speaking, with a notable Cornish element, and were drawn much more largely from the south and southwest than those of the eastern counties were to be. The settlement of these was begun when the land office was opened in Wisconsin in 1834; and the first agricultural settlements were made in 1835. Land was then obtainable by direct entry upon government domain, at $1.25 the acre provided

---

[1]*Ibid.*, 67–8.
[2]J. Schafer, *Wisconsin Domesday Book. Town Studies*, vol. i (Madison, Wisc., 1924).
[3]*Four Wisconsin Counties* (1927), *The Wisconsin Lead Region* (1932), *The Winnebago-Horicon Basin* (1937).

there were no other bid; by the purchase of state and particularly school lands, on which credit was allowed; or by purchase from a previous holder who had himself bought from the
land office either intending to farm or only to hold for a rise.[1]
The more prosperous of the settlers chose land combining high
prairie with woodland and meadows, and within reach of a
market; and until the building of the railroad made deeper
penetration practicable, their settlements clung to the areas
within easy distance of water transport, whether by lake, river,
or canal. The poorer settlers were driven to the forested area,
since they could not afford to pay the speculator's price nor to
buy the timber to build upon the prairies; but they numbered
among them a few backwoodsmen from the Old Northwest
who settled in the woods for choice. The population of 1850
was more than one-third foreign born, the largest groups being
British and German, followed at some distance by the Norwegians. The bulk of the native born were from Vermont and
New York; and the New Yorkers were probably in large
measure New Englanders at one remove. Into the pine forests
of the northern part of the state, opened by the Indian cessions
of 1837 and 1848, went the lumber men, supplying the
market provided by the settlement of the prairie states and
made accessible by the possibility of floating lumber down
the Wisconsin, the Mississippi, or the Fox River canal;
the hardwood, since it could not be floated, having to await
the coming of the rail-road. Round the lumber camps
gathered such agricultural settlement as they afforded a
market to, exploiting later the alternative outlet afforded
by the railroads that were built in the first instance for the
transport of the lumber.

With this knowledge of the demographical foundation, the
political history of the state can be intelligently followed.
During the Territorial period from 1836 to 1848 the lead region
was predominant; but its supremacy was challenged by the
lake-shore counties which secured a lead in population in
1837, and by 1841 Whig east was clearly ranged against Demo-

---

[1] J. Schafer, *Four Wisconsin Counties* (Madison, Wisc., 1927), pp. 74–80.

cratic southwest. As late as the election of 1856, however, the southwest retained allies in the east among the poorer German and Irish settlers in the forest counties opposed to the more prosperous farmers of native, English, or Welsh stock; and it needed the influence of the Forty-eighters to rally the German vote to the support of the Republican party in 1860. The broad division in early Wisconsin politics, that is to say, was a division between the old and the new immigration into the Mississippi valley; and the outstanding feature in the political history of Wisconsin down to 1860 is the disappointment of the expectations of the old by the success of the new.

The case is the same in the states of the Old Northwest bordering upon the Ohio. The history of their settlement is earlier and of their public lands more complicated; and there has been no such detailed study of it as Schafer attempted in Wisconsin. But enough has been done, particularly in the study of the history of Illinois, to make the outlines clear. Except for the early French colonies upon the Mississippi, the first settlement of Illinois was that of the pioneers from Maryland, Virginia, and the Carolinas filtering into the woodlands of the southern counties. Since the sale of public lands did not start until 1814, they were, to begin with, unless purchasers from the French or their assigns, mere lawless squatters with no secure title to their improvements.[1] Among them was a sprinkling of foreign and northern settlers; but they remained predominant down to 1830. In the twenties there began to arrive from the east a new kind of settler in the northern counties. By the end of the decade this immigration had become a great influx from New England. Dependent, like the southern pioneers, upon water transport, the new settlers also kept within reach of it; and like the southerners they also were at first attracted to the timber lands, the prairies being popularly supposed to be evidence of poorer soil and their settlement

[1] A. C. Boggess, *The Settlement of Illinois, 1778–1830* (Chicago, 1908), p. 100; B. W. Bond, jr., *The Civilization of the Old Northwest* (New York, 1934), pp. 180–91, 294–302.

being in any case more expensive by reason of the difficulty of procuring water and the cost of hauling wood for buildings and fences. In the early years a willingness to go upon the prairies was shown by the English immigrants who were men of capital; but the prairie district of eastern Illinois was only sparsely settled before 1850, and its effective use awaited the coming of the railroad. The growth of community life among the settlers of the northern counties was much more rapid than in the south. In Ohio the history of land titles and of settlement was more complicated. In addition to mere squatting by the land companies in the Ohio and Miami Purchases which had subsequently to be regularized, there had been indiscriminate locations in the Virginia Military District and in Clark's Grant and unmethodical sales of surveyed lands by the Connecticut Land Company in the Western Reserve, as well as the orderly disposal of townships. Intermingled in the southern counties along the Ohio river with the backwoodsmen of Western Pennsylvania, Virginia and Kentucky, were immigrants from New England and New Jersey and a French settlement at Gallipolis. Lying both geographically and historically between Ohio and Illinois, Indiana partook of the character of each—the population of its southern counties more heterogeneous than in Illinois, its broad regional division less perplexed than Ohio's. In this area between the Great Lakes and the Ohio river, as in Wisconsin, the origin and distribution of settlement determined political history; and the first broad division to show itself was the division between the immigration moving up from the Ohio and that moving down from the Lakes. The situation is at its simplest in Illinois. There, the immigration of the thirties produced a cleavage between the northern counties and the southern part of the state that became known as Egypt. The retention of the support of the lower counties without the frustration of the ambitions of the upper became the most difficult task of the leaders of the Democratic party; and canals and railroads demanded by the one were so designed as not to alienate the other, but to be such, if might be, as would promote a reconciliation of divergent interests. But the two parts of the state were in disagreement about slavery; and as the sectional conflict grew in the nation at large, Whigs and Democrats in Egypt drew together, and during the Civil War opposition to the administration continued to be powerful there. In Indiana the picture was very similar.[1] In Ohio also southern influence was at first predominant, showing itself among other ways in the organization of local government upon a southern model. But political divisions began earlier and were not so clearly regional, arising in the first instance from a conflict between a New England federalist settlement on the Ohio at Marietta, controlling the territorial government, and back country Jeffersonian settlers demanding the erection of a state; and although the southern element dominated the constitutional convention of 1802 and retained control of the state until the middle of the century, and southern trade continued for long to be of great importance, slavery, though but by one vote, was excluded from the state from the outset and anti-slavery activities were always numerous though unpopular in the southern counties. The effect upon the history of Ohio of its indeterminate geographical character and the competition of the east-west with the south-north lines of communication was that no one section or city out-distanced the rest.

The settlement of the fifth of the states created out of the Old Northwest, the state of Michigan, was delayed by the failure to regularize land titles embarrassed by French and British grants, and by the forbidding aspects of its shores as they were seen from the Lakes. Almost the only white men in Michigan before 1805 were the French Canadians at Detroit and in the shore settlements; and there was very little American penetration before 1812 and at that date scarcely a farm cultivated by a white man more than ten miles from the border.[2] The first public land sales were held in 1818, and effective settlement did not begin until after the opening of the Erie Canal and the first great influx did not occur until the years 1829–32. Consequently

[1] L. Esarey, *A History of Indiana*, 2 vv. (Fort Wayne, Ind., 1924), i, 230–9, 243–4, 245n., 271–8, 310–15; ii, 963.
[2] G. H. Fuller, *Economic and Social Beginnings of Michigan . . . 1805–1837* (Lansing, Mich., 1916), p. 489.

although there was a division between the settlers advancing by way of Detroit and those entering the open country upon the borders of Ohio and Indiana who had a southern element among them, party lines were not so clearly determined by the distribution of the several immigrant stocks as elsewhere, but rather by differences in wealth within a homogeneous population and by those regional locations that the possession or the lack of capital dictated.

The settlement of the Middle Border, with the notable exception of Missouri, the only slave state of the Middle West, differed radically from that of the Old Northwest. It came later in time, not beginning effectively before the forties. As it moved away from the Mississippi it became dependent upon railroads. It developed its own rather different legal problems. It was effected by a more homogeneous population. And although there was a distinct regional distribution of foreign elements among the immigrants, this had less political significance than in the Old Northwest; and it was the nature of the country rather than the history of settlement that determined the social cleavages that subsequently occurred. Partly, perhaps, because of this, but partly also because the growth of its own historical activities has been more recent, the basic monographic studies of the settlement of the Middle Border have not yet been written. Valuable work has however been done upon the history of public land policy in both Iowa and Nebraska.

The settlement of the Middle Border occurred in the main after the passage of the pre-emption and graduation acts, and much of it after the passage of the homestead act. But settlement often ran ahead of survey; railroad land grants withdrew great areas from settlement under the laws regulating the disposal of the public domain; the Morrill act of 1862, providing for the endowment of the states with public lands for the support of colleges of agricultural and mechanical sciences, frequently resulted in the anticipation of the homesteader by the location of agricultural college scrip; and the pre-emption act, the homestead act itself, and the survey deposit system established by the legislation of 1862-79 that authorized the survey of townships at the expense of settlers ready to pay for the survey if their payments were treated as deposits in part discharge of the price of the land itself, one and all facilitated the acquisition of title, without settlement, by speculators or by cattle companies.

A clear and most precise account of the mechanics of land purchase in a particular area is contained in the study of *Iowa Public Land Disposal* by R. L. Lokken (*cf.* map 4). The settlers in Iowa met two difficulties. The machinery of public land disposal was not put in operation soon enough for them; and when it operated it was not entirely suited to their situation. They accordingly made laws of their own concerning the matter, which they observed themselves and secured the observance of by others. Except in the small Half-Breed Tract of 1824, Iowa was not entered until after the Black Hawk Purchase of 1832. But settlers went in freely from 1833 onwards; and settlement ran ahead of survey. When the first sales in the Iowa country occurred in 1838, there were already 23,242 persons on the ground. No attempt had been made to enforce the act of 1807 prohibiting settlement upon the unsurveyed domain, although that act had been specifically made applicable to the Black Hawk Purchase; but the pre-emption act was not yet upon the statute book, and the temporary act of 1834 granting exemption from that of 1807 had expired in 1836, too soon to be of use, for what it was worth to them, to the farmers of Iowa. These found themselves, therefore, in danger of being out-bid at the land sales and losing the homes that they had made. And neither the renewals of the suspending act in 1838 and 1840, nor the pre-emption act, when it came in 1841, much helped their case, for these applied only to surveyed land. To provide for the regulation of what was thus lawless occupation and to prevent dispossession by purchase at the land sales of a legal title by a newcomer, they formed themselves into Claim Associations that entered upon a plat what were agreed to be the just claims of their members, provided a court of appeal in matters of dispute, appointed persons to bid off the tracts at public sale, and saw to it that things were made uncomfortable for anyone who had the temerity to bid against them. And where, because settlement had run ahead of survey and there were no section lines to go by, areas roughly equivalent to the legal claim had been stepped-out with such accuracy as might be but failed properly to coincide with surveyor's plot when at last that was made, neighbour had to deal with neighbour and convey to him such fractions of land as fell beyond the lines. But even when the translation of moral right into legal title had been provided for, there were still practical difficulties to be overcome. The journey to the land office to make entry might be long, and was indeed, before the removal of business from Cincinnati to Dubuque in 1838, one of some 1,200 to 1,300 miles. The raising of money to pay even the minimum price was often difficult, and was made more so if land sales were fixed at a time of year unsuitable to a farming community. And land offices, or the banks where the deposit of the receipts from sales was made, could be particular about what they would accept, refusing notes of small denomination or of any but specified banks, or accepting, even, only silver and gold. So that there readily grew up a class of agents who would buy in a claim and re-sell to the claimant on credit, agreeing to deed to him at a later date and at a price that paid them for their service.

In Nebraska, while the plats of the first surveyed townships were not delivered to the land offices until June, 1856, and the first land sales were proclaimed for 6 September, 1858, settlement had in fact begun immediately upon the extinction of Indian title in 1854. Such settlement was in Nebraska authorized by an act of 22 July, 1854, the settler being required, when the survey had been completed, to select those 160 acres the survey of which fell in most nearly with the land that he had located upon, rectifying any lack of correspondence by private deals with his neighbours. But this in Nebraska, as elsewhere, afforded no protection either to anyone, not resident at the date of the act, who was unable to meet the pre-emption payment before the day of sale or for acres beyond the 160, which might go at auction to an outside bidder; and it so happened that the first demands for payment came at a time of falling prices. In consequence, there was much indebtedness at high rates of interest; and, in spite of the defence of the settlers by Claims Clubs, large purchases were made at auction by the speculators. Nor was the homestead act, when it came, a full solution of these problems. It did not operate in railroad or in state lands, and its operation in the public domain could be forestalled by the location of college scrip. And in the area then coming into occupation the farmer met a new competitor in the stockman, and found pitted against him the resources of the corporation in the shape of a cattle company seeking, by the purchase of proved-up pre-emption claims and commuted homesteads, to acquire the waterfront on streams and lakes that secured the undisturbed use of the grazing on the hinterlands. The homestead act, framed with an eye to conditions prevailing in the area between the Alleghany mountains and the 98th meridian, was unsuited to conditions on the plains; and it had been carried at the moment when the work that it should have promoted was for the most part done.

The history of the lower Mississippi valley has been much less adequately studied than that of the Middle West (map 5). We know something about the colonial background. Although there are serious gaps in our knowledge of the history of Louisiana during the second generation of French rule between 1732 and 1769, the profuse documentation of the Spanish empire has made it possible to recover in astonishing detail the obscure annals of the Spanish frontier in Texas; and careful studies have been made of the foundation of the French colony in Louisiana and of the early history of French and Spanish rivalry in the Gulf. The history of Spanish policy in Florida is known in so far as it is part of the story of Anglo-Spanish conflict in the border areas;[1] and that of the lower Mississippi valley in the years of tension after 1783, which ended in the final extrusion of foreign powers, has been very fully examined and delineated with great clarity.

[1] *Cf. supra,* pp. 51–2, 69–70.

11

Our knowledge of the history of the area south of the Ohio river in the nineteenth century is very much more fragmentary. The history of the settlement of Kentucky and Tennessee has been embarrassed by a romantic tradition from which that of Kentucky has hardly yet been redeemed; and there has been no detailed study of the American settlement of Mississippi or Louisiana. We depend upon work relating to Tennessee, Alabama, and the Southwest. The history of the American southwest before 1830 is that of the Indian tribes, of the penetration of white traders into Indian territory, and of the settlement of Arkansas. Of the last, we have as yet only the first sketch. It is only in Tennessee and Alabama that the foundations have been firmly laid. There the picture is one of the reproduction of a society very closely resembling that of the Atlantic coast, with the river counties playing the part of the tidewater. The first settlements in Tennessee were those of backwoodsmen dependent upon and content with land communication with the east. They were followed by settlers who were cultivators of cotton and tobacco, who needed river transportation; who turned their faces, therefore, to the Mississippi and the Ohio; and who peopled the Cumberland valley with large plantations and a slave population. In consequence the line of political cleavage ran between the mountain settlements of East Tennessee and the wealthier counties of the western parts of the state, growing into a rivalry between an up-country agrarian party and a commercial interest careful of public credit and favourable to internal improvements. There are indications that the situation was somewhat similar in Arkansas, and that there also there was a division between the planters of the river valleys and the settlers of the back country. The picture is certainly similar in Alabama, although the physical structure of that state is more complicated. Before 1812, white settlement in the area that was to become Alabama was restricted to a settlement of traders upon the lower Tombigbee with its centre at St. Stephens, and one of planters from Georgia who took up lands in the triangle between the southern boundary of Tennessee and the Tennessee river opened to settlement in 1809. Immigration upon any considerable scale only began after 1815. It was then the immigration of two clearly differentiated groups. Into the upper valley of the Alabama river and into the northern triangle there moved tidewater planters, and small farmers, few of them of great wealth and most of them drawn from the piedmont rather than from the tidewater of the Atlantic states, but becoming in their new home planters using slave labour. Into the hill country between the Tennessee and the headwaters of the Alabama and the Black Warrior, and into the red hills of the southeast, there moved the backwoodsmen of Tennessee, Virginia, and North and South Carolina. The agricultural economy of the state was thus divided and sub-divided. Both classes of settlers early became growers of cotton. But whereas, on the plantation, cotton was the main interest, to the backwoodsman it was a cash crop of subsidiary importance in what was in intention a self-sufficient economy. At the same time, among the planters themselves there were radical differences in origin and practice. Both in the northern triangle and in the upper valley of the Alabama river, tidewater planters and farmers from the piedmont were intermingled; and there was often a conflict of interest between the owners of the large plantation and the small farmers dependent upon the middleman for the marketing of their cotton. To the radical divergence of interest between the hill counties and the river counties there is therefore added in Alabama a division within the cotton-planting group itself, and a regional rivalry between two river valleys. It is out of the permutations and combinations of these factors that the political history of Alabama is built.

Imperfect though our knowledge of the history of the settlement of the lower Mississippi valley still is, it is nevertheless sufficient to make clear that the character and influence of that settlement were radically different from those of the Middle West. The settlement, it is true, was no mere extension of the old South. It partook in some respects of the character of the West; and it developed divergencies of interest within itself. It affected profoundly the economy of the old South; and it opened a new and more sinister chapter in the history of slavery in the United States. But it suffered no decisive change in the source from which it was drawn and no diversion of its course.

BIBLIOGRAPHICAL NOTE

The history of the settlement of the Mississippi valley is fundamentally the history of migration, immigration, and public land policy. To its understanding, a study of the history of transportation is essential. Upon these foundations, but only when these foundations have been laid, it is possible to build an intelligible account of the political experience of the several states that were created in the Valley. Only when that has been done can national history be fully understood.

i. For population figures, see American Council of Learned Societies, *Report of the Committee on Linguistic and National Stocks in the Population of the United States* (reprinted from the *Annual Report of the American Historical Association for the Year 1931*. Govt. Printing Office: Washington, D.C., 1932); E. Young, Chief of the Bureau of Statistics, *Special Report on Immigration* (Govt. Printing Office: Washington, D.C., 1871); *Statistical Review of Immigration, 1820–1910*. Reports of the Immigration Commission. 61 Cong., 3 Sess., S. Doc. 756 (Govt. Printing Office: Washington, D.C., 1911); U.S. Bureau of Foreign and Domestic Commerce, *One Hundred Years of American Immigration*. Daily Consular and Trade Reports, no. 245 (Govt. Printing Office: Washington, D.C., 1919). For population maps, see Bureau of the Census, *A Century of Population Growth from the First Census of the United States to the Twelfth, 1790–1900* (Govt. Printing Office: Washington, D.C., 1909) and *Statistical Atlas of the United States*, Dept. of Commerce, Bureau of the Census (Govt. Printing Office: Washington, D.C., 1914). For general statistics, see *Historical Statistics of the United States, 1789–1945; a Supplement to the Statistical Abstract of the United States* (Department of Commerce: Washington, D.C., 1949).

ii. For the history of migration, immigration, and settlement, see:—F. Mood (ed.), *The Early Writings of Frederick Jackson Turner* (Univ. of Wisconsin Press: Madison, Wisc., 1938); F. J. Turner, *Rise of the New West, 1819–1829*, being vol. xiv of 'The American Nation' (Harper: New York, 1906); and *The Frontier in American History* (Holt: New York, 1920) in which the famous essay was reprinted; F. L. Paxson, *The History of the American Frontier, 1763–1893* (Macmillan: New York, 1924); D. E. Clark, *The West in*

American History (Thomas Y. Crowell: New York, 1937); R. A. Billington, *Westward Expansion; a History of the American Frontier* (Macmillan: New York, 1949).

A. B. Hulbert, *Soil: its Influence on the History of the United States* (Yale Univ. Press: New Haven, Conn., 1930); Lois K. Mathews, *The Expansion of New England, the Spread of New England Settlement and Institutions to the Mississippi River, 1620–1865* (Houghton, Mifflin: New York, 1909); Lois K. M. Rosenberry, *Migrations from Connecticut prior to 1800*. Tercentenary Pamphlet Series, xxviii (Connecticut Tercentenary Commission: New Haven, Conn., 1934); L. D. Stilwell, *Migration from Vermont, 1776–1860* (Vermont Historical Soc.: Montpelier, Vt., 1937).

J. R. Commons, *Races and Immigrants in America* (Macmillan: New York, 1907); G. M. Stephenson, *A History of American Immigration, 1820–1924* (Ginn: Boston, 1926); M. L. Hansen, *The Atlantic Migration, 1607–1860*, and *The Immigrant in American History* (Harvard Univ. Press: Cambridge, Mass., 1941, 1940); C. Wittke, *We Who Built America; the Saga of the Immigrant* (Prentice-Hall: New York, 1939); R. Ernst, *Immigrant Life in New York City, 1825–1863* (King's Crown Press: New York, 1949); O. Handlin, *Boston's Immigrants, 1790–1865* (Harvard Univ. Press: Cambridge, Mass., 1941); S. C. Johnson, *A History of Emigration from the United Kingdom to North America, 1763–1912* (Routledge, 1913); J. Van der Zee, *The British in Iowa* (State Hist. Soc. of Iowa: Iowa City, Ia., 1922); W. F. Adams, *Ireland and Irish Emigration to the New World from 1815 to the Famine* (Yale Univ. Press: New Haven, Conn., 1932); A. B. Faust, *The German Element in the United States*, 2 vv. (The Steuben Society of America: New York, 1909; revd. ed. 1927); J. L. Rosenberger, *The Pennsylvania Germans* (Univ. of Chicago Press: Chicago, 1923); W. A. Knittle, *Early Eighteenth Century Palatine Emigration* (Dorrance: Philadelphia, 1937); D. Cunz, *The Maryland Germans; a History* (Princeton Univ. Press; Princeton, N.J., 1948); J. A. Hawgood, *The Tragedy of German America* (Putnam's: New York, 1940); R. L. Biesele, *The History of the German Settlements in Texas, 1831–1861* (Press of Von Boeckmann-Jones: Austin, Tex., 1930); R. Sallet, *Russlanddeutsche Siedlungen in den Vereinigten Staaten von Amerika.* Reprinted from 'Jahrbuch der Deutsch-Amerikanischen historischen Gesellschaft von Illinois' (Chicago, 1931); Irmgard Erhorn, *Die deutsche Einwanderung der Dreissiger und Achtundvierziger in die Vereinigten Staaten und ihre Stellung zur nordamerikanischen Politik* (Hans Christian: Hamburg, 1937); H. Motteli, *Die schweizerische Auswanderung nach Nord-Amerika, mit besonderer Berücksichtigung der Kolonie Neu-Glarus und der Auswanderungs-Propaganda von Nat. Rat. Dr. Joos* (H.

Bayer u. Sohne: Langensalza, 1920); B. H. Wabeke, *Dutch Emigration to North America, 1624–1860* (Netherlands Information Bureau: New York, 1944); K. C. Babcock, *The Scandinavian Element in the United States*. Univ. of Illinois Studies in the Social Sciences, iii, no. 3 (Urbana, Ill., 1914); T. C. Blegen, *Norwegian Migration to America*, and *Norwegian Migration to America; the American Transition* (Norwegian-American Hist. Assoc.: Northfield, Minn., 1931, 1940); C. C. Qualey, *Norwegian Settlement in the United States* (Norwegian-American Hist. Assoc.: Northfield, Minn., 1938); J. S. Lindberg, *The Background of Swedish Emigration* (Univ. of Minnesota Press: Minneapolis, Minn., 1930); Florence E. Janson, *The Background of Swedish Immigration, 1840–1930* (Univ. of Chicago Press: Chicago, Ill., 1931); H. Nelson, *The Swedes and the Swedish Settlements in North America*, 2 vv. Skrifter Utgivna av Kungl. Humanistika Vetenskapssamfundet i Lund, xxxvii (G. W. K. Gleerup: Lund, 1943).

R. C. Downes, *Frontier Ohio, 1788–1803* (F. J. Heer Printing Co.: Columbus, O., 1935); J. S. Davis, *Essays in the Earlier History of American Corporations*, 2 vv. (Harvard Univ. Press: Cambridge, Mass., 1917); T. T. Belote, *The Scioto Speculation and the French Settlement at Gallipolis*. Univ. of Cincinnati Studies, ii, 3 (Cincinnati, O., 1907); A. C. Boggess, *Settlement of Illinois, 1778–1830*. Chicago Hist. Soc. Coll., v (Chicago, Ill., 1908); W. V. Pooley, *The Settlement of Illinois from 1830 to 1850*. Bulletin of the Univ. of Wisconsin, i, no. 4 (Madison, Wisc., 1908); P. W. Gates, *The Illinois Central Railroad and its Colonization Work* (Harvard Univ. Press: Cambridge, Mass., 1934); B. F. Lathrop, *Migration into East Texas, 1835–1860* (Texas State Hist. Assoc.: Austin, Tex., 1949).

iii. There are two general studies of the history of public land policy, B. H. Hibbard, *A History of the Public Land Policies* (Macmillan: New York, 1924) and R. M. Robbins, *Our Landed Heritage; the Public Domain, 1776–1936* (Princeton Univ. Press: Princeton, N.J., 1942). They supersede an early essay on the subject, S. Sato, *History of the Land Question*. Johns Hopkins Univ. Studies, iv, nos. 7–9 (Johns Hopkins Press: Baltimore, Md., 1886). The subject is treated in fuller detail in P. J. Treat, *The National Land System, 1785–1820* (E. B. Treat: New York, 1910); R. G. Wellington, *The Political and Sectional Influence of the Public Lands, 1828–1842* (Riverside Press: Cambridge, Mass., 1914); and G. M. Stephenson, *Political History of the Public Lands, 1840–1862* (Badger: Boston, 1917). There are a few special studies: Amelia C. Ford, *Colonial Precedents of our National Land System*. Bul. of the Univ. of Wisc., no. 352 (Madison, Wisc., 1910); M. Egleston, *The Land System of the New England Colonies*. Johns Hopkins Univ. Studies, iv, nos. 11–2 (Johns Hopkins Press:

Baltimore, Md., 1886); C. F. Emerick, *The Credit System and the Public Domain*. Pubs. of the Vanderbilt Southern Hist. Soc., no. 3 (Cumberland Presbyterian Publ. Ho.: Nashville, Tenn., 1899); R. T. Hill, *The Public Domain and Democracy*. Col. Univ. Studies, 100 (Columbia Univ. Press: New York, 1910); Helene S. Zahler, *Eastern Working Men and National Land Policy, 1829–1862* (Columbia Univ. Press: New York, 1941). But these all deal, in the main, with law and policy. What is needed also is the history of the system at work, and of that, as yet, we have only the scantiest accounts. It is a very difficult subject, requiring much local and technical knowledge for its successful study; and only a few monographs have been published. Following them from east to west, they are S. G. McLendon, *History of the Public Domain of Georgia* (The Harrison Company: Atlanta, Ga., 1924); C. E. Sherman, *Original Ohio Land Subdivisions*. Ohio Co-operative Topographic Survey. Final Rept. pt. iii (Columbus, O., 1925); W. E. Peters, *Ohio Lands and their History* (the author: Athens, O., 1930); R. L. Lokken, *Iowa Public Land Disposal* (State Hist. Soc. of Iowa: Iowa City, Ia., 1942); B. F. Shambaugh (ed.) *Constitution and Records of the Claim Association of Johnson County Iowa* (State Hist. Soc. of Iowa: Iowa City, Ia., 1894); J. Schafer, *Wisconsin Domesday Book. Town Studies*, vol. i (State Hist. Soc. of Wisconsin: Madison, Wisc., 1924); R. McKitrick, *The Public Land System of Texas, 1823–1910*, Bulletin of the Univ. of Wisconsin, no. 905 (Madison, Wisc., 1918); A. S. Lang, *Financial History of the Public Lands in Texas*. Baylor Bulletin, xxxv, no. 3 (Baylor Univ.: Waco, Tex., 1932); H. O. Brayer, *William Blackmore*, vol. i, *The Spanish-Mexican Land Grants of New Mexico and Colorado, 1863–1878* (Bradford-Robinson: Denver, Colo., 1949); C. H. Shinn, *Land Laws of Mining Districts*. Johns Hopkins Univ. Studies, ii, no. 12 (Johns Hopkins Press: Baltimore, Md., 1884); W. W. Robinson, *Land in California; the Story of Mission Lands, Ranchos, Squatters, Mining Claims, Railroad Grants, Land Scrip, Homesteads* (Univ. of California Press: Berkeley, Calif., 1948).

iv. One of the curiosities of American historiography is that so little expert attention has been given to the history of transportation. Transportation has obviously been a matter of the first importance in the settlement and the development of the continent; yet it is possible to count upon the fingers of one's hands the books of first-rate quality devoted to the subject. B. H. Meyer, *History of Transportation in the United States before 1860* (Carnegie Institution of Washington: Washington, D.C., 1917) is an early digest, compiled before much monographic work had been done. There are illuminating chapters in Ellen C. Semple: *American History and its Geographic*

Conditions (Houghton, Mifflin: Boston, 1903; revd. ed., 1933); the study of the subject state by state has been begun in W. J. Wilgus, *The Role of Transportation in the Development of Vermont* (Vermont Hist. Soc.: Montpelier, Vt., 1945); and W. J. Lane, *From Indian Trail to Iron Horse; Travel and Transportation in New Jersey* (Princeton Univ. Press: Princeton, N.J., 1939). U. B. Phillips, *A History of Transportation in the Eastern Cotton Belt* (Columbia Univ. Press: New York, 1908) is a valuable more general work; and E. C. Kirkland, *Men, Cities and Transportation; a Study in New England History, 1820-1900*, 2 vv. (Harvard Univ. Press: Cambridge, Mass., 1948) is a model of the way in which the subject can be treated. But add perhaps half a dozen first-rate works upon the history of particular railroads, and the rest is, at best, undistinguished and at the worst unscientific and incompetent.

On the history of roads, see A. B. Hulbert, *Historic Highways*, 16 vv. (Arthur H. Clark: Cleveland, O., 1902-5), which though learned is the work of an antiquary and topographer rather than an historian; F. J. Wood, *The Turnpikes of New England* (Marshall Jones: Boston, 1919); Mary Verhoeff, *The Kentucky Mountains; Transportation and Commerce, 1750 to 1911*. Filson Club Publication no. 26 (John P. Morton: Louisville, Ky., 1911); W. C. Plummer, *The Road Policy of Pennsylvania* (Univ. of Pennsylvania Press: Philadelphia, 1925); J. A. Durrenberger, *Turnpikes; a Study of the Toll Road Movement in the Middle Atlantic States and Maryland* (Southern Stationery & Printing Co.: Valdosta, Ga., 1931); and J. S. Young, *A Political and Constitutional Study of the Cumberland Road* (Chicago Univ. Press: Chicago, Ill., 1904).

On the history of canal and river transport, more work has been done. T. C. Purdy, 'Report on the Canals of the United States', in 'Report on the Agencies of Transportation in the United States'. Department of the Interior. Census Office. [*Tenth Census*. Final Vol. iv] (Govt. Printing Office: Washington, D.C., 1883); and, moving from south to north and from east to west, W. F. Dunaway, *History of the James River and Kanawha Company*. Col. Univ. Studies, 236 (Columbia Univ. Press: New York, 1922); Corra Bacon-Foster, *Early Chapters in the Development of the Potomac Route to the West*. Records of the Columbia Historical Society, xv (Columbia Hist. Soc.: Washington, D.C., 1912); G. W. Ward, *The Early Development of the Chesapeake and Ohio Canal Project*. Johns Hopkins Univ. Studies, xvii, nos. 9-11 (Johns Hopkins Press: Baltimore, Md., 1899); W. S. Sanderlin, *The Great National Project; a History of the Chesapeake and Ohio Canal*. Johns Hopkins Univ. Studies, lxiv, no. 1 (Johns Hopkins Press: Baltimore, Md., 1946); T. B. Klein, *The Canals of Pennsylvania and the System of Internal Improvements of the Commonwealth*. Excerpt from Part iv, 'Report of the Secretary of Internal Affairs of Penn-sylvania' (State Printer: Harrisburg, Pa., 1900); A. L. Bishop, *The State Works of Pennsylvania.* Connecticut Academy of Arts and Sciences, xiii, pp. 149–298 (Yale Univ. Press: New Haven, Conn., 1907); J. W. Livingood, *The Philadelphia-Baltimore Trade Rivalry, 1780–1860* (Pennsylvania Historical and Museum Commission: Harrisburg, Pa., 1947); C. L. Jones, *Economic History of the Anthracite-Tidewater Canals* (published for the University: Philadelphia, 1908); C. S. Bowyer, *Waterways of New Jersey; History of Riparian Ownership and Control over the Navigable Waters of New Jersey* (Chew & Sons: Camden, N.J., 1915); E. H. Mott, *Between the Ocean and the Lakes; the Story of Erie* (J. S. Collins: New York, 1899); H. W. Hill, *An His-torical Review of Waterways and Canal Construction in New York State.* Buffalo Hist. Soc. Publications, xii (Buffalo, N.Y., 1908); N. E. Whitford, *History of the Canal System of the State of New York*, 2 vv. Supplement to the Annual Report of the State Engineer and Sur-veyor of the State of New York, 1905 (State Printer: Albany, N.Y., 1906); F. H. Severance (ed.), *Canal Enlargement in New York State. Papers on the Barge Canal Campaign and related Topics*, and *The Holland Land Co. and Canal Construction in Western New York.* Buffalo Hist. Soc. Publications, xiii, xiv (Buffalo, N.Y., 1909, 1910).

C. H. Ambler, *History of Transportation in the Ohio Valley* (Arthur H. Clark: Glendale, Calif., 1932); A. B. Hulbert, *The Ohio River; a Course of Empire* (Putnam's: New York, 1906); Mary Verhoeff, *The Kentucky River Navigation.* Filson Club Publication no. 28 (John P. Morton: Louisville, Ky., 1917); W. F. Gephart, *Transportation and Industrial Development in the Middle West.* Col. Univ. Studies, 89 (Columbia Univ. Press: New York, 1909); C. C. Huntington & C. P. McClelland, *History of the Ohio Canals* (Ohio State Arch. & Hist. Soc.: Columbus, O., 1905); E. L. Bogart, *Internal Improvements and State Debt in Ohio* (Longmans: New York, 1924); E. J. Benton, *The Wabash Trade Route.* Johns Hopkins Univ. Studies, xxi, nos. 1–2 (Johns Hopkins Press: Baltimore, Md., 1903); J. W. Putnam, *The Illinois and Michigan Canal.* Chicago Hist. Soc. Coll., x (Univ. of Chicago Press: Chicago, Ill., 1918); R. G. Plumb, *History of the Naviga-tion of the Great Lakes.* [House] Committee on Railways and Canals (Govt. Printing Office: Washington, D.C., 1911); J. C. Mills, *Our Inland Seas, their Shipping and Commerce for Three Centuries* (McClurg: Chicago 1910); F. H. Dixon, *Traffic History of the Mississippi River System.* National Waterways Commission, doc. no. 11 (Govt. Print-ing Office: Washington, D.C., 1909); G. W. Stephens, *Some Aspects of Intersectional Rivalry for the Commerce of the Upper Mississippi Valley.* Washington Univ. Studies. Humanistic Ser., x, no. 2 (St. Louis, Mo., 1923); W. W. Belcher, *The Economic Rivalry between St. Louis and*

Chicago, 1850–1880. Col. Univ. Studies, 529 (Columbia Univ. Press: New York, 1947); L. D. Baldwin, *The Keelboat Age on Western Waters* (Univ. of Pittsburgh Press: Pittsburgh, Pa., 1941); Mildred L. Hartsough, *From Canoe to Steel Barge on the Upper Mississippi* (Univ. of Minnesota Press: Minneapolis, Minn., 1934); L. C. Hunter, *Steamboats on the Western Rivers* (Harvard Univ. Press: Cambridge, Mass., 1949): W. J. Petersen, *Steamboating on the Upper Mississippi* (State Hist. Soc. of Iowa: Iowa City, Ia., 1937); G. B. Merrick, *Old Times on the Upper Mississippi; the Recollections of a Steamboat Pilot from 1854 to 1863* (Arthur H. Clark: Cleveland O., 1909).

The best introduction to the history of American railroads is W. M. Daniels, *American Railroads; Four Phases of their History* (Princeton Univ. Press: Princeton, N.J., 1932). E. R. Johnson, *American Railway Transportation* (Appleton: New York, 1903; 2nd ed. rvd., 1908) is a useful elementary survey of American railroad economics; but the prime authority is W. Z. Ripley, *Railroads, Rates and Regulation*, and *Railroads, Finance and Organization* (Longmans: New York, 1912, 1915). On this aspect of the subject see, also, F. A. Cleveland & F. W. Powell, *Railroad Promotion and Capitalization in the United States* (Longmans: New York, 1909); F. C. Hicks (ed.), *High Finance in the Sixties* (Yale Univ. Press: New Haven, Conn., 1929); J. B. Phillips, *Freight Rates and Manufactures in Colorado; a Chapter in Economic History.* Colorado Univ. Studies no. vii, no. 1 (Boulder, Colo., 1909); H. O. Brayer, *William Blackmore*, 2 vv., vol. ii, *Early Financing of the Denver and Rio Grande Railway and Ancillary Land Companies* (Bradford-Robinson: Denver, Colo., 1949); R. H. Maybee, *Railroad Competition and the Oil Trade* (Extension Press, State Teachers College: Mt. Pleasant, Mich., 1940); J. H. Gordon, *Illinois Railway Legislation and Commission Control since 1870.* University of Illinois Bulletin, i, no. 12 (University Press: Urbana, Ill., 1904); J. F. Doster, *Alabama's First Railroad Commission, 1881–1885* (the author: University, Ala., 1949); R. A. Lively, *The South in Action; a Sectional Crusade against Freight Rate Discrimination.* James Sprunt Studies, xxx (Univ. of N. Carolina Press: Chapel Hill, N.C., 1949). The first volume of I. L. Sharfman, *The Inter-State Commerce Commission*, 4 vv. in 5 (Commonwealth Fund: New York, 1931–7), a technical work of great erudition, is of much value to the student of railroad history. The political history of the railroads is dealt with in L. H. Haney, *A Congressional History of Railways to 1850* and *1850–1887.* Bulletin of the University of Wisconsin. Economics and Pol. Sci. Ser., iii, no. 2, and vi, no. 1 (Madison, Wisc., 1908, 1910); J. B. Sanborn, *Congressional Grants of Land in Aid of Railways.* Bulletin of the University of Wisconsin, no. 30 (Madison, Wisc., 1899); S. Daggett, *Railroad Reorganization* (Harvard Univ. Press: Cambridge, Mass.,

1908); E. G. Campbell, *The Reorganization of the American Railroad System, 1893–1900.* Col. Univ. Studies, 434 (Columbia Univ. Press: New York, 1938); F. H. Dixon, *Railroads and Government; their Relations in the United States, 1910–1921* (Scribner's: New York, 1922); D. P. Locklin, *Railroad Regulation since 1920* (McGraw Hill Book Co.: New York, 1928).

The separate histories of the several roads are, for the most part, undistinguished work. Few of them have been written by professional historians; and of those that have, Gates's notable study of the Illinois Central is a study rather of land disposal than of railroad construction and operation. Omitting the entirely insufficient, the student has to make what he can of a very mixed collection, though recent publications make it clear that scientific work upon the subject is getting under way. The books that must be included are:— G. P. Baker, *The Formation of the New England Railroad Systems; a Study of Railroad Combination in the Nineteenth Century* (Harvard Univ. Press: Cambridge, Mass., 1937); A. F. Harlow, *Steelways of New England* (Creative Age Press: New York, 1945); E. C. Kirkland, *Men, Cities and Transportation,* 2 vv. (Harvard University Press: Cambridge, Mass., 1948); E. E. Chase, *Maine Railroads; a History of the Development of the Maine Railroad System* (A. J. Houston: Portland, Me., 1926); F. B. C. Bradlee, *The Eastern Railroad; a Historical Account of Early Railroading in Eastern New England,* and *The Boston and Lowell Railroad, the Nashua and Lowell Railroad, and the Salem and Lowell Railroad* (The Essex Institute: Salem, Mass., 1922 (2nd ed.) and 1918); Thelma M. Kistler, *The Rise of Railroads in the Connecticut River Valley.* Smith College Studies in History, xxiii, nos. 1–4 (Northampton, Mass., 1938); W. A. Lucas, *From the Hills to the Hudson; a History of the Paterson and Hudson River Railroad, the Paterson and Ramapo, and the Union Railroads* (Pierce Business Book: New York, 1944); E. Hungerford, *Men and Iron. The History of the New York Central* (Thomas Y. Crowell: New York, 1938); F. W. Stevens, *The Beginnings of the New York Central Railroad; a History* (Putnam's: New York, 1926); E. Hungerford, *The Story of the Rome, Watertown and Ogdensburgh Railroad* (R. M. McBride: New York, 1922); *A Century of Progress, History of the Delaware and Hudson Company, 1823–1923* (J. B. Lyon & Co., printers: Albany, N.Y. Published by the Company, 1925); J. I. Bogen, *The Anthracite Railroads; a Study in American Railroad Enterprise* (The Ronald Press: New York, 1927); H. W. Schotter, *The Growth and Development of the Pennsylvania Railroad Company* (Allen, Lane & Scott: Philadelphia, 1927); M. W. Schlegel, *Ruler of the Reading; the Life of Franklin B. Gowen, 1836–1889* (Archives Publishing Co. of Pennsylvania: Harrisburg, Pa., 1947); E. Hungerford, *The Story of the Baltimore*

and Ohio Railroad, 1827–1927, 2 vv. (Putnam's: New York, 1928);
M. Reizenstein, *The Economic History of the Baltimore and Ohio Railroad.* Johns Hopkins Univ. Studies, xv, nos. 7–8 (Johns Hopkins Press: Baltimore, Md., 1897); J. P. Nelson, *Address; the Chesapeake and Ohio Railway* (Mitchell & Hotchkiss: Richmond, Va., 2nd ed. 1916); W. Way, jr., *The Clinchfield Railroad; the Story of a Trade Route across the Blue Ridge Mountains* (Univ. of N. Carolina Press: Chapel Hill, N.C., 1931); A. C. Brown, *The Old Bay Line* (Dietz Press: Richmond, Va., 1940); C. K. Brown, *A State Movement in Railroad Development; the Story of North Carolina's first Effort to establish an east and west Trunk Line Railroad* (Univ. of N. Carolina Press: Chapel Hill, N.C., 1928); S. M. Derrick, *Centennial History of South Carolina Railroad* (State Co.: Columbia, S.C., 1930); H. D. Dozier, *A History of the Atlantic Coast Line Railroad* (Houghton, Mifflin: Boston, 1920); C.R. Fish, *The Restoration of the Southern Railroads.* Univ. of Wisconsin Studies in the Social Sciences & History, no. 2 (Madison, Wisc., 1919).

F. F. Hargrave, *A Pioneer Indiana Railroad; the Origin and Development of the Monon* (Wm. B. Burford Printing Co.: Indianapolis, Ind., 1932); W. K. Ackerman, *Early Illinois Railroads.* Fergus Hist. Ser., no. 23 (Fergus Printing Co.: Chicago, Ill., 1884); H. G. Brownson, *The History of the Illinois Central Railroad to 1870.* Univ. of Illinois Studies in the Social Sciences, iv (Urbana, Ill., 1915); P. W. Gates, *The Illinois Central Railroad and its Colonization Work* (Harvard Univ. Press: Cambridge, Mass., 1934); T. D. Clark, *A Pioneer Southern Railroad from New Orleans to Cairo* (Univ. of N. Carolina Press: Chapel Hill, N.C., 1936); J. H. Hollander, *The Cincinnati Southern Railway.* Johns Hopkins Univ. Studies, xii, nos. 1–2 (Johns Hopkins Press: Baltimore, Md., 1894); E. M. Coulter, *The Cincinnati Southern Railroad and the Struggle for Southern Commerce, 1865–1872* (American Historical Society, Inc.: Chicago, Ill., 1922); J. L. Kerr, *The Story of a Southern Carrier; the Louisville & Nashville* (Young & Ottley: New York, 1933); P. W. Ivey, *The Père Marquette Railroad Company.* Michigan Hist. Pubs., Univ. Ser., v (Michigan Historical Commission: Lansing, Mich., 1919); [J. P. Kaysen], *The Railroads of Wisconsin, 1827–1937* (The Railway and Locomotive Hist. Soc., Inc.: Baker Library, Harvard Business School: Cambridge, Mass., 1937); J. W. Cary, *Organization and History of the Chicago, Milwaukee, and St. Paul Railway Company* (Cramer, Aikens & Cramer: Milwaukee, Wisc., 1892); R. C. Overton, *Burlington West; a Colonization History of the Burlington Railroad* (Harvard Univ. Press: Cambridge, Mass., 1941); J. Grodinsky, *The Iowa Pool; a Study in Railroad Competition, 1870–84* (Univ. of Chicago Press: Chicago, 1950); J. W. Million, *State Aid to Railways in Missouri.* Univ. of Chicago Economic Studies, no. 4 (Chicago, Ill., 1896).

G. L. Albright, *Official Explorations for Pacific Railroads, 1853–5.*
Univ. of California Pubs. in History, xi (Univ. of California Press:
Berkeley, Calif., 1921); R. E. Riegel, *The Story of the Western Railroads*
(Macmillan: New York, 1926); J. P. Davis, *The Union Pacific Railway*
(Griggs: Chicago, Ill., 1894); H. K. White, *History of the Union
Pacific Railway* (Univ. of Chicago: Chicago, Ill., 1895); N. Trottman,
History of the Union Pacific; a Financial and Economic Survey (Ronald
Press: New York, 1923); J. D. Galloway, *The First Transcontinental
Railroad; Central Pacific, Union Pacific* (Simmons-Boardman: New
York, 1950); G. L. Anderson, *General William J. Palmer; a Decade
of Colorado Railroad Building, 1870–1880* (Colorado College: Colorado
Springs, Colo., 1936); H. A. Hubbard, *A Chapter in Early Arizona Trans-
portation History; the Arizona Narrow Gauge Railroad Company.* Arizona
Univ. Social Science Bull., no. 6 (Univ. of Arizona: Tucson, Ariz.,
1934); C. S. Potts, *Railroad Transportation in Texas*, Univ. of Texas
Bull., no. 119 (Univ. of Texas, Austin, Tex., 1909); S. Daggett,
Chapters on the History of the Southern Pacific (Ronald Press: New York,
1922); G. Kennan, *E. H. Harriman; a Biography*, 2 vv. (Houghton,
Mifflin: Boston, 1922); E. V. Smalley, *History of the Northern Pacific
Railroad* (Putnam's: New York, 1883); J. B. Hedges, *Henry Villard
and the Railways of the North West* (Yale Univ. Press: New Haven,
Conn., 1930); J. G. Pyle, *The Life of James J. Hill*, 2 vv. (Doubleday,
Doran: Garden City, N.Y., 1917).

v. Building upon a knowledge of the course of settlement, the
writing of the history of the Middle West has made great progress.
The area so named includes the Old Northwest and the Middle
Border, namely, the states of Ohio, Indiana, Illinois, Michigan and
Wisconsin, and those of Minnesota, Iowa and Missouri, with the
eastern parts of North and South Dakota, Nebraska and Kansas.
Upon the history of this area we have now a substantial literature,
composed of scientific state histories, the work of single writers or
of coöperative effort, together with a number of competent mono-
graphs. Of these publications the most notable are, C. Wittke (ed.)
The History of the State of Ohio, 6 vv. (Ohio State Arch. & Hist. Soc.:
Columbus, O., 1941–4); R. E. Chaddock, *Ohio before 1850.* Col.
Univ. Studies, 82 (Columbia Univ. Press: New York, 1908); E. A.
Holt, *Party Politics in Ohio, 1840–1850.* Ohio Historical Collections,
i (Ohio State Arch. & Hist. Soc.: Columbus, O., 1931); L. Esarey,
A History of Indiana from its Exploration to 1850 (W. K. Stewart:
Indianapolis, Ind., 1915), and *A History of Indiana from 1850 to the
Present* (B. F. Bowen: Indianapolis, Ind., 1918), 3rd ed., *A History
of Indiana*, 2 vv. (Hoosier Press: Fort Wayne, Ind., 1924); C. W.
Alvord (ed.), *The Centennial History of Illinois*, 5 vv. + Introductory

Volume (Illinois Centennial Commission. McClurg: Chicago, Ill., 1915–22); M. M. Quaife, *Chicago and the Old Northwest, 1673–1735* (Univ. of Chicago Press: Chicago, 1913); G. N. Fuller, *Economic and Social Beginnings of Michigan . . . 1805–1837*. Michigan Hist. Pubs., Univ. Ser., i (Michigan Historical Commission: Lansing, Mich., 1916); F. B. Streeter, *Political Parties in Michigan, 1837–1860*. Michigan Hist. Pubs., Univ. Ser., iv (Michigan Historical Commission: Lansing, Mich., 1918); H. M. Dilla, *The Politics of Michigan, 1865–1878*. Col. Univ. Studies, 118 (Columbia Univ. Press: New York, 1912); J. Schafer, *A History of Agriculture in Wisconsin, Four Wisconsin Counties, The Wisconsin Lead Region*, and *The Winnebago-Horicon Basin* (State Hist. Soc. of Wisconsin: Madison, Wisc., 1922, 1927, 1932, 1937); M. M. Quaife, *Wisconsin, its History and its People*, 2 vv. (S. J. Clarke Publ. Co.: Chicago, Ill., 1924); F. Merk, *Economic History of Wisconsin during the Civil War Decade*. Pubs. of the State Hist. Soc. of Wisconsin. Studies, i (Madison, Wisc., 1916); W. W. Folwell, *A History of Minnesota*, 4 vv. (Minnesota Hist. Soc.: Saint Paul, Minn., 1921–30); M. E. Jarchow, *The Earth Brought Forth; a History of Minnesota Agriculture to 1885* (Minnesota Hist. Soc.: Saint Paul, Minn., 1949); I. B. Richman, *Ioway to Iowa* (State Hist. Soc. of Iowa: Iowa City, Ia., 1931); and F. C. Shoemaker, *Missouri's Struggle for Statehood, 1804–1821* (Stephens Printing Co.: Jefferson City, Mo., 1916). There are in addition monographic studies of particular aspects of Middle Western history, J. D. Hicks, *The Constitutions of the Northwest States* (Univ. of Nebraska: Lincoln, Neb., 1923); H. J. Webster, *History of the Democratic Party Organization in the Northwest, 1824–1840* (F. Heer Printing Co.: Columbus, O., 1915); C. C. Cleveland, *The Great Revival in the West, 1797–1805* (Univ. of Chicago Press: Chicago, Ill., 1915); D. R. Fox (ed.), *Sources of Culture in the Middle West* (Appleton-Century: New York, 1934); J. M. Miller, *The Genesis of Western Culture; the Upper Ohio Valley, 1800–1825* (Ohio State Arch. & Hist. Soc.: Columbus, O., 1938); W. H. Venable, *The Beginnings of Literary Culture in the Ohio Valley* (Clarke: Cincinnati, O., 1891); R. L. Rusk, *The Literature of the Middle Western Frontier*, 2 vv. (Columbia Univ. Press: New York, 1925); Dorothy A. Dondore, *The Prairie and the Making of Middle America: Four Centuries of Description* (Torch Press: Cedar Rapids, Ia., 1926). B. W. Bond, jr., *The Civilization of the Old Northwest . . . 1788–1812* (Macmillan: New York, 1934) deals generally with the earlier period; and H. C. Hubbart, *The Older Middle West, 1840–1880* (Appleton-Century: New York, 1936) is an able summary of the work on the later years.

vi. The situation is very different below the Ohio river. The history of the Spanish and French colonial empires in the lower Mississippi valley has not yet been, by any means, fully worked out; and modern scientific study of the history of the several states of the Union that have succeeded to them is still only fragmentary.

There are two general works, written before the results of research in the archives were available, J. Wallace, *The History of Illinois and Louisiana under French Rule* (Clarke: Cincinnati, O., 1893), and A. Franz, *Die Kolonisation des Mississippitales bis zum Ausgange der französischen Herrschaft* (G. Wigand: Leipzig, 1906). On the beginnings, there are I. J. Cox, *The Early Exploration of Louisiana* (Univ. of Cincinnati: Cincinnati, O., 1906), and W. E. Dunn, *Spanish and French Rivalry in the Gulf Region of the United States, 1678–1702.* Univ. of Texas Studies in History, no. 1 (Austin, Tex., 1917); and the wealth of Spanish documentation has made it possible to draw an astonishingly detailed picture of the far Spanish frontier in H. E. Bolton, *Texas ini the Middle Eighteenth Century.* Univ. of California Pubs. in History, ii (Univ. of California Press: Berkeley, Calif., 1915). The classical work on the history of Louisiana is C. Gayarré, *History of Louisiana,* 4 vv., 3rd ed. (Hawkins: New Orleans, 1885; 4th ed., Hansell: New Orleans, 1903);[1] and there is a recent general history É. Lauvrière, *Histoire de la Louisiane française, 1673–1939.* Louisiana State Univ., Romance Languages Ser., iii (Louisiana State Univ. Press: University, La., 1940). The early part of the eighteenth century is adequately covered by P. Heinrich, *La Louisiane sous la Compagnie des Indes, 1717–1731* (E. Guilmoto: Paris [1908]); but M. de Villiers du Terrage, *Les dernières années de la Louisiane française* (E. Guilmoto: Paris, 1904), while based on manuscript sources and reproducing much in full, is a confused and unscientific work; and there is a gap between the two books extending from 1732 to 1752 that is not adequately filled by a chapter in the work by Wallace cited above. Nancy M. M. Surrey, *Commerce of Louisiana during the French Régime, 1699–1763.* Col. Univ. Studies, 167 (Columbia Univ. Press: New York, 1916) is a useful collection of information on economic affairs. More work has been done on the years after 1763 by H. E. Bolton, *Athanase de Mézières and the Louisiana-Texas Frontier, 1768–1780.* 2 vv. (Arthur H. Clarke: Cleveland, O., 1914); Vera L. Brown, *Anglo-Spanish Relations in the Closing Years of the Colonial Era, 1763–1774.* Reprinted from the 'Hispanic American Historical Review' (Baltimore, Md., 1923); and J. W. Caughey, *Bernado de*

---

[1]First published as (a) *Louisiana: its Colonial History and Romance* (Harper & Bros.: New York, 1851), and *Louisiana: its History as a French Colony* (J. Wiley: New York, 1852); (b) *Histoire de la Louisiane,* 2 vv. (Magne et Weisse: New Orleans, 1846–7); English translation, *History of Louisiana,* 2 vv. (Redfield: New York, 1854, 1855); (c) *History of Louisiana,* vol. iii (1803–1861) (W. J. Widdleton: New York, 1866).

Gálvez in Louisiana, 1776–1783. Pubs. of the Univ. of California at Los Angeles in Social Sciences, iv (Univ. of California Press: Berkeley Calif., 1934). L. Houck, *The Spanish Régime in Missouri.* 2 vv. (R. R. Donnelley: Chicago, Ill., 1909), and J. A. Robertson, *Louisiana under the Rule of Spain, France, and the United States, 1785–1807.* 2 vv. (Arthur H. Clark: Cleveland, O., 1911) are documentary collections. On the Revolutionary period, see P. C. Phillips, *The West in the Diplomacy of the American Revolution.* Univ. of Illinois Studies in the Social Sciences, ii, nos. 2–3 (Urbana, Ill., 1913), and, particularly, A. B. Darling, *Our Rising Empire, 1763–1803* (Yale Univ. Press: New Haven, Conn., 1940). The difficult and confused story of the southwest between the establishment of independence and the Louisiana Purchase is treated with masterly clarity in A. P. Whitaker, *The Spanish-American Frontier, 1783–1795* (Houghton, Mifflin: New York, 1927), and *The Mississippi Question, 1795–1803* (Appleton-Century: New York, 1934). See also F. A. Ogg, *The Opening of the Mississippi* (Macmillan: New York, 1904); J. W. Caughey, *Mc-Gillivray of the Creeks* (Univ. of Oklahoma Press: Norman, Okla., 1938); W. F. McCaleb, *The Aaron Burr Conspiracy* (Dodd: New York, 1903); M. Serrano y Sanz, *El Brigadier Jaime Wilkinson* (Tip. de la 'Revista de arch., bibl. y museos': Madrid, 1915); E. W. Lyon, *Louisiana in French Diplomacy, 1759–1804* (Univ. of Oklahoma Press: Norman, Okla., 1934); F. P. Renaut, *La question de la Louisiane, 1796–1806* (E. Champion: Paris, 1918); E. S. Brown, *Constitutional History of the Louisiana Purchase.* Univ. of California Pubs. in History, x (Univ. of California Press: Berkeley, Calif., 1920); T. M. Marshall, *A History of the Western Boundary of the Louisiana Purchase, 1819–1841.* Univ. of California Pubs. in History, xi (Univ. of California Press: Berkeley, Calif., 1914); I. J. Cox, *The West Florida Controversy, 1798–1813* (Johns Hopkins Press: Baltimore, Md., 1918); and H. B. Fuller, *The Purchase of Florida* (Burrows: Cleveland, O., 1906).

Satisfactory studies of the history of the states of the lower Mississippi valley are few. The history of Kentucky and Tennessee has been a prey to romance, and is yet barely recovered from the hands of the amateurs; and the details of settlement are more difficult to trace than in the areas of later occupation. The outlines of the early history of Kentucky have been drawn in T. Bodley, *History of Kentucky before the Louisiana Purchase in 1803* (S. J. Clarke Publishing Co.: Chicago, Ill., 1928) and *Our First Great West* (John P. Morton: Louisville, K., 1938); and that of Tennessee has been dealt with in a series of volumes by S. C. Williams, *Dawn of Tennessee Valley and Tennessee History* (Watauga Press: Johnson City, Tenn., 1937), *Tennessee during the Revolutionary War* (Tenn. Hist. Commission: Nashville, Tenn., 1944), *History of the Lost State of Franklin*

(Press of the Pioneers: New York, 1933), and *The Beginnings of West Tennessee; in the Land of the Chickasaws, 1541–1841* (Watauga Press: Johnson City, Tenn., 1930); to which are to be added T. P. Abernethy, *From Frontier to Plantation in Tennessee* (Univ. of N. Carolina Press: Chapel Hill, N.C., 1932); S. J. Folmsbee, *Sectionalism and Internal Improvements in Tennessee, 1796–1845* (East Tennessee Hist. Soc.: Knoxville, Tenn., 1939); and Blanche H. Clark, *The Tennessee Yeoman, 1840–1860* (Vanderbilt Univ. Press: Nashville, Tenn., 1942). The founder of modern historiography in Alabama was T. M. Owen. There are two general histories of the state, T. M. Owen, *History of Alabama and Dictionary of Alabama Biography,* 4 vv. (S. J. Clarke Publ. Co.: Chicago, Ill., 1921), and A. B. Moore, *History of Alabama and her People,* 3 vv. (American Hist. Soc., Inc.: Chicago, Ill., 1927); and the political structure of the state is made clear in T. P. Abernethy, *The Formative Period in Alabama* (Alabama Dept. of Archives & Hist.: Montgomery, Ala., 1922), to which are to be added, T. H. Jack, *Sectionalism and Party Politics in Alabama, 1819–1842* (Banta Publ. Co.: Menasha, Wisc., 1919); L. Dorman, *Party Politics in Alabama from 1850 through 1860* (Alabama Dept. of Archives & Hist.: Montgomery, Ala., 1935); M. C. Boyd, *Alabama in the Fifties.* Col. Univ. Studies, 353 (Columbia Univ. Press: New York, 1931); C. S. Davis, *The Cotton Kingdom in Alabama* (Alabama Dept. of Archives & Hist.: Montgomery, Ala., 1939); W. E. Martin, *Early History of Internal Improvements in Alabama.* Johns Hopkins Univ. Studies, xx, no. 4 (Johns Hopkins Press: Baltimore, Md., 1902). There is a study by S. W. Martin of *Florida during the Territorial Days* (Univ. of Georgia Press: Athens, Ga., 1944); and one by W. B. Posey of *The Development of Methodism in the Old Southwest, 1783–1824* (Weatherford Printing Co.: Tuscaloosa, Ala., 1933). Of the American settlement of Mississippi and Louisiana there has been no detailed study. Of that of the southwest more has been written, although the history of Arkansas after the early years is as dark as that of any part of the Union. For the rest, see E. E. Dale, *The Indians of the Southwest* (Univ. of Oklahoma Press: Norman, Okla., 1949); G. Foreman, *Indians and Pioneers; the Story of the American Southwest before 1830* (Yale Univ. Press: New Haven, Conn., 1930), and *Advancing Frontier, 1830–1860* (Univ. of Oklahoma Press: Norman, Okla., 1933); E. B. Wesley, *Guarding the Frontier: a Study of Frontier Defense from 1815 to 1825* (Univ. of Minnesota Press: Minneapolis, Minn., 1935); R. N. Richardson, *The Comanche Barrier to South Plains Settlement* (Arthur H. Clark Co.: Glendale, Calif., 1933); L. W. Newton & H. P. Gambrell, *Social and Political History of Texas* (South West Press: Dallas, Tex., 1932); W. C. Binkley, *The Expansionist Movement in Texas, 1836–1850.* Univ. of California Pubs. in Hist., xiii (Univ. of

right which should set limits to the authority it would shortly be powerless to control. The origin of sectional conflict is thus discovered to reside largely in the history of the Mississippi valley and of the Pacific coast and it is to be remembered that the withdrawal of the Southern votes from Congress was immediately followed by public land legislation, railroad legislation, and tariff legislation that laid the foundations of the modern economic system, and that the aim of Congress during the so-called period of reconstruction was directed largely to preventing a reversal of the economic policy of the North.

While such an interpretation shows that matters of substance lay behind the logomachy of constitutional debate, that debate has also come to be better understood by virtue of recent constitutional studies. The South had already lost hope of equality in the presidency or in the House. By the admission of California in 1850, it lost the power to defend itself in the Senate; and it failed to restore its position by making a slave state of Kansas. In these circumstances, it fell back upon the constitutional principles that had been victorious in the Philadelphia Convention of 1787 and the ratifying conventions of 1787–8. Legislative absolutism threatened now, not in the states, but at the centre. But the enemy was the same, and the same issues were at stake. 'We claim', said Yancey at Charleston in 1860, 'the benefit of the Constitution that was made for the protection of minorities. In the march of events, feeling conscious of your numerical power, you have aggressed upon us. We hold up between us and your advancing columns of numbers that written instrument which your fathers and our fathers made, and by the compact of which, you with your power were to respect us and our rights. Our and your fathers made it that they and their children should for ever observe it; that upon all questions affecting the rights of the minority, the majority should not rely upon their voting numbers, but should look, in restraint upon passion, avarice, and lust for power, to the written compact, to see in what the minority was to be respected, and how it was to be protected, and to yield an implicit obedience to that compact. You, in your voting power, are not accustomed to scan its provisions as closely as we, who, less in number, find in the instrument the only peaceable solution of difficulties that otherwise would lead us to defend ourselves with arms.'[1]

While moral repugnance to slavery has not been set aside as a factor to be taken into account, it has a much less prominent place in the story than it used to have. It is now recognized that the conflict was more deep-rooted and more complicated than used to be supposed. It is coming to be held that the issues of right and wrong were less clear-cut than had been assumed. And the civil war itself is beginning to fall into place as an episode in the history of a social and economic revolution and as a chapter in a constitutional conflict that is not yet determined.

'When Jay and Adams . . . in the peace negotiations of 1782 . . . secured the Mississippi boundary for the United States,' Mr. Hockett has observed, 'they unwittingly prepared the overthrow of the political order to which they were attached.'[2] The settlement of the Mississippi valley caused an immense disturbance in the communities of the Atlantic seaboard. This disturbance was not limited to the American continent; and what happened upon the western shores of the Atlantic ocean did not differ essentially from what happened upon the eastern, though it is with the western only that we are here concerned.

The effect upon the North Atlantic states was to give a new direction to the employment of northern capital and to northern business activity. In place of a commerce that had been dislocated by the cumulative effects of the exclusion of the Americans from the British commercial system upon the establishment of independence and of the wars of the disordered years between 1793 and 1815, there developed an industrial activity stimulated in the first instance by the long interruption of the foreign supply of industrial goods, and, as it grew, finding in the West an open and ever-expanding market for

[1] *Cit.*, D. L. Dumond, *The Secession Movement, 1860–1861* (New York, 1931), p. 4, n. 5.
[2] H. C. Hockett, *Western Influences on Political Parties to 1825* (Columbus, O., 1917), p. 42.

all that it could produce. There followed a growing demand for industrial labour and a diversion of capital investment to the erection of industrial plant and the building of a network of internal communications. And there was required the creation of a national monetary and banking system. Northern agriculture went down before the impact of competition from the virgin and more fertile soils of the Mississippi valley. The stony fields of New England were abandoned; and the tillers migrated either to new farms in the Middle West or to the growing industrial towns of the east. Much of the poorer ground reverted to the wild; and most of such farms as survived were converted to pasture and to the supply of neighbouring industrial and urban communities with hay, dairy produce, potatoes, and truck. The consequence was the transformation of northern society and the loosening of all its accustomed habits. In predominant economic opinion there was a shift from a faith in free trade to faith in high protection. In politics, the North became at once more nationalist and more democratic: more nationalist, because its interests came to transcend the boundaries of states; more democratic, because of the growth of an industrial proletariat and by reason of the need, in order to retain that indispensable instrument of its prosperity, to enter into competition with western states in political liberality. In religion, the foundations of belief were broken up, and an excited activity led to a variety of intellectual and emotional adventures. Upon the South the effect of the settlement of the valley was very different. With its capital invested in real estate and in slaves that partook of the nature of real estate, the South was not in a position to share directly in the industrial expansion that occurred in the Northeast or in the exploitation of the internal market. Instead, it was led to concentrate its activity upon the production of a single crop, cotton, for the supply of the factories of the North and of western Europe. Moreover, in large areas of the old South the soil was exhausted, and the planters, unable to compete with the produce of the new lands of the Gulf and the lower Mississippi, found themselves with a redundant labour force that was both a capital

investment they were unwilling to lose and a social liability of
which they could not readily rid themselves. But they discovered
a remedy for their distress in the very feature of it that promised
to be their most grave embarrassment; and they became the
breeders and suppliers of slave labour for the new plantations
of the uplands of the old South and of the rich bottoms of the
Mississippi valley. In consequence there grew up a new and
revolting domestic slave trade, and there occurred a hardening
in the attitude of the South towards slavery. While, therefore,
to the South as well as to the North, the settlement of the Mississippi valley brought enlarged markets, agrarian revolution,
and rural emigration, there were great dissimilarities; and set
over against a North which became increasingly industrial,
proletarian, and nationalist, there grew a South devoted to the
production of a staple crop with slave labour, vitally interested
in foreign trade, and dominated by the movement of prices in a
world market. 'If', it has been observed, 'Webster ceased to be
a particularist after 1824 and became a nationalist by 1830, it
was because the interests of New England had undergone a
similar change; or, if Calhoun deserted about the same time
the cause of nationalism and became the most ardent of sect-
ionalists, it was also because the interests of his constituents . . .
had become identified with particularism.'[1]

Of this radical change in the character of the North we have
as yet only a fragmentary account. The great body of monographic work remains to be done. It will need to stretch from
the history of individual business houses to that of religious
beliefs; and when the story has been worked out what will have
been written will be a history of an intellectual, as well as of a
social and economic, revolution. But the North Atlantic states
have an immense population; their history in the nineteenth
century is highly involved; their metropolitan character gives
a national importance to their political affairs that diverts the
attention of the state historian from his proper task; the sheer
bulk of their records is itself overwhelming; and their historians,
having a longer past to look back upon, have been preoccupied

[1] W. E. Dodd, *Expansion and Conflict* (Boston, 1915), p. v.

with colonial and early republican events. The history of the nineteenth century has not, therefore, in this region received the same attention that has been devoted to it in the Middle West; and this phenomenon is the historiographical counterpart of the tardiness with which the nations of western Europe have addressed themselves to the writing of their own domestic histories during this period.

Of the transformation of the South we have a fuller knowledge if only because the process was so much simpler. The increased demand for cotton, consequent first upon the growth of the English cotton industry and then upon that of New England, coupled with the invention of the cotton gin making profitable the growth of the short staple variety of cotton that alone could be produced on the uplands, led to a rapid extension of the cotton area and the extrusion of the small farmers by the planters. This concentration upon a staple crop resulted in an ever-growing disparity in the commercial and industrial strength of North and South and to an increasing dependence of the South upon the North for credit and for industrial goods. While Southern capital was locked up in land and slaves, and credit facilities in the South were poorly developed, mobile capital accumulated rapidly in the North with the mounting profits of industry and transport. By the eighteen-fifties, southern agriculture was almost completely commercialized: except in the mountains, even the farmer who was not himself a planter produced no longer for his own consumption but for sale; and the South, like the Northeast, had become an importer of foodstuffs. Southern commerce, in spite of the great increase in the export of Southern staples, was rapidly out-distanced by Northern; for the South Atlantic ports remained almost stationary in population and in the volume of their imports from the thirties onwards, and the growth of New Orleans was greatly retarded after 1835. Added to this, the fiscal system increased the drain upon the liquid resources of the South. The tariff was the principal provider of federal revenue, a disproportionate part of the funded debt was held in the North, and a further advantage was enjoyed by the

North in the deposit of the bulk of federal funds in Northern banks. Except in the fall, when the cotton bills were drawn against New York, the domestic exchange rates were commonly in favour of the North. The situation was felt to be irksome by the old South as early as the thirties, although it was not until the fifties, when the dream of the alliance of South and North-west had been broken and the commercial dependence of South upon Northeast had become inescapably obvious, that the old South had the full sympathy of the Southwest. Yet the response to the situation was not, either before 1850 or after, a simple increase in the sectional diversity of economic ideas. It was indeed the opposite, though that did not in itself make for harmony. It took the form of plans to promote Southern indus-try and commerce, and was an adoption in the state of a policy that its proponents condemned in the Union. What the South sought was the diversification of its agriculture; the develop-ment of its industrial resources, and particularly the establish-ment of cotton manufactures; the improvement of its banking system; and in general the modernization of its economy and the creation of a body of Southern business men in order to reduce its dependence upon the North. Its attitude towards the protec-tive tariff, therefore, changed materially during the forties. The South ceased to be uniformly opposed to the idea of pro-tective legislation, bounties, and navigation laws. It began to seek the encouragement of Southern manufactures by means of the discriminatory taxation of manufactured goods coming from non-slave holding states or imported through the North, or by the grant of loans, bounties, drawbacks or tax exemptions. It extended public credit or gave direct capital assistance to railroads and other internal improvements, and to shipping companies. And it indulged in campaigns to encourage the consumption of the productions of home industries. All this was done in order to promote Southern economic independence, and it was accompanied by the hope of direct trade with Europe. But it bred in the South, nevertheless, a class of men whose economic ideas were not essentially different from those of like-circumstanced persons in the North or the West. In

consequence, tariffs, as a matter of principle and as distinguished from particular tariff rates, ceased during the fifties to
arouse strong sectional feeling. The tariff and all that it stood
for was as much a source of division within the South as
between the sections. Even so it was some decline, rather than
any growth, in the new economic thought of the South, during
those years, that increased the tension. The prosperity of
Southern agriculture, and particularly of cotton, during the
fifties, that led to some relief in the dependence of the South
upon Northern or foreign credit, encouraged less rather than
greater diversity in Southern agriculture, and brought a
reaction against alterations in the general economic structure of
the South; and it caused a rise in the demand for slaves and
an agitation for the reopening of the foreign slave trade. The
result of the impact of West upon South was thus the creation
in the South, not of a more complex, but of a more homogeneous civilization, and its geographical extension into the
lower Mississippi valley; for the Southwest, for all that it
differed from the old South, was part of the cotton kingdom.
And the upshot was a new nation *in posse*, sharing many of the
nationalist tenets of the statesmen of the Union, but affirming
them of a different geographical area.

As the economic and social structure of North and South
thus diverged, each section became the more unwilling to see
the Union controlled by the other. To the prosperity of the
North, national legislation relating to the public lands, transportation, the banks, and the tariff was vital. To the South,
foreign immigration, internal improvements, a more stringent
monetary system, and protective duties designed to promote
Northern interests were a burden or a menace. The state of
power in Washington became, therefore, a matter of crucial
importance. Josiah Quincy had remarked in 1811 that 'the
proportion of the political weight of each sovereign state . . .
depends upon the number of the states, which have a voice
under the compact';[1] and, as a later observer has added, 'as

[1] *Cit.*, A. B. Hart, *American History Told by Contemporaries*, 5 vv. (New York,
1919–29), iii, 411.

the development of the West was a prime cause of the disturbance of the old order and the source of many of the new issues, so its growth in political power made it a leading factor in determining the readjustment.'[1] To the original thirteen states, six slave and seven free, seventeen new states were added between 1791 and 1848, nine slave and eight free, producing a Senate of sixty members equally divided. But while thus holding its own in the number of states, the South was outdone in population, and consequently reduced in the House and the Electoral College to a minority, without hope of redress. The predicament was described by Calhoun in an often-quoted speech made in the Senate on 19 February, 1847.

'Mr. President,' he said, 'it was solemnly asserted on this floor some time ago, that all parties in the non-slave holding States had come to a fixed and solemn determination upon two propositions. One was,—that there should be no further admission of any States into this Union which permitted, by their constitutions, the existence of slavery; and the other was,—that slavery shall not hereafter exist in any of the territories of the United States; the effect of which would be to give to the non-slaveholding States the monopoly of the public domain, to the entire exclusion of the slaveholding States. . . .

'Sir, there is no mistaking the signs of the times; and it is high time that the Southern States—the slaveholding States, should inquire what is now their relative strength in this Union, and what it will be if this determination should be carried into effect hereafter. Already we are in a minority—I use the word "we" for brevity's sake—already we are in a minority in the other House,—in the electoral college,—and I may say, in every department of this Government, except, at present, in the Senate of the United States—there for the present we have an equality . . . And this equality in this body is one of the most transient character. . . .

'Sir, if this state of things is to go on—if this determination, so solemnly made, is to be persisted in, where shall we stand, as far as this Federal Government of ours is concerned? We shall be at the entire mercy of the non-slaveholding States. . . . [2]

In a single generation the South had travelled from a position

[1]H. C. Hockett, *Western Influences on Political Parties to 1825* (Columbus, O., 1917), p. 85.
[2]*The Works of John C. Calhoun*, 6 vv. (New York, 1854–61), iv, 340–2.

of apparently assured predominance to the brink of a precarious future. To the intense conservatism of rural habits of life and thought, the vigorous but chaotic progress brought about in the North by the advent of industrialism was hateful. The thought of subordination to Northern rule was intolerable. To it there were two barriers. They were the preservation of at least a power of obstruction in the Senate, or, failing that, an assurance of the submission of an otherwise omnipotent majority to the control of the Constitution. In the anxious eyes of the South, the events of the decade between 1850 and 1860 were evidence that it could put its trust in neither.

The unimpedible growth of the West precluded any merely conservative solution. The admission of California as a free state in 1850 tipped the balance in the Senate against the South. The first question to be asked and answered was whether, as had heretofore always been the case, that balance could be restored. Its answering was soon necessitated by the operation of the same expansive force that gave rise to it; and the answer seemed to the South to be something more than a permanent relegation of that region to a position of inferiority. It showed also, in the eyes of the South, that its opponents were ready to use the power that was theirs without regard to the limits set by the Constitution. It amounted, indeed, to an affirmation of the absolutism of the majority.

The debate, the issue of which seemed to the South to be so conclusive, arose over the erection of new states in the Territory of Nebraska, which lay north of the line 36° 30′ (map 6). From that area slavery had been excluded by the act of 1820, admitting the state of Missouri and commonly known as the Missouri Compromise. On the 23rd of January, 1854, there was reported to the Senate from the committee on territories a bill to organize governments for the Territories of Kansas and Nebraska. It contained a declaration that the Missouri Compromise had been superseded by the principles adopted in 1850 to regulate the status of slavery in the territory newly acquired from Mexico, with the effect of removing the prohibition of slavery north of 36° 30′ and leaving the people of the Territories themselves to determine whether or not slavery should be permitted during the Territorial period. The conventional interpretation of these proceedings used to be to attribute them to the personal ambition of Stephen A. Douglas, one of the Senators from Illinois. A northern Democrat, seeking Southern support for his candidature for the presidency, he made, it is said, an unscrupulous bid for Southern votes by opening to slavery an area of unsettled territory from which it had been excluded by an agreement of some thirty years' standing. The more thorough study of the history of the Mississippi valley has, however, shown that to be too superficial a view, and has revealed the operation of forces far less personal and far more complicated. The acquisition of Pacific coast territory from Mexico and the immigration of population into California, together with the growth of settlements in Oregon, rendered it increasingly desirable to free the Oregon and Santa Fé trails from the presence of Indians and awakened competition between the sections and within the sections for the eastern terminal of a proposed transcontinental railroad. In these circumstances, and now that the motive of separating the Indians from contact with the British was no longer operative, it became the policy of the Indian Department to clear the great transcontinental routes and form a chain of settlements connecting the Mississippi valley with the Pacific coast, locating the Indians in two separate groups, one to the north, in the Dakotas, and the other to the south, in Oklahoma, with a white population between them. At the same time, the organization of the territory west of Missouri was necessary if the transcontinental terminus was to be at either Chicago or St. Louis. But these were changes the South had strong reasons to dislike and possessed effective power to obstruct. The decision taken twenty years before to devote to Indian Territory the area between the Platte and the Red rivers had aroused the jealousy of the South because, while it effectively barred its own westward expansion, it left Iowa open to the settlers of the North. But that grievance had been alleviated by the annexation of Texas in 1845. The change of policy now proposed

offered no new opportunity to the South; and, since the area
to be freed for settlement and necessary to be organized in
order to make practicable a northern location of the eastern
terminal lay above the line 36° 30′, it was subject to the act of
1820. The effect of its settlement would before long be the
application of new free states for admission to the Union. A
price, therefore, must be paid for the necessary Southern
acquiescence; and its payment was made the more exigent
by the local situation in the states of Missouri and Illinois,
each of which reproduced in microcosm the problems of the
Union at large. Opinion in the state of Missouri was divided
between a desire for the organization of the Nebraska country
and the fear of the effect upon slavery in Missouri of the
erection of a free state upon its western border. This found
expression in the rivalry of two Missouri politicians, T. H.
Benton and D. R. Atchison, and drove the latter, in order to
retain his leadership in the western counties where his strength
lay, to seek a solution satisfactory to both the expansionists and
the slaveholders. At the same time, in the state of Illinois the
increasing sectional tension in the nation at large threatened
to create a division within the Democratic party between its
members in the northern and southern parts of the state.
Accordingly, Stephen A. Douglas, the dominant figure in the
Democratic party in Illinois and one of its leaders in the Union,
himself a heavy investor in Chicago real estate, keenly interested
in railroad development in Illinois, and an ardent expansionist,
found that, as chairman of the Committee on Territories, he was
faced at the national level with the same problem as Atchison
in Missouri, and was driven to seek a solution that would
gratify the demand for the organization of Nebraska without
awakening the implacable hostility of the slave-owners and the
slave states. That solution, both in Missouri and in Congress,
was to buy Southern renunciation of the eastern terminal of
the transcontinental line, and Southern acquiescence in the
opening to settlement of the new lands north of 36° 30′, by the
repeal of the Missouri Compromise and the concession thereby
to the South of the opportunity to redress the balance in the

Senate. The bargain had for the South a double attraction. It afforded at least a chance of a recovery of power. And properly interpreted, it might be held to affirm a principle. If the first of the two states, into which it was ultimately agreed that the territory should be divided, should enter the Union as a slave state, the South might hope to continue to block in the Senate the enactment of legislation obnoxious to it. If, on the contrary, it was driven to rely upon the defences of the Constitution, those defences would be strengthened by the repudiation of a long-accepted claim of legislative authority to abridge a constitutional right.

But the doctrine of squatter sovereignty or territorial self-determination had serious defects. It might, in the first place, be held to be a predication in respect of the majority of the electorate of a Territory of just that absolute and unlimited legislative authority that the South was now so unwilling to see erected at the centre: and in the second, intended as it was to operate in a community that was growing daily in population, lacking as it did any definition of the achievement of selfhood, and according equal validity to every determination, it invited the organization of rival immigrations designed to capture the Territory for their respective promoters. Two things followed. There emerged in Kansas a state of faction degenerating into violence and the commission of atrocities such as the twentieth century has since become only too familiar with; and there was started a constitutional debate about the limits of legislative authority with respect to slavery in the Territories that was brought to a head by the judgments delivered in the Supreme Court in the Dred Scott case in 1857. The election in Kansas, first of a pro-slavery Territorial Assembly and a free soil Constitutional Convention, and then of a free soil Assembly and a pro-slavery Convention, the one in each case acrimoniously accusing the other of irregularity, was a failure in self-determination. The admission of a free state organized by the free soil Convention was accordingly blocked by the Senate; and admission under a constitution adopted by the pro-slavery Convention was blocked by the House, on the ground of the

refusal of the Free Soil settlers to participate in the election of
the Convention and of the Convention candidly to submit its
handiwork to a popular vote when the confidence of Free Soil
in electoral proceedings had been restored. And when Congress
ultimately insisted that admission must wait upon submission
to the fairly ascertained will of the people of Kansas, that
people preferred to remain out of the Union rather than to
enter it with a constitution they could not approve. But
squatter sovereignty was not only a failure as a practical device.
It also stirred the most difficult and controversial constitutional
issues. The repeal of the Missouri Compromise had been
accepted in different quarters for quite different reasons. It
was regarded by some as a means of taking the problem of
slavery out of federal politics and relegating it to a sphere where,
without any derogation of popular authority, it would do less
damage to the cohesion of parties. It appeared to others to be
a reaffirmation of the principle that popular authority was
exercised within limits set by the Constitution and had no title
to discriminate between the kinds of property to which the
guarantees of the Constitution should apply; and to these
minds it followed that what Congress itself did not enjoy it had
no power to confer upon another. The act started, therefore,
not merely a struggle for power, but also a battle of interpretation. The ambiguity so necessary to secure the adoption of the
measure was impracticable in the execution of it; and the course
of events in Kansas forced asunder the incongruous elements
that made up the Democratic party. When the pro-slavery
Lecompton Constitution was not candidly submitted to the
people of Kansas, but their choice was limited to accepting it
either with or without clauses relating to slavery, the omission
of which would leave rights in slaves already imported into
the Territory still fully protected, the application of the
state for admission divided the party and the cabinet itself.
Some saw in these proceedings a denial of the principle of self-
government; but some looking only to their strict legality,
held that the Kansas-Nebraska Act had required the decision
to be that of actual residents, taken in their own way and legally

expressed, and thought it was not for Congress to reject an application for admission because the people had seen fit to adopt a procedure Congress did not like. If there was some disingenuousness in the argument from legality, the division of opinion nevertheless bespoke a deep-seated incompatibility of temper. A belief in the validity of the occasional will expressed in a popular fiat was set over against a care for the permanent reason embodied in the law. And the issue was more starkly posed upon a higher plane. The incompatibility of the pronouncement of the Supreme Court in the Dred Scott case, delivered on the 6th of March, 1857, with the attribution to the people of a Territory of sovereign authority to pass upon the right to hold slaves within the Territory during the Territorial period was unambiguous. If an act of Congress that prohibited a citizen from holding or owning a particular kind of property in a particular area of the United States was not warranted by the Constitution and was void, no act of Congress could confer authority to pass such law upon any other body. So radical a clash of opinion not only split the national parties, but also impaired the authority of the Supreme Court. It is now known that the intention of the Court to deliver its verdict upon the Dred Scott case without bringing into question the validity of the Missouri Compromise was frustrated by the anti-slavery members of the Court. But it is also true that some Southern leaders, and perhaps one Southern member of the bench, together with James Buchanan, the President-elect himself, who looked hopefully to the Court for a pronouncement that would relieve him of an unwelcome responsibility, wanted a political declaration; and it is certain that the discreet interference of Buchanan reinforced the influence of parties. And at the time, the odium was placed wholly upon the Chief Justice, who was accused of serving as the tool of the slave-owning interest. The effect was to undermine Northern respect for the Court and to produce threats of its reconstruction, which in turn convinced the South that the loyalty of the North to constitutional decisions in conflict with its interest was not to be relied upon.

The lesson drawn by the South from these events was not

13

Senate debate on the Kansas-Nebraska bill in 1854, 'which is greatest in numbers? According to the present census, all the slaveholders in the United States do not amount to four hundred thousand. What number of free laborers are there who ought to have the benefit of this great Territory? Probably fully thirteen millions are to be offset against about four hundred thousand.'[1] There was already, it was said in the same debate, a threat that the North 'will assume a jurisdiction equal to their numerical power and strength; and that northern justice is not to be trusted.'[2] 'Would it not be utterly impossible,' it was asked, 'to preserve this Union after a distinct declaration from one portion of it that it would not respect the rights of the other?'[3] 'Apart from the question of slavery,' Toombs had written in 1851, 'another great question is rising up before us [to] become a "fixed fact" in American politics. It is, and has [been] the will of a majority, sometimes called the higher law, in antagonism to our constitutional compact. If the first succeeds, we have no safety except in secession; if the latter, "liberty and union, may be forever one and inseparable".'[4] 'Our greatest danger to-day,' he concluded in May, 1860, 'is that the Union will survive the Constitution. The great body of your enemies in the North who hate the Constitution, and daily trample it under their feet, profess an ardent attachment to the Union —and, I doubt not, feel such attachment for the Union unrestrained by the Constitution.'[5] 'I have no more regard,' said Butler in the course of a debate in the Senate in February 1854, 'for the despotism of a democracy than I have for any other despotism. Unless it can be controlled, unless limitations can be imposed upon a democracy, it becomes no less despotic than any other form of government. The very name may give it the power to do injustice. I want a Government that can be controlled by rule, and not one that has to be reformed by revolu-

---

[1] *The Congressional Globe*, vol. xxviii, pt. 1 (Washington, D.C., 1854), p. 339a.
[2] *Appendix to the Congressional Globe*, n.s. . . . vol. xxxi (Washington, D.C., 1854), p. 292a.   [3] *Ibid.*, p. 294b.
[4] U. B. Phillips (ed.), The Correspondence of Robert Toombs, Alexander H. Stephens, and Howell Cobb. *Annual Report of the American Historical Association for the Year 1911*, vol. ii (Washington, D.C., 1913), p. 229.
[5] *Ibid.*, p. 476.

tion; a Government that rests upon some *veto* power against irresponsible will.'[1] In 1860, what the South saw itself subject to was 'the exercise of unlimited power by a sectional majority which may have possession of the machine':[2] 'the absolute control of a sectional majority without restraints from the Constitution, which hereafter would be whatever they wished it':[3] 'the supreme despotism of numbers' knowing 'no restraint but its own will.'[4] That was not the Union of 1789. 'If one section should get possession of this machinery, and not only destroy the limitations and conditions of its action, but direct that action to ends and purposes not only different from, but hostile to, those for which this political organism was created,' wrote Hunter with reference to a government common to the members of the Union, 'they destroy the Union as it was formed by the fathers, and seek to substitute another for it.'[5] In that case, the last defence of the rights of the minority had gone, and the only remedy was to leave the Union. 'We seceded,' said Jefferson Davis in 1864, 'to rid ourselves of the rule of the majority.'[6]

The dispute cut deep. It raised two fundamental issues. The first was whether the occasional fiat of the popular will was to prevail, and the checks and balances designed to make difficult its free and rapid translation into sovereign commands were to be discarded. The second was whether the justice of majority rule is not dependent upon the homogeneity of the electorate; whether, when there is a gross heterogeneity between the majority and the minority, the rule of numbers is anything more than an act of power, carrying no conviction and to be tolerated only so long as it must.[7] It had hitherto been of the very essence of the American system that the distinct interior

---

[1]*Appendix to the Congressional Globe*, n.s. . . . vol. xxxi (Washington, D.C., 1854), p. 238c.

[2]C. H. Ambler, *op. cit.*, p. 344.   [3]*Ibid.*, p. 340.

[4]*Cit.*, D. L. Dumond, *The Secession Movement, 1860–1861* (New York, 1931), p. 119, n. 6.

[5]C. H. Ambler, *op. cit.*, pp. 343–4.

[6]J. G. Nicolay & J. Hay, *Abraham Lincoln; a History*, 10 vv. (New York, 1890), ix, 210.

[7]*Cf.* R. F. Nichols, *The Disruption of American Democracy* (New York, 1948), p. 197.

groups were guaranteed security from the imposition without their own assent of measures peculiarly affecting their
interests. The plan of a consolidated nation, of a single people
arbitrarily divided into electoral districts of homogeneous
population, had been considered and rejected in 1787, precisely
because homogeneity had not been achieved. The time might
now be ripe for reconsideration. But there could be no question
of the revolutionary character of the change that there would
be if the decision of 1787 were to be reversed. 'All agencies,'
said Butler in the Senate in 1854, 'that are employed to fuse
the people of the United States into an entirety is [*sic*] wrong.
It is giving up to party and to party organization the controlling power contemplated in the Constitution.'[1] 'The attempt',
it was said of a proposal in a Whig convention in Georgia in
1852 to weight the votes of states in proportion to population,
'is made to connect this convention with the wildest sort of
democracy—the democracy of numbers. For the first time the
large States presume to control the sovereignty of the States.
The principle contended for will uproot your constitution and
the sovereign character of the States will be prostituted to
numbers.'[2] The language may have been intemperate; but
the conclusion was logical if the assessment of the evidence
was just.

Yet the right of self-government, defended with so much
passion and with such political acumen and grasp of principle,
was to be exercised in order to preserve the institution of slavery.
It was a disastrous and a forlorn case on which to make the
test. As one of their leaders put it, the Southern people had
'retreated from each position, to one of the greatest weakness,
that which is based upon the question of slavery and in many
cases, merely in the abstract.'[3] That it was the line chosen upon
which to fight was due in part to the exigencies of political
tactics, in part to an inability to face the task of reorganizing

[1] *Appendix to the Congressional Globe*, n.s. . . . vol. xxxi (Washington, D.C., 1854),
p. 240a.
[2] *Cit.*, A. C. Cole, *The Whig Party in the South* (Washington, D.C., 1918), p. 247.
[3] O. Crenshaw, *The Slave States in the Presidential Election of 1860* (Baltimore, 1945),
p. 225.

a social structure that had been heedlessly allowed to grow up and was desperately difficult to escape from. There was a large number of persons in the South in 1860 who would in the political jargon of to-day be described as 'appeasers'. Enthralled by the astounding material progress of the United States, they looked forward to the submersion of political disputation in the common pursuit of wealth. To the political philosophers they appeared as renegades. But they were not attentive to academic argument, and it was necessary to touch their pockets. The easiest way to rally the South to the defence of a speculative principle was to persuade it that a material interest was in immediate jeopardy; and in order to arouse the requisite alarm trivial events must be magnified or atrocities, if need be, invented.

Faced with the monstrous anomaly of slavery in 1860, it is difficult to appreciate by what slow degrees the institution had fastened itself upon Southern society and become the thing it was. The supply of labour in the mainland colonies, in the early years of their history, was derived from the importation of indentured servants ranging from convicts to well-to-do apprentice planters. But since there was an unlimited supply of virtually free land, such labour, when it had served its term, could not be retained at a wage that was economically bearable. It became necessary, therefore, if the plantation system was to survive, to procure a supply of labour that was not subject to a constant leakage; and such a supply was found in negro slaves imported from Africa. Imports were not made in any large numbers before the last quarter of the seventeenth century. Between 1670 and 1730 the situation was revolutionized. By 1800 the number of negro slaves in the United States amounted to about a million. By that date, however, economic conditions had changed. By the middle of the eighteenth century all the more desirable lands east of the mountains had been taken up. In a relatively more complex society labour was not so difficult to obtain. Moreover, after 1755 the balance of trade was adverse; and negroes were a very costly import. Alarm at the social dangers created by the presence of so large an alien population was reinforced by fear of the over-production of staple crops and an anxiety to reduce the difficulty of making sterling remittances by checking the importation of one of the most costly of commodities. Philanthropy found itself strengthened. After the establishment of independence, the slave trade was prohibited as from the year 1808; and there was a general expectation, shared by the South, that the institution of slavery would die out. Instead, it got a new lease of life when the production of cotton became the main occupation of the South; and between 1830 and 1850 a defence of the institution upon principle was gradually formulated.

A slave was by origin a captive in war; at first a Moor, a Muslim enemy of Christianity, captured by the Portuguese in battle; and then a negro similarly acquired, when the activities of Portugal extended to the Guinea Coast. When the demand grew to exceed the supply thus directly provided, the slave was then procured by purchase from an African sovereign who had himself acquired him, in accordance with African custom, by capture in war, by judicial condemnation, or by the sale of himself by the slave. Slaves began, therefore, though servants for life, by being capable of redemption and persons whose children were not themselves slaves. But when they were carried across the Atlantic, the possibility of redemption was destroyed; the offspring of the slave became themselves slaves, because it was difficult to see what else to do with them; and the rule that the status of the children followed that of the mother was established. Yet no illegality or moral obliquity attached to the institution unless the war or the judicial condemnation that had led to enslavement had itself been unjust; and it being impossible for the buyer in America to find this out for himself, he was absolved from the duty of enquiring into it by the development of the doctrine that the third possessor, who was normally the European trader, had a prescriptive right. Thus American slavery was not an absolute, arbitrary, despotical power of one over another. The legal character of slavery was regarded as being either quasi-contractual or one of a status in which the relation of master and slave was regulated by law.

In the one view, the right to the person of the slave was derived from the right to his labour; and that right was a right for the term of his life, though the owner upon his part was required to give protection and support. In the other view, although the right to his labour involved the control of his will, the slave nevertheless upon his part retained certain rights against his owner. He was protected from cruel oppression, maiming or mutilation; he had a right of resistance to murderous violence; homicide with malice committed upon him was murder; he was conceded limited rights of property; and he was held to have a moral personality and to be capable of salvation.

Upon this foundation it was possible to build a doctrine of moral justification. Both right reason and the divine law taught that punishment was just and that the status of men was various; and slavery was but one among many forms of social subordination. The system was in accordance with the inescapable inequalities of nature; but it was one of mutual rights and obligations. Master and slave were of one family; and the authority of the one over the other rested upon divine fiat. The slave, incapable of self-control, was better off as a slave than he would be as a freedman; he enjoyed a social security denied to a member of the proletariat; and he was only in rare and exceptional cases the victim of brutality. His legal character of a chattel personal was a device to distinguish him from real property and not one intended to assimilate his condition to that of a mere chattel. He retained his personality; and he, and not his owner, was in certain cases responsible to the law.

Yet colonial and state law, both common and statutory, which regulated these relations, often frustrated the more benevolent tendencies of the system and rendered humane purposes exceedingly difficult to effect. On the one hand, public interest set limits to the exercise of the rights of owners, and police regulations restricted both the manumission and education of slaves. On the other, care for the rights of property embarrassed the legislative regulation of the relations of master and slave, and impeded charity. Humanity dictated the legalisation of slave marriages, the limitation of the pledge of slaves as security for debt, and the formulation of systems of entails and primogeniture so as to prevent forced sales and the division of families. But the courts often found themselves constrained to defeat these good intentions. A testator in Maryland was held not to be entitled, in order to effect the emancipation of his slaves by his will, to direct that his debts be satisfied out of his real estate, even if that were sufficient. 'The creditors are the first objects . . . It is not in his [the testator's] power to confine them [the creditors] to a particular fund for the satisfaction of their debts . . . to turn them over from the natural fund, to one more uncertain, and less accessible.'[1] There might even be an obligation to inhumanity. An executor was bound to break up a family if sale in parcels would bring more than sale in one lot, since 'he is not to indulge his charities at the expense of others'.[2] Slaves hired out as apprentices must if necessary be coerced so that they might learn their trade and not contract habits of obstinacy; and their indulgence at the expense of their owner brought liability to an action for damages.[3] 'If the master contract . . . that the slave shall be emancipated upon his paying to his master a sum of money, or rendering him some stipulated amount of labor, although the slave may pay the money, . . . or perform the labor, yet he cannot compel his master to execute the contract, because both the money and the labor of the slave belong to the master, and could constitute no legal consideration for the contract.'[4] In January, 1855, an agreement was entered into between the slave Redmond and his owner Osborn, that if Redmond would pay Osborn $550 plus 10 per cent interest since 1852, the date of his purchase, Osborn would give him his freedom. $501 were paid at once, and the balance and interest were offered in August. Nevertheless Redmond was sold by Osborn. 'Manumission,' the Missouri court said, 'is a mere gratuity under our laws, and a mere intention or promise by the master, not consummated in the manner pointed out by law, however solemn the form in which

[1]Helen T. Catterall (ed.), *Judicial Cases concerning American Slavery and the Negro*, 5 vv. (Washington, D.C., 1926–37), iv, 76.
[2]*Ibid.*, ii, 59.   [3]*Ibid.*, ii, 210–11.   [4]*Ibid.*, v, 251.

such promise may be made, can confer no power or capacity
on the slave to have it enforced; it endows him with none of the
attributes of a freeman; his condition or *status* is not in the least
changed or affected in its legal relations; and there is nothing,
therefore, of which the law can take cognizance, nor any
ground on which the plaintiff can base his claim to relief, however strongly it might appeal, under circumstances of apparent
hardship, to conscience or the moral sense.'[1] Moreover, the
development of the law in the Border States and the deep south
diverged. Whereas in Delaware a negro was presumed to be
free, and in Maryland hearsay evidence was admitted to prove
descent from a free white ancestress, in all other slave states a
contrary view was taken by the courts; and while in one section
the emphasis came to be laid more and more upon the slave
as a person, in the other he was more and more rigidly held to
be mere property. 'All who have examined the earlier cases in
our books,' said a justice of the Virginia court of appeals in
1831, 'must admit, that our judges (from the purest motives, I
am sure) did, *in favorem libertatis*, sometimes relax, rather too
much, the rules of law, and particularly the law of evidence.
Of this, the court in later times, has been so sensible, that it has
felt the propriety of gradually returning to the legal standard,
and of treating these precisely like any other questions of
property.'[2] In Maryland, litigation about property in slaves
tended in the course of the nineteenth century to become concerned with such questions as emancipation, the emancipatory
effect of importations in contravention of state law, settlement,
the rendition of fugitives, or the suppression of the foreign slave
trade. In the deep south the records of the courts reveal a
hardening of the resistance to any improvement in the legal
status of the slave, despite continual efforts by particular owners
to secure the emancipation of individuals. And while in this
area there is outspoken condemnation of brutality, a growing
readiness to recognize a right in a slave to resist murderous
violence, a steady refusal to accept confessions obtained under
threats, and a frequent endeavour to secure to slaves a just trial

[1]*Ibid.*, v, 214.   [2]*Ibid.*, i, 164.

and to protect the liberty of free persons of colour, there is evidence of gross cruelty in the rougher communities; and in the eight states of which it was made up there were, apart from the killing of slaves in fight and the shooting of fugitives, twenty-four reported cases of death from excessive and inhuman punishment between 1817 and 1862. In Missouri, Arkansas, and Texas conditions were distinguished by the insecurity of property in slaves. In Missouri this was due to the near neighbourhood of free soil, in Arkansas and Texas to the fact that those areas were a market for the less desirable slaves from the older communities and the recourse of embarrassed planters who ran their property there to escape sale for debt. Accordingly the dealers, since they traded so largely in slaves of dubious value, were neither over-scrupulous about warranties of soundness nor too particular in their enquiries into title; and the courts were much occupied with disputes arising from these conditions. Thus the development of the institution took different courses in different areas; and the conflict of laws multiplied.

The perplexity of the Southern mind was increased and its sense of alarm deepened by the outbreak at this juncture of the conflict between science and religion. Any attack upon the divine inspiration of the bible or upon the validity of the biblical history of the human race threatened to undermine that moral justification of slavery that was most easily and generally accepted, and to drive the defenders of the institution back upon doctrines of mere naked power that were both crude in themselves and inconsistent with the stand being taken by the South in the defence of fundamental law. If the generally held beliefs in a common humanity and the brotherhood of man were to be exploded, and they were to be replaced by a doctrine of the multiple origin of races such as pre-Darwinian scientific thought gave colour to, then the common system of rights and obligations dissolved. One race standing in a relation of mere power to another, men subordinated to the will of an alien race had no rights, but only a claim, as of grace, to its charity; and the subjection of the negro would differ from that of any other animal only in degree, but not in kind. The Christian

ideal itself was thus put in jeopardy. The conversion or baptism
of the slave must be prohibited, since it would make him a
member of the Christian community and confer upon him
fundamental rights incompatible with that relation of mere
power upon which his condition of slavery must now be held
to depend. And such ideas were not only in conflict with the
teaching of the churches. They had troublesome political implications. If it was thought that the allegiance of man was
wholly absorbed in his racial groups and his duty fully discharged so long as he was faithful to it, the whole conception of
a fundamental law and inalienable rights received a shock, and
absolutism was advanced. It was not a long step from the belief
that different races were in a state of nature with respect to one
another to the belief that each independent political community was total. The defence of slavery became, therefore,
paradoxically involved in the defence of inalienable rights.
The overthrow of the religious justification of slavery was the
work of that same heretical mind that would erect a popular
despotism. In both fields of debate what was at issue was a conception of law and a system of rights and obligations. And the
asperity of the debate was not mitigated by the fact that the
South was itself divided upon these matters.

One of the recurrent perplexities of American history is the
fact that opposition to absolutism in the Union or the state may
always arise from either of two motives, and that political
alliances have frequently had no more durable foundation
than common animosity. An exercise of absolute authority
may be resented because it is absolute or merely because it is
thought to rest in the wrong hands. For the moment, both
objectors can agree to seek its overthrow. But they do so for
quite different reasons. The one wants the restraint, the other
merely the transfer of authority. This constantly repeated
phenomenon recurred in the act of secession. There were no
more ardent believers in popular sovereignty than some of the
Southern members of Buchanan's cabinet. When they transferred their allegiance to the Confederacy, they did not change
their political skins. They only changed the predication of their

nationalist ideas. They opposed to popular sovereignty, not the rule of law, but popular sovereignty. Their challenge was not one of permanent reason to occasional will, but of will to will. Of the degree to which this radical division within the Southern mind was a cause of the failure of the Confederacy no adequate study has yet been made.

The act of secession was not as foolhardy as defeat has since made it look. It was not hopeless to expect, before April, 1861, that the Union might acquiesce in separation; and there were times during the war when it was not madness to think that it might be forced to do so. But there were two insuperable obstacles to the political or geographical feasibility of secession. There was no ground in logic to accept the self-determination of the particular unit that called itself the Confederacy; and when one of the Democratic leaders in the Tennessee valley said that 'if the people of South Alabama should succeed in putting the State out of the Union, he favoured putting the valley out of the State,'[1] there was really no answer to him except to deny the validity of secession as a political remedy at all. At the same time, the whole of American history pointed to the unity of the Mississippi valley; and the dream of a state consisting of the valley and the South Atlantic area, though not yet wholly renounced by the South, had by now become foolish.

It is remarkable how little scientific work of the first quality has yet been done upon the history of the conduct of the American Civil War. Few of the indispensable preliminary monographic studies have yet been written. There is a large literature dealing with operations in the field; and this includes a few works of the highest reputation, and has been notably enriched in recent years by Southern contributions to the history of the Confederacy. But even here the history of recruitment, organization, supply, and transport has been little studied. The history of the decisions made upon issues of policy at the highest level is in process of detailed examination. But

[1] O. Crenshaw, *The Slave States in the Presidential Election of 1860* (Baltimore, 1945), pp. 255-6.

in the elucidation of what went on in Congress and in party caucus, at the state capitals and among the rank and file, in the newspaper offices and the departments, it is hardly an exaggeration to say that almost everything remains to be done. About the ultimate reasons for the military failure of the Confederacy, when it had come so near to success, we still do no more than generalize and speculate. All this is due in part, no doubt, to the peculiar technical difficulties of the history of war, to the daunting complexity of its problems, and in this case to the copiousness of the records. But it is also due in part to the violent interruption of accustomed ways that demands of the narrator, also, a change of habit and a shift of attention from what has hitherto interested him to something new.

It is the political and constitutional aspect of the war that has received the most penetrating examination by the historians. There is good authority for insisting that the war, at bottom, was not about slavery.[1] That was the view explicitly stated by Lincoln himself. The war was not undertaken in order to overthrow slavery; it might have been successfully concluded without its abolition. The matter was constitutionally one for the states; and Lincoln neither desired, nor was he politically in a position, to impose a policy upon them. The Emancipation Proclamation when it came was regarded by him as a measure of limited scope, doubtful legality, and inadequate effect;[2] and at the time it had greater importance as a political demonstration than as a social reform. The measures of Congress showed a more uncompromising intention; but they often had little practical effect. To the slaves in the loyal states, freedom came by state enactment; to those whose owners were in rebellion, it came in practice as an incident of war—to a relatively few, by capture, civilian service, or enlistment; to the great majority, when the fact of their finding themselves within the field of military operations gave reality and some semblance of legality to a proclamation

[1] *Cf.* J. Macy, *Political Parties in the United States, 1846–1861* (New York, 1900), p. 271; J. G. Randall, *Lincoln the President*, 2 vv. (New York, 1945), ii, 126–7.
[2] *Cf.* Randall, *op. cit.*, ii, 141.

issued in virtue of the president's powers as commander-in-chief. To those in any state within the Confederacy not designated on 1 January, 1863, as an area in rebellion and being then represented in Congress, had there been one, freedom would not by virtue of the presidential proclamation have come at all. That slavery so vanished is but another illustration of the way in which war accelerates the pace rather than alters the direction of social change. But if the fact that the formal identification of the North with the cause of freedom added, as it was designed to add, fervour to the prosecution of the war is indisputable, the acceleration of emancipation had results by no means fortunate for the negro. His release was an act of alien force. Social and political rights were conferred upon him, not on his merits, but because he could be made an instrument of continuing Northern control. And they were subsequently taken away from him, not for his shortcomings, but as a step in the recovery of self-government by the South. Traditionally regarded with hostility by his white competitors, unable to meet them successfully when thrown upon his own resources, dependent upon the Republican party for his new-found social and political privileges, unwelcome as a member of trade unions which saw in that party their principal opponent, he was reduced to an even greater extent than in the days of slavery to employment in agriculture and domestic service. As an agriculturalist, in default of a sufficient acreage of confiscated lands for the fulfilment of plans to turn him into a peasant proprietor, and for lack of resources from which he could pay rent or the planter wages, he became a share-cropper and relapsed into a state of peonage to his creditor.

It was in tune with the history of emancipation that the matters of controversy continued throughout the war and in the immediately post-war years to be, as they had been in the fifties, predominantly political and constitutional. That war should produce a growth of executive power was no more than was to be expected; and although the increase in the power of the presidency was to continue, what happened was not revolutionary. Neither were the invasions of the liberty of the subject, although they were serious, more in themselves than an aberration from which a return might confidently be expected on the restoration of peace. But issues of fundamental importance were raised by the necessity of defining the nature of the war and by the claims advanced by the legislature. The war at the outset was conceived as an operation for the suppression of a rebellion raised by disloyal persons within states whose power to withdraw from the Union was denied. Upon this principle the Southern troops were banditti, their ships pirates, and their captures unlawful. But the blockade of the Confederate ports was a measure that needed for its sanction a different doctrine. Blockade is a belligerent right. It assumes a state of public war. Its exercise in the eyes of the world converted rebellion into lawful warfare. The Confederate armies became belligerents, their ships lawful cruisers, and their captures good prize. 'It was,' wrote Lord Russell, ' . . . your own government which, in assuming the belligerent right of blockade, recognized the Southern States as Belligerents. Had they not been belligerents the armed ships of the United States would have had no right to stop a single British ship upon the high seas.'[1] The principles of conduct continued throughout to be ambiguous. Foreign relations, constitutional law, and the task of emancipation were all bedevilled by the confusion; and when the war ended it was uncertain whether the states whose plan to secede had been flatly defeated were in the Union or out of it. This paradoxical result was the more unhappy in that it gave scope to the ambitions of a legislature dominated by politicians who had little or no respect for any legal or constitutional inhibitions obnoxious to their interests. The radical Republicans have been described as aiming at 'sectional supremacy, social revolution, capitalistic exploitation, and such a program of future party ascendancy as would make the Radicals the controlling element in the whole country.'[2] Kept in check, so long as he lived, by the wisdom and political skill

---

[1] Note of 4 May, 1865. *Cit.*, Q. Wright, *The Control of American Foreign Relations* (New York, 1922), p. 38, n. 2.
[2] J. G. Randall, *Lincoln the President*, 2 vv. (New York, 1945), ii, 205.

of Lincoln, they found their opportunity under his successor; and they came very near to erecting just that legislative despotism which the South had feared and against the threat of which it had revolted.[1]

The re-embodiment of the states of the late Confederacy in the persons of their loyal inhabitants, the re-establishment of their relations with the federal government, and their resumption of their place in the Union threatened, unless there were electoral reform, to result in a paradoxical increase in the political power of those very persons who had just suffered so crushing a military defeat. The emancipation of the negro had raised him from three-fifths of a man to a whole man for the purpose of calculating the number of representatives to be returned by his state to the lower house of Congress. Yet unless he were enfranchised, the additional representatives that the South had thus become entitled to would be returned by the Southern whites. The toleration of so unjust a consequence called for a large generosity; and its concession might jeopardize that new economic policy the adoption of which the removal of Southern representation from Congress had made possible and upon the maintenance of which the prosperity of the interests represented by the Radicals depended. 'The bare idea,' wrote John Jay to Salmon P. Chase in January, 1867, ' of the rebel states casting their votes for election in 1868—the blacks being excluded—& giving us again a democratic & rebel gov. is altogether intolerable.'[2] The reconstruction of the Southern states successfully effected by the president by the end of 1865, upon the assumption that all that was needed was the re-establishment of loyal state governments, was accordingly rejected; and the task was undertaken anew by Congress itself. Returned to the arbitrary rule of military government, the Southern states were deemed to be out of the Union, and were required to pay for their readmission to it by the acceptance of measures calculated to alter their political complexion

---

[1] *Cf.* R. F. Nichols, *The Disruption of American Democracy* (New York, 1948), p. 332.
[2] Diary and Correspondence of Salmon P. Chase. *Annual Report of the American Historical Association for the Year 1902*, vol. ii (Washington, D.C., 1903), p. 519.

14

and to insure to the Radicals the support of their representatives in Congress. The aim of these measures was the creation of a Republican party in the South by means of the endowment of the negro with social and political rights. Great ingenuity was required to validate so large a degree of federal intervention in what had hitherto been the affairs of the several states; the policy was developed experimentally; the measures in which it took shape increased steadily in severity; they included two further constitutional amendments in addition to the Thirteenth; they raised the widest constitutional issues and altered radically the relation of all the states to the Union; and they failed in the long run to achieve either the happiness of the negro or the desired political ends.

Resenting presidential reconstruction as an executive usurpation, and unwilling while the future of the freedman was still unassured to relegate the mastery of his fate to his former owners, Congress refused admission to the reconstructed states, finding a justification for its action in the doctrine either that they were conquered provinces at the mercy of the victor or that they had at best forfeited their rights and were reduced to the status of a Territory the terms of whose admission to statehood might be prescribed by Congress. This frustration of presidential policy accomplished, Congress passed to measures of ever-increasing severity directed first to a national guarantee of the civil and political rights of the freedman; then to reconstruction *de novo* and the adoption, under military direction, of constitutions containing provisions dictated by Congress; and finally, after re-admission, to enforcement in face of a Southern determination to eliminate the negro from politics. These proceedings involved both a revolution in the basis of citizenship and an arbitrary intervention in the affairs of the states under the authority of legislation adopted nearly two years after the cessation of hostilities and only legally justifiable on the theory that the war had not ended. The Civil Rights Act of 1866 and the Fourteenth Amendment of 1868 provided for the first time that definition of United States citizenship that had heretofore been made impracticable by lack of agreement upon the status of the free negro in the eyes of the United States; and they placed the civil rights of these citizens under the protection first of the federal government and then of the federal Constitution, preventing their abridgment by acts of the states. It is not correct to say that this, for the first time, created a dual citizenship or for the first time created a federal guarantee of civil rights. Since the establishment of the Constitution, citizens of the states had been citizens of the United States; and every citizen had both owed a dual allegiance and enjoyed United States as well as state rights. Neither did the Fourteenth Amendment provide a federal guarantee of the enjoyment by citizens of the United States of those rights that accrued to them by virtue of citizenship of a state. But the act and the Amendment specified the persons whose civil rights the Union would protect, including by definition among those persons free people of colour and therefore the emancipated slaves, and enlarged the body of rights thus protected. More specifically, and with less ambiguity of intention and effect, Congress invaded what had hitherto been the preserve of the states to regulate the franchise. This end was sought by indirection in the Fourteenth Amendment, which provided that representation of a state in the lower house of Congress should be reduced in proportion to the denial of the franchise to its citizens. But by the second Reconstruction Act of 1867 the enfranchisement of the negro was directly imposed. The commanders of the military districts into which the South had now been divided were required by the act to register as voters in the election of the state constitutional conventions, called to begin again the task of reconstruction, all those persons defined as citizens by the Civil Rights Act; and the conventions so elected were required to include negro suffrage in the constitutions that they framed and to submit these constitutions to an electorate composed upon the same rule. By the Fifteenth Amendment the reversal of these arrangements was sought to be prevented by making it a requirement of the Constitution that 'the right of citizens of the United States to vote shall not be denied or abridged by the United States or any State on

account of race, colour, or previous condition of servitude.'
And when the Southern states, once again freed from military
government and restored to the control of their own domestic
affairs, showed an intention to circumvent these provisions and
to deprive the negro of those rights intended to be secured to
him, a series of further measures was enacted by Congress for
the punishment of the offenders, the federal supervision of
elections, the trial by federal courts of cases arising under the
acts, and the use if necessary of federal troops to enforce
the law.

It was a scant mitigation of these arbitrary and despotic
proceedings that two of them were not simple legislative enactments, but took the form of amendments to the Constitution.
These, indeed, at least required the approval of some among the
Southern states. But the ratification of the Fourteenth Amendment was made part of the price of the re-admission of Arkansas,
North and South Carolina, Florida, Louisiana, and Alabama,
and that of the Fifteenth was added to the price paid by Virginia, Mississippi, Texas, and Georgia. To the states whose
affairs they were intended primarily to regulate, they were
mere acts of power.

Such absolutism, as was inevitable under the American Constitution, brought the legislature into conflict with the executive
and the judiciary. A number of vetoes of what he regarded as
unwise and unconstitutional legislation led to an open quarrel
between Andrew Johnson and Congress and to a narrowly
defeated attempt by Congress to impeach the president. The
adoption of a more discreet attitude failed to save the Supreme
Court from a similar challenge to its authority. In the case
ex parte McCardle, in 1867, the Court was deliberately shorn
of jurisdiction by the repeal, before it could deliver judgment,
of certain provisions of reconstruction legislation upon which
the appellant relied.

Yet so deeply ingrained was the American respect for the
rule of law that the threat that there would be established the
unfettered rule of the legislature was not realized. The defeat
of the impeachment; the survival of the Supreme Court; the

refusal by it to accept the more extravagant interpretations of the Fourteenth Amendment or to allow the transfer of the protection of all civil rights to the federal government; the continuance of dual citizenship and divided loyalties; and the discredit of the Radicals by the gross corruption and inefficiency shown by them in both the state and federal spheres—all these set bounds to the authority of the federal legislature. If in the eighteen-eighties it was commonly assumed by the more advanced political thinkers that the national will expressed in the national legislature should prevail without hindrance, and that the system of checks and balances was cumbersome and out of date, these were still but notional speculations and were not yet the substance of an existing political structure. It remained yet to be seen whether the ideas of 1787 were to be jettisoned or should continue to prevail.

BIBLIOGRAPHICAL NOTE

i. The impact of the settlement of the Mississippi valley upon the Atlantic states, and the domestic history of those states during the years between the close of the war of 1812 by the Treaty of Ghent in 1815 and the outbreak of the Civil War in 1861 have as yet been but imperfectly studied. The best introduction to the subject is H. C. Hockett, *Western Influences on Political Parties to 1825.* Ohio State Univ. Bulletin, xxii, no. 3 (Columbus, O., 1917). A group of studies of agrarian, industrial, and social history provides a general view of the economic changes that occurred, namely, P. W. Bidwell & J. I. Falconer, *History of Agriculture in the Northern United States, 1620–1860* (Carnegie Institution of Washington: Washington, D.C., 1925); L. C. Gray, *History of Agriculture in the Southern States to 1860*, 2 vv. (*Ibid.*, 1933); V. S. Clark, *History of Manufactures in the United States, 1607–1860* (*Ibid.*, 1916; revd. ed., 1928); Alice F. Tyler, *Freedom's Ferment; Phases of American Social History to 1860* (Univ. of Minnesota Press: Minneapolis, Minn., 1944); H. W. Farnam, *Chapters in the History of Social Legislation in the United States to 1860* (Carnegie Institution of Washington: Washington, D.C., 1938); and J. R. Commons *et al., History of Labor in the United States.* 4 vv. (Macmillan: New York, 1918–35). The best part of A. M. Schlesinger, jr., *The Age of Jackson* (Little, Brown: Boston, 1945) is an able survey of working class politics in the North Atlantic states during this period; and there are two more specialized studies of the subject, R. B. Morris, *Government and Labor in Early America* (Columbia Univ. Press: New York, 1946), and N. J. Ware, *The Industrial Worker, 1840–1860* (Houghton, Mifflin: New York, 1924). But the monographic literature upon the history of the several states is still fragmentary. It includes J. T. Adams, *New England in the Republic, 1776–1850* (Little, Brown: Boston, 1926); Caroline F. Ware, *The Early New England Cotton Manufacture; a Study in Industrial Beginnings* (Houghton, Mifflin: New York, 1931); Van Wyck Brooks, *The Flowering of New England, 1815–1865* (Dutton: New York, 1936); A. B. Darling, *Political Changes in Massachusetts, 1824–1848.* Yale Hist. Pubs., xv (Yale Univ. Press: New Haven, Conn., 1925); J. C. Meyer, *Church and State in Massachusetts, 1740–1833* (Western Reserve Univ. Press; Cleveland, O., 1930); O. & Mary F. Handlin, *Commonwealth; a Study of the Role of Government in the American Economy; Massachusetts, 1774–1861* (New York Univ. Press: New York, 1947); S. E. Morison, *The Maritime History of Massachusetts, 1783–1860* (Houghton, Mifflin: Boston, 1921); J. M. Morse, *A Neglected Period of Connecticut's History, 1818–1850.* Yale Hist. Pubs., xxv (Yale Univ. Press: New Haven, Conn., 1933); Margaret E. Martin, *Merchants and Trade of the Connecticut River Valley, 1750–1820.* Smith College Studies in History, xxiv, 1–4 (Northampton, Mass., [1939]); C. Williamson, *Vermont in Quandary 1763–1825* (Vermont Hist. Soc.: Montpelier, Vt., 1949); D. McW. Ludlum, *Social Ferment in Vermont, 1791–1850* (Columbia Univ. Press: New York, 1939); D. R. Fox, *Decline of Aristocracy in the Politics of New York.* Col. Univ. Studies, 198 (Columbia Univ. Press: New York, 1919); D. M. Ellis, *Landlords and Farmers in the Hudson-Mohawk Region, 1700–1850* (Cornell Univ. Press: Ithaca, N.Y., 1946); I. Mark, *Agrarian Conflicts in Colonial New York, 1711–1775.* Col. Univ. Studies, 469 (Columbia Univ. Press: New York, 1940); W. R. Fee, *The Transition from Aristocracy to Democracy in New Jersey, 1789–1829* (Somerset Press: Somerville, N.J., 1933); R. J. Ferguson, *Early Western Pennsylvania Politics* (Univ. of Pittsburgh Press: Pittsburgh, Pa., 1938); P. S. Klein, *Pennsylvania Politics, 1817–1832* (Hist. Soc. of Pennsylvania: Philadelphia, 1940); Marguerite G. Bartlett, *The Chief Phases of Pennsylvania Politics in the Jacksonian Period* (H. R. Haas: Allentown, Pa., 1919); H. R. Mueller, *The Whig Party in Pennsylvania.* Col. Univ. Studies, 230 (Columbia Univ. Press: New York, 1922); L. Hartz, *Economic Policy and Democratic Thought; Pennsylvania, 1776–1860* (Harvard Univ. Press: Cambridge, Mass., 1948); M. R. Eiselen, *The Rise of Pennsylvania Protectionism* (Univ. of

Pennsylvania Press: Philadelphia, 1932). Of the changes in the South Atlantic states there is a general review in F. M. Green, *Constitutional Development in the South Atlantic States, 1776–1860* (Univ. of N. Carolina Press: Chapel Hill, N.C., 1930); and there are a few more particular studies, J. G. Blandi, *Maryland Business Corporations. 1783–1852.* Johns Hopkins Univ. Studies, lii, 3 (Johns Hopkins Press: Baltimore, Md., 1934); C. H. Ambler, *Sectionalism in Virginia from 1776 to 1861* (Univ. of Chicago Press: Chicago, Ill., 1910); H. H. Simms, *The Rise of the Whigs in Virginia, 1824–1840* (William Byrd Press: Richmond, Va., 1929); W. K. Boyd, *The Federal Period, 1783–1860,* being vol. ii of the *History of North Carolina.* 6 vv. (Lewis Pub. Co.: Chicago, Ill., 1919); H. M. Wagstaff, *State Rights and Political Parties in North Carolina, 1776–1861.* Johns Hopkins Univ. Studies, xxiv, 7–8 (Johns Hopkins Press: Baltimore, Md., 1906); A. R. Newsome, *The Presidential Election of 1824 in North Carolina.* James Sprunt Studies in Hist. and Pol. Sci., xxiii, no. 1 (Univ. of N. Carolina Press: Chapel Hill, N.C., 1939); J. G. de R. Hamilton, *Party Politics in North Carolina, 1835–1860.* James Sprunt Pubs., xv, nos. 1–2 (The Seeman Printery: Durham, N.C., 1916); C. C. Norton, *The Democratic Party in Ante-Bellum North Carolina, 1835–1861* (Univ. of N. Carolina Press: Chapel Hill, N.C., 1930); R. H. Taylor, *Ante-Bellum South Carolina; a Social and Cultural History.* James Sprunt Studies in Hist. and Pol. Sci., xxv, no. 2 (Univ. of N. Carolina Press: Chapel Hill, N.C., 1942); P. Murray, *The Whig Party in Georgia, 1825–1823. Ibid.,* xxix (*Ibid.,* 1948); and U. B. Phillips, 'Georgia and State Rights'. *Annual Report of the American Historical Association for the Year 1901,* pt. ii (Govt. Printing Office: Washington, D.C., 1902).

These are all, in the main, political in outlook. For the agrarian conditions that lay behind politics, see, in addition to the items on p. 197, J. Schafer, *The Social History of American Agriculture* (Macmillan: New York, 1936); P. W. Bidwell, 'Rural Economy in New England at the Beginning of the Nineteenth Century'. Connecticut Academy of Arts & Sciences, *Transactions,* xx (New Haven, Conn., 1916); H. F. Wilson, *The Hill Country of Northern New England; its Social and Economic History, 1790–1930* (Columbia Univ. Press: New York, 1936); and A. Craven, *Soil Exhaustion as a Factor in the Agricultural History of Virginia and Maryland, 1606–1860.* Univ. of Illinois Studies in the Social Sciences, xiii, 1 (Urbana, Ill., 1926).

The growing political tension that resulted from the divergence between the history of the North and of the South found expression in conflicts over public land policy, transportation, and the tariff. The literature of the first and second of these has been dealt with above, pp. 150–7. The standard authority upon the history of the tariff is F. W. Taussig, *The Tariff History of the United States.* 8th ed. (Putnam's: New York, 1931).

Upon the successive political crises that these conflicts resulted in during the second quarter of the century, see F. C. Shoemaker, *Missouri's Struggle for Statehood* (Stephens Printing Co.: Jefferson City, Mo., 1916); Florence Weston, *The Presidential Election of 1828* (The Ruddick Press: Washington, D.C., 1938); D. F. Houston, *A Critical Study of Nullification in South Carolina.* Harvard Hist. Studies, iii (Longmans, Green: New York, 1908); F. Bancroft, *Calhoun and the South Carolina Nullification Movement* (Johns Hopkins Press: Baltimore, Md., 1928); C. S. Boucher, *The Nullification Controversy in South Carolina* (Univ. of Chicago Press: Chicago, Ill., 1916); S. R. Gammon, *The Presidential Campaign of 1832.* Johns Hopkins Univ. Studies, xl, 1 (Johns Hopkins Press: Baltimore, Md., 1922); E. M. Carroll, *Origins of the Whig Party* (Duke Univ. Press: Durham, N.C., 1925); and G. R. Poage, *Henry Clay and the Whig Party* (Univ. of N. Carolina Press: Chapel Hill, N.C., 1936).

ii. There is a learned, if rather baffling survey of 'What historians have said about the causes of the Civil War' by H. K. Beale in *Theory and Practice in Historical Study; a Report of the Committee on Historiography* (Social Science Research Council: New York, 1946). The reason that it is baffling is that, while the literature is immense, too much of it is argument and too little of it the result of a scientific investigation of the facts. But much has indeed lately been done to elucidate the events of the decade preceding the war. The most authoritative summaries of this are H. H. Simms, *A Decade of Sectional Controversy, 1851–1861* (Univ. of N. Carolina Press: Chapel Hill, N.C., 1942), and, on a more generous scale, A. Nevins, *Ordeal of the Union,* 2 vv., and *The Emergence of Lincoln,* 2 vv. (Scribner's: New York, 1947, 1950). A. Craven, *The Coming of the Civil War* (Scribner's: New York, 1942) is an interpretation that is more openly expressed in the title of a volume of lectures, *The Repressible Conflict, 1830–1861* (Louisiana State Univ. Press: University, La., 1939). G. F. Milton, *The Eve of Conflict. Stephen A. Douglas and the Needless War* (Houghton Mifflin: Boston, 1934) is a lucid and vivid account of the political events of the decade that is written from a similar point of view, but does not add substantially to what was previously known, save in respect to the history of party management.

On the several histories of the parties during the decade, see J. Macy, *Political Parties, 1846–1860* (Macmillan: New York, 1900); A. C. Cole, *The Whig Party in the South* (American Historical Assoc.:

Washington, D.C., 1913); R. F. Nichols, *The Democratic Machine*, *1850–1854*. Col. Univ. Studies, 248 (Columbia Univ. Press: New York, 1923), *Franklin Pierce* (Univ. of Pennsylvania Press: Philadelphia, 1931), and *The Disruption of American Democracy* (Macmillan: New York, 1948), forming a continuous history of the Democratic party from 1850 to 1861; T. C. Smith, *The Liberty and Free Soil Parties in the Northwest*. Harvard Hist. Studies, vi (Harvard Univ. Press: Cambridge, Mass., 1897); H. D. A. Donovan, *The Barnburners . . . 1830–1852* (New York Univ. Press: New York, 1925); M. Evangeline Thomas, *Nativism in the Old Northwest, 1850–1860* (Catholic Univ. of America: Washington, D.C., 1936); F. Curtis, *The Republican Party*, 2 vv. (Putnam's: New York, 1904); and A. W. Crandall, *The Early History of the Republican Party* (Gorham Press: Boston, 1930). G. W. Van Vleck, *The Panic of 1857* (Columbia Univ. Press: New York, 1943) is a lucid explanation of the complication of political by economic crisis. The place of the antislavery movement in this story is still debated, but it is not so large as it once looked to be. The most important books are D. L. Dumond, *Anti-Slavery Origins of the Civil War in the United States* (Univ. of Michigan Press: Ann Arbor, Mich., 1939); Mary S. Locke, *Anti-Slavery in America, 1619–1808* (Ginn: Boston, 1901); Alice D. Adams, *Neglected Period of Anti-Slavery in America, 1808–1831* (Ginn: Boston, 1908); E. L. Fox, *The American Colonization Society, 1817–1840*. Johns Hopkins Univ. Studies, xxxvii, 3 (Johns Hopkins Press: Baltimore, Md., 1919); A. E. Martin, *The Anti-Slavery Movement in Kentucky prior to 1850*. Filson Club Pub., no. xxix (Standard Print Co. of Louisville: Louisville, Ky., 1918); G. H. Barnes, *The Anti-Slavery Impulse, 1830–1844* (Appleton-Century: New York, 1933); W. H. Siebert, *The Underground Railroad from Slavery to Freedom* (Macmillan: New York, 1898); Henrietta Buckmaster, *Let My People Go; the Story of the Underground Railroad* (Harper's: New York, 1941); R. B. Nye, *Fettered Freedom; Civil Liberties and the Slavery Controversy, 1830–1860* (Michigan State College Press: East Lansing, Mich., 1949); W. S. Savage, *The Controversy over the Distribution of Abolition Literature, 1830–1860* (Association for the Study of Negro Life and History, Inc.: Washington, D.C., 1938); Mary B. Putnam, *The Baptists and Slavery, 1840–1845* (G. Wahr: Ann Arbor, Mich., 1913); C. B. Swaney, *Episcopal Methodism and Slavery, with Sidelights on Ecclesiastical Politics* (R. G. Badger: Boston, 1926); J. N. Norwood, *The Schism in the Methodist Episcopal Church, 1844; a Study of Slavery and Ecclesiastical Politics*. Alfred Univ. Studies, i (Alfred, N.Y., 1923); and Madeleine H. Rice, *American Catholic Opinion in the Slavery Controversy*. Col. Univ. Studies, 508 (Columbia Univ. Press: New York, 1944). A. Y. Lloyd, *The Slavery Controversy, 1831–1860* (Univ. of N.

Carolina Press: Chapel Hill, N.C., 1939) is a belligerent re-statement of the older Southern view.[1]

The most radical changes in the interpretation of the events of the fifties are due to the influence of Turner and of Beard. Events in Washington take on a new appearance in the light of the study of the settlement of the Mississippi valley, and what was before written of in terms of the personal ambitions of politicians is now seen to have arisen from more deep-seated causes; while the constitutional issues have been made clearer by the study of the origins of the Constitution itself. The career of Stephen A. Douglas and the crucial Kansas-Nebraska Act of 1854 are better understood. Their elucidation was the work of P. O. Ray, *The Repeal of the Missouri Compromise* (Arthur H. Clark: Cleveland, O., 1909) and of a group of articles by F. H. Hodder that have unfortunately never been gathered together in book form, namely, 'Genesis of the Kansas-Nebraska Act'. *Wisconsin Hist. Soc. Proceedings, 1912*, pp. 69–86 (Madison, Wisc., 1913), 'The railroad background of the Kansas-Nebraska Act' (*Mississippi Valley Hist. Rev.*, xii (1925–6), pp. 3–22), and 'Some aspects of the English bill for the admission of Kansas'. *Annual Report of the American Historical Assoc. for the year 1906*, i, pp. 199–210 (Govt. Printing Office: Washington, D.C., 1908). To the first of these Ray replied in 'The genesis of the Kansas-Nebraska Act'. *Annual Report of the American Historical Assoc. for the Year 1914*, i, pp. 259–80 (*Ibid.*: Washington, D.C, 1916). To them are to be added, J. C. Malin, *Indian Policy and Westward Expansion*. Bulletin of the Univ. of Kansas, Humanistic Studies, ii, no. 3 (Lawrence, Kan., 1921), and *John Brown and the Legend of Fifty-six*. Memoirs of the American Philosophical Society, vol. xvii (Am. Philosophical Soc.: Philadelphia, 1942); M. M. Quaife, *The Doctrine of Non-intervention with Slavery in the Territories* (Chamberlin: Chicago, 1910); A. Johnson, *Stephen A. Douglas; a Study in American Politics* (Macmillan: New York, 1908); A. C. Cole, *The Era of the Civil War, 1848–1870*, being vol. iii of the 'Centennial History of Illinois' (Illinois Centennial Commission: Springfield, Ill., 1919); R. R. Russell, *Improvement of Communications with the Pacific Coast as an Issue in American Politics, 1783–1864* (Torch Press: Cedar Rapids, Ia., 1948); O. Lewis, *Sea Routes to the Gold Fields* (Knopf: New York, 1949); and G. D. Harmon, *Aspects of Slavery and Expansion, 1848–60*. Lehigh Univ. Pubs., iii, no. 7 (Bethlehem, Pa., 1929). Almost equally important has been the more careful study of the closely associated history of the Dred Scott decision, where again the drama of individual villainy has had thrown upon it a colder light,

---

[1] *Cf. Am. Hist. Rev.*, xlv (1940), 663-4; *Mississippi Valley Hist. Rev.*, xxvi (1939-40), 419-21; *Journal of Southern Hist.*, vi (1940), 271-3

so that the part played by Roger B. Taney is now seen to be different from what it was long represented to have been. The discussion has been extensive, but the salient facts and the most authoritative interpretations will be found in E. S. Corwin, *The Doctrine of Judicial Review* (Princeton Univ. Press: Princeton, 1914); Helen T. Catterall, 'Some antecedents of the Dred Scott case' (*American Hist. Rev.*, xxx (1923-4), pp. 56-71), and *Judicial Cases concerning American Slavery and the Negro*, 5 vv. (Carnegie Institution of Washington: Washington, D.C., 1926-37), v, pp. 113-22, 198-200; C. Warren, *The Supreme Court in United States History*, 2 vv. (Little, Brown: Boston; revd. ed., 1926); F. H. Hodder, 'Some phases of the Dred Scott case' (*Mississippi Valley Hist. Rev.*, xvi (1929-30), pp. 3-22); C. B. Swisher, *Roger B. Taney* (Macmillan: New York, 1935); and R. F. Nichols, *The Disruption of American Democracy* (Macmillan: New York, 1948).

In the study of the history of secession, the Middle Western school has been reinforced by a new school of Southern history. This Southern historiography has drawn its strength in part from the men who went out from Johns Hopkins in the closing years of last century, and in part from the influence of the Middle Western school itself. Its most vigorous centres have been North Carolina, Alabama and, more recently, Louisiana. A new coöperative *History of the South* in 10 volumes (Louisiana State Univ. Press: Baton Rouge, La., 1947+) is now in course of publication, and includes a volume by C. S. Sydnor on *The Development of Southern Sectionalism, 1819–1848* (1948). The monographic literature of the secession movement is, R. S. Cotterill, *The Old South. The Geographic, Economic, Social, Political and Cultural Expansion, Institutions, and Nationalism of the Ante-Bellum South* (Arthur H. Clark: Glendale, Calif., 1936); C. Eaton, *A History of the Old South* (Macmillan: New York, 1949); R. R. Russel, *Economic Aspects of Southern Sectionalism, 1840–1861.* Univ. of Illinois Studies in the Social Sciences, xi, nos. 1–2 (Urbana, Ill., 1924); J. G. Van Deusen, *The Ante-Bellum Southern Commercial Conventions.* Trinity College Hist. Soc. Papers, xvi (Duke Univ. Press: Durham, N.C., 1926), and *Economic Bases of Disunion in South Carolina.* Col. Univ. Studies, 305 (Columbia Univ. Press: New York, 1928); C. S. Boucher, *The Ante-Bellum Attitude of South Carolina towards Manufacturing and Agriculture.* Washington Univ. Humanistic Studies, iii, pt. ii, no. 2 (St. Louis, Mo., 1916); H. Wender, *Southern Commercial Conventions, 1837–1859.* Johns Hopkins Univ. Studies, xlviii, 4 (Johns Hopkins Press: Baltimore, Md., 1930); W. J. Cash, *The Mind of the South* (Knopf: New York, 1941); C. Eaton, *Freedom of Thought in the Old South* (Duke Univ. Press: Durham, N.C., 1940); J. T. Carpenter, *The South as a Conscious Minority* (New York Univ. Press: New York, 1930); U. B. Phillips, *The Course of the South to*

Secession; an Interpretation (Appleton-Century: New York, 1939);
D. L. Dumond, *The Secession Movement, 1860–1861* (Macmillan:
New York, 1931); D. L. Dumond (ed.), *Southern Editorials on Seces-*
sion. Publications of the American Hist. Assoc. (Appleton-Century:
New York, 1931); H. T. Shanks, *The Secession Movement in Virginia,*
1847–1861 (Garrett & Massie: Richmond, Va., 1934); J. C.
Sitterson, *The Secession Movement in North Carolina.* James Sprunt
Studies in Hist. & Pol. Sci., xxiii, no. 2 (Univ. of N. Carolina Press:
Chapel Hill, N.C., 1939); P. M. Hamer, *The Secession Movement in*
South Carolina, 1847–1852 (H. R. Haas: Allentown, Pa., 1918); C. S.
Boucher, *The Secession and Cooperation Movements in South Carolina,*
1848 to 1852, and *South Carolina and the South on the Eve of Secession,*
1852–1860. Washington Univ. Studies. Humanistic Ser., v. no. 2,
vi, no. 2 (St. Louis, Mo., 1918, 1919); H. S. Schultz, *Nationalism and*
Sectionalism in South Carolina, 1852–60; a Study of the Movement for
Southern Independence (Duke Univ. Press: Durham, N.C., 1950);
Laura A. White, *Robert Barnwell Rhett; Father of Secession* (Century:
New York, 1931); R. H. Shryock, *Georgia and the Union in 1850* (Duke
Univ. Press: Durham, N.C., 1926); F. G. Davenport, *Ante-Bellum*
Kentucky (Mississippi Valley Press: Oxford, O., 1943); Minnie C.
Boyd, *Alabama in the Fifties.* Col. Univ. Studies, 353 (Columbia Univ.
Press: New York, 1931); C. S. Davis, *The Cotton Kingdom in Alabama*
(Alabama State Dept. of Archives & Hist.: Montgomery, Ala.,
1939); C. P. Denman, *The Secession Movement in Alabama* (*Ibid.,* 1933);
P. L. Rainwater, *Mississippi; Storm Center of Secession, 1856–1861*
(Otto Claitor: Baton Rouge, La., 1938); W. M. Caskey, *Secession*
and Restoration of Louisiana (Louisiana State Univ. Press: University,
La., 1938); and R. W. Shugg, *Origins of Class Struggle in Louisiana.*
A Social History of White Farmers and Laborers during Slavery and after,
1840–1875 (Louisiana State Univ. Press: University, La., 1939).

iii. The understanding of the large and difficult subject of the
history of negro slavery in the United States is being gradually
advanced by the publication of regional studies. The institution
varied so much from time to time and place to place that firm ground
can only be reached by the patient study of local cases; and varying
widely though they do in quality, each of these studies has its value.
The most important investigations of the problem in its wider
aspects are A. H. Stone, *Studies in the American Race Problem* (Doubleday, Page: New York, 1908); G. Myrdal, *An American Dilemma; the*
Negro Problem and Modern Democracy, 2 vv. (Harper's: New York,
1944); C. H. Wesley, *Negro Labor in the United States, 1850–1925*
(Vanguard Press: New York, 1927); and S. D. Spero & A. L. Harris,
The Black Worker (Columbia Univ. Press: New York, 1931). Upon

Southern plantation life, see U. B. Phillips, *Life and Labor in the Old South* (Little, Brown: Boston, 1929); F. P. Gaines, *The Southern Plantation; a Study in the Development and Accuracy of a Tradition*. Col. Univ. Studies in English and Comparative Literature (Columbia Univ. Press: New York, 1924); J. H. Easterby (ed.), *The South Carolina Rice Plantation as revealed in the Papers of Robert F. W. Allston* (Univ. of Chicago Press: Chicago, Ill., 1945); U. B. Phillips & J. D. Glunt, *Florida Plantation Records from the Papers of George Noble Jones*. Pubs. of the Missouri Hist. Soc. (St. Louis, Mo., 1927); J. S. Bassett, *The Southern Plantation Overseer as revealed in his Letters*. Smith College Fiftieth Anniversary Publications (Northampton, Mass., 1925); W. T. Jordan, *Hugh Davis and his Alabama Plantation* (Univ. of Alabama Press: University, Ala., 1948); C. S. Sydnor (ed.), *A Gentleman of the Old Natchez Region. Benjamin L. C. Wailes* (Duke Univ. Press: Durham, N.C., 1938); W. H. Stephenson, *Alexander Porter, Whig Planter of Old Louisiana* (Louisiana State Univ. Press: Baton Rouge, La., 1934); and E. A. Davis (ed.), *Plantation Life in the Florida Parishes of Louisiana, 1836–1846, as reflected in the Diary of Bennet H. Barrow* (Columbia Univ. Press: New York, 1943). Upon the institution of slavery itself see, W. S. Jenkins, *Pro-Slavery Thought in the Old South* (Univ. of N. Carolina Press: Chapel Hill N.C., 1935), an ungainly but important book; T. E. Drake, *Quakers and Slavery in America*. Yale Hist. Pubs., li (Yale Univ. Press: New Haven, Conn., 1950); S. B. Weekes, *Southern Quakers and Slavery*. Johns Hopkins Univ. Studies, extra vol. xv (Johns Hopkins Press: Baltimore, Md., 1896); C. G. Woodson, *The Education of the Negro prior to 1861* (Putnam's: New York, 1915); U. B. Phillips, *American Negro Slavery* (Appleton: New York, 1918); W. E. B. DuBois, *The Suppression of the African Slave Trade to the United States of America*. Harvard Hist. Studies, i (Harvard Univ. Press: Cambridge, Mass., 1896); F. Bancroft, *Slave-Trading in the Old South* (J. H. Furst: Baltimore, Md., 1931); W. H. Collins, *The Domestic Slave Trade of the Southern States* (Broadway Publishing Co.: New York, 1904); J. C. Carroll, *Slave Insurrections in the United States, 1800–1865* (Chapman & Grimes: Boston, 1938). To these more comprehensive studies are to be added a group of works on the history of slavery in particular areas, L. J. Greene, *The Negro in Colonial New England*. Col. Univ. Studies, 494 (Columbia Univ. Press: New York, 1942); H. S. Cooley, *A Study of Slavery in New Jersey*. Johns Hopkins Univ. Studies, xiv, 9–10 (Johns Hopkins Press: Baltimore, Md., 1896); E. R. Turner, *The Negro in Pennsylvania, 1639–1861* (American Hist. Assoc.: Washington, D.C., 1911); J. R. Brackett, *The Negro in Maryland*. Johns Hopkins Univ. Studies, extra vol. vi (Johns Hopkins Univ. Press: Baltimore, Md., 1889); J. M. Wright, *The Free Negro in Maryland, 1634–1860.* Col. Univ. Studies, 222 (Columbia Univ. Press: New York, 1921); J. C. Ballagh, *A History of Slavery in Virginia.* Johns Hopkins Univ. Studies, extra vol. xxiv (Johns Hopkins Univ. Press: Baltimore, Md., 1902); T. M. Whitfield, *Slavery Agitation in Virginia, 1829–1832. Ibid.,* extra vol., n.s., x (*Ibid.,* 1930); B. B. Munford, *Virginia's Attitude toward Slavery and Secession* (Longman's: New York, 1909); L. P. Jackson, *Free Negro Labor and Property Holding in Virginia, 1830–1860* (Appleton-Century: New York, 1942); J. S. Bassett, *Slavery and Servitude in the Colony of North Carolina* and *Slavery in the State of North Carolina.* Johns Hopkins Univ. Studies, xiv, 4–5, xvii, 7–8 (Johns Hopkins Univ. Press: Baltimore, Md., 1896, 1899); R. H. Taylor, *The Free Negro in North Carolina* and *Slaveholding in North Carolina.* James Sprunt Hist. Pubs. xvii, 1, xviii, 1–2 (Univ. of N. Carolina Press: Chapel Hill, N.C., 1926); J. H. Franklin, *The Free Negro in North Carolina, 1790–1860* (Univ. of N. Carolina Press: Chapel Hill, N.C., 1943); J. S. Bassett, *The Anti-Slavery Leaders of North Carolina.* Johns Hopkins Univ. Studies, xvi, 6 (Johns Hopkins Press: Baltimore, Md., 1898); H. M. Henry, *The Police Control of Slavery in South Carolina* (Emory & Henry College: Emory, Va., 1914); R. B. Flanders, *Plantation Slavery in Georgia* (Univ. of N. Carolina Press: Chapel Hill, N.C., 1933); Ruth Scarborough, *Opposition to Slavery in Georgia.* Contributions to Education of George Peabody College for Teachers, no. 97 (Nashville, Tenn., 1933); C. T. Hickok, *The Negro in Ohio, 1802–1870* (Press of the Williams Publishing & Electric Co.: Cleveland, O., 1896); F. U. Quillin, *The Color Line in Ohio* (George Wahr: Ann Arbor, Mich., 1913); N. D. Harris, *Negro Servitude in Illinois* (A. C. McClurg: Chicago, Ill., 1904); H. A. Trexler, *Slavery in Missouri, 1804–1865.* Johns Hopkins Univ. Studies, xxxii, 2 (Johns Hopkins Press: Baltimore, Md., 1914); I. E. McDougle, *Slavery in Kentucky, 1792–1865* (The Journal of Negro History: Washington, D.C., 1918); C. P. Patterson, *The Negro in Tennessee, 1790–1865.* Univ. of Texas Bulletin, no. 2205 (Austin, Tex., 1922); J. B. Sellers, *Slavery in Alabama* (Univ. of Alabama Press: University, Ala., 1950); C. S. Sydnor, *Slavery in Mississippi* (Appleton-Century: New York, 1933); V. A. Moody, *Slavery on Louisiana Sugar Plantations* (Cabildo: New Orleans, La., 1924). Helen T. Catterall (ed.) *Judicial Cases concerning American Slavery and the Negro,* 5 vv. (Carnegie Institution of Washington: Washington, D.C., 1926–37), a work of immense labour and great erudition, gathers together a mass of material from the law reports relating to the character of the institution.

iv. The most authoritative recent account of the central crisis itself will be found in J. G. Randall, *The Civil War and Reconstruction*

(D. C. Heath: Boston, 1937). On the events of the winter of 1860–1861, see R. F. Nichols, *The Disruption of American Democracy* (Macmillan: New York, 1948); P. G. Auchampaugh, *James Buchanan and his Cabinet on the Eve of Secession* (priv. ptd.: Lancaster, Pa., 1926); Z. T. Johnson, *The Political Policies of Howell Cobb.* George Peabody College for Teachers Contributions to Education, no. 55 (Nashville, Tenn., 1929); W. N. Brigance, *Jeremiah Sullivan Black* (Univ. of Pennsylvania Press: Philadelphia, 1934); E. D. Fite, *The Presidential Campaign of 1860* (Macmillan: New York, 1911); O. Crenshaw, *The Slave States in the Presidential Election of 1860.* Johns Hopkins Univ. Studies, lxiii, no. 3 (Johns Hopkins Press: Baltimore, 1945); L. T. Lowrey, *Northern Opinion of Approaching Secession, Oct. 1859–Nov. 1860.* Smith College Studies in Hist., iii, 4 (Northampton, Mass., 1918); H. C. Perkins (ed.) *Northern Editorials on Secession,* 2 vv. (Appleton-Century: New York, 1942); P. S. Foner, *Business and Slavery; the New York Merchants and the Irrepressible Conflict* (Univ. of N. Carolina Press: Chapel Hill, N.C., 1941); Mary Scrugham, *The Peaceable Americans of 1860–1861; a Study in Public Opinion.* Col. Univ. Studies, 219 (Columbia Univ. Press: New York, 1921); C. F. Dunham, *The Attitude of the Northern Clergy toward the South, 1860–1865* (Gray Company: Toledo, O., 1942).

On the military conduct of the war the literature is very large. The best introductions to it are, Ellen C. Semple, *American History and its Geographic Conditions* (Houghton Mifflin: Boston, 1903; revd. ed. 1933); W. B. Wood & J. E. Edmonds, *The Civil War in the United States, with special reference to the Campaigns of 1864 and 1865* (Methuen, 1905; revd. ed., 1937); and M. F. Steele, *American Campaigns.* 1 vol. & atlas. Publication of General Staff, Second Section, no. 13. War Dept. doc. no. 324 (Byron S. Adams: Washington, D.C., 1909). Military administration is dealt with in F. A. Shannon, *The Organization and Administration of the Union Army, 1861–1865,* 2 vv. (Arthur H. Clark: Cleveland, O., 1928); A. H. Meneely, *The War Department, 1861; a Study in Mobilization and Administration.* Col. Univ. Studies, 300 (Columbia Univ. Press: New York, 1928); and Ella Lonn, *Desertion during the Civil War* (Century: New York, 1928): transportation, in F. P. Summers, *The Baltimore and Ohio in the Civil War* (Putnam's: New York, 1939). J. G. Nicolay and J. Hay, *Abraham Lincoln,* 10 vv. (Century: New York, 1890) is very largely a military history; and there are two classical studies of Southern generalship, G. F. R. Henderson, *Stonewall Jackson and the American Civil War,* 2 vv. (Longmans, 1898), and D. S. Freeman, *R. E. Lee; a Biography,* 4 vv. (Scribner's: New York, 1934–5).

The most penetrating study of the constitutional problems aroused by the war is still W. A. Dunning, *Essays on the Civil War and Recon-*

struction (Macmillan: New York, 1897), a book that seems rather curiously to have fallen out of American esteem, for it is now seldom spoken of by American writers with the warmth that it deserves. It belongs to a group of formative works produced in that and the following decade; and nothing that has been written since on this aspect of the subject really supersedes it, although J. G. Randall, *Constitutional Problems under Lincoln* (Appleton: New York, 1926) adds much detail. The study of one aspect of the subject has been elaborated in W. Gray, *The Hidden Civil War; the Story of the Copperheads* (Viking Press: New York, 1942), and G. F. Milton, *Abraham Lincoln and the Fifth Column* (Vanguard Press: New York, 1942).

An admirable introduction to the Lincoln literature is provided by D. M. Potter's lecture, *The Lincoln Theme and American National Historiography* (Clarendon Press: Oxford, 1948). There is a select bibliography by P. M. Angle, *A Shelf of Lincoln Books; a Critical, Selective Bibliography of Lincolniana* (Rutgers Univ. Press: New Brunswick, N.J., 1946); and a full list in J. Monaghan, *Lincoln Bibliography, 1839–1939*, 2 vv. Collections of the Illinois State Hist. Library, Bibliographical Series, iv, v (Illinois State Hist. Library: Springfield, Ill., 1943, 1945). The standard authorities on Lincoln are now, for the early years, A. J. Beveridge, *Abraham Lincoln, 1809–1858*, 2 vv. (Houghton Mifflin: Boston, 1928), and for the first two years of the war, J. G. Randall, *Lincoln the President; Springfield to Gettysburg*, 2 vv. (Dodd, Mead: New York, 1945). While the older literature upon Lincoln and the war is immense, modern scientific works, although they are now multiplying, are not yet very numerous and have not yet got, chronologically, to the end of the story. They are, D. W. Riddle, *Lincoln Runs for Congress* [1846] (Rutgers Univ. Press: New Brunswick, N.J., 1948); R. H. Luthin, *The First Lincoln Campaign* (Harvard Univ. Press: Cambridge, Mass., 1944); W. E. Baringer, *Lincoln's Rise to Power* (Little, Brown: Boston, 1937), and *A House Dividing; Lincoln as President Elect* (Abraham Lincoln Assoc.: Springfield, Ill., 1945); C. E. Macartney, *Lincoln and his Cabinet* (Scribner's: New York, 1931); B. J. Hendrick, *Lincoln's War Cabinet* (Little, Brown: Boston, 1946); R. S. West, jr., *Gideon Welles; Lincoln's Navy Department* (Bobbs-Merrill: Indianapolis, Ind., 1943); H. J. Carman & R. H. Luthin, *Lincoln and the Patronage* (Columbia Univ. Press: New York, 1943); W. B. Hesseltine, *Lincoln and the War Governors* (Knopf: New York, 1948); D. M. Potter, *Lincoln and his Party in the Secession Crisis*. Yale Hist. Pubs., xiii (Yale Univ. Press: New Haven, Conn., 1942); J. S. Tilley, *Lincoln Takes Command* (Univ. of N. Carolina Press: Chapel Hill, N.C., 1941); T. H. Williams, *Lincoln and the Radicals* (Univ. of Wisconsin Press: Madison, Wisc., 1941); K. P. Williams, *Lincoln Finds a General*, 2 vv. (Macmillan:

New York, 1949); J. Monaghan, *Diplomat in Carpet Slippers; Abraham Lincoln deals with Foreign Affairs* (Bobbs-Merrill: Indianapolis, Ind., 1945). J. G. Nicolay & J. Hay, *Abraham Lincoln*, 10 vv. (Century: New York, 1890) fails almost entirely to convey that first-hand political information that its authors possessed in such abundance. Very rarely in the course of the ten volumes is anything included that was not already a matter of public knowledge, such as the description of Lincoln's first meeting with Grant (viii, 340–4).

Not very much has yet been written upon the domestic history of the Northern or Border states during the war. There are two relatively early studies, E. D. Fite, *Social and Industrial Conditions in the North during the Civil War* (Macmillan: New York, 1910), and W. B. Weeden, *War Government, Federal and State, in Massachusetts, New York, Pennsylvania, and Indiana, 1861–1865* (Houghton Mifflin: Boston, 1906). And there are a few studies of the history of particular states during the war: Edith E. Ware, *Political Opinion in Massachusetts during Civil War and Reconstruction*. Col. Univ. Studies, 175 (Columbia Univ. Press: New York, 1916); J. R. Lane, *Political History of Connecticut during the Civil War* (Catholic Univ. of America Press: Washington, D.C., 1941); S. D. Brummer, *Political History of New York State during the Period of the Civil War*. Col. Univ. Studies, 103 (Columbia Univ. Press: New York, 1911); C. M. Knapp, *New Jersey Politics during the Period of the Civil War and Reconstruction* (W. F. Humphrey: Geneva, N.Y., 1924); S. L. Davis, *Pennsylvania Politics, 1860–1863* (The Bookstore, Western Reserve Univ.: Cleveland, O., 1935); G. H. Porter, *Ohio Politics during the Civil War*. Col. Univ. Studies, 105 (Columbia Univ. Press: New York, 1911); A. C. Cole, *The Era of the Civil War*, being vol. iii of the 'Centennial History of Illinois' (Illinois Centennial Commission: Springfield, Ill., 1919); K. M. Stampp, *Indiana Politics during the Civil War* (Indiana Hist. Bureau: Indianapolis, Ind., 1949); F. Merk, *Economic History of Wisconsin during the Civil War Decade*. Pubs. of the State Hist. Soc. of Wisconsin. Studies, i (Madison, Wisc., 1916); O. B. Clark, *The Politics of Iowa during the Civil War and Reconstruction* (Clio Press: Iowa City, Ia., 1911); Sceva B. Laughlin, *Missouri Politics during the Civil War* (the author: Salem, Or., 1930); E. C. Smith, *The Borderland in the Civil War* (Macmillan: New York, 1927); E. M. Coulter, *The Civil War and Readjustment in Kentucky* (Univ. of N. Carolina Press: Chapel Hill, N.C., 1926); T. Speed, *The Union Cause in Kentucky, 1860–1865* (Putnam's: New York, 1907); J. W. Patton, *Unionism and Reconstruction in Tennessee, 1860–1869* (Univ. of N. Carolina Press: Chapel Hill, N.C., 1934); and J. C. McGregor, *The Disruption of Virginia* (Macmillan: New York, 1922).

Not very much is yet known about the internal history of the

15

Confederacy, and J. C. Schwab, *The Confederate States of America, 1861–1865; a Financial and Industrial History of the South during the Civil War* (Scribner's: New York, 1901) is still the fullest general account. But new work is under way, and there is an important group of modern studies: R. S. Henry, *The Story of the Confederacy* (Bobbs-Merrill: Indianapolis, Ind., 1931); C. W. Ramsdell, *Behind the Lines in the Southern Confederacy* (Louisiana State Univ. Press: Baton Rouge, La., 1944); B. J. Hendrick, *Statesmen of the Lost Cause; Jefferson Davis and his Cabinet* (Little, Brown: Boston, 1939); R. W. Patrick, *Jefferson Davis and his Cabinet* (Louisiana State Univ. Press: Baton Rouge, La., 1944); W. M. Robinson, jr., *Justice in Grey; a History of the Judicial System of the Confederate States of America* (Harvard Univ. Press: Cambridge, Mass., 1941); F. L. Owsley, *State Rights in the Confederacy* (Univ. of Chicago Press: Chicago, Ill., 1925); A. B. Moore, *Conscription and Conflict in the Confederacy* (Macmillan: New York, 1924), C. E. Cauthen, *South Carolina goes to War, 1860–1865.* James Sprunt Studies in Hist. and Pol. Sci., xxxii (Univ. of N. Carolina Press: Chapel Hill, N.C., 1950); Ella Lonn, *Desertion of Alabama Troops from the Confederate Army.* Col. Univ. Studies, 378 (Columbia Univ. Press: New York, 1932), and *Salt as a Factor in the Confederacy* (Neale: New York, 1933); F. L. Owsley, *King Cotton Diplomacy* (Univ. of Chicago Press: Chicago, Ill., 1931); S. B. Thompson, *Confederate Purchasing Operations Abroad* (Univ. of N. Carolina Press: Chapel Hill, N.C., 1935); and F. E. Vandiver, *Confederate Blockade Running through Bermuda, 1861–1865; Letters and Cargo Manifests* (Univ. of Texas Press: Austin, Tex., 1947).

v. Work on the history of Reconstruction began with a group of political and constitutional studies that came from Johns Hopkins and Columbia, the latter inspired by Dunning. But this political approach to the subject is now recognized to be insufficient by itself, and more recent work has turned attention to the economic aspects. The important books are: C. E. Chadsey, *The Struggle between President Johnson and Congress over Reconstruction.* Col. Univ. Studies, 19 (Columbia Univ. Press: New York, 1896); H. K. Beale, *The Critical Year; a Study of Andrew Johnson and Reconstruction* (Harcourt, Brace: New York, 1930), a book that broke new ground; G. F. Milton, *The Age of Hate; Andrew Johnson and the Radicals* (Coward McCann: New York, 1930); C. H. Coleman, *The Election of 1868.* Col. Univ. Studies, 392 (Columbia Univ. Press: New York, 1933); A. Nevins, *Hamilton Fish; the Inner History of the Grant Administration* (Dodd, Mead: New York, 1936); T. S. Barclay, *The Liberal Republican Movement in Missouri* (State Hist. Soc. of Missouri: Columbia, Mo., 1926); B. B. Kendrick, *The Journal of the Joint Committee of Fifteen on*

Reconstruction, 39th Congress, 1865–1867. Col. Univ. Studies, 150
(Columbia Univ. Press: New York, 1914); H. E. Flack, *The Adoption
of the Fourteenth Amendment.* Johns Hopkins Univ. Studies, extra vol.
xxvi (Johns Hopkins Press: Baltimore, Md., 1908); J. M. Mathews,
Legislative and Judicial History of the Fifteenth Amendment. Johns Hopkins
Univ. Studies, xxvii, 6–7 (*Ibid.*, 1909); H. D. Farish, *The Circuit
Rider Dismounts; a Social History of Southern Methodism, 1865–1900*
(Dietz Press: Richmond, Va., 1938); W. S. Meyers, *The Self-
Reconstruction of Maryland, 1864–1867.* Johns Hopkins Univ. Studies,
xxvii, 1–2 (Johns Hopkins Press: Baltimore, Md., 1909); H. J.
Eckenrode, *The Political History of Virginia during the Reconstruction.*
Johns Hopkins Univ. Studies, xxii, 6–8 (*Ibid.*, 1904); A. W. Moger,
The Rebuilding of the Old Dominion (Edwards: Ann Arbor, Mich.,
1940); J. G. de R. Hamilton, *Reconstruction in North Carolina.* Col.
Univ. Studies, 141 (Columbia Univ. Press: New York, 1914);
J. P. Hollis, *The Early Period of Reconstruction in South Carolina.*
Johns Hopkins Univ. Studies, xxiii, 1–2 (Johns Hopkins Press:
Baltimore, Md., 1905); F. B. Simkins & R. H. Woody, *South
Carolina during Reconstruction* (Univ. of N.C. Press: Chapel Hill,
N.C., 1932); E. C. Woolley, *The Reconstruction of Georgia.* Col.
Univ. Studies, 36 (Columbia Univ. Press: New York, 1901);
C. Mildred Thompson, *Reconstruction in Georgia, 1865–1872.* Col.
Univ. Studies, 154 (*Ibid.*, 1915); W. W. Davis, *The Civil War
and Reconstruction in Florida.* Col. Univ. Studies, 131 (*Ibid.*, 1913);
E. M. Coulter, *The Civil War and Readjustment in Kentucky* (Univ. of
N. Carolina Press: Chapel Hill, N.C., 1926); J. W. Patton, *Unionism
and Reconstruction in Tennessee, 1860–1869* (Univ. of N. Carolina
Press: Chapel Hill, N.C., 1934); P. Clayton, *The Aftermath of the
Civil War in Arkansas* (Neale: New York, 1915); T. S. Staples,
Reconstruction in Arkansas. Col. Univ. Studies, 245 (Columbia Univ.
Press: New York, 1923); W. L. Fleming, *Civil War and Reconstruction
in Alabama* (Columbia Univ. Press: New York, 1905); J. W. Garner,
Reconstruction in Mississippi (Macmillan: New York, 1901); J. R.
Ficklen, *History of Reconstruction in Louisiana.* Johns Hopkins Univ.
Studies, xxviii, 1 (Johns Hopkins Univ. Press: Baltimore, Md.,
1910); G. W. McGinty, *Louisiana Redeemed; the Overthrow of Carpet-
Bag Rule, 1876–1880* (Pelican Publishing Co.: New Orleans, La.,
1941); C. W. Ramsdell, *Reconstruction in Texas.* Col. Univ. Studies,
95 (Columbia Univ. Press: New York, 1910). Upon the negro during
Reconstruction, see P. Lewinson, *Race, Class and Party; a History of
Negro Suffrage and White Politics in the South* (Oxford Univ. Press:
New York, 1932); P. S. Peirce, *The Freedman's Bureau.* Univ. of Iowa
Studies in the Social Sciences, iii, no. 1 (Iowa City, Ia., 1904);
Laura J. Webster, *The Operation of the Freedman's Bureau in South*

VI

Integration and Reform

THE history of the United States during the two generations that passed between the close of the period of Reconstruction in 1877 and the outbreak of the second World War in 1939 has been the subject of a wealth of historical studies that has no parallel in Great Britain. But only slowly and imperfectly is the general structure of this period revealing itself. To the normal obstacle of proximity there has been added that of the swiftness, scale and complexity of events both in the internal history of the United States and in the history of its relations to the external world. The historian, accordingly, has had to be content with the observation of here a phenomenon and there a phenomenon of which the origin and development can be studied, while he holds in suspense any attempt to judge how their relations with one another may finally be established. And the reader of the papers and monographs that have been published may well be baffled by the disparity and deficiency of the fragments out of which he struggles to make an intelligible whole.

Certain radical changes of circumstance are at once obvious to anyone looking back upon these years; and certain changes of political temper have as obviously flowed from them. But these are no sooner perceived than conflicting forces make their appearance, and the simplicity of the explanation is perplexed. The two most conspicuous changes in circumstance have been the closing of the frontier revealed by the census of 1890 and the revolution in the external economic relations of the United States consummated by the events of the first World

War. The one meant that land capable of conversion into a farm without heavy capital expenditure was no longer to be had for the payment of a $10.00 fee, and that the self-reliant habits of the frontier were no longer sufficient; the other, that an economic structure adapted to a passive balance of payments that had prevailed for three hundred years was out of date. The conjunction of the two within a generation, supervening as it did upon developments in social and economic structure which had themselves been greatly accelerated by the Civil War, induced radical changes in American political ideas and in the aims and methods of state and federal government. The result was a process of national integration that elevated public welfare and reasons of state into a criterion of political behaviour both at home and abroad. Yet if at first sight this promises to provide a theme that will comprehend the whole history of the period, it will not in fact do so. The contemporary mind was captured by the enlarged conception of the function of the state and the new enthusiasm that served it. But there is commonly a lag in public thinking. The solution of the problem of yesterday engages the public mind of to-day while the problem of to-day treads unnoticed upon its heel. Seized of the urgency of national integration, the American intelligence was unmindful of new challenges, whether from without or from within, to the omnicompetence of the nation. Yet in fact, sectionalism had been sunk in patriotism only to give place to new interior groups as ready as the old to claim the undivided allegiance of their members; and externally the new-found nationalism met obstacles both economic and political to its growing belief in its own self-sufficiency. The history of these new complexities must be added, therefore, to the story of a change in character and growth in strength answering new national needs. In the domestic history of the United States it comes to be necessary to substitute for the study of a nation a study of ' . . . a society of great collective aggregates'.[1] 'La démocratie,' it has been observed of another country, 'est, semble-t-

---

[1] R. Hofstadter, *Social Darwinism in American Thought, 1860–1915* (Philadelphia, 1945), p. 99.

il, à la recherche d'un moyen qui permette de peser des interêts collectifs, au lieu de compter les opinions individuelles.'[1] Upon the other hand, the sovereignty of the nation has likewise been diminished by the recognition, if only under the pressure of economic necessity, of membership of a larger whole. And there have been raised constitutional issues of great difficulty, embarrassing the simplicities of democratic nationalism with new confusions.

Victory in the Civil War spelled the prevalence of national over sectional interest and opened the way for the establishment of a popular absolutism at the federal level. But certain obstacles remained to block such an event. During the years of Reconstruction the union was a union achieved by force. And that union was not yet either a consolidated or an absolute state: for its citizens still owed a dual allegiance and could oppose sovereign to sovereign; and the popular fiat, at whatever level, was still subject to the control of a written constitution guarded by an independent judiciary. Two questions, therefore, awaited an answer. Could the newly-asserted principle of national supremacy be infused with life? And if it could, what was to become of divided sovereignty, of the rule of law, and of its guardian the Supreme Court?

The legal mould of the new national ideal was a revised conception of citizenship. The essential purpose in 1787 had been to establish a rule of law setting bounds to the authority of the several states, so that they might be restrained from injustice towards their members and from actions that were harmful to the interests of a larger whole. The bill of rights that was written into the new federal constitution was an exception to the pursuit of this end, and was intended to protect the citizens of the several states from the invasion of their inalienable rights by the new federal sovereign itself. Eighty years later, the boot was on the other foot; and the essential purpose of the Fourteenth and Fifteenth Amendments to the Constitution was to protect the rights of the citizens of the

[1]W. Martin, *Histoire de la Suisse* (Paris, 1929), p. 317.

larger whole from invasion by the sovereign authority of the parts. The distinction is subtle; and the history of citizenship in the United States is a highly complex matter of which no satisfactory or exhaustive study has yet been made. The establishment in 1787 of rights beyond the reach of the several states and of corresponding obligations to a higher law created a dual citizenship and a divided allegiance; and of the obligations of this dual citizenship secession had been a repudiation. But the Fourteenth and Fifteenth Amendments went further in this matter than the purpose of 1787. Not only were the citizens of a state to be amenable to a higher law and their inalienable rights guaranteed against invasion whether by state or union; but the civil rights of a new category, the citizens of the nation, were now intruded within the several states and their preservation guaranteed by an external authority.

This change, prompted by an anxiety to shelter the freedman, and bearing at first a negative and even a punitive aspect, quickly gathered impetus from a variety of confluent events. The conduct of the war itself and the patriotic devotion that it called for; the pecular circumstances of the settlement of the last unoccupied areas in the West; the economic and social transformation of the South after its defeat; and the emergence of social problems insusceptible of self-regulatory solution and beyond the scope of state control—all these alike fostered national consciousness and activity. By the end of the century there had developed reunion and a revived Southern patriotism, a belief in dynamic and not merely inhibitory federal government, and an exuberant self-confidence in foreign affairs. There were differences of opinion about the pace of reform and about the particular national instruments to be employed to promote it. But national integration and opposition to national integration appeared to make the sum of politics.

If the ardent and belligerent temper of the war years was itself, during the period of Reconstruction, often a disruptive rather than a unionist influence—for it was easy to exploit for partisan ends—no one will question the ultimate effect of the war upon the growth of the national spirit. The conduct, with whatever shortcomings, of large national affairs by federal departments and voluntary societies developed new national abilities. The very physical apparatus of life had to be adapted to a national scale. Most conspicuously, the Civil War promoted through traffic upon the railroads. Built initially to serve local needs, although the process of consolidation began in the fifties, the railroads were still physically and administratively ill-adapted to national purposes. No company before the war operated more than a thousand miles of line; and seven changes were necessary on a journey from New York to the Mississippi. The conduct of military operations on two widely separated fronts required both through freight and through passenger traffic. The standardization of material was stimulated and the process of consolidation accelerated. Federal legislation in 1866 authorizing through routes and through bills of lading removed some of the obstacles created by the terms of charters granted by the states to the railroads.[1] The maximum length of line under single operation increased between 1870 and 1880 to 5,000 miles, and after 1890 to 10,000; to be followed by the great consolidations of 1900 to 1910. But the cohesive impulse of the Civil War upon the social structure of the United States and the impetus that that gave to the adaptation of the instrumentalities of American life to use upon a larger scale have as yet been only roughly assessed.

The history of the last American frontier and of its influence upon the growth of the nation has on the contrary been the subject of a group of illuminating studies. It fell within the province of the dominant Mississippi valley school. Just as the settlers of the Middle West hesitated when they first reached the prairies of Illinois, so the whole migratory advance paused before moving out of the woods to settle the plains lying beyond the 98th meridian (map 7). For something like a generation the fertile soils of the eastern prairies and the arid lands that lay beyond them were a mere obstacle to be overcome when the emigrant left the shelter of the woodlands on the long journey to the Pacific coast. For this, the reasons were

[1] W. Z. Ripley, *Railroads: Rates and Regulation* (New York, 1913), p. 443.

simple enough, although it took W. P. Webb's book on *The Great Plains* (1931) to make them clear. In the first place, rich as much of the land was it could only be exploited when there had been provided a ready means of access to markets; and since the rivers that drained the area ceased in their upper reaches to be navigable, this meant that exploitation must await the building of railroads. In the second, no movement out upon the plains could be successful until the settlers changed their woodland habits to new ones adapted to the peculiar demands of the plains. On the prairies of Illinois the settler had been daunted by the lack of timber for cabin and fence, the want of shelter from wind and sun, the physical labour of breaking the prairie sod, the lack of easily reached water, the difficulties of transportation, and a superstition that an absence of timber denoted a poverty in the soil. Beyond the 98th meridian he found a land altogether devoid of timber and of surface water except along the river bottoms; and this was inhabited by mounted Indians who were a foe very different from what the Indian of the woods had ever been. He had therefore to learn, Professor Webb argues, to substitute for the bucket well, the rail fence, and the long rifle, a new set of tools—the small-bore well and windmill, barbed-wire fencing, and the revolver. It took him time to do so; and he was not ready until somewhere about the year 1880. By then two competitors had forestalled him. Since the close of the Civil War a cattle industry had spread over the great plains; and in the seventies mining began in the eastern foothills of the Rocky Mountains. There are three chapters, therefore, in the history of the last frontier; and the history of the break-up of the last of the great Indian reserves is an appendix to them. Those dealing with the cattle industry and with the agrarian settlement have been written, though they may still be subject to revision. That dealing with mining has hardly been begun. The mountain states are only just starting to gather together the materials upon which the historian must draw, and the history of the mining areas has in the main yet to be worked out.

The cattle industry of the Great Plains had a dual origin,

and it flourished between the close of the Civil War and the end of the century. An embryonic northern industry grew up on the ranges of what was to become western Montana in the forties and fifties, to serve the needs of the emigrants by the Oregon trail and of the western posts; and in the sixties further development was stimulated by the demands of the mining camps in Colorado and Montana, of the builders of the Union Pacific, and of the contractors who supplied the Indian reservations. In the South, in the forty years before the Civil War, there developed a cattle industry devoted to the marketing of the practically wild cattle of Texas, which were exported to New Orleans and other Gulf ports. After the war, these two centres of cattle production were joined. Stock accumulated in Texas during the war and was depleted elsewhere; and high prices drew supply to meet demand. Already, between 1858 and 1862, the markets of Colorado had been served by Mexicans of the upper Rio Grande; and a herd had occasionally been driven from Texas to the northern ranges. In 1865 this drive began on a large scale. But the Baxter trail, which was the first to be chosen, lay too much to the east, running through lands that were being rapidly settled; and the passage of the herds met with the stiff resistance of the settlers. This caused a reversion to the export of cattle by water, with the Red River and the Mississippi substituted for the Texan ports and New Orleans as the line of traffic. But the trade was difficult to handle; and a severe outbreak of Texas fever in Illinois led to its break-up in 1869 at the instance of the Illinois farmers. The solution came with the extension of the trans-continental railroads and the establishment, beyond the line of agricultural settlement, of stations at which the cattle could be received for shipment. The drive could now go further west and avoid the obstacles of the Baxter trail. Its destination was first the shipping point established at Abilene in 1866 and moved further west to Dodge City in 1872. And this trail led, moreover, to new markets as well as to new ways to old ones. As the buffalo vanished, the demand for cattle for the Indian reservations grew; and a new call came upon a more important scale for cattle to stock the northern ranges. Out of these elements the cattle industry of the great plains was organized between 1867 and 1880. In the north, the cattle were fed on open ranges on which a right of pasturage was enjoyed by the general consent of neighbouring cattlemen, but without legal title to the soil; and the ranges spread over Colorado, southwestern Wyoming, western Montana, and Dakota. From the south there continued to come the cattle driven over the trail. From both sources beasts went to supply the packing industry of Chicago. In the following decade the system was transformed by the substitution of the fenced ranch for the open range. This resulted from changes both in the market and in the west itself. The first successful export of dressed beef to Great Britain in 1875 and the growing export of live cattle from 1880 onwards were followed by a rapid rise in prices. The consequence was heavy investment in the early eighties and the overstocking of the ranges. This highly speculative position was struck by a fall in the prices and by the peculiarly severe winters of 1885–6 and 1886–7. At the same time the tide of settlement advanced with the advance of the railroads, and was further encouraged by the abnormal humidity of the semi-arid area during the years from 1876 to 1885. The arrival of the settlers threatened to obstruct access to the watering places; and sheep began to compete with cattle for the pasturage. The industry was driven to revise its assumptions and to modify its structure. It was clear that it was fallacious to regard the cattlemen as the merely temporary occupiers of the ranges where they would be succeeded by the farmers. There was now no further frontier for the cattlemen to move to; and the arid plains were discovered to be at that date no place for the farmer. Something more permanent and better organized than the rough and ready habits of the open range was needed; and on the prairies, where the farmers and the cattlemen met, the open range was incompatible with the farm. The answer was the fenced ranch and the more scientific production of a better quality of beef. After 1873 the practice had begun of driving Texan cattle northwards to be fattened on the ranges; and with the growing

scarcity of range there developed a similar partnership between
the ranges and the cornbelt. It was found to be to the interest
of the one to sell its animals earlier and not for immediate
slaughter but for fattening for the market by corn-feeding; and
to the interest of the other to avoid the burden of keeping breed-
ing animals or of feeders during their earlier stages. But for this
partnership to be successful it was necessary to provide cattle
for the ranges free from Texas fever and cattle more easily
handled upon the farm than the half-wild stock of the south.
Imports from the east had already begun to compete upon the
ranges with the Texan stock; and attention was now turned to
the improvement of breeds: and these needed for their proper
care the privately owned pasture and the irrigated forage crop.
The effect of this change in the north was the decline of the
drive. It was clearly threatened by the middle eighties. It
was virtually over by 1900. Instead there developed ranches
in Texas, New Mexico, and Oklahoma, and trunk-line communications between Texas and the northern ranges.

These events raised difficult problems in land title. In the
early stages the cattlemen were opposed to the idea that they
needed any legal title to land over which their stock could
range at will; and the land law framed for the farms of the
humid area east of the 98th meridian was ill-suited to one
where it took anything from ten to thirty acres to furnish grass
enough for a range steer. Since attempts to secure an amendment of the law that would permit of the purchase or leasing
of grazing lands were unsuccessful, when the ranges threatened
to become overcrowded and the industry had to be more
closely organized, the cattlemen had recourse to entry under
the Pre-emption, Homestead, or Desert Land Acts of tracts
that provided the water and thus carried effective control,
without legal title, of the area dependent upon that particular
source of supply. These entries were sometimes made by their
employees and deeded by them to the firm. Often they were
fraudulent pre-emption or homestead entries made by persons
willing, for a consideration, to deed to the cattle company on
completion. In either case the entry was followed by the illegal

fencing of the dependent area. As the management of the herds became more careful and a sound title to a larger area became more necessary, recourse was had also to the purchase of lands sold at foreclosure or for taxes, or to the purchase of railroad lands and the unauthorized fencing-in of government lands along with the alternate railroad sections.

Agricultural settlement beyond the 98th meridian had, as has already been said, to wait upon the railroads. The first considerable construction of railroads in the trans-Mississippi West occurred in the first tier of states beyond the river during the years 1851–6. But the roads were poorly built, and except in Texas their financial organization was unsound. They were reduced to ruin by the panic of 1857. During the war, construction was resumed; and with the removal of Southern representation from Congress the way was opened for the passage of the legislation that was necessary for the undertaking of the trans-continental lines. The Union Pacific and the Central Pacific were built between 1863 and 1869, and local systems were extended to the second tier of trans-Mississippi states. After a set-back by the panic of 1873, the advance was resumed; and the trans-continental system was completed between 1881 and 1893. Between 1866 and 1880 the farmer moved into the prairies of eastern Dakota, Nebraska, and Kansas; from the late seventies to the middle eighties there was a boom in trans-Mississippi settlement that carried him into the arid lands, to meet there the drought that set in in 1887 and lasted for ten years. It was a far less self-sufficient frontier than any that had been settled to the east of it. It was in greater measure than ever before the creature of the railroads; for these had here been built, not to link existing communities, but to make possible the founding of communities at all. Its inhabitants were not pioneers in the old sense. They had no advance guard like the screen of backwoodsmen who had covered the progress of earlier frontiers, moving ahead of the permanent settlers and making the first rough clearings; and they themselves were collected from the eastern states or were immigrants brought direct from the Atlantic ports, and were

hopped, like men in a game of halma, over the heads of their
forerunners out onto the margin of the advance. They sought
no self-sufficient livelihood provided by their own exertions
eked out with such help as neighbours might afford. At best,
they were men who ran an agricultural business; at worst,
'hands' in a farm factory that was soon to be mechanized.
They depended upon distant supplies for much that was
essential to them; they produced for distant markets over which
they had no control; and they were at the mercy of a system
of transportation that had no competitor, and that had made
and could un-make them. They had trusted, moreover, to an
accident of climate and to the uncovenanted indulgence of
outraged nature, cultivating in their habitual way land
that called for the special practices of arid farming and breaking the sod that alone protected the soil from erosion by wind
and water. When the drought struck them, therefore, not only
did they suffer grievously in their individual fortunes, but their
calamity was felt far beyond their borders. The real estate
boom that had accompanied the settlement had caused the
payment of inflated prices for farms and town lots, and had
encouraged excessive optimism about what was in any case
speculative railroad building. When the crops failed, the
burden of mortgage debt and heavy local taxation continued
unabated. In consequence, interest payments failed; there was
a collapse of land values; and there took place an almost complete abandonment of the extreme western settlements and a
large exodus from the central trans-Mississippi area, while
acute distress was felt by the surviving farmers in this central
and even in the eastern areas of the new settlement.

At the same time that this occurred there was acute agrarian
distress in the South. The emancipation of the slave and the
collapse of the plantation system had made necessary a reconstruction of Southern economy. Widespread sales of land at
nominal prices led to the substitution for the planter of the
small farmer whether as owner or tenant. With this disappearance of the plantation economy a new system was required for
the importation and distribution of consumer goods. Instead

of the wholesale trade with the planter who himself acted as the distributor, a retail trade grew up to supply the needs of the white farmers and the now self-dependent freedman. For lack of an adequate Southern banking system, the credit required by this new class of farmers was provided by a system of crop mortgage against store account. It encouraged a single-crop agriculture. Cotton was the product that could mostly readily find a market and most easily be handled by the creditor; and it was to his advantage that groceries, hay, and fertilizers should be bought from the store rather than that these purchases should be made less necessary by the diversification of the farm. At the same time, Northern capital was invested heavily in the building and extension of southern railroads, and these roads were integrated with the northern systems. Thus there grew up a new South that had much in common with the last frontier in the west. It continued to produce, as the old South had produced, for a distant market over which it had no control. But it was now, also, in large measure a land of small, indebted farmers, looking for their supplies to the manufacturing plant and the great commercial houses of the east and the Middle West, and served by a railroad system that was ceasing to be amenable to local control.

Upon these two already embarrassed communities there bore with peculiar severity a steady fall in prices and a rise in interest rates engendered by forces operating far beyond their borders. From their sufferings emerged an agrarian agitation, beginning with the Farmers' Alliances of the late seventies and early eighties and leading to the formation of the People's Party of 1892 and the capture by William Jennings Bryan of the Democratic nomination in 1896. That the movement in the end pinned its faith to the adoption of monetary policies of more than doubtful validity, and that it took as its leader a man who belonged to a world of rural simplicities that was rapidly vanishing, is of less importance than that it broke across the division of North and South and the boundaries of established political parties and forced attention to new problems of national scope that it had hitherto been to the interest of those parties to evade. Rejecting any theory of over-production as palpably absurd in the presence of a great volume of obviously unsatisfied consumptive capacity, and neglecting their own errors of judgment, the aggrieved sought the explanation of their troubles in a number of injustices inflicted upon them by alien powers. They were the victims, it seemed to them, of the malpractices of the railroads in particular and of the manipulation, by distinct and adverse interests, of the economic system in general: high railroad rates and discriminatory practices that operated to the disadvantage of particular shippers or particular places of shipment or delivery; land monopoly, and particularly large railroad holdings, that deprived the economically distressed of their traditional recourse; a tariff system that enhanced the price of what they bought when the prices of what they sold were settled in a world market; and a monetary system that had failed to supply a circulating medium either adequate in volume to the growing number of transactions or elastic enough to meet the seasonal variations in demand. And these things, to which they attributed their plight, were beyond their immediate control, and must be dealt with, if dealt with at all, at the federal level. It was in line with the traditions of the frontier, that was by nature a community of debtors, that the sovereign remedy should have seemed to lie in a change in monetary policy; and this suited the needs of the silver mining interest that had grown up in the mountain states of Nevada, Colorado, and Montana between 1860 and 1890, and was now suffering from a fall in demand consequent upon changes in European monetary policy between 1872 and 1876. And that they put their faith in this particular cure for their uneasiness was a fact of much political importance. It was a choice that drove them to look beyond the boundaries of states and sections. Because the reform so ardently desired needed, beyond question, the exercise of national authority, its inclusion in state platforms would have been futile. There could thus be no evasion by local option of the profound differences of opinion on the matter within the Democratic party, and no escape for

16

the South from the division of the white vote that it was so keenly anxious to avoid.

At the root of the monetary problem lay the perennial and unsolved difficulty of securing a supply of currency corresponding to the volume of business to be transacted. The effect of the Banking Act of 1863 had been that the amount of the circulating medium was determined, not upon grounds of national policy, but as a consequence of bank practice; and between 1886 and 1889 emissions fell by $1 million. The unhappy memory of the depreciation of the greenbacks issued during the war, and the bitter experience of the repudiation of Confederate notes had, however, discredited paper. Reflation by means of the monetization of silver was therefore a welcome alternative. It received support from a variety of interests; and its advocates won a number of modest legislative victories between 1878 and 1890 that have been adjudged, while falling short of the intentions of their promoters, to have offset factors that would have led to severe contraction.[1] But the cause was embarrassed by the assumption that any level of prices, once attained, must be supported, and by the logical difficulty of reconciling the frank intention of the mining interests that the price of silver should rise with the argument that the use of silver would have an inflationary influence. In the event, the creditors were badly frightened; the industrial workers failed to respond to the advocacy of a policy that promised a rise in prices; and the appreciation of gold was checked by the discoveries in Alaska and the increased output of the South African mines. Pressure from the silver states was relieved by the production of gold in Colorado and the rise in the price of domestic lead that was secured by the Dingley tariff of 1897. And recovery occurred without recourse to cheap money. Since, indeed, the most serious falls in agricultural prices had occurred upon the world market in the prices of wheat and cotton, substantial inflation of the domestic price-structure would in fact have embarrassed rather than relieved the agricultural com-

---

[1] J. P. Hütter, *L'incidence économique de la frappe de monnaie d'argent aux États-Unis de 1878 à 1893* (New York, 1938), pp. 41–5.

munity; and it may be that the silver movement should be regarded, when stripped of its more temporary and local features, as one of the first manifestations of resistance to the necessity of re-adjustment upon the part of a group who were becoming high-cost producers and should have been directing themselves to a new and different economic activity. Yet, if the cry of the 'people' *versus* the 'money power', with its belief that the gold standard was the prime cause of the distresses of the West and South after 1887 and its panacea of free silver, led the reformers on a false scent and resulted in their defeat and temporary eclipse, the episode forced upon the national attention a group of economic and social problems that, excepting the regulation of the currency, had not before been dealt with upon a national scale.

These problems, moreover, although most readily recognized upon the frontier were not peculiar to any section. Already gaining weight and momentum in the fifties, their development had been greatly accelerated by the war; and gathering speed they now broke upon a bewildered public that was at a loss to know how to deal with them. They were all, in one way or another, the result of the growth of the business corporation. This growth had been fostered under the aegis of the several states, where by separate legislative acts of incorporation special privileges had been conferred upon groups of private persons in return for the performance of public services or some other promotion of the public interest. The first effect of the Revolution had been to strengthen the control of the legislature over such bodies. With the disappearance of the royal charter that was beyond the reach of the colonial legislature came the belief that the legislature that now made could alter or unmake also.[1] But during the first half of the nineteenth century two further changes occurred. There grew up the idea that an act of incorporation was a contract creating rights, beyond the

[1] J. S. Davis, *Essays in the Earlier History of American Corporations*, 2 vv. (Cambridge, Mass., 1917), i, 49–72; *cf.* W. B. Munro, *The Government of American Cities* (New York, 1919), p. 5; O. & Mary F. Handlin, *Commonwealth: a Study of the Role of Government in the American Economy: Massachusetts, 1774–1861* (New York, 1947), p. 163.

recall of the legislature, to be enjoyed by these fictitious persons like the inalienable rights of the real persons in whose image they were made. At the same time, with the increasing employment of incorporation as a form of industrial and commercial organization, there was a weakening of the idea of an association of private persons for a public purpose who were endowed, for that reason, with a power of assessment; and there was a tendency to substitute for it that of a body of investors in a stock whose purpose was the earning of dividends and whose corporate privileges came to be regarded as a franchise. Before the Civil War, this situation was tempered by the wide distribution of corporate privileges and by the survival in the several states of a strong sense of social responsibility. Because of the absence of gross distinctions of class, there was at first no popular jealousy of the conferment of the privileges of incorporation; and when hostility towards corporations that exercised these privileges for purely private ends began to be felt, the obvious recourse seemed to be to reduce the advantage by making it more readily and more generally available. This was effected by legislation providing for incorporation by mere registration. And the aim, it has been observed, was rather to secure that anyone might become a capitalist and speculator than that a limited class of such persons should be socially controlled.[1] Yet, all the time, because of a long tradition of state action to promote the common interest that arose naturally from the popular character of state governments, state regulation of government-granted privilege was easily accepted; and the idea of inalienable rights was offset by a tendency to restrict those of a private corporation by the doctrine of affection with public interest. After the Civil War, three changes occurred simultaneously. The sphere of corporate activity broke across the boundaries of states and escaped the jurisdiction of state legislatures; the smaller competitors began to go to the wall before the monopolists; and doctrines of *laissez-faire* came to prevail. The problem had taken a new shape.

[1] *Journal of Economic History*, vi (New York, 1946), p. 82.

Of the new corporate monopoly the railroad was the earliest and most obvious example. Serious public discontent with the behaviour of the railroads first showed itself in the late sixties. It was prompted by the evidence of waste in the construction of the roads and of the jobbery and corruption practised by the promoters, by extortionate railroad charges, and by the growing recourse to pooling agreements by the companies. It was reinforced by the experience of the financial panic of 1873, which was due in a large measure to the over-building and mismanagement of the roads; and by the alienation of the good will of the West, where most of the new construction had taken place, when financial control passed, as it had by that date, to the East and to Europe, and when the progress of consolidation resulted in the concentration of management in eastern cities, the organization of through routes and the reduction of services to places of less importance. State and local support ceased in the West; opposition to federal aid to the railroads grew; the Grangers demanded between 1869 and 1874 the regulation of the railroads by state legislation; federal control began to be exercised over the bond-aided roads; and there arose a call for more extensive federal intervention upon the strength of the commerce clause of the Constitution. The complaint was that the roads failed to supply the services that were needed at rates that were reasonable, that they were becoming monopolies, and that they abused their power by discriminating between shippers and localities, extorting favours for favours granted; and it soon became evident that the several states were not suitable instruments for their better discipline. The function of the railroads in widening the market by lowering the cost to the marginal producer made them masters of the fortunes of the shippers, and enabled them to determine the place of manufacture and the point of distribution of manufactured goods by the wholesale to the retail dealer. Their weapons were the grant of personal rebates and local discrimination by means of varying charges for long and short hauls, the zonal rates of the trunk-line system, the Southern plan of basing points, and the postage-stamp rates of the trans-

Mississippi traffic. Neither through services nor non-discriminatory rates, that grew in importance with the growth of the traffic in livestock and grain to the seaboard for export, could be enforced by various and uncoördinated state enactments; and the state legislatures were not themselves without reproach. Federal intervention was sought first in the sixties to secure the building of bridges, in particular over the Ohio and the Mississippi, where there was a conflict between the rival interests of railroads and river navigation. It was sought next in order to secure through freights and through bills of lading, and the control of rates; and there was even an agitation for the construction of a federal road connecting the Mississippi valley with the eastern ports. It was called upon to promote the regulation of the conditions of the livestock traffic, and for the insurance of safety. After 1874, when a substantial reduction in rates followed upon the rate wars that had resulted in the establishment of the trunk-like system and upon the improvements in railroad mechanics and the economics of operation, it was looked to for the control, not so much of excessive, as of discriminatory rates, the spectacular abuse of which by the Standard Oil Company was conspicuously revealed by the report of the Hepburn Committee of the New York legislature in 1879. Public anxiety was increased by the rising threat of monopoly as pooling and other agreements spread, and by the rising volume of speculation and fraud in railroad finance and the growing lawlessness of the companies. The issue was clinched by the decision of the Supreme Court in the case of the Wabash, St. Louis & Pacific Railway Co. v. Illinois in 1886, when the Court held that a distinction must be made between the exercise of state jurisdiction over interstate commerce pending congressional action where the effect was substantially confined within the state and diversity of treatment could be tolerated, and the exercise of such a jurisdiction when it clearly affected matters in which a diversity of treatment would not be tolerable; that a right of continuous transport was essential to that freedom of commerce the Constitution was intended to guarantee; and that if the regulation of such transport was necessary it must be regulation by federal authority. The problem thus cast upon the nation might be dealt with in a variety of ways. But thenceforth there could be no doubt but that to deal with it in one way or another was an inescapable national responsibility.

Railroads were, however, only a single if peculiarly obvious case of the problems created by the growth of the business corporation and the tendency to monopoly. The scale of the American market, and the freedom and intensity of the struggle within it, encouraged large-scale organization and were both a temptation and a spur to combinations of businesses engaged in particular branches of production or distribution. Taking a variety of legal forms, such combinations resulted, upon the one hand, in the creation of what amounted in substance to a monopoly but rested upon the mere size and efficiency of business organization, or in the establishment, upon the other, of complete or nearly complete monopoly by means of the control of the whole or nearly the whole supply of a particular commodity or service, or the enjoyment, by virtue of patent, charter, or other legal grant, of some special privilege. Prompted, probably in a greater degree than has commonly been allowed, by a desire to avoid the waste and losses of unregulated production, they were nevertheless ruthless and unscrupulous in the treatment of their competitors, and waged economic warfare upon them; and in pursuit of their ends they corrupted the government agencies and the legislatures that had the disposal of franchises, charters, patents and other sources of artificial monopoly. And once established they were in a position to exploit the consumer and exercise a tyrannical power over the labour that they employed. They effected, it is true, substantial economies, making great savings in industrial waste and cross freights, promoting the use of more efficient organization and plant, checking over-production and reducing the irregularity of the demand for labour; and it is arguable that the consumer was, in the long run, not badly, though he might have been better, served. But what was immediately obvious was the ruin of competitors, the scale of profits, the exploitation of the opportunity for gross over-capitalization, and the helplessness of labour. And the effect was to arouse the fear and hatred of rival, consumer, and employee. But it was in line with established ideas about the business corporation that it was the misfortunes, not of the consumer or of the employee, but of the competitor that were the first to awaken sympathy. Labour had to have recourse, not to protection by public regulation, but to the mere opposition of power to power; and a new and more vigorous chapter opened in the history of American trade unions. Yet here, again, the problems were national in scope and insusceptible of solution at the state level.

The response to these problems was determined by the prevailing climate of opinion. Where public interest may be the interest of either the state or the union, there will be a disposition when it is predicated of the one for private right to appeal to the other. Before the Civil War no broad regulation of economic enterprise throughout the country had been attempted by Congress; and the formulation of rules setting limits in the public interest to what private persons might be permitted to do had, in the main, been the act of the several states. In consequence the most important commerce cases that had come before the Supreme Court of the United States had related, not to the federal regulation of commerce, but to state laws encroaching upon the federal sphere or violating rights guaranteed by the federal Constitution. In dealing with these, the tendency of the Court, particularly during the chief-justiceship of Roger B. Taney (1836–64), had been to uphold the police power of the states against limitation by the national authority. But the aim of the appellants to federal jurisdiction had been the prevention of regulation; and nationalism thus became the ally of *laissez-faire*. Of the intellectual domination exercised by the doctrine of *laissez-faire*, with which the tradition of the Supreme Court could be made so neatly to fit, and of the way in which this gave place between 1885 and 1915 to a new view of the functions of the state, an account has been written by R. Hofstadter in a study of *Social Darwin-*

ism in American Thought, 1860-1915 that is one of the most illuminating contributions yet made to the understanding of this period. By 1880, intellectual circles in the United States had been converted to a general acceptance of the teaching of Darwin; and the social implications of it, as they were displayed in the volumes of Herbert Spencer's *Synthetic Philosophy* and his separate *Study of Sociology*, first published serially in 1872–3, had obtained a wide currency, enjoying their greatest vogue between 1870 and 1890. Of this individualist and *laissez-faire* school the most effective American exponent was W. G. Sumner, described by Dr. Hofstadter as combining 'the functions of a great Puritan preacher, an exponent of the classical pessimism of Ricardo and Malthus, and a popularizer and assimilator of evolution.'[1] And Sumner went beyond Spencer in accepting the trade union as a competitive instrument preferable to the alternative of recourse to state regulation. To this school of thought the first important challenge was offered by L. F. Ward's *Dynamic Sociology* published in 1883. It advocated governmental regulation as politically justifiable now that political power had passed to the people, and as intellectually justifiable on the ground that social forces were susceptible of use, as physical forces were used, to promote social welfare; and in place of natural determinism it offered artificial choice, purposeful activity, social engineering, the planned control of society by society as a whole. Such a social philosophy was what the critics of the shortcomings of American society between 1870 and 1900 were looking for. It provided, at the same time, a theoretical foundation for the social gospel that was growing out of the experiences of the clergy, and particularly of those working in the urban communities; and it suited the teachings of Henry George and Edward Bellamy. Its content was deepened, after the turn of the century, by two notable events in the history of ideas. Pragmatism lent its authority to what Dr. Hofstadter describes as 'active human effort in the bettering of life'; and a change in economic thought occurred that put an

---

[1] R. Hofstadter, *Social Darwinism in American Thought, 1860–1915* (Philadelphia, 1944), p. 37.

emphasis upon the historical and statistical method, and upon the acceptance of relativity and a less dogmatic orthodoxy, of which the beginning had been marked by the foundation of the American Economic Association in 1885. It was also reinforced by two other contemporary intellectual developments. A discussion of the nature of sovereignty, having its roots in the experiences of the Civil War, powerfully stimulated by the German training of so many of the leading American thinkers of the period, was begun with J. N. Pomeroy's *Introduction to the Constitutional Law of the United States*, of 1875; and culminated in the publication of J. W. Burgess's two volumes on *Political Science and Comparative Law* in 1890–1 and W. W. Willoughby's volume on *The Nature of the State* in 1896. It led to the exposition of the doctrine of the legal omnipotence of the state. Simultaneously, the reconciliation of North and South became the source of a powerful national emotion. Sharing a common sorrow, and discovering a common pride in the prowess of the combatants and the character and genius in particular of Lee, the sections united in nursing the heroic and romantic traditions of the war and of Southern civilization; and a new Southern literature grew up that was written for, and in the main supported by, not a Southern but an American or indeed a Northern, public, as Dr. Buck has pointed out.

Thus in a variety of ways the idea of a dynamic national policy came to possess the more active and progressive minds in many walks of life.[1] ' . . . No century of slow and half-understood experience,' wrote Henry Adams in 1889, 'could be needed to prove that the hopes of humanity lay thenceforward, not in attempting to restrain the government from doing whatever the majority should think necessary, but in raising the people themselves till they should think nothing necessary but what was good.'[2] And there is a consequent unity in the fifty years that lie between the first administration of Grover Cleveland and the New Deal of the nineteen-thirties. From the first tentative steps of the one to the full vigour of the other

---

[1] *Cf.* J. Bryce, *The American Commonwealth*, 3 vv. (1888), ii, 411.
[2] H. Adams, *History of the United States of America*, 9 vv. (1909–17), i, 130.

there is a steady progression. The observation of Bryce in 1888 that 'the State is not to them, as to Germans or Frenchmen, and even to some English thinkers, an ideal moral power, charged with the duty of forming the characters and guiding the lives of its subjects. It is more like a commercial company, or perhaps a huge municipality created for the management of certain business in which all who reside within its bounds are interested, levying contributions and expending them on this business of common interest, but for the most part leaving the shareholders or burgesses to themselves,'[1] has been invalidated by the exercise of a national absolutism in the name of public welfare. And this makes comparatively easy the orderly apprehension of many difficult subjects. Each separately is full of technical complexities, and each separately will need its own literature for its full exploration. But each falls readily into its place in a single story of national organization. From the first measures of the eighties and nineties there is a continuous development through the administrations of Theodore Roosevelt and Woodrow Wilson to the achievements of the thirties. In the first place, the closing of the frontier called for a new immigration policy and for the conservation of natural resources. The first general federal immigration law, enacted in 1882, was followed by a series of more and more stringent measures prompted by the increase of pauperism and insanitary conditions in the great cities, the jealousy of organized labour for the preservation of its standards, and the immense immigration of the years between 1900 and 1914. They culminated in the highly restrictive act of 1921. With the disappearance in 1890 of the last of the free land, the end of the period of mere reckless consumption of the accumulations of the ages was in sight. Much has been written about the building of new homes in the West; and it is indeed a patent truth that the sparsely inhabited hinterland has been made the abode of a new society. But the pioneer, moving out from the Atlantic seaboard across the continent, was set first upon extracting a living, and as much more than a living as could be had, from the virgin re-

[1] *The American Commonwealth*, 3 vv. (1888), iii, 472–3.

sources of the unexploited wilderness. 'Vermont', writes a recent student of the early history of that state with reference to a time half a century after its settlement had begun, ' . . . had never been an agricultural community in the true sense. The people, in obedience to their pioneer necessities, had ruined the state rather than cultivated it.'[1] The game, the forests, the water-power, the fertility of the soil, the very soil itself were wasted under the spur of urgent and reckless necessity or the temptation of profit. And in the course of the century, as county was added to county and state to state, tier by tier the devastation moved across the continent, the wastage as opportunity offered extending to coal, oil, natural gas, and minerals. The scientists and the responsible officers of the federal government began in the seventies and eighties to call public attention to the improvidence of this prodigal destruction of the national wealth; and an agitation for the adoption of measures of conservation gathered weight in the nineties. The first effective action was taken by Theodore Roosevelt in the opening years of the new century; and conservation became thenceforth a widely debated matter of public policy. Within the fixed horizon of the closed frontier the nation then addressed itself to the mastery of a rapidly changing economy. The increase of urbanization and the multiplication of wage-earners made more insistent the demand for municipal reform and for the regulation of the hours and conditions of labour. The menace of the selfishness and irresponsibility of the great aggregations of capital and of their special manifestations in the shape of railroad and power companies called for an insistence upon the overriding claims of public interest and the invention of an instrument of government competent to make that claim prevail; and a new organ was developed in the shape of the commission, beginning in the federal sphere with the Interstate Commerce Commission of 1887, and designed to secure the application of the right reasoning of properly informed and technically qualified persons to novel social problems. The con-

[1] L. D. Stillwell, *Migration from Vermont, 1776–1860.* Proceedings of the Vermont Historical Society (Montpelier, Vt., 1937), p. 154, *cf.* 232.

stitutional responsibility of the federal government for monetary policy presented the necessity of a choice between the creation of self-regulatory conditions or a managed currency, variously answered in the Federal Reserve Act of 1913 and the experiments of the New Deal. Under the impact of two wars, the negative measures of the last quarter of the nineteenth century designed to restore conditions of free competition gave place to positive measures of control; and by legislative enactment and judicial interpretation the federal police power was immensely enlarged. And in order that these new responsibilities might be adequately discharged great efforts were made to reform the civil service, to improve the way in which the national budget is framed, and to re-organize the executive departments.

To this immense task of national organization, shared in so large a measure by all modern states, there were added three subordinate problems, of which two were peculiarly American. They were those of the adjustment of the relation of federal power to the powers of the states, the determination whether effective political leadership was to be exercised by the legislature or the executive, and the identification of the place of the Supreme Court in what was tending increasingly to become the omnicompetent state. In respect to the first, the mere scale of modern economic operations has been decisive and the sixty years have seen the progressive interference of federal authority in matters hitherto regarded as lying within the province of the states. In respect to the second, down to the Civil War policy making had been the function of Congress, and Bryce thought in 1888 that Congress would, 'did it possess a better internal organization, be even more plainly than it now is the supreme power in the government.'[1] But in fact, a change had already begun; and the experience of Cleveland was of more than personal significance. At the outset of his first administration he conceived of his duty as 'executive work', like the governorship of the state of New York that he had regarded as 'a business engagement between the people of the

[1] *The American Commonwealth*, 3 vv. (1888), i, 304; *cf.* 350, but see also iii, 655–6.

State and myself, in which the obligation on my side is to perform the duties assigned to me with an eye single to the interests
of my employers'. But by the time of his second administration
he was ready to constrain Congress to give effect to presidential
policy and to appeal if necessary from the representatives to the
represented. 'Behind these direct representatives of the people,'
he wrote in September, 1893, 'there was a sentiment that
actually *drove* them to duty'; and with that sentiment he
thought of himself as being in alliance.[1] Since that date there
have been fluctuations, and there may well be more; but the
general trend is unmistakable. Presidential leadership has grown
enormously; and on critical occasions the president now becomes a more efficient vehicle of the popular will than the
legal representatives of the people assembled in Congress.
Of the effect of recent history upon the place of the Supreme
Court in the political structure of the United States it is more
difficult to form an opinion. McLaughlin has observed, 'In
the eighteenth century a fixed constitution was the ideal of
men ending or hoping to end the long struggle between super-
imposed government and personal safety; by the end of the
nineteenth century the fixed Constitution, with the balanced
system so dear to the men of the earlier days, was considered
the stronghold of conservatism, which was secured by the
complexity of the governmental system.'[2] It is certainly the
case that the reverence shown by the Court during the last
decades of the nineteenth century for the doctrine of *laissez-
faire* brought it into ill repute; and the growth in the twentieth
century of belief in popular absolutism has discredited the
conception of judicial review. Yet the Court has shown, as it
showed during the period of Reconstruction, remarkable
powers of survival; and it may be in process of resuming that
creative function that it discharged during the earlier years of
its history. The infinitely complex and rapidly moving problems of modern society will not yield to legislative fiat alone.

[1] A. Nevins (ed.), *Letters of Grover Cleveland, 1850–1908* (Boston, 1933), pp. 99,
18, 334, 351, 377.
[2] A. C. McLaughlin, *A Constitutional History of the United States* (New York, 1936),
pp. 723–4.

They call also for more skilled and more subtle ratiocination; and this, in respect at least to those matters not relegated because of their technical character to a specially qualified body, the Court can provide.

BIBLIOGRAPHICAL NOTE

i. It has always to be borne in mind by the student of this period of American history that he is dealing with rapidly increasing orders of magnitude. It is important therefore to keep an eye upon statistics. Of these there are two convenient historical collections, A. P. Andrew, *Statistics for the United States, 1867–1909*. National Monetary Commission. 61 Cong., 2 Sess., S. Doc. 570 (Govt. Printing Office: Washington, D.C., 1910), and *Historical Statistics of the United States, 1789–1945; a Supplement to the Statistical Abstract of the United States* (Department of Commerce: Washington, D.C., 1949). To these may be added, the *Statistical Atlas*. Prepared under the supervision of Henry Gannett, Geographer of the Twelfth Census (United States Census Office: Washington, D.C., 1903). On population, see also W. S. Thompson & P. K. Whelpton, *Population Trends in the United States* (McGraw Hill Book Co.: New York, 1933).

ii. There is a valuable general sketch of the history of the period by C. A. Beard, *Contemporary American History, 1877–1913* (Macmillan: New York, 1914). But the best approach to an understanding of it is offered by a group of studies of social ideas and their gradual embodiment in new political machinery. The most valuable of these are R. Hofstadter, *Social Darwinism in American Thought, 1860–1915* (Univ. of Pennsylvania Press: Philadelphia, 1944); E. R. Lewis, *A History of American Political Thought from the Civil War to the World War* (Macmillan: New York, 1937); and H. S. Commager, *The American Mind; an Interpretation of American Thought and Character since the 1880's* (Yale Univ. Press: New Haven, Conn., 1950). To these are to be added, C. E. Merriam, *American Political Ideas; Studies in the Development of American Political Thought, 1865–1917* (Macmillan: New York, 1920; revd. ed. 1929); F. E. Haynes, *Social Politics in the United States* (Houghton, Mifflin: Boston, 1924); C. McA. Destler, *American Radicalism, 1865–1901*. Connecticut College Monograph, no. 3 (New London, Conn., 1946); J. Dorfman, *The Economic Mind in American Civilization*, vol. iii, *1865–1918* (Viking Press: New York, 1949); S. Chugerman, *Lester F. Ward* (Duke Univ.

Press: Durham, N.C., 1939); T. H. Greer, *American Social Reform Movements; their Pattern since 1865* (Prentice Hall: New York, 1949); J. Dombrowski, *The Early Days of Christian Socialism in America* (Columbia Univ. Press: New York, 1936); C. H. Hopkins, *The Rise of the Social Gospel in American Protestantism, 1865–1915* (Yale Univ. Press: New Haven, Conn., 1940); H. F. May, *Protestant Churches and Industrial America* (Harper's: New York, 1949); H. J. Browne, *The Catholic Church and the Knights of Labor* (Catholic Univ. of America Press: Washington, D.C., 1949). P. H. Buck, *The Road to Reunion, 1865–1900* (Little, Brown: Boston, 1937) is an original and valuable study of the growth of national sentiment. A. K. Weinberg, *Manifest Destiny; a Study of Nationalist Expansionism in American History* (Johns Hopkins Press: Baltimore, Md., 1935) traces the operation of that sentiment in foreign affairs.

C. B. Swisher, *American Constitutional Development* (Houghton, Mifflin: Boston, 1943), while covering the whole period of the history of the United States, is fuller for the years since 1865 and is the first authoritative survey of the constitutional changes that occurred during that time. It is amplified in a group of special studies, Professor Swisher's own monograph on *Roger B. Taney* (Macmillan: New York, 1935); B. R. Twiss, *Lawyers and the Constitution; how 'laissez-faire' came to the Supreme Court* (Princeton Univ. Press: Princeton, N.J., 1942); B. F. Wright, jr., *The Contract Clause of the Constitution* (Harvard Univ. Press: Cambridge, Mass., 1938); B. R. Trimble, *Chief Justice Waite, Defender of Public Interest* (Princeton Univ. Press: Princeton, N.J., 1938); and W. L. King, *Melville Weston Fuller, Chief Justice of the United States, 1888–1910* (Macmillan: New York, 1950). I. F. Sharfman, *The Interstate Commerce Commission,* 4 vv. in 5 (The Commonwealth Fund: New York, 1931–7) is an important and illuminating study of a new instrument of government, but is only in part historical.

iii. Because, doubtless, of the dominant influence of the Middle Western school, the most thoroughly explored aspect of the period is the history of the West. Katharine Coman, *Economic Beginnings of the Far West*, 2 vv. (Macmillan: New York, 1912; revd. ed. in 1 vol., 1925); W. P. Webb, *The Great Plains* (Ginn, 1931); D. E. Clark, *The West in American History* (Thomas Y. Crowell: New York, 1937); and E. Dick, *Vanguards of the Frontier; a Social History of the Northern Plains and Rocky Mountains from the Earliest White Contacts to the Coming of the Homemaker* (Appleton-Century: New York, 1941) are general works covering more than these years. Of the importance of Webb's book something has been said above at pp. 35, 217–18. The early phases of the penetration of the trans-Mississippi West are dealt with in C. Goodwin, *The Trans-Mississippi West, 1803–1853* (Appleton: New York, 1922); E. W. Gilbert, *The Exploration of Western America, 1800–1850* (Cambridge Univ. Press: Cambridge, 1933); and J. C. Bell, *Opening a Highway to the Pacific, 1838–1846.* Col. Univ. Studies, 217 (Columbia Univ. Press: New York, 1921). The works more particularly devoted to the last chapter in the history of settlement are, F. L. Paxson, *The Last American Frontier* (Macmillan: New York, 1910); N. Anderson, *Desert Saints; the Mormon Frontier in Utah* (Univ. of Chicago Press: Chicago, Ill., 1942); E. Dick, *Sod-house Frontier, 1854–1890* (Appleton: New York, 1937); W. C. Holden, *Alkali Trails; or Social and Economic Movements of the Texas Frontier, 1846–1900* (The Southwest Press: Dallas, Tex., 1930); C. C. Rister, *The South-Western Frontier, 1865–1881* (A. H. Clark: Cleveland, O., 1928), *Southern Plainsmen* (Univ. of Oklahoma Press: Norman, Okla., 1938), and *Land Hunger; David L. Payne and the Oklahoma Boomers* (*Ibid.*, 1942); R. Gittinger, *Formation of the State of Oklahoma.* Univ. of California Pubs. in Hist., vi (Univ. of California Press: Berkeley, Calif., 1917); and H. O. Brayer, *William Blackmore*, vol. i, *The Spanish-Mexican Land Grants of New Mexico and Colorado, 1863–1878* (Bradford-Robinson: Denver, Colo., 1949). The period is also covered in vol. v of the 'Economic History of the United States', F. A. Shannon, *The Farmers' Last Frontier; Agriculture, 1860–1897* (Farrar & Rinehart: New York, 1945). The history of the cattle industry takes a prominent place, and it has been the subject of a group of special studies, L. Pelzer, *The Cattlemen's Frontier; a Record of the Trans-Mississippi Cattle Industry from Oxen Trains to Pooling Companies, 1850–1890* (Arthur H. Clark: Glendale, Calif., 1936); E. E. Dale, *The Range Cattle Industry* and *Cow Country* (Univ. of Oklahoma Press: Norman, Okla., 1930, 1942); E. S. Osgood, *The Day of the Cattleman* (Univ. of Minnesota Press: Minneapolis, Minn., 1929); J. A. Hopkins, jr., *Economic History of the Production of Beef Cattle in Iowa* (State Hist. Soc. of Iowa: Iowa City, Ia., 1928); O. B. Peake, *The Colorado Range Cattle Industry* (Arthur H. Clark: Glendale, Calif., 1937); and R. G. Cleland, *The Cattle on a Thousand Hills; Southern California, 1850–1870* (Huntington Library: San Marino, Calif., 1941). The study of the history of mining has barely been begun, and there are only one or two monographs on the subject, W. J. Trimble, *The Mining Advance into the Inland Empire.* Univ. of Wisconsin Bulletin, no. 638 (Madison, Wisc., 1914); C. H. Shinn, *Land Laws of Mining Districts.* Johns Hopkins Univ. Studies, ii, 12 (Johns Hopkins Press: Baltimore, Md., 1884), and *Mining Camps; a Study in American Frontier Government*, edited by J. H. Jackson (Knopf: New York, 1948); and T. A. Rickard, *A History of American Mining* (McGraw Hill Book Co.: New York, 1932). On the extravagant misuse of the hitherto untouched riches of the continent, see C. R. Van Hise, *The Conservation of Natural Resources in the United States* (Macmillan: New York, 1910).

The political aspects of the last phases of the settlement have been the subject of two valuable monographs, S. J. Buck, *The Granger Movement . . . 1870–1880.* Harvard Hist. Studies, xix (Harvard Univ. Press: Cambridge, Mass., 1913), and J. D. Hicks, *The Populist Revolt; a History of the Farmers' Alliance and the People's Party* (Univ. of Minnesota Press: Minneapolis, Minn., 1931). There have also been a few local studies, more numerous for the South than for the Northwest, F. E. Haynes, *Third Party Movements since the Civil War, with special reference to Iowa* (State Hist. Soc. of Iowa: Iowa City, Ia., 1916), and *James Baird Weaver* (*Ibid.*, 1919); P. R. Fossum, *The Agrarian Movement in North Dakota.* Johns Hopkins Univ. Studies, xliii, no. 1 (Johns Hopkins Press: Baltimore, Md., 1925); A. F. Bentley, *The Condition of the Western Farmer as illustrated by the Economic History of a Nebraska Township* (Johns Hopkins Press: Baltimore, Md., 1893); D. M. Robison, *Bob Taylor and the Agrarian Revolt in Tennessee* (Univ. of N. Carolina Press: Chapel Hill, N.C., 1935); R. L. Hunt, *A History of the Farmer Movements in the Southwest, 1873–1925* (A. & M. College of Texas: College Station, Tex., 1935); R. C. Martin, *The People's Party in Texas; a Study in Third Party Politics* (Univ. of Texas Press: Austin, Tex., 1933); J. B. Clark, *Populism in Alabama* (Auburn Print Co.: Auburn, Ala., 1927); W. du B. Sheldon, *Populism in the Old Dominion; Virginia Farm Politics, 1885–1900* (Princeton Univ. Press: Princeton, N.J., 1935); S. A. Delap, *The Populist Party in North Carolina.* Trinity College Hist. Soc. Papers, xiv (Durham, N.C., 1922); S. Noblin, *Leonidas Lafayette Polk, Agrarian Crusader* (Univ. of N. Carolina Press: Chapel Hill, N.C., 1949); F. B. Simkins, *The Tillman Movement in South Carolina* (Duke Univ. Press: Durham, N.C., 1926), and *Pitchfork Ben Tillman* (Louisiana State Univ. Press: Baton Rouge, La., 1944); R. P. Brooks, *The Agrarian Revolution in Georgia, 1865–1912.* Univ. of Wisconsin Bulletin, no. 639. Hist. Ser., iii, 3 (Madison, Wisc., 1914); A. M. Arnett, *The Populist Movement in Georgia.* Col. Univ. Studies, 235 (Columbia Univ. Press: New York, 1922); C. Vann Woodward, *Tom Watson, Agrarian Rebel* (Macmillan: New York, 1938); W. W. Brewton, *Life of Thomas E. Watson* (the author: Atlanta, Ala., 1926); and R. C. McGrane, *William Allen; a Study in Western Democracy* (Ohio State Arch. & Hist. Soc.: Columbus, O., 1925).

iv. On the monetary history that figured so largely in the thoughts of the West, see D. R. Dewey, *Financial History of the United States* (Longmans: New York, 6th ed., 1918); A. D. Noyes, *Forty Years of*

American Finance, 1865–1907 (Putnam's: New York, 2nd ed., 1909); A. B. Hepburn, *History of Currency in the United States* (Macmillan: New York, revd., ed., 1924), M. S. Wildman, *Money Inflation in the United States* (Putnam's: New York, 1905); F. Simiand, *Inflation et stabilisation alternées; le développement économique des États-Unis* (F. Loviton: Paris, 1934); J. P. Hütter, *La question de la monnaie d'argent aux États-Unis des origines à 1900*, and *L'incidence économique de la frappe de monnaie d'argent aux États-Unis de 1878 à 1893* (E. C. Stechert: New York, 1938). On the panic of 1893, see O. M. W. Sprague, *History of Crises under the National Banking System.* National Monetary Commission. 61 Cong., 2 Sess., S. Doc. 538 (Govt. Printing Office: Washington, D.C., 1910); and W. J. Lauck, *The Causes of the Panic of 1893* (Houghton, Mifflin: Boston, 1907). F. P. Weberg, *The Panic of 1893* (The Catholic Univ. of America: Washington, D.C., 1929) is a jejune academic exercise.

The literature of railroad history has been dealt with above, pp. 154–7.

v. The history of the commercial and industrial areas has, in this as in former periods, been much less worked upon than the history of the West. There is an illuminating introductory study, T. C. Cochran & W. Miller, *The Age of Enterprise; a Social History of Industrial America* (Macmillan: New York, 1942); and much factual information will be found in V. S. Clark, *History of Manufactures in the United States*, 3 vv. (Carnegie Institution of Washington; Washington, D.C., 1929), and E. R. Johnson *et al.*, *History of Domestic and Foreign Commerce of the United States*, 2 vv. (*Ibid.*, 1915).

The history of modern business corporations only becomes intelligible when seen against the earlier history of incorporation in the several states; and the Social Science Research Council has put in hand a valuable series of investigations of which three have been published, O. & Mary F. Handlin, *Commonwealth; a Study of the Role of Government in the American Economy: Massachusetts, 1774–1861* (New York Univ. Press: New York, 1947); L. Hartz, *Economic Policy and Democratic Thought: Pennsylvania, 1776–1860* (Harvard Univ. Press: Cambridge, Mass., 1948); and J. W. Cadman, jr., *The Corporation in New Jersey; Business and Politics, 1791–1875* (Harvard Univ. Press: Cambridge, Mass., 1949). In the study of recent developments it becomes increasingly difficult to distinguish between historical work and that which belongs strictly to other branches of learning. But there is much historical matter in C. R. Van Hise, *Concentration and Control: a Solution of the Trust Problem in the United States* (Macmillan: New York, new ed., 1914); J. W. Jenks & W. E. Clark, *The Trust Problem* (Doubleday & Page: New

York, 4th ed., 1917); J. D. Clark, *The Federal Trust Policy*. Johns Hopkins Univ. Studies. Extra vol., n.s., xv (Johns Hopkins Univ. Press: Baltimore, Md., 1931); O. W. Knauth, *The Policy of the United States towards Industrial Monopoly*. Col. Univ. Studies, 138 (Columbia Univ. Press: New York, 1914); and A. A. Berle, jr., & G. C. Means, *The Modern Corporation and Private Property* (Macmillan: New York, 1933). There have also now been written a number of studies of particular industries, some of them more and some less historical in method and varying much in scope and quality. They are, T. A. Rickard, *A History of American Mining* (McGraw Hill Book Co.: New York, 1932); H. R. Mussey, *Combination in the Mining Industry*. Col. Univ. Studies, 60 (Columbia Univ. Press: New York, 1905); E. Jones, *The Anthracite Coal Combination in the United States* (Harvard Univ. Press: Cambridge, Mass., 1914); P. H. Giddens, *The Birth of the Oil Industry* (Macmillan: New York, 1938); C. C. Rister, *Oil! Titan of the Southwest* (Univ. of Oklahoma Press: Norman, Okla., 1949); Ida M. Tarbell, *The History of the Standard Oil Company*, 2 vv. (Macmillan: New York, 1904–11); A Nevins, *John D. Rockefeller*, 2 vv. (Scribner's: New York, 1940); R. H. Maybee, *Railroad Competition and the Oil Trade* (Extension Press, State Teachers College: Mt. Pleasant, Mich., 1940); A. Berglund, *The United States Steel Corporation, a Study of the Growth and Influence of Combination in the Iron and Steel Industry*. Col. Univ. Studies, 73 (Columbia Univ. Press: New York, 1907); B. J. Hendrick, *The Life of Andrew Carnegie*, 2 vv. (Doubleday, Doran: Garden City, 1932); G. Harvey, *Henry Clay Frick* (Scribner's: New York, 1928); Ida M. Tarbell, *Life of Elbert H. Gary; the Story of Steel* (Appleton: New York, 1925); J. V. Woodworth, *American Tool Making and Interchangeable Manufacturing* (Page: London, 1921); M. B. Hammond, *The Cotton Industry* (Macmillan: New York, 1897); M. T. Copeland, *The Cotton Manufacturing Industry of the United States*. Harvard Econ. Studies, viii (Harvard Univ. Press: Cambridge, Mass., 1912); A. H. Cole, *The American Wool Manufacture*, 2 vv. (Harvard Univ. Press: Cambridge, Mass., 1926); P. L. Vogt, *The Sugar Refining Industry in the United States; its Development and Present Condition* (Univ. of Pennsylvania Press: Philadelphia, 1908); R. G. Blakey, *The United States Beet Sugar Industry and the Tariff*. Col. Univ. Studies, 119 (Columbia Univ. Press: New York, 1912); Nannie M. Tilley, *The Bright-Tobacco Industry, 1860–1929* (Univ. of N. Carolina Press: Chapel Hill, N.C., 1948); W. N. Baer, *The Economic Development of the Cigar Industry in the United States* (The Art Print Co.: Lancaster, Pa., 1933); R. A. Clemen, *The American Livestock and Meat Industry* (Ronald Press: New York, 1923); C. B. Kuhlmann, *The Development of the Flour-Milling Industry in the United States* (Houghton, Mifflin: Boston, 1929). Something has also been done to write the history of the industrialization of the South in B. B. Kendrick & A. M. Arnett, *The South Looks at its Past* (Univ. of N. Carolina Press: Chapel Hill, N.C., 1935); B. Mitchell, *The Rise of the Cotton Mills in the South.* Johns Hopkins Univ. Studies, xxxix, no. 2 (Johns Hopkins Press: Baltimore, Md., 1921); B. & G. S. Mitchell, *The Industrial Revolution in the South* (Johns Hopkins Press: Baltimore, Md., 1930); H. Thompson, *From the Cotton Field to the Cotton Mill; a Study of Industrial Transition in North Carolina* (Macmillan: New York, 1906); and Ethel M. Armes, *The Story of Coal and Iron in Alabama* (Chamber of Commerce: Birmingham, Ala., 1910). But the most valuable recent work has been that done upon the history of individual business houses and individual industrial towns.

The scope and quality of work being done upon business history may be judged by the masterly *Guide to Business History. Materials for the Study of American Business History and Suggestions for their Use* by Henrietta M. Larson (Harvard Univ. Press: Cambridge, Mass., 1948). The most important studies of individual firms are, H. J. Thornton, *The History of the Quaker Oats Company* (Univ. of Chicago Press: Chicago, Ill., 1933); R. M. Hower, *History of an Advertising Agency: N. W. Ayer & Son at Work, 1869–1939* (Harvard Univ. Press: Cambridge, Mass., 1939); G. S. Gibb, *The Whitesmiths of Taunton: a History of Reed & Barton, 1824–1943 (Ibid.,* 1943); R. M. Hower, *History of Macy's of New York, 1858–1919 (Ibid.,* 1943); C. W. Moore, *Timing a Century; History of the Waltham Watch Company (Ibid.,* 1945); S. B. Clough, *A Century of American Life Insurance; a History of the Mutual Life Insurance Company of New York* (Columbia Univ. Press: New York, 1946); Evelyn H. Knowlton, *Pepperell's Progress; History of a Cotton Textile Company, 1844–1945* (Harvard Univ. Press: Cambridge, Mass., 1948); T. C. Cochran, *The Pabst Brewing Company* (New York Univ. Press: New York, 1948); G. S. Gibb, *The Saco-Lowell Shops; Textile Machinery Building in New England, 1813–1949* (Harvard Univ. Press: Cambridge, Mass., 1950); T. R. Navin, *The Whitin Machine Works since 1831; a Textile Machinery Company in an Industrial Village (Ibid.,* 1950); S. E. Morison, *The Ropemakers of Plymouth; a History of the Plymouth Cordage Company, 1824–1949* (Houghton Mifflin: Boston, 1950).

Constance McL. Green, *Holyoke, Massachusetts; a Case History of the Industrial Revolution in America.* Yale Hist. Pubs., xxxiv (Yale Univ. Press: New Haven, Conn., 1939) is a model of what urban history can contribute to the illustration of this period, and Mrs. Green has added to it a *History of Naugatuck, Connecticut (Ibid.,* 1948). W. B. Munro, *The Government of American Cities* (Macmillan: New York, 1912) is a useful general introduction to the subject. Other valuable histories of individual towns are E. L. Bogart,

Peacham; the Story of a Vermont Hill Town (Vermont Hist. Soc.: Montpelier, Vt., 1948); Vera Shlakman, *Economic History of a Factory Town; a Study of Chicopee, Massachusetts.* Smith College Studies in Hist., xx, 1–4 (Northampton, Mass., 1935); S. L. Wolfbein, *The Decline of a Cotton Textile City; a Study of New Bradford.* Col. Univ. Studies, 507 (Columbia Univ. Press: New York, 1944); H. C. Syrett, *The City of Brooklyn, 1865–1898.* Col. Univ. Studies, 512 (Columbia Univ. Press: New York, 1944); T. J. Wertenbaker, *Norfolk; Historic Southern Port* (Duke Univ. Press: Durham, N.C., 1931); G. M. Capers, jr., *The Biography of a River Town; Memphis, its Heroic Age* (Univ. of N. Carolina Press: Chapel Hill, N.C., 1939); B. McKelvey, *Rochester, the Water-Power City, 1812–1854*, and *Rochester, the Flower City, 1855–1890* (Harvard Univ. Press: Cambridge, Mass., 1945, 1949); G. Ross, *Cleveland; the Making of a City* (World Publishing Co.: Cleveland, O., 1950); Bessie L. Pierce, *A History of Chicago*, 2 vv. (Knopf: New York, 1937, 1940); D. Garwood, *Crossroads of America; the Story of Kansas City* (Norton: New York, 1948); G. B. Catlin, *The Story of Detroit* (The Detroit News: Detroit, Mich., 1923); B. Still, *Milwaukee; the History of a City* (State Hist. Soc. of Wisconsin: Madison, Wisc., 1948); Mildred L. Hartsough, *The Twin Cities as a Metropolitan Market; a Regional Study of the Economic Development of Minneapolis and St. Paul.* Univ. of Minnesota Studies in the Social Sciences, xviii (Minneapolis, Minn., 1925); and A. Binns, *Northwest Gateway; a History of the Port of Seattle* (Doubleday, Doran: Garden City, N.Y., 1941).

The first serious study of the history of organized labour was made by J. R. Commons at Wisconsin between 1904 and 1934,[1] and bore fruit in J. R. Commons *et al.*, *A Documentary History of American Industrial Society*, 10 vv. (A. H. Clark: Cleveland, O., 1910–11) and a *History of Labor in the United States*, 4 vv. (Macmillan: New York, 1918–35). There is a more summary treatment by one of the contributors to the larger work, S. Perlman, *History of Trade Unionism in the United States* (Macmillan: New York, 1922); a more recent general survey in F. R. Dulles, *Labor in America; a History* (Thomas Y. Crowell: New York, 1949); and a study of a special aspect of the subject in Marion C. Cahill, *Shorter Hours; a Study of the Movement since the Civil War.* Col. Univ. Studies, 380 (Columbia Univ. Press: New York, 1932). N. J. Ware, *The Labor Movement in the United States, 1860–1895* (Appleton: New York, 1929) is a highly condensed and a difficult, but valuable and important, book that deals with the crucial transition from the Knights of Labor to the American Federation of Labor. It is continued by L. Wolman, *The Growth of American Trade Unions, 1880–1923* (National Bureau

[1] *Cf.* J. R. Commons, *Myself* (New York, 1934), pp. 128–38.

of Economic Research: New York, 1924), and L. L. Lorwin, *The American Federation of Labor* (Brookings Institution: Washington, D.C., 1933). The two leaders, of the Knights and of the Federation respectively, have left their own record, T. V. Powderley, *Thirty Years of Labor, 1859–1889* (Excelsior Publishing House: Columbus, O., 1889), H. J. Carman & P. N. Guthrie (eds.), *The Path I Trod; the Autobiography of Terence V. Powderley* (Columbia Univ. Press: New York, 1940), and S. Gompers, *Seventy Years of Life and Labor; an Autobiography*, 2 vv. (Dutton: New York, 1925); and there are two secondary studies of Gompers, R. H. Harvey, *Samuel Gompers, Champion of the Toiling Masses* (Stanford Univ. Press: Stanford Univ., Calif., 1935), and L. S. Reed, *The Labor Philosophy of Samuel Gompers*. Col. Univ. Studies, 327 (Columbia Univ. Press: New York, 1930). The study of the history of labour in the several states has barely begun. There are I. B. Cross, *A History of the Labor Movement in California* (Univ. of California Press: Berkeley, Calif., 1935); L. Eaves, *A History of California Labor Legislation, with an Introductory Sketch of the San Francisco Labor Movement*. Univ. of California Pubs. in Economics, ii (Univ. Press: Berkeley, Calif., 1910); and E. H. Downey, *History of Labor Legislation in Iowa* (State Hist. Soc. of Iowa: Iowa City, Ia., 1910). Some of the outstanding events in labour history have been the subject of special studies, S. Yellen, *American Labor Struggles* (Harcourt, Brace: New York, 1936); J. W. Coleman, *Labor Disturbances in Pennsylvania, 1850–1880* (Catholic Univ. of America: Washington, D.C., 1936); *Official History of the Great Strike of 1866 on the Southwestern Railway System* (Bureau of Labor Statistics and Inspection: Jefferson City, Mo., 1887); H. David, *The History of the Haymarket Affair; a Study in the American Social-Revolutionary and Labor Movements* (Farrar & Rinehart: New York, 1936); A. C. Hutson, jr., *The Coal Miners' Insurrection of 1891 in Anderson County, Tennessee*. East Tenn. Hist. Soc. Pub., vii (Knoxville, Tenn., 1935); D. L. McMurray, *Coxey's Army; a Study of the Industrial Army Movement of 1894* (Little, Brown: Boston, 1929); and A. Lindsey, *The Pullman Strike; the Story of a Unique Experiment and of a Great Labor Upheaval* (Univ. of Chicago Press: Chicago, Ill., 1942). There are also studies of two of the protagonists in the Pullman strike, McA. Coleman, *Eugene V. Debs, a Man Unafraid* (Greenberg: New York, 1930); R. Ginger, *The Bending Cross; a Biography of Eugene Victor Debs* (Rutgers Univ. Press: New Brunswick, N.J., 1949); W. R. Browne, *Altgeld of Illinois, 1847–1902* (B. W. Heubsch: New York, 1924); and H. Barnard, *'Eagle Forgotten'; the Life of John Peter Altgeld* (Duell, Sloan & Pearce: New York, 1938). The history of the relations of government with organized labour is discussed in E. Berman, *Labor Disputes and the President of the United States*. Col. Univ. Studies,

249 (Columbia Univ. Press: New York, 1924); B. M. Rich, *The Presidents and Civil Disorder* (The Brookings Institution: Washington, D.C., 1941); H. L. Hurwitz, *Theodore Roosevelt and Labor in New York State, 1880–1900.* Col. Univ. Studies, 500 (Columbia Univ. Press: New York, 1943); and F. Frankfurter & N. Greene, *The Labor Injunction* (Macmillan: New York, 1930). The histories of individual unions are few, scattered, very various in quality and hard to come by. They are D. J. McDonald & E. A. Lynch, *Coal and Unionism; a History of the American Coal Miners' Union* (Lynald Brooks: Silver Spring, Md., 1940); C. Evans, *History of the United Mine Workers of America from the year 1860 to 1900*, 2 vv. (priv. ptd.: Indianapolis, 1918–20); J. S. Robinson, *The Amalgamated Association of Iron, Steel, and Tin Workers.* Johns Hopkins Univ. Studies, xxxviii, no. 2 (Johns Hopkins Press: Baltimore, Md., 1920); F. T. Stockton, *The International Molders' Union of North America.* Johns Hopkins Univ. Studies, xxxix, no. 3 (*Ibid.*, 1921); W. F. Bucknam, *A History of Boston Division Number Sixty-one Brotherhood of Locomotive Engineers* (Bliss: Boston, 1906); B. R. Brazeal, *The Brotherhood of Sleeping Car Porters; its Origin and Development* (Harper's: New York, 1946); L. Stuckey, *The Iowa Federation of Labor.* Univ. of Iowa Studies in the Social Sciences, iv, 3 (Iowa City, Ia., 1915); E. Staley, *History of the Illinois State Federation of Labor* (Univ. of Chicago Press: Chicago, Ill., 1930); G. A. Stevens, *New York Typographical Union No. 6; Study of a Modern Trade Union and its Predecessors* (State Dept. of Labor: Albany, N.Y., 1912); Augusta E. Galster, *The Labor Movement in the Shoe Industry, with special reference to Philadelphia* (The Ronal Press: New York, 1924); C. J. Stowell, *Studies in Trade Unionism in the Custom Tailoring Trade* (Journeyman Tailors' Union of America: Bloomington, Ill., 1913); and W. Carsel, *A History of the Chicago Ladies' Garment Workers' Union* (Normandie House: Chicago, Ill., 1940).

vi. If in dealing with the literature relating to economic events it is difficult to distinguish what may be regarded as historical works from what is contemporary discussion, it is still more so in the realm of politics. There is a large literature on political science dealing with American experience that is not historical in method and must be omitted here. Upon the subject of political structure and upon political parties and party history, the classical works are J. Bryce, *The American Commonwealth*, 3 vv. (Macmillan, 1888), and *Modern Democracies*, 2 vv. (Macmillan, 1921); and M. Y. Ostrogorsky, *La démocratie et l'organisation des partis politiques*, 2 vv. (Calmann-Levy: Paris, 1903; new ed. in 1 vol., 1912). The latter work was first published in translation, *Democracy and the Organization of Political Parties*, 2 vv. (Macmillan: New York, 1902); of the American section there is a separate issue, *Democracy and the Party System in the United States* (Macmillan: New York, 1910). *The American Commonwealth* is for this period an original authority rather than an historical work; and, except for a number of political biographies, there has been little historical investigation of the fortunes of the established parties. The important books are H. C. Thomas, *The Return of the Democratic Party to Power in 1884.* Col. Univ. Studies, 203 (Columbia Univ. Press: New York, 1919); A. Nevins, *Grover Cleveland* (Dodd, Mead: New York, 1932); and G. H. Knoles, *The Presidential Campaign and Election of 1892* (Stanford Univ. Press: Stanford Univ., Calif., 1942). There are two historical studies of machine politics in the period, H. F. Gosnell, *Boss Platt and his New York Machine* (Univ. of Chicago Press: Chicago, Ill., 1924), and Edith Dobie, *The Political Career of Stephen Mallory White; a Study of Party Activities under the Convention System* (Stanford Univ. Press: Stanford Univ., Calif., 1927); and there is a group of books on the closely allied topics of the civil service and military pensions, C. R. Fish, *The Civil Service and the Patronage.* Harvard Hist. Studies, xi (Longmans, Green: New York, 1905); D. H. Smith, *The United States Civil Service Commission. Its History, Activities, and Organization* (Johns Hopkins Press: Baltimore, Md., 1928); F. M. Stewart, *The National Civil Service Reform League* (Univ. of Texas: Austin, Tex., 1929); W. D. Foulke, *Fighting the Spoilsmen; Reminiscences of the Civil Service Reform Movement* (Putnam's: New York, 1919); J. W. Oliver, *History of Civil War Military Pensions.* Univ. of Wisconsin Bulletin, no. 844 (Madison, Wisc., 1917); W. H. Glasson, *History of Military Pension Legislation in the United States.* Col. Univ. Studies, 32. (Columbia Univ. Press: New York, 1900), and *Federal Military Pensions in the United States* (Oxford Univ. Press: New York, 1918).

VII

New Complexities

'IT was national integration', it has been said, 'which triumphed at Appomattox. It was national integration which marked every important development in the years that followed.'[1] But the apparent simplicity of the history of national integration and reform is deceptive. J. F. Rhodes, much praised for the tolerance shown in his *History of the United States from the Compromise of 1850* (7 vv., 1893–1906), betrayed a new bitterness in the supplementary volume dealing with the years 1877 to 1898. It had become possible to write without prejudice of the conflict between North and South; but new fissures were opening, and an ironmaster found it difficult to write without prejudice about the relations of capital and labour. The trust and the trade union, if not also the party machine, each showed a tendency towards self-sufficiency, each becoming increasingly a law to itself, obedient only to the dictates of its own necessity, calling for the undivided and unlimited allegiance of its members, placing itself in a relation of mere power to the other and to the community, so that there unconsciously emerged a conception of 'total' business[2] and 'total' unionism, corresponding to total war in the political state, that knew no rule of behaviour but success and offered as flat a challenge to the new patriotism as any sectional division with its roots in geography.

Of this development the history has as yet been very imperfectly examined. In the business world, the change had its roots in the differentiation of the private from the public corp-

[1] P. H. Buck, *The Road to Reunion, 1865–1900* (Boston, 1937), p. vii.
[2] *Cf.* T. C. Cochran & W. Miller, *The Age of Enterprise* (New York, 1943), pp. 75–6, 88–9.

oration and in the acquisition by the corporations of rights
beyond the reach of legislative control; and in its course two
stages are observable. There occurred first the shedding of
social responsibility and the growth of the doctrine of the
responsibility of the corporation solely to the stockholders.
When George M. Pullman was examined before the Chicago
Strike Commission in 1894 he betrayed a confusion of mind
that obviously troubled him. He admitted under pressure at
one point in his evidence that the decision of his company to
keep the construction division at Pullman running by the
acceptance of orders for execution at less than cost was a
philanthropic act designed to assist the workers. But he had
already committed himself to a stricter line, forswearing this
improper tenderness.

> I would have no right [he said] to take the stockholders' money
> to give one set of mechanics a higher rate than the market price,
> or higher than we were paying other men—that is, to give them
> a contribution, as I understand you to say that if we had made
> profits, why, divide them. We can only divide profits in a corpora-
> tion to its stockholders.
>
> 335 (Commissioner Worthington). Let me ask you, then, what
> right you had to take these contracts at a loss of $400 on a car in
> order to keep the men at work, if that does not involve exactly
> the same principle?—Ans. No; because there is a business ele-
> ment in that that you will readily understand, that there would
> be damage resulting to the property of the Pullman company as
> well as to the men and as to everybody living in the vicinity. If I
> could by a contribution of money in that way secure the dis-
> bursement of $500,000 or $1,000,000, my excuse for it to my
> stockholders would be that it would save that amount that would
> otherwise be lost indirectly.[1]

Business was business. It was a dereliction of duty and a confusion of thought to allow other considerations to intervene.
And the ethical defence of this point of view was found in the
faith that the general interest would be automatically fulfilled
by the self-adjustment of competing endeavours. But the
development of the business corporation did not stop here. The
weakening of responsibility to society in the name of respon-

[1] *Report on the Chicago Strike of June to July, 1894, by the United States Strike Commission* (Washington, D.C., 1895), p. 565, *cf.* 567.

sibility to the shareholders was followed by a weakening of the sense of responsibility to the shareholders in the name of responsibility to the enterprise. Growth in size and the separation of ownership from control have resulted in investing a group of managers with something like an arbitrary authority. ' . . . we have reached the condition,' it has been observed, 'in which the individual interest of the shareholder is definitely made subservient to the will of the controlling group of managers even though the capital of the enterprise is made up of the aggregated contributions of perhaps many thousands of individuals. The legal doctrine that the judgment of the directors must prevail as to the best interests of the enterprise is, in fact, tantamount to saying that in any given instance the interests of the individual may be sacrificed to the economic exigencies of the enterprise as a whole, the interpretation of the board of directors as to what constitutes an economic exigency being practically final.'[1] The consequence has been the emergence of interior groups of great strength, ceasing to exercise their powers in trust either for their creators, the state, or their owners, the shareholders, and tending to autarchy.

In response to this change in the business corporation there opened a new phase in the history of the American trade union that pointed in the same direction. In the course of the eighties predominance in the world of organized labour passed from the Knights of Labor to the American Federation of Labor. Shaken by the failure of the strike on the Gould railroad system in the southwest in 1886 and by the defeat of the Chicago packers in the autumn of that year, and dominated by a group who had captured control of the executive in 1884 to the exclusion of the trade union element, the Knights rapidly lost support and by 1886 were clearly on the decline. Their place was taken by the trade unions, which had revived on a national scale between 1880 and 1885, and after a false start at Terre Haute in 1881 found an instrument for the pursuit of their aims in the American Federation of Labor, organized under

[1] A. A. Berle, jr., & G. C. Means, *The Modern Corporation and Private Property* (New York, 1935), pp. 277–8.

the lead of Samuel Gompers and the group in the Cigar Makers Union that had been denied its opportunity within the ranks of the Knights. The change had more than a domestic significance. The aim of the Knights had been revolutionary. They had desired the overthrow of the wage system; and standing for the organization of all workers, they had fostered the idea of class conflict. Yet it was with the reform of society as a whole that they were concerned. The trade union movement, on the contrary, limited itself to purely industrial aims, and became the advocate of the interests of an interior group of a society whose general structure it accepted. Although these unions have usually avoided incorporation, and there is thus a formal distinction between them and the business corporation, the histories of the two show striking similarities. The unions, like the trusts, have tended to operate with an undivided mind and a ruthless disregard of the public interest and to foster a controlling group ready, in the name of the exigencies of the enterprise, to show an almost equal disregard for the welfare of individual members of it. Here, also, the Chicago enquiry of 1894 was illuminating. There was revealed a sense of isolation in the mind of labour and, by no means without reason, a lack of faith in the justice of the law and a mistrust in the fairness of the whole apparatus of the legal system. The consequence was a refusal to accept compulsory arbitration as a solution, and reliance, instead, upon the opposition of organization to organization.

> Should injustice be perpetrated upon a citizen of this country by any foreign power, [said one of the leaders of the strike] when a representative of this country goes forward to seek redress for that injury or injustice it will never be necessary for us to strike to protect that citizen, but we will always be met by a spirit of conciliation and arbitration, and it will never be necessary for this Government to strike and use its weapons, because its force is recognized. And upon that same principle I said that the force of labor would never have to strike when it had the good sense to get solidly in line, when its force would be recognized.[1]

[1] *Report on the Chicago Strike of June–July, 1894, by the United States Strike Commission* (Washington, D.C., 1895), p. 44, cf. 30–1, 161, 173–4.

In default of a law that is accepted as common to them both, group is opposed to group in a relation of mere strength. It is an application in the domestic field of the international doctrine of the balance of power; and it amounts to a system of domestic power politics. And as in the international field so here there is a tendency to make the necessity of the group the criterion of right and wrong to its servants.

Thus, as Professor Swisher has observed, in the United States the 'constitutional system as conventionally conceived operates in conflict, in rivalry, and in interchange of authority with two powerful groupings of agencies which in the language of political science are not governments at all', but which quite palpably exercise over their members the authority of governments and act externally after the manner of governing powers.[1] And when what these groups do may make or mar the fortunes of communities and frustrates the policy of the state whether at home or abroad, no interpretation of the period in which they have grown up that sees only a process of national integration is sufficient. The labours of the historian who tries to explain events without a due regard for the behaviour of these bodies or an understanding of their springs of action will be futile. Yet historians have barely begun to observe them and know next to nothing about their internal politics. The subject is obviously one of great difficulty. Few can regard it dispassionately; and the original records are still only rarely available. The conventional categories, moreover, obstruct clear thinking. The accepted assumptions require the student who treats of these matters to discuss the relations of the state with what are conceived of as subordinate entities differing fundamentally in their nature from the state itself; and if these conceptions were liberalized in America by the existence of two distinct embodiments of the state, this was offset, in the climate of opinion resulting from the successful suppression of a great rebellion, by the anxiety for union and the great unwillingness of patriotism to face the prospect of new division. It has been difficult,

[1] C. B. Swisher, *The Post-War Constitution*. Reprinted from the *Boston University Law Review*, vol. xxviii (April, 1948), p. 144.

therefore, to see the facts as they were and not as society would have had them. They have been repugnant to the prevailing temper; and they have been ill-suited to the dominant theme. They have been among the discards that the current hypothesis has had no place for. And they await their historians.

The changing condition of American foreign relations, upon the other hand, has given a great impetus to the study of American diplomatic history. Much of this history is the history of the exercise of the new-found power of the United States and has called for no abatement of unionist fervour. The change has, in fact, been in many respects but the external expression of that re-integration that has occurred within the nation and as such easy to chronicle without disturbance of the generally accepted habits of mind and feeling. And it is also the case that the other aspect of American foreign relations, the external challenge to the absolutism of the sovereign national authority, has been less easy to overlook and less difficult to accept than the challenge offered by the interior group. The very pace and scale of world events during the last half-century have forced the movement of political thought in this sphere; and there was, furthermore, a deeply-rooted political tradition that assisted the acceptance of the new circumstances. The Articles of Confederation were an apt model for a league of nations. American devotion to the maintenance of the rule of law, the part played by the United States in promoting recourse to the peaceful settlement of international disputes, the existence within the American political system of dual allegiance and divided sovereignty, all predisposed the American mind, divided though it might remain, to accept American membership of a larger whole and to recognize its implications. American historiography responded accordingly. A new school of diplomatic history was founded; and the beginnings have been made of the study of those far-reaching changes in the external relations of the United States that have added a new complexity to the situation and call for radical modifications of nationalist doctrine.

Concurrently with the discovery by the newly-integrated

nation of a fresh challenge to the uniqueness and all-sufficiency of its authority at home, it also found its autonomy progressively diminished by the growing necessity of participation in the affairs of a larger society, and its sovereignty increasingly hedged about by obligations of obedience, if not yet to superior jurisdictions, at least to international undertakings that it could not afford to neglect. During the fifty-four years between Cleveland's first inauguration and the outbreak of the second World War, the United States experienced a radical alteration in its economic relations with the external world. The change was twofold. On the one hand the accumulation of wealth and the rapid growth of industrial production in the United States, led to the repatriation of foreign investments in the States and to the decreasing dependence of the States upon foreign supplies of industrial goods. Upon the other, United States capital itself began to seek overseas investment and certain branches of United States manufacture to experience the need for markets more extensive than the United States itself could afford. These changes, strongly felt in the generation between 1884 and 1914, were enormously accelerated by the events of the first World War. The nation that in 1914 was, on balance, a debtor, came out of the war in 1918 a creditor upon a huge scale. The conditions that had governed external economic relations since the days of the first settlement had been radically and permanently altered. Neither economically nor politically was the United States thenceforth to be able to go its own way regardless of events abroad or to be wholly unfettered by foreign obligations in the determination of its national policy. The exuberant nationalism of the nineties and the early years of the new century, and the naval expansion that accompanied it, which were so congenial to the patriotic enthusiasm bred by reunion, discovered a concrete and practical objective and became more than an expression of national sentiment. And in proportion as American foreign policy responded to changed economic circumstance it discovered a countervail to the self-regarding absolutism of American imperialism. The impracticability of autarky, the failure to build a viable economy in which foreign trade should be a subordinate, if not an almost trivial, incident, constrained the nation to become party to international engagements that abridged the freedom of self-determination.

Very little secondary work of outstanding importance on the diplomatic history of the United States was published before 1900, except on the diplomatic history of the Revolution and the early national period prior to the war of 1812. At the turn of the century there began to appear books of weight dealing generally with foreign relations, but lying upon the boundary between history and politics. But before 1914, except that some pioneer work had been done upon the history of the relations of the United States with the Far East, monographic studies that were to be of permanent value were, again excepting works relating to the early period, virtually limited to the field of Latin American policy. This tendency to turn in the first instance to the history of American diplomacy in the Far East and in Latin America had its origin in the preoccupations of American statesmanship and was to leave its mark. It was in respect to these areas of diplomatic activity that American thought about the foreign relations of the United States was most mature. The treatment of the history of diplomatic relations with the European powers in respect to European problems has been by comparison jejune and fragmentary, and, except when it has had as its subject the recurrent disputes about maritime rights, all too often a study of the superficial and the relatively trivial. And it has suffered perhaps more than most historical subjects from the facility with which dissertations to be submitted for higher degrees can be compiled by the almost mechanical juxtaposition of the papers of a couple of chancelleries, so that the literature of the subject is peculiarly unequal in quality. It has required the revolutionary change in the economic relations of the United States with the rest of the world to reveal what is needed for a full understanding of the relations of the United States with Europe during the nineteenth century; and out of that a new historiography may be expected to grow.

18

The break-up of the Spanish Empire reproduced once more a situation that had occurred again and again in the course of modern history, and was likely to have the familiar consequences. From every area that had disintegrated, or in which integration was imperfect and was being resisted, there had come appeals for help from dissentient groups to their kith and kin beyond the frontier. To these appeals there had in the past been all too often, sooner or later, a response; and whenever the consequences of that response were an undue accretion to the power that went to the rescue, counter-intervention was liable to follow for the sake of preserving the balance. The appeals had been very various. But whether dynastic, provincial, religious, political or economic, they had been essentially those of a dissentient interior group that was in revolt against, or opposed to absorption in, a larger society. Various also were the circumstances that led in the several instances to the fall into the temptation that these appeals offered. But whatever the particular ground of response, the consequence of successful intervention had been uniform. Sooner or later it was war between the powers. And most of their wars had this origin. To this process of competitive partition, of intervention followed by counter-intervention, leading to war between the competitors, European statesmanship knew two alternatives. They were either a refusal to countenance disintegration, an insistence that the sick man must not die, or partition by agreement. The Monroe Doctrine offered a third solution. It proposed at once an acceptance of disintegration and an insistence that to the appeals for aid there should be no response. It grew very naturally out of the particular circumstances of the United States. It was suited to the combination of an extreme unwillingness to tolerate the substitution of virile for effete European power in Latin America, with the risk that such power so situated would bring support to the discontented minorities of the United States itself, and an extreme unwillingness to participate in a process of competitive partition that would be likely radically to deflect the course of constitutional development at home, by rendering impracticable the liberality that was the American ideal and necessitating the adoption of authoritarian and alien practices.

The full implications of the system enunciated in Monroe's message to Congress of 2 December, 1823, as an alternative to the extension to the western hemisphere of the European principle of a balance, were only developed by experience; and changes in circumstance, producing more subtle dangers than the flagrant threat of direct military intervention followed by political partition, eventually wrought changes in doctrine that at one period amounted almost to a translation of defence into aggression. To the United States the Doctrine soon came to mean something more than a refusal to deal with the problem created by the disintegration of the Spanish Empire by the time-honoured method of competitive intervention and partition. It was in due course construed as an affirmation of the principle of self-determination; and at the same time the notice of opposition to further European colonization was expanded into a refusal to recognize the validity of any transfer of territory to a European power even were that the desire of its inhabitants. Therein lay the germs of a denial to any other nation of the right to obstruct a change in the balance of power that was favourable, or to promote one that was unfavourable, to the interests of the United States. And in the course of the nineteenth century the simplicities of the policy of non-intervention were circumvented by novel events. The migration, not of settlers but of traders, and not, on any significant scale at all, of persons, but of capital created interests within the jurisdiction of Latin American states that might be jeopardized by unjust or discriminatory treatment and that foreign governments felt themselves obliged to protect to the best of their ability. Loss could arise from the closing, perhaps at the instigation of competitors, of a door that had been open, or by acts of native ill-will or incompetence; and when foreign interests grew out of all proportion to legitimate foreign influence, native governments the more naturally lacked the ability or the will to deal justly with the outlanders whose disturbance of the established economy awakened alike resentment and cupidity. The appeals that then flowed to their several governments from the injured and defrauded traders and investors created new risks of European intervention, and with them new factors entered into United States policy. The interests of American nationals in the protection of their property and the promotion of their competitive advantage, and the reawakened anxieties of the Department of State thus called forth an extension of the Doctrine that for a time came very near to an assertion of the hegemony of the United States in the western hemisphere.

The interest of the United States in the Far East was very different from its interest in Latin America, yet the situation in the Far East was one to which the history of Latin America was very relevant. There, too, a great and ancient empire was in a state of disintegration; its government was incapable of affording to foreigners such protection to their persons and property as they were accustomed to, or of observing the rules of comity towards neighbouring states: and its conflicting factions were liable to appeal to foreign aid in pursuit of their domestic quarrels. From one or all of these circumstances foreign intervention was likely to arise and would be liable to result in the acquisition by the intervening power of privileges or territory that would alter its position in relation to other powers and lead to efforts upon their part to restore the balance. There, too, as in Latin America, there was a choice between a variety of answers to the problem. There might be an insistence that imperial rule would not completely break down and that nobody need interfere; there might be competitive intervention and war between the competitors over the division of the spoil; there might be partition by agreement, after the African model; or there might be an application in the Far East of the principles of the Monroe Doctrine. The early success of Japan in ridding itself of limitations upon its autonomy, the rapid modernization of the country, and the defeat of China in the Sino-Japanese war of 1894-5, with its revelation of the weakness of that state and the danger of the foundation of a Japanese empire at its expense, threatened the loss to the western powers of their commercial opportunities and a radical disturbance of the balance of power. This precipitated the adoption of the customary measures. At the close of the nineteenth century the partition of China was commonly expected. To the United States such a prospect was as un-welcome, although for rather different reasons, as the prospect of the partition of Latin America had been; and a Monroe Doctrine was once again appropriate to a combination of an extreme anxiety not to be excluded with an extreme unwilling-ness to take a share in partition or to assume imperial respon-sibilities the discharge of which might prove difficult without changes in the structure of American government foreign to its genius.

The United States at an early date enjoyed a large share in the China trade. By 1820, American shipping in the Far East was second only to that of Great Britain; and with the develop-ment of the clipper, around 1840, a smaller and swifter ship than the East Indiaman, great prominence was won in the tea trade. But on the diversion of American energies to the settle-ment and exploitation of the Mississippi valley, interest declined in overseas trade; and except for ginseng and furs no large American export was available for the supply of the Far Eastern market. The United States failed to meet the competi-tion of Great Britain when the iron ship appeared. American-China shipping that stood at 2,609,390 tons to the British 2,862,214 in 1864 fell to 129,127 to the British 20,496,347 in 1894. When, therefore, in the middle of the century, the United States, having acquired a long Pacific coast-line, was led to participate in the opening-up of Japan partly by a need to protect the whalers of the north Pacific ocean from the hostility of the Japanese when they were driven upon the coasts of Japan by bad weather or in search of supplies, and partly by the need of the steamship service between San Francisco and Shanghai for coaling stations and fresh provisions on the way, Americans were less interested than Europeans in Asiatic markets. Negligible as a military or naval power, traditionally hostile to the imperial ambitions of European states, and without colonial plans of its own, the United States took a more liberal stand than the rest of the western world towards the oriental nations. Sympathy went out to the efforts of Japan to reorganize herself upon a western model; a view of the rights of extraterritoriality was taken that was more tolerant than that of the European powers, and American nationals were surrendered to the operation of Chinese or Japanese law without restriction except that it must be administered in American consular courts; and a greater readiness was shown to release Japan from the control of a conventional tariff and an earlier willingness to restore Japanese juridical autonomy. Drawing upon the experience of the one first-class diplomatic problem to which American statesmanship had had hitherto to address itself, American policy in the Far East thus came in the last quarter of the nineteenth century to rest upon three principal propositions. They were that the threatened partition of the Far East among the European powers must be opposed; that the greatest danger lay in conflict between China and Japan; and that a solution might be found in the performance by Japan in the Far East of the rôles played by the United States in the Americas and Great Britain in the Atlantic. On the outbreak of the Sino-Japanese war of 1894-5, therefore, while much sympathy was felt for the Japanese case in Korea, the main object of United States policy was to secure a settlement without the intervention of the European powers; and a very active though unofficial part was taken in the peace negotiations. And when American fears were realized and the powers took steps to restore the balance that had been upset by the demonstration of Chinese weakness and Japanese strength, and forestalled danger by themselves acquiring concessions from China, the United States formally proposed in the Hay notes of 1899-1900 what was already implicit in American Far Eastern policy, the application of the solution of the problem formerly presented by the disintegration of the Spanish empire to the problem now presented by the disintegration of China. To the traditional European policy of competitive partition the United States opposed the principles of territorial integrity and the open door. It was a Far Eastern version of the Monroe Doctrine.

The policy of the United States in the Far East was not, however, without its ambiguities and confusions. The Spanish-American war of 1898 was the first notable manifestation of an American imperialism that extended beyond the continental mainland; and the acquisition of the Philippine Islands, though an accident of a war that had a Caribbean origin, looked very much like the adoption rather than the rejection of the European model in Far Eastern policy. At the same time, American capital had begun to look for profitable employment overseas and American interest in foreign markets was changing and growing; while the expectation that Japanese naval power would play in the China sea the part in the execution of a Far Eastern Monroe Doctrine that was played by Great Britain in the Atlantic had proved to be an illusion. The situation was not so simple, nor the American mind so sure, as appears to a first view.

The first step towards clarification was the change in the attitude of the United States towards Japan that occurred between 1895 and 1909. The belief in Japan as the protector of the integrity of China led to the welcome of the Anglo-Japanese alliance of 1902 as a support to Japanese opposition to the designs of Russia and ensured sympathy with Japan in the Russo-Japanese war of 1904-5. But the extent of the Japanese victory, the temper displayed by the Japanese in the course of the negotiations at Portsmouth in 1905, and the wider knowledge of Far Eastern affairs derived from the very able presentation of the Russian case gave pause to American enthusiasm; and doubt was fed by the emergence of conflicts of economic interest. The new search for overseas employment by American capital was vividly illustrated by the schemes of E. H. Harriman. Whereas in the forties J. M. Forbes had withdrawn his capital from the China trade to invest it in the building of railroads in Michigan, E. H. Harriman at the end of the century turned to Asia to find the scope that America was too small to afford him. In control of the Illinois Central by 1883 and master by

1900 of the whole of the trans-continental railroad system of the United States save for the Hill lines of the Great Northern and Northern Pacific, he launched in 1905 a plan to acquire the Japanese and Russian railways in Manchuria and trackage rights over the Trans-Siberian, only to find himself blocked by the Japanese. The more ardently nationalist elements in Japan bitterly resented the moderation of the terms of the Treaty of Portsmouth, and regretted in particular the failure to secure a large indemnity. In face of that failure, the Manchurian railway was the only financial asset secured from Russia that would help materially to meet the cost of the war. It was not surprising, therefore, that Japan decided to retain sole control and rejected in October, 1905, Harriman's proposals for the joint operation of the line and of various mines and other appurtenant enterprises by a syndicate representing both governmental and financial interests. At the same time the growing desire of the United States for new overseas markets began to produce complaints of Japanese obstruction. The new Japanese tariff was held to show an intention to discriminate against foreign nations; and a heavy fall in American trade with China was attributed to Japanese competition and to an anti-American prejudice that was fostered by Japan. To these sources of American disillusionment and mutual estrangement there was added in 1906 a dispute about the treatment of Japanese immigrants in the United States, having its deeper roots in a rising alarm at the extent and character of oriental immigration on the Pacific coast and its immediate origin in a resolution of the San Francisco board of education to send all Chinese, Japanese, and Korean children to a separate 'oriental school'. So rapidly, in fact, did relations deteriorate that by 1907–8 there was a very general expectation of a Japanese-American conflict; and the exercise of skill and restraint by both governments was needed to control the less responsible elements in their respective countries. The mistrust and dislike of Japan thus suddenly engendered was fully confirmed by the events of the next decade. The foundation of the Chinese Republic in 1911 and the promise of the modernization of China won the sympathy of America, and added to the fervour with which the doctrine of territorial and administrative integrity was upheld and to the importance of the doctrine of the open door; while the steady pursuit of the imperial designs of Japan from the annexation of Korea in 1910 to the Twenty-One Demands of 1915, the Sino-Japanese military agreement of 1918, and the military operations in Siberia and Manchuria of 1918–22, revealed Japan as the most dangerous enemy of Chinese independence. And when, moreover, a new crisis in Japanese-American relations developed in 1918–21, the centre of gravity in naval matters had shifted from the North Atlantic to the Pacific, and the prospect of a Japanese-American conflict was a much more grave affair than it had been in 1907–8. But this discovery in Japan, not of the St. George of which a too-hopeful imagination had dreamed but of the dragon itself, worked no change in the fundamental principles of the policy of the United States in the Far East. A different instrument must be employed now that it was clear that Japan would not play the part for which she had been too innocently cast; and public sympathy had shifted from the Japan whose once admired enthusiasm for westernization had degenerated into imperialism, and was transferred to China, whose feet it seemed had been set upon the road to democracy. But the Nine Power Treaty that was the work of the Washington Conference of 1921–2 only set out more firmly and with more authority the doctrine of the Hay notes. By it the signatories guaranteed the territorial and administrative integrity of China and renounced the policy of spheres of interest, reaffirmed and defined the doctrine of the open door, and pledged themselves not to enter into treaties incompatible with these principles. On Far Eastern policy the American mind was now clear. Once the illusion about Japan had been dispelled, there was no doubt what the issues were or that they were issues about which America cared; and, until disillusionment began to be aroused about the conduct of China herself, there was no doubt which was black and which was white, who was the wolf and who the lamb.

Upon the European conflict that broke out in 1914 the United States could bring to bear no such maturity of experience as it by then had gained in respect to the problems of Latin America and the Far East. The ostensible American interest, it is true, was the interest of a neutral in the maintenance of its maritime rights, and that involved ancient disputes upon which the American mind had long been exercised and about which there had been no lack of acute and penetrating thought. But grave as these problems were, and great as the tension was that their discussion at one stage produced in Anglo-American relations, they would not by themselves have caused the entry of the United States into the war. That resulted from a combination of the rapidly changing economic relations of the United States with the rest of the world and the challenge offered by the concept of total war and the concept of the absolute state that lay behind it. It was the vital importance of American supplies to the Allies that drove Germany to unrestricted submarine warfare; and it was the lawlessness of that warfare and the growing entanglement of American welfare with the welfare of the Allies that finally determined the action of the United States. In this way, not only was the nation drawn into a conflict the responsibility for which the American public had not believed to lie at the door of any one power, and into a maze of international disputes and economic, colonial and imperial rivalries of which it had a very imperfect knowledge and which it had been in the habit of regarding with impartial disapprobation, but it also found itself in the face of circumstances that assorted ill with the predominant trend to national integration that was the result of internal politics. The revelation upon the one hand of the logical consequences of the doctrine of unlimited national sovereignty, and upon the other of the increasing dependence of American prosperity upon the prosperity of other countries, exposed the insufficiency of a mere patriotism that was no longer politically acceptable or economically viable. But that the recognition of so radical a change should be slow and reluctant was only to be expected. It called for the direction of attention to an unfamiliar field and the modification of what had only recently been accepted as laudable aims of public policy. In the event, uncertainty about the merits of the quarrels between the European powers and a tenacious confidence that absolutism was all right so long as it was democratic impeded the sacrifice of sovereignty in response to political argument; and it needed the concrete evidence of economics to exert an effective persuasion upon the American mind.

The general intellectual level of the debate upon the Treaty of Versailles and the League of Nations was incomparably below that of the debate upon the Constitution that had taken place a hundred and thirty years before; and the outstanding impression left by the study of it is one of its unreality. For this there were various reasons. The structure of American society had changed profoundly since 1787, and matters of high policy were no longer the preserve of an educated class. The president had deliberately kept the lawyers at arm's length, when the essential problems were largely juridical. Preparation had not been commensurate with the magnitude of the issues. The initial American work upon the draft of the Covenant had been astonishingly casual; the president was neither fully qualified, nor could he have been expected to spare the time, to master in all their intricate technicality the problems that so novel a plan gave rise to; and there was a lack of competent departmental support, for which he himself was to blame. In these circumstances, the issue was so presented that every man thought himself entitled to express an opinion on it; and the debate became a debate between laymen. It was confused by inaccuracy and want of information. It was bewildered by disputes about hypothetical cases. It continually strayed, to participate with little understanding in the domestic and foreign controversies of other powers. And there can be no question but that the situation was exploited to serve partisan ends. But all these were adventitious causes of argumentative disorder. The root of the matter was that no sufficiently concrete American interest was at stake to engage the practical skill of any substantial and politically effective body of business or professional men; that the debate continued throughout to be highly theoretical; and that at this juncture the American mind was filled with a patriotic enthusiasm that took its rise in national reunion and had been strengthened by war, and was in no mood to allow the diminution of the authority of the Union by one iota.

If surrender of a measure of sovereignty could plausibly be shown to be a contradiction in terms and any invasion resisted as incompatible with the national welfare, the economic situation was nevertheless intractable. The change from the position of a debtor to that of a creditor was the most far-reaching event of modern American history. It occurred with great rapidity between 1914 and 1918. But it had long been in preparation, and war only accelerated the arrival of a state of affairs that must in any case have come about sooner or later. The dependence of America upon foreign capital for the building of a new civilization in the wilderness was drawing to an end. The closing of the frontier revealed by the census of 1890 coincided with radical changes in external economic relations. A threefold shift was then taking place in the composition of American foreign trade and the external balance of payments; and at the same time there was a change in the relation of export to internal trade. There was in process a shift from the export of agricultural products to the export of manufactured goods, a shift from the import of manufactured goods to an import of tropical products, and a fall in interest payments, partly offset by a growth in the volume of immigrant remittances and tourist expenditure. A large volume of American railroad securities was returned from Europe as a result of the American financial panic of 1893, and after 1898 the railroads became dependent upon United States capital; in 1898 the United States became a net exporter of manufactured goods; by 1913 the value of exports of manufactured goods was nearly half the total value of all exports. The repatriation of $2 billion of foreign-owned American securities by the autumn of 1916, the prodigious Allied purchases of the products of American farms and factories, and the immense foreign loans that made them possible, were not, therefore, events that deflected the line of development. They brought about more quickly what was already in train. But the change was nevertheless revolutionary. Both the alteration in the composition of the account and the reversal of the balance of payments called inescapably for radical adjustments in the internal economic structure and the foreign economic policy of the United States.

In no area of the American economy was this call for re-adjustment more urgent than in agriculture. There, the influence of the first World War was directly contrary to what was desirable and had an effect the flat opposite of the pre-war trend. The combination of the export of an immense agricultural surplus with the maintenance of a highly restrictive schedule of duties upon imports was feasible so long as there was a large foreign debt to service and ultimately to refund. But the disposal of that surplus became difficult when the balance of payments changed, and doubly difficult as American farmers became, in comparison with other sources of supply, high-cost producers. When that happened there was need both for the restriction and the diversification of agricultural production, and for an increase of imports. Yet the course of events encouraged, instead of reducing, resistance to the necessary adjustment to new circumstances. In a long view the general trend of American agriculture is clear. In the forty years between 1899 and 1939 net farm output increased by about half, compared with a fourfold increase of manufacturing output and an increase of 75 per cent in population; while there occurred a change in the composition of that output by a fall, on the one hand, in grains and meat animals and the virtual disappearance of hay, and a rise, on the other, in dairy products, poultry and eggs, citrus fruit, and sugar. This led to a fall in the proportion of the population engaged in agriculture.[1] But that trend was deflected from its course in 1914. The effect of a war that in the long run greatly reduced the

[1] H. Barger & H. H. Landsberg, *American Agriculture, 1899–1939* (New York, 1942), pp. 19–20, 26–8, 245-6.

capacity of foreign markets to absorb American agricultural surpluses was to induce an expansion of the farm area by some fifty million acres, to stimulate the continuance on a large scale of the production of the basic crops, and to accelerate a process of mechanization that reduced the flexibility of farm costs. By the eighteen-nineties international shipments of wheat and flour amounted on the average to some 400m. bushels a year, of which the United States net exports averaged about 44 per cent, amounting to a third of the United States wheat production. The peak was reached in the period from 1897-8 to 1902-3, when the United States net export averaged 219m. bushels and was nearly half the world trade. Between 1900 and 1910, although the total trade increased, the United States share began to go down, the leading place being taken by Russia. The effect of the outbreak of war was that in 1914-15 United States exports reached a record figure and were over 60 per cent of all international shipments; and after the entry of the United States itself into the war, great efforts were made to increase production, resulting in a crop in 1919 second only in volume to the record crop of 1915 and double in value, while it was treble in value that of 1909. This expanded acreage was maintained after the war, fresh areas in the western parts of the Great Plains taking the place of land east of the Mississippi returned to other uses. In consequence, agrarian readjustment, hard enough to achieve before, became the most stubborn of all the problems with which the United States had to deal; at one and the same time its intrinsic difficulty and the unwillingness to face the problem alike increased. By 1923, wheat exports were down to a third of the 1919 figure.[1] Cotton exports fell away in the same year to less than half, in value, the exports of 1920, and they had been lower in 1922. The farmers were in distress. Post-war opinion, however, was in no mood to apply the obvious remedy. Industry was enjoying great if meretricious prosperity; and nationalist doctrines were in vogue. A variety of measures was adopted to assist the farmer to continue to produce what he could no longer sell and to buy what he could

[1] J. S. Davis, *Wheat and the AAA* (Washington, D.C., 1935), p. 7.

no longer afford to pay for, partly in the belief that all that needed to be dealt with was a temporary disturbance and partly in consequence of a reluctance to face facts and the sheer impracticability of change at the pace and upon the scale that was in theory desirable. By the Emergency Tariff Act of 27 May, 1921, and the Fordney-McCumber Tariff of 1922, agriculture was accorded a higher measure of protection in the domestic market; and the Agricultural Credit Act of 1923 provided relief to the indebted farmer by the increase of credit facilities. The War Finance Corporation was revived in 1921 to assist in the export of farm products; and the Federal Farm Board was established for the same purpose in 1929. The railroads were induced to grant special export rates; agricultural products were dumped abroad at uneconomic prices; and heavy foreign loans were made to enable people to buy what they could not pay for out of their own resources. These public measures were ably seconded by the efforts of private business firms. The art of salesmanship was much advanced, and the habit of purchase by instalments was encouraged. The effect was to promote some recovery between 1922 and 1929 from the low prices of 1920–1, to reduce at least in appearance the disparity between agricultural depression and industrial prosperity, and to mask the shrinkage of agricultural purchasing power. But no sufficient or lasting result was obtained. By far the most important cash crop was wheat; and in terms of four, five or six year averages the production of 1926–31 was the largest reached to that date in the history of the United States. Yet acreage was being expanded in Canada, Australia, and Argentina by low-cost methods, the U.S.S.R. was resuming its exports, European yields were increasing, the restrictions imposed by importing countries were multiplying, United States price-raising devices were nothing but an embarrassment in international markets, and only large capital outflows enabled the United States to maintain a substantial export surplus without serious disturbances in the balance of payments. The trend of agricultural exports, therefore, was generally downwards; there was a chronic weakness in prices; and the exchange value of farm products for other goods deteriorated. When there was an abrupt curtailment of American foreign lending in 1929, and in consequence of this event and other sources of disturbance and instability there set in the great economic depression of 1929–32, Europe was both in a position and under compulsion to curtail imports from the United States. In 1930–1, Soviet and Australian exports of wheat increased, and trade barriers in Europe were multiplied. World wheat prices by the end of 1930 were below the levels of the nineties and unprecedentedly low in terms of other commodities. The fall of agricultural prices in the United States was catastrophic. Wheat went down from $1.07 a bushel in January, 1930, to 31.6c. in December, 1932; cotton, from 16c. a pound in December, 1929, to 5.4c. in December, 1932; corn, from 78c. a bushel in 1929 to 18.8c. in 1932. The gross income of American farmers fell from over $11m. in 1929 to under $5m. in 1932. In February, 1930, the Federal Farm Board set up the Grain Stabilization Corporation to support the domestic wheat market; and purchases were also made, with Farm Board support, by the Farmers' National Grain Corporation. The effect was to check exports and further to increase the carry-over. In 1931, the United States crop was the largest since 1919; and the United States wheat supply in that year was the largest in history and double the ordinary domestic usage.[1] By August, 1933, the prospective carry-over of cotton was equal to the annual average world consumption of American cotton during three previous seasons; and there, also, the operations of the Federal Farm Board had priced the United States product out of the world market.[2]

But if it is true that between 1921 and 1933 'post-war Republicanism formulated national policies on the premise of the self-contained nation, the consequence of which policies it did not accept,'[3] it is the case that the New Deal also, in its first phase, was an experiment in self-sufficiency. In one point

[1] J. S. Davis, *Wheat and the AAA* (Washington, D.C., 1935), p. 23.
[2] H. I. Richards, *Cotton and the AAA* (Washington, D.C., 1936), p. 14.
[3] J. M. Jones, jr., *Tariff Retaliation. Repercussions of the Hawley-Smoot Bill* (Philadelphia, 1934), p. 301.

of view it was the fulfilment of the ideals of Theodore Roosevelt and Woodrow Wilson, the elevation of public above private purpose, the consummation of national integration. But in another, it also called for national isolation. A managed currency needed freedom from control by international monetary agreements; the operation of the Codes of Fair Competition, securing the regulation of the conditions of employment and the adoption of minimum prices, required the exclusion of competition from producers not subject to such restraints; and even in agriculture a nationalist solution was attempted. One of the prime causes of the depression and of its persistence, it was argued, was the distress into which American agriculture had fallen, and aid to this industry was necessary to any general recovery. The task, as it was conceived, was to extend to farmers the benefits of 'protection', and by removing the disparity between agricultural and other prices to restore the ability of farmers to buy industrial goods.[1] The aim of the Agricultural Adjustment Act, as defined in the act itself, was 'to establish and maintain such balance between the production and consumption of agricultural commodities and such marketing conditions therefor, as will re-establish prices to farmers at a level that will give agricultural commodities a purchasing power with respect to articles farmers buy, equivalent to the purchasing power of agricultural commodities in the base period'; and the base period, for all agricultural commodities except tobacco, was August, 1909, to July, 1914. The means chosen to achieve this end were a combination of crop-restriction, with a view to an increase of price, and benefit, or parity, payments, in return for the restriction of acreage, pending such re-adjustment of supply and demand as would result in parity without subvention. The acreage to be taken out of production was to be agreed by the individual farmer with the Secretary of Agriculture; and benefit payments were to be made to co-operating producers in proportion to the grower's share of the domestically consumed crop in a base period or to the estimated yield per acre of the land ploughed up. The working formula

[1] J. S. Davis, *Wheat and the AAA* (Washington, D.C., 1935), p. 40.

19

was 'national average farm price per bushel sold + gross benefit payments = parity'. The farmer, that is to say, provided that he coöperated in the effort to raise current average farm prices, was guaranteed the receipt of the 'fair exchange value' of what he produced, the 'fair exchange value' being the price that would give the commodity the same purchasing power with respect to what he bought that it had in the base period, the difference between current average farm prices and the 'fair exchange value' being provided at first out of the pockets of the domestic consumer and later out of those of the taxpayer. But the lesson learned by 1934–5 was that, while farm income had been substantially improved, that improvement was in the main due to benefit payments. The Act failed to secure the fulfilment of the pledge in the Wheat Agreement of 1933 to reduce the harvested acreage in 1934 by 15 per cent, and had little effect upon wheat prices. The immediate difficulties of the wheat growers were removed by the drought of 1934.[1] In cotton, the plantings in 1934 and 1935 were considerably below the permitted acreage, but it is doubtful whether this voluntary restriction could have been maintained in face of an improvement in price; and such rise as was secured had the effect of reducing the foreign consumption of United States cotton and ended in the accumulation of large stocks in government hands.[2]

The effort to solve the farm problem within the frontiers of the United States, that had been continuous since 1920, was thus a failure; and the logic of these events wrought a radical change in the fundamental assumptions of the New Deal. If the restoration of the parity of economic prosperity between the agrarian and industrial sections of American society was essential to economic revival, and if the American farm problem was insoluble without a substantial recovery of the demand in foreign markets for American agricultural products, autarky was impracticable. What had begun as an experiment

[1] J. S. Davis, *Wheat and the AAA* (Washington, D.C., 1935), pp. 110–14.
[2] H. I. Richards, *Cotton and the AAA* (Washington, D.C., 1936), pp. 256–7, 259–60, 265–6, 291; W. Diebold, jr., *New Directions in Our Trade Policy* (New York, 1941), p. 83.

in self-sufficiency developed into a new American economic foreign policy, of which the first overt sign was the Reciprocal Trade Agreements Act of 1934. Although this act marks one of the turning-points of recent American history it was not, however, without its paradoxes and confusions of thought; nor indeed was it free of divided aims. In all the experiments in agricultural policy during the years that followed the first world war there was an underlying assumption that the loss of overseas markets for United States agricultural products was only temporary; and the aim both of the Wheat Agreement of 1933 and of the cotton policy of the Roosevelt administration was to conserve the United States share of the world market and to prevent the substitution of other sources of supply. The United States was peculiarly affected by the increasing recourse by foreign countries to discriminatory bilateral agreements for the protection of their agricultural producers; and the trade agreements programme was designed to rectify this. It was in accordance with this that the prime object of the most important agreement entered into under the act, the Anglo-American Trade Agreement of 1938, was to increase agricultural exports.[1] Yet parity was not a concept that was internationally viable; the re-establishment of prices to American farmers at a level that would give agricultural commodities a purchasing power, with respect to articles American farmers bought, equivalent to the purchasing power of those commodities in 1909–14, did not make sense in international markets; and there was an element of absurdity in an attempt to extend the benefits of United States 'protection' to the American farmer by the recovery of markets beyond the reach of that shelter. Moreover, the most conspicuous feature of United States foreign trade in this period was the emergence of the predominance of manufactured in place of unmanufactured exports; so that the discovery of a more active interest in foreign trade might rather and more rationally have been expected to have had its origin in industrial than in agrarian

[1] C. Kreider, *The Anglo-American Trade Agreement* (Princeton, 1948), pp. 117, 120, 138.

quarters. But that it did not was due in part to a difference in the relative importance of foreign to total trade in agricultural and industrial products, and in part to an ambiguity of purpose. It was not until a fortnight after the Reciprocal Trade Agreements Act had received the president's signature that it was certain which of two federal agencies would be entrusted with its execution or which of two conflicting policies it was intended to serve. On the one hand stood the secretary of state, Cordell Hull, committed to the policy of tariff reduction by means of reciprocal agreements and the generalization of the concessions made in each of them; on the other, George N. Peek, in charge of a 'temporary committee' appointed in December, 1933, and holding the office of Special Adviser on Foreign Trade established in March, 1934, empowered to develop foreign purchasing power by the use of barter and other international arrangements as well as tariff agreements, confident of the ability of the United States to solve its problems within its own boundaries, and a believer in high tariffs and bilateral deals on a conditional most-favoured-nation basis. The president appeared to hesitate between them; and the expectation for a while was that the execution of the act would be entrusted to Peek. Only on the 29th of June was the announcement made that the responsibility was to rest with the State Department; and the influence of Peek was not finally removed until his office lapsed with the adverse decision of the Supreme Court on the National Industrial Recovery Act in 1935.[1] Even when Hull's interpretation of the purposes of the Reciprocal Trade Agreements had prevailed, the new policy was embarrassed by the definition in the preamble to the act of the aim that the executive was to keep in view. The act 'not only defines limits to the concessions which shall be made but also states a definite condition upon which they are to be awarded.'[2] The grant of authority to the president to enter into foreign trade agreements was 'for the purpose of expanding

[1] H. J. Tasca, *The Reciprocal Trade Policy of the United States* (Philadelphia, 1938), pp. 82–91.
[2] J. D. Larkin, *Trade Agreements. A Study in Democratic Methods* (New York, 1940), p. 44.

foreign markets for the products of the United States'. The agreements, that is to say, were not to correct the imbalance created by the emergence of the United States as a creditor upon an immense scale, but only to raise the level at which that imbalance was struck. Yet, for all these hesitations and confusions of thought, the Reciprocal Trade Agreements Act opened a new chapter in the history of American foreign relations; and it also raised a constitutional issue of the first importance. It was a sign of recognition that the prosperity of the United States was not self-contained, but was in the last analysis dependent upon the prosperity of a larger whole; it spelled a change in the aims of tariff reformers, who had hitherto concentrated their attention upon the substitution of national for special interests in the construction of tariffs and had been negligent of the effect of these tariffs upon foreign trade; and the pursuit of the aims now in mind required a technical change that amounted to a denial of the exclusive control of the tariff to the legislature, for the act removed something that had hitherto lain within the province of mere legislative fiat into that of international negotiation. The new policy involved the regulation by binding agreements of what had hitherto been variable in accordance with electoral fluctuations or legislative caprice. Because legislatures cannot conveniently negotiate, it required an executive invasion of what had hitherto been a legislative power. A high, autonomous, single-schedule tariff, without any other means of exercising persuasion upon foreign countries than the penal provisions of article 317 of the Emergency Tariff of 1921, by which the president was empowered to impose additional duties upon, or wholly to exclude, goods coming from countries that discriminated against the trade of the United States, was too clumsy an instrument to serve the needs of a community that recognized the dependence of its prosperity upon access to foreign markets. But a negotiated, or conventional, tariff not only could not be the work of Congress, it also tied the hands of that body and of the people.

The change in the objective of tariff policy and the evolution of tariff-making procedure was slow and reluctant; and it was by no means complete in 1934. The widespread discontent with the high protective policy established during the Civil War, which found expression in the eighties, was at first directed mainly to checking the exploitation of the American consumer by the protected interests; and this was the principal object of the tariffs of 1883, 1894, and 1913. But the agricultural losses that resulted from the growth of the protective movement in Europe, beginning with the German tariff of 1879 and the surrender by France and Great Britain in 1882 of the Cobden Treaty of 1860, together with the growing importance of large-scale manufacture in the United States and the increasing interest of United States industrialists in exports, prompted attempts to use the tariff also as a means of securing entry into foreign markets. The problem was twofold. It was in part that of devising machinery by means of which international agreements could be negotiated relating to a matter that lay in a special degree within the province of the legislature; in part, it was that of finding inducements sufficient to persuade foreign countries to make the desired concessions. The failure of Congress itself in international tariff negotiations was almost complete. The treaty with Cuba of 1902 was negotiated under the authority of the tariff act of 1897, and was ratified by Congress. But not one of the seven commercial treaties negotiated under section 4 of that measure was acted upon by Congress, and the treaties lapsed; the reciprocity arrangement with Canada, of 1911, proposed to be effected by concurrent legislation, was rejected by Canada after adoption by Congress; and because of the outbreak of war in 1914, no use was made by the executive of the power to negotiate commercial agreements, subject to Congressional ratification, granted by the tariff act of 1913. The tariff act of 1909 provided for a two-column tariff of minimum and maximum rates, and authorized the president to extend the privilege of the minimum schedule to countries found not to be discriminating against the United States. But these provisions proved to be too rigid. Some concessions were obtained by the threat to impose the maximum rates. But the president had no power of selection, but must apply the maximum rates, if at all, to all imports from the discriminating country; and in consequence the minimum rates were applied in 1910 to the entire commercial world, in spite of the fact that full equality of treatment was not always conceded to United States products. Such progress as was made before 1914 in the promotion of the foreign trade of the United States by the use of the tariff was, apart from advantages secured in the Cuban market, the result of recourse to a new constitutional device. This was the grant to the executive by Congress of powers to give effect to contingency legislation, whereby the president acted as the agent of the law-making department in ascertaining and declaring the event upon the occurrence of which the expressed will of the legislature was to take effect, his action operating either to impose specified penalties upon, or to concede specified favours to, foreign countries. In accordance with this plan the executive concluded eleven agreements under the threat of the application of the penal provisions of the tariff act of 1890 and nine agreements under the provisions of the act of 1897. But while the influence of these agreements was favourable to the trade of the United States, it was not far reaching. The countries with whom they were concluded took too small a proportion of United States exports, or the specified products to which they related were too few, to produce results of any importance. The report of the Tariff Commission on Reciprocity and Commercial Treaties, of 1919, was an exposition of the failure of the measures thus far adopted to meet the growing need of the United States for easier access to export markets. Two things had been made clear by the experience of thirty years. The regulation of commercial relations by means of treaties requiring full congressional or even merely senatorial ratification was impracticable; and neither the grant to the executive of authority to withhold the imposition of penal duties or to grant reductions of duty upon specified conditions, nor the grant of authority to offer the advantages of a minimum schedule had provided means of sufficient flexibility for successful tariff negotiations.

The first step towards the adaptation of commercial policy to the new needs of United States foreign trade was the renunciation in 1923 of conditional most-favoured-nation treatment as its governing principle. The foundations of this change of policy were laid in the Tariff Commission's report of 1919. 'So far as commercial policy and commercial negotiations are concerned,' said the Commission, 'the evidence presented in the present report indicates that a policy of special arrangements, such as the United States has followed in recent decades, leads to troublesome complications. Whether as regards our reciprocity treaties or as regards our interpretation of the most-favoured-nation clause, the separate and individual treatment of each case tends to create misunderstanding and friction with countries which, though supposed to be not concerned, yet are in reality much concerned. When each country with which we negotiate is treated by itself, and separate arrangements are made with the expectation that they shall be applicable individually, claims are none the less made by other States with whom such arrangements have not been made. Concessions are asked; they are sometimes refused; counter concessions are proposed; reprisal and retaliation are suggested; unpleasant controversies and sometimes international friction result. . . . A great gain would be secured, now that the United States is committed to wide participation in world politics, if a clear and simple policy could be adopted and followed. The guiding principle might well be that of equality of treatment. . . . Equality of treatment should mean that the United States should treat all countries on the same terms, and in turn require equal treatment from every other country. So far as concerns general industrial policy and general tariff legislation, each country—the United States as well as others—should be left free to enact such measures as it deems expedient for its own welfare. But the measures adopted, whatever they be, should be carried out with the same terms and the same treatment for all nations.'[1] But the Commission was divided in opinion; and

[1] *Reciprocity and Commercial Treaties.* United States Tariff Commission (Washington, D.C., 1919), p. 10.

illuminating history and lucid analysis issued in ambiguous recommendations. The logical conclusion was not drawn until the matter was again taken up in 1922. The final abandonment of the traditional attitude of the United States was announced in a circular letter from the secretary of state to United States diplomatic officers dated 18 August, 1923. 'The principle of equality of treatment,' the secretary of state wrote, 'has made great progress and it is now considered to be in the interest of the trade of the United States, in competing with the trade of other countries in the markets of the world, to endeavour to extend the acceptance of that principle. The enlarged productive capacity of the United States developed during the World War has increased the need for assured equality of treatment of American commerce in foreign markets.'[1] But the United States had returned in 1913 to a single-column autonomous tariff, and so long as that was retained it was a matter of little practical importance to foreign countries whether the conditional or the unconditional form of the most-favoured-nation clause was approved. Until the United States should enter into trade agreements involving a number of duty reductions, all that foreign countries gained by the adoption by the United States of the unconditional form was an equality in exclusion from the American market; and for that they would not be ready to make any counter-concessions of substance. The Emergency Tariff of 1921, the Fordney-McCumber Tariff of 1922, the Hawley-Smoot Tariff of 1930, and the Revenue Act of 1932 were more highly protective than any of the measures that had preceded them, and the so-called 'flexible' provisions of the acts of 1922 and 1930 embodied a principle that would, if carried to its logical conclusion, bring international trade altogether to an end. 'In order to . . . put into force and effect the policy of the Congress by this Act intended,' ran section 315 of the Fordney-McCumber tariff, 'whenever the President, upon investigation of the differences in costs of production of articles wholly or in part the growth or product of the United

[1] *Papers Relating to the Foreign Relations of the United States, 1923*, vol. i (Washington, D.C., 1938), p. 121.

States and of like or similar articles wholly or in part the growth or product of competing foreign countries, shall find it thereby shown that the duties fixed in this Act do not equalize the said differences in cost of production . . . he shall, by such investigation, ascertain such differences and determine and proclaim the changes in classification or increases or decreases in any rate of duty provided in this Act shown by said ascertained differences in such costs of production necessary to equalize the same.' Yet, even so, these were developments that were to have an important bearing on a revised commercial policy. Not only was the authority of the executive to impose or remove specified rates of duty upon enumerated articles, when certain conditions were fulfilled, extended to an authority to change rates, vary classifications, and alter the basis of valuation within specified limits, but the 'flexible' provisions of the acts of 1922 and 1930 conferred upon him virtually dictatorial powers. The provision was designed as 'the constant guardian of domestic interests from the close of one congressional tariff revision to the close of the next';[1] but it had far-reaching and unforeseen constitutional implications. By the ascertainment of the differences in foreign and domestic costs and the proclamation of rates of duty necessary to eliminate such differences, the president could overthrow upon one ground rates deliberately established by Congress upon another. He might reduce, for example, a duty on goods coming from Canada on the ground that the costs of production were virtually equal, when the rate had in fact been deliberately fixed by Congress so as to protect the American producer against the competition of imports from that source. He was, moreover, unavoidably endowed with the power of reclassification, if the principle of cost-equalization was to be applied to items included within basket clauses, although this necessarily involved the power to frame new paragraphs or write new language into the statute. This power to make alterations in rates of duty to meet differences of foreign and domestic costs was restricted, when the statutory rates were specific, within a margin of 50 per cent,

[1] J. D. Larkin, *The President's Control of the Tariff* (Cambridge, Mass., 1936), p. 38.

but the president might well go beyond that when the rate was *ad valorem*, by means of a change in the basis of valuation from 'foreign value' to 'American selling price'. And, since he was also empowered to take into account, in determining differences in foreign and domestic costs, 'other advantages and disadvantages in competition' (1922) or 'other relevant factors that constitute an advantage or disadvantage in competition' (1930), he might prescribe rates that were in fact quite inconsistent with any cost-equalization standard at all. It was plausibly argued that such powers left so wide a discretion as to make the acts of the executive essentially legislative in character. It was at least difficult to see how they could be brought within the definition of a 'delegation to find on a fact and not to determine a policy' that was the boundary set by the doctrine of contingency legislation.[1]

The period between 1921 and 1933, when a highly nationalist and protectionist policy prevailed, thus saw the fashioning of tools for which the leaders in that period themselves had little use but which were indispensable if the tariff was to be employed to promote the foreign trade of the United States. When Cordell Hull took the lead in 1931–2 in a demand for the reduction of tariffs and secured the inclusion in the Democratic platform of 1932 of an approval of reciprocal tariff agreements, and when this resulted in the Reciprocal Trade Agreements Act of 1934, both the constitutional machinery for the negotiation of such agreements and the inducements to persuade foreign countries to enter into them were substantially more efficient than they had been at the close of the first World War. In both respects, it is true, the process of evolution was incomplete. The authority of the president to negotiate agreements under the act was strictly defined both in scope and purpose; and it was argued that there was no abbreviation of Congressional power. 'Under the Trade Agreements Act,' ran a report of the House Committee on Ways and Means of 5 May, 1943,

---

[1] J. D. Larkin, *The President's Control of the Tariff* (Cambridge, Mass., 1936), chs. iii–iv; Q. Wright, *The Control of American Foreign Relations* (New York, 1922), p. 302, *cf.* 101–6.

changes in our tariff rates are made, so far as our domestic law is concerned, by the President's proclamation under the authority of the Trade Agreements Act. Changes in the tariff rates are not made by the agreements, *per se*. The agreements are merely the means provided in the act for getting foreign concessions in return for our concessions. The agreements are also the mechanism through which, pursuant to the bargaining standard of the act, within prescribed limitations, our rates are fixed. Since changes in our tariff rates, i.e., our domestic law, are made by the President's proclamation pursuant to authority granted by Congress in the Trade Agreements Act there is no constitutional necessity for the agreements to be submitted subsequently to the Congress for approval or review. In this respect the principle underlying the trade-agreements procedure is entirely different from the theory of treaty procedure under which the Executive, without any prior authorization from Congress and without any limitations, negotiates on the basis of what he thinks advisable and then submits the treaty to the Senate for its approval. Under the latter procedure the Constitution provides that the treaty itself, when approved by two-thirds of the Senate, becomes the supreme law of the land. Trade agreements, on the other hand, of themselves, never become the law of the land, but the rates established in the trade agreement become domestic law solely by reason of the President's proclamation based on the authority of the Trade Agreements Act. In this sense the legal basis of tariff changes under the Trade Agreements Act is precisely the same as changes made in the tariff by Presidential proclamation pursuant to the authority granted the President under the 'flexible' provisions of section 315 of the Tariff Act of 1922 and section 336 of the Tariff Act of 1930. It is precisely the same procedural principle as that on which the Interstate Commerce Commission is authorized by Congress to fix fair and reasonable railroad rates.[1]

And, on the other hand, although the United States now had a three-decker tariff consisting of the Hawley-Smoot rates, the Cuban rates, and the Trade Agreement rates, and had something therefore to offer in return for foreign concessions, the value to foreign countries of the adherence by the United States to the principle of unconditional most-favoured-nation treatment was sensibly tempered by the device of restricting concessions to the principal supplier, by the elaboration of the

[1] *78 Cong., 1 Sess., H. Rept. 409*, pp. 47–8.

sub-classification of tariff schedules, and by the operation of the 'invisible tariff'. Yet a great change had occurred, and a new element had been introduced into national politics.

This realization of the inadequacy of the doctrine of self-sufficiency extended beyond the economic sphere. But it was in the economic sphere that the conclusion was least escapable and the consequence most concrete. That the McKinley tariff of 1890, which first clearly enunciated the principle of high protective rates as in themselves a sound and proper economic policy, and first clearly set up the ideal of reserving the American market for the American producer, sought also for the first time to use the tariff to force the entry of United States goods into foreign markets was a symbol of the perplexity of old purposes, at the height of their achievement, by new needs. Externally as well as internally, from without as well as from within, from above as well as from below, there came a challenge to the sufficiency of national integration and public service as a standard of judgment and a criterion of behaviour. Just when the public imagination was captured by the new patriotism and old divisions were forgotten in a new enthusiasm, the self-sufficiency of the nation met the challenge of loyalties to other groups both interior and exterior; and nationalism found itself assaulted upon two fronts.

BIBLIOGRAPHICAL NOTE

i. The study of the last fifty years in the history of the United States is more advanced than that of the same period in the history of Great Britain. There is a supplementary volume to the 'American Nation' that carries the narrative down to the entry of the United States into the first World War, F. A. Ogg, *National Progress, 1907–1917* (Harper's: New York, 1918). A preliminary outline of the continuation of the story will be found in J. C. Malin, *The United States after the World War* (Ginn, 1930), D. L. Dumond, *Roosevelt to Roosevelt* (Holt: New York, 1937), and L. M. Hacker, *American Problems of To-day; a History of the United States since the World War* (Crofts: New York, 1938). A more elaborate survey of *American*

Democracy and the World War is being written by F. L. Paxson, vol. i, *Pre-War Years, 1913–1917*, vol. ii, *America at War, 1917–1918*, vol. iii, *Post-War Years; Normalcy, 1918–1923* (Houghton Mifflin: Boston, 1936, 1939, and Univ. of California Press: Berkeley, Calif., 1948). A. D. Noyes, *The War Period of American Finance, 1908–1925* (Putnam's: New York, 1926) treats one aspect in more detail; and C. B. Swisher, *American Constitutional Development* (Houghton Mifflin: Boston, 1943) carries the study of another down to the forties. Three valuable biographies deal with the administrations of the first three presidents of the century, H. F. Pringle, *Theodore Roosevelt* (Harcourt, Brace: New York, 1931) and *The Life and Times of William Howard Taft*, 2 vv. (Farrar & Rinehart: New York, 1939); and R. S. Baker, *Woodrow Wilson, Life and Letters*, 8 vv. (Doubleday, Doran: Garden City, N.Y., 1927–39), with its supplement, *Woodrow Wilson and World Settlement*, 3 vv. (*Ibid.*, 1922). The first two volumes of Baker's *Life* are one of the best of academic biographies. Its last two volumes, dealing with the months of war from 1917 to November, 1918, are little more than fragmentary excerpts from Wilson's private papers. Volumes iii to vi are a very able narrative of the New Jersey governorship and the first years of the presidency. But like so much political biography they are for the period they cover both too long and too short; and there is still no detailed account of the last months of the administration. H. C. F. Bell has written a single-volume study, *Woodrow Wilson and the People* (Doubleday, Doran: Garden City, N.Y., 1945); and there is a more specialized monograph by A. S. Link, *Wilson; the Road to the White House* (Princeton Univ. Press: Princeton, N.J., 1947).

ii. There has been very little detailed scientific study of the domestic history of the United States during the years 1900 to 1921. The more notable books are G. E. Mowry, *Theodore Roosevelt and the Progressive Movement* (Univ. of Wisconsin Press: Madison, Wisc., 1946); C. G. Bowers, *Beveridge and the Progressive Era* (Houghton Mifflin: Boston, 1932); E. E. Robinson, *The Presidential Vote, 1896–1932* (Milford, 1934); C. H. Wooddy, *The Growth of Federal Government, 1915–1932* (McGraw Hill Book Co.: New York, 1934); W. P. G. Harding, *The Formative Period of the Federal Reserve System* (*During the World Crisis*) (The Riverside Press: Cambridge, Mass., 1925); and W. Diamond, *The Economic Thought of Woodrow Wilson*, Johns Hopkins Univ. Studies, lxi, 4 (Johns Hopkins Press: Baltimore. Md., 1943). Something has already been said above (pp. 243–8) about the literature relating to the history of business and of organized labour. To the books there listed there should be added, P. F. Brissenden, *The I.W.W.; a Study of American Syndicalism*. Col.

Univ. Studies, 193 (Columbia Univ. Press: New York, 1919); Z. Chafee, jr., *Freedom of Speech* (Harcourt, Brace & Howe: New York, 1920), revised and re-issued as *Free Speech in the United States* (Harvard Univ. Press: Cambridge, Mass., 1941); and R. L. Garis, *Immigration Restriction* (Macmillan: New York, 1928). There is a wealth of material on the history of the civilian aspects of the first World War in the volumes included in the *Economic and Social History of the World War* edited by J. T. Shotwell for the Carnegie Endowment for International Peace, and in B. Crowell & R. F. Wilson, *How America Went to War; an Account from Official Sources of the Nation's War Activities, 1917–1920*, 6 vv. (Yale Univ. Press: New Haven, Conn., 1921); G. B. Clarkson, *Industrial America in the World War* (Houghton Mifflin: Boston, 1923); and W. F. Willoughby, *Government Organization in Wartime and After* (D. Appleton: New York, 1919). The military conduct of the war has received more strictly historical treatment in J. G. Harbord, *America in the World War* (Houghton Mifflin: Boston, 1933), *The American Expeditionary Forces* (Evanston Publ. Co.: Evanston, Ill., 1929), and *The American Army in France, 1917–1919* (Little, Brown: Boston, 1936); B. J. Hendrick & W. S. Sims, *The Victory at Sea* (Doubleday, Page: Garden City, N.Y., 1920); and T. G. Frothingham, *The Naval History of the World War*, vol. iii, *The United States in the War, 1917–1918* (Harvard Univ. Press: Cambridge, Mass., 1926).

iii. The change in the foreign relations of the United States that occurred at the turn of the century led to the growth of a school of diplomatic history that is now one of the best equipped branches of American historiography; and the masterly and indispensable *Guide to the Diplomatic History of the United States, 1775–1921*, by S. F. Bemis and Grace G. Griffin (Govt. Printing Office: Washington, D.C., 1935) gives a view both of what has been done to make available the original documents upon which the writing of this history must be based and of what has been written.

If there is set aside the diplomatic history of the American Revolution and of the War of 1812, which is intimately associated with that of the European powers and on which there is a substantial literature of an early date, it is true to say that the competent study of American diplomatic history is of quite recent origin. At the turn of the century there began to appear books of weight that dealt generally with the foreign relations of the United States but that lay upon the boundary between history and politics, such as J. W. Foster, *A Century of American Diplomacy* (Houghton Mifflin: Boston, 1900), and *The Practice of Diplomacy as illustrated in the Foreign Relations of the United States* (Houghton Mifflin: Boston, 1906); J. H. Latané,

America as a World Power, 1897–1907 (Harper's: New York, 1907);
A. C. Coolidge, *The United States as a World Power* (Macmillan: New
York, 1908); and A. T. Mahan, *The Interest of America in International
Conditions* (Little, Brown: Boston, 1910); and in A. B. Hart, *The
Foundations of American Foreign Policy* (Macmillan: New York, 1901)
there was provided the first bibliographical tool designed for students
of the subject. But before 1914, scientific work was virtually restricted to the history of the relations of the United States with Latin
America. J. M. Callahan, *The Diplomatic History of the Southern Con-
federacy* (Johns Hopkins Press: Baltimore, Md.), appeared in 1901;
and some pioneer work was done on the history of the relations of
the United States with the Far East in J. M. Callahan, *American
Relations in the Pacific and the Far East, 1784–1900.* Johns Hopkins
Univ. Studies, xix, 1–3 (Johns Hopkins Press: Baltimore, Md.,
1901); J. W. Foster, *American Diplomacy in the Orient* (Houghton:
Boston, 1903); Mary R. Coolidge, *Chinese Immigration* (Holt: New
York, 1909); and F. W. Williams, *Anson Burlingame and the first
Chinese Mission to Foreign Powers* (Scribner's: New York, 1912). But
most of the work was devoted to the history of relations with Latin
America. The Spanish-American war of 1898 produced H. E. Flack,
Spanish-American Diplomatic Relations preceding the War of 1898. Johns
Hopkins Univ. Studies, xxiv, 1–2 (Johns Hopkins Press: Baltimore,
Md., 1906); E. J. Benton, *International Law and the Diplomacy of the
Spanish-American War* (Johns Hopkins Press: Baltimore, Md., 1908);
and F. E. Chadwick, *The Relations of the United States and Spain*, vol. i,
Diplomacy, vols. ii–iii, *The Spanish-American War* (Scribner's: New
York, 1909, 1911). At the same time, the serious study of the history
of relations with Latin America in a wider field was also begun with
L. M. Keasbey, *The Nicaragua Canal and the Monroe Doctrine* (Putnam's
New York, 1896); I. D. Travis, *The History of the Clayton-Bulwer
Treaty.* Pubs. of the Michigan Pol. Science Assoc., iii, 8 (Ann Arbor,
Mich., 1900); F. L. Paxson, *The Independence of the South American
Republics* (Ferris: Philadelphia, 1903); B. H. Carroll, *Die Annexion
von Texas; ein Beitrag zur Geschichte der Monroe-Doktrin* (Inaugural-
Dissertation. Berlin, 1904); T. B. Edgington, *The Monroe Doctrine*
(Little, Brown: Boston, 1904); H. B. Fuller, *The Purchase of Florida*
(Burrows: Cleveland, O., 1906); J. S. Reeves, *American Diplomacy
under Tyler and Polk* (Johns Hopkins Press: Baltimore, Md., 1907);
E. D. Adams, *British Interests and Activities in Texas, 1838–1846*
(Johns Hopkins Press: Baltimore, Md., 1910); and G. L. Rives,
The United States and Mexico, 1821–1848, 2 vv. (Scribner's: New York,
1913); while there appeared the first three important studies of the
Monroe Doctrine to be written by foreign scholars, W. F. Reddaway,
The Monroe Doctrine (University Press: Cambridge, 1898); H. Pétin,

Les États-Unis et la doctrine de Monroe (Rousseau: Paris, 1900); and H. Kraus, *Monroedoktrin, in ihren Beziehungen zur amerikanischen Diplomatie und zum Völkerrecht* (Guttentag: Berlin, 1913). Upon these foundations the modern school of American diplomatic history has been built since the outbreak of the first World War: and most of the best work has continued to be done in the fields of Latin American and of Far Eastern relations.

The historical literature upon the relations of the United States with Latin America is now extensive. A convenient guide to it will be found in R. A. Humphreys, *Latin America: a Selective Guide to Publications in English* (Royal Institute of International Affairs, 1949). The standard authority upon the history of the Monroe Doctrine is now D. Perkins, *The Monroe Doctrine, 1823–1826* (Harvard Univ. Press: Cambridge, Mass., 1927), *The Monroe Doctrine, 1826–1867* (Johns Hopkins Press: Baltimore, Md., 1933), and *The Monroe Doctrine, 1867–1907 (Ibid., 1937)*. On the history of the policy of the United States in the Far East the most important books are T. Dennett, *Americans in Eastern Asia* (Macmillan: New York, 1922); A. W. Griswold, *The Far Eastern Policy of the United States* (Harcourt, Brace: New York, 1938); K. S. Latourette, *The History of the Early Relations between the United States and China, 1784–1844.* Connecticut Academy of Arts & Sc., Transactions, xxii (Yale Univ. Press: New Haven, Conn., 1917); P. J. Treat, *Japan and the United States, 1853–1921*, revd. ed. continued to 1928 (Stanford Univ. Press: Stanford, Calif., 1928), and *Diplomatic Relations between the United States and Japan, 1853–1895*, 2 vv. (*Ibid.*, 1932); E. H. Zabriskie, *American-Russian Rivalry in the Far East; a Study in Diplomacy and Power Politics, 1895–1914* (Univ. of Pennsylvania Press: Philadelphia, 1946); T. Dennett, *Roosevelt and the Russo-Japanese War* (Doubleday, Page: Garden City, N.Y., 1925); T. A. Bailey, *Theodore Roosevelt and the Japanese-American Crisis* (Stanford Univ. Press: Stanford, Calif., 1934); Mary R. Coolidge, *Chinese Immigration* (Holt: New York, 1909); Y. Ichihashi, *Japanese in the United States* (Stanford Univ. Press: Stanford, Calif., 1932), and *The Washington Conference and After (Ibid., 1928)*; H. L. Stimson, *The Far Eastern Crisis* (Harper's: New York, 1936); T. A. Bisson, *American Policy in the Far East, 1931–1940* (Institute of Pacific Relations: New York, 1940); and Ethel B. Dietrich, *Far Eastern Trade of the United States (Ibid., 1940)*.

iv. On the diplomacy of Woodrow Wilson the literature is already substantial. The works that treat the subject historically are, H. Notter, *The Origins of the Foreign Policy of Woodrow Wilson* (Johns Hopkins Press: Baltimore, Md., 1937); C. Seymour, *American*

Diplomacy during the World War (Johns Hopkins Press: Baltimore, Md., 1934), and *American Neutrality, 1914–1917* (Yale Univ. Press: New Haven, Conn., 1935); Alice M. Morrissey, *The American Defence of Neutral Rights, 1914–1917* (Harvard Univ. Press: Cambridge, Mass., 1939); C. C. Tansill, *America Goes to War* (Little, Brown: Boston, 1938); T. A. Bailey, *The Policy of the United States towards Neutrals, 1917–1918* (Johns Hopkins Press: Baltimore, Md., 1942); and L. I. Strakhovsky, *The Origins of American Intervention in North Russia, 1918* (Princeton Univ. Press: Princeton, N.J., 1937). The more strictly legal aspects of the subject are dealt with in C. C. Hyde, *International Law, chiefly as interpreted and applied by the United States*, 2 vv. (Little, Brown: Boston, 1922); J. W. Garner, *International Law and the World War*, 2 vv. (Longmans, 1920); and C. Savage, *Policy of the United States toward Maritime Commerce in War*, vol. ii, *1914–1918* (Govt. Printing Office: Washington, D.C., 1936).

R. S. Baker's three volumes on *Woodrow Wilson and World Settlement* (1922) noted above (p. 286) were the first full historical account of the American part in the making of peace. But brilliantly written though they were, they are also not without serious inaccuracies. There are now available, T. A. Bailey, *Woodrow Wilson and the Lost Peace* (Macmillan: New York, 1944); A. Nevins, *Henry White, Thirty Years of American Diplomacy* (Harper's: New York, 1930); D. H. Miller, *The Drafting of the Covenant*, 2 vv. (Putnam's: New York, 1928); D. F. Fleming, *The United States and the League of Nations, 1918–1920* (Putnam's: New York, 1932); C. A. Berdahl, *The Policy of the United States with respect to the League of Nations*. Publications of the Graduate Institute of International Studies, no. 4 (Librairie Kundig: Geneva, 1932); and R. J. Bartlett, *The League to Enforce Peace* (Univ. of N. Carolina Press: Chapel Hill, N.C., 1944). There has been a good deal of detailed study of American foreign relations since 1920. The more important of the distinctively historical works are G. H. Blakeslee, *Recent Foreign Policy of the United States; Problems in American Cooperation with other Powers* (Abingdon Press: New York, 1925); J. W. Garner, *American Foreign Policies* (New York Univ. Press: New York, 1928); F. H. Simonds, *American Foreign Policy in the Post-War Years* (Johns Hopkins Press: Baltimore, Md., 1935); D. F. Fleming, *The United States and World Organization, 1920–1933* (Columbia Univ. Press: New York, 1938); R. L. Buell, *The Washington Conference* (Appleton: New York, 1922); Y. Ichihashi, *The Washington Conference and After* (Stanford Univ. Press: Stanford Univ., Calif., 1928); D. H. Miller, *The Peace Pact of Paris; a Study of the Briand-Kellogg Treaty* (Putnam's: New York, 1928); and the State Department publication, *Peace and War; United States Foreign Policy,*

1931–1941 (*documented edition*) (Govt. Printing Office: Washington, D.C., 1943). And since 1928, the history of American foreign relations has been recorded in a series of annual volumes, C. P. Howland, *Survey of American Foreign Relations, 1928* [etc.], 4 vv. (Yale Univ. Press: New Haven, Conn., 1928–31), and W. Lippmann, W. O. Scroggs *et al.*, *The United States in World Affairs, 1931* [etc.] (Harper & Bros.: New York, 1932+). But the decisive relations have been economic, and to these there is an introduction in B. H. Williams, *Economic Foreign Policy of the United States* (McGraw-Hill: New York, 1929), and there is a masterly survey of them in *The United States in the World Economy*. Economic Series, no. 23. U.S. Department of Commerce (Govt. Printing Office: Washington, D.C., 1943).

v. There are three useful introductory studies of the history of the New Deal written by Englishmen, A. Steel-Maitland, *The New America* (Macmillan, 1934), E. M. Hugh-Jones & E. A. Radice, *An American Experiment* (Milford, 1936), and A. S. J. Baster, *The Twilight of American Capitalism* (King, 1937); and there are two more strictly historical American studies, L. M. Hacker, *A Short History of the New Deal* (Crofts: New York, 1934), and B. Rauch, *The History of the New Deal, 1933–1938* (Creative Age Press: New York, 1944). There are more detailed studies of certain aspects of the crisis in S. E. Harris, *Twenty Years of Federal Reserve Policy, including an extended discussion of the Monetary Crisis, 1927–33*, 2 vv. (Harvard Univ. Press: Cambridge, Mass., 1933); L. S. Lyon *et al.*, *The National Industrial Recovery Administration; an Analysis and Appraisal* (Brookings Institution: Washington, D.C., 1935); C. F. Roos, *NRA. Economic Planning* (Principia Press: Bloomington, Ind., 1937); and E. E. Robinson, *The Presidential Vote, 1936* (Stanford Univ. Press: Stanford Univ. Calif., 1940).

A good deal has been done to elucidate the recent changes in American agriculture, although much that has been written lies upon the frontier between history and economics. The books of a rather more historical than analytical character are A. Tilden, *The Legislation of the Civil War Period considered as a Basis of the Agricultural Revolution in the United States* (Univ. of S. California Press: Los Angeles, Calif., 1937); L. Rogin, *The Introduction of Farm Machinery in its Relation to the Productivity of Labor in the Agriculture of the United States during the Nineteenth Century* (Univ. of California Press: Berkeley, Calif., 1931); H. Barger & H. H. Landsberg, *American Agriculture, 1899–1939* (National Bureau of Economic Research: New York, 1942); E. F. Dummeier, R. B. Heflebower & T. Norman, *Economics with Applications to Agriculture*, 3rd ed. (McGraw-Hill: New York, 1950); J. S. Davis, *On Agricultural Policy*,

1926–1938. Misc. Pubs. no. 9 (Food Research Institute: Stanford Univ. Calif., 1939); Persia C. Campbell, *American Agricultural Policy* (King, 1933); O. M. Kile, *The Farm Bureau through Three Decades* (Waverly Press: Baltimore, Md., 1948); E. G. Nourse *et al.*, *Three Years of the Agricultural Adjustment Administration* (Brookings Institution: Washington, D.C., 1937); J. S. Davis, *Wheat and the AAA* (*Ibid.*, 1935); H. I. Richards, *Cotton and the AAA* (*Ibid.*, 1936); H. B. Rowe, *Tobacco under the AAA* (*Ibid.*, 1935); and D. A. FitzGerald, *Livestock under the AAA* (*Ibid.*, 1935).

vi. Upon the background of the recent history of the commercial policy of the United States see, F. W. Taussig, *The Tariff History of the United States*, 8th ed. (Putnam's: New York, 1931), to which is to be added the authoritative volume issued by the United States Tariff Commission, *Reciprocity and Commercial Treaties* (Govt. Printing Office: Washington, D.C., 1919), in the preparation of which Taussig played a large part; and P. W. Bidwell, *Tariff Policy of the United States* (Council on Foreign Relations: New York, 1933), a valuable introductory survey written on a smaller scale and in less technical terms. W. McClure, *A New American Commercial Policy as evidenced by Section 317 of the Tariff Act of 1922*. Col. Univ. Studies, 255 (Columbia Univ. Press: New York, 1924) is of small importance, since the concession of unconditional most-favoured-nation treatment was ineffectual in the circumstances. The history of the Hawley-Smoot tariff is the subject of E. E. Schattschneider, *Politics, Pressures and the Tariff; a Study of Free Private Enterprise in Pressure Politics as shown in the 1929–1930 Revision of the Tariff* (Prentice-Hall: New York, 1935), and J. M. Jones, *Tariff Retaliation: Repercussions of the Hawley-Smoot Bill* (Univ. of Pennsylvania Press: Philadelphia, 1934). The radical change in policy is recorded in W. A. Brown, jr., *The United States and the Restoration of World Trade* (Brookings Institution: Washington, D.C., 1950); W. Diebold, *New Directions in our Trade Policy* (Council on Foreign Relations: New York, 1941); H. O. Davis, *America's Trade Equality Policy* (American Council on Public Affairs: Washington, D.C., 1942); H. J. Tasca, *The Reciprocal Trade Policy of the United States* (Univ. of Pennsylvania Press: Philadelphia, 1938); J. D. Larkin, *The President's Control of the Tariff* (Harvard Univ. Press: Cambridge, Mass., 1936); and C. Kreider, *The Anglo-American Trade Agreement; a Study of British and American Commercial Policies, 1934–1939* (Princeton Univ. Press: Princeton, N.J., 1943).

LIST OF WORKS CITED

ABBOTT, W. C., *New York in the American Revolution*, 105
ABERNETHY, T. P., *From Frontier to Plantation in Tennessee*, 161
— *The Formative Period in Alabama*, 161
— *Western Lands and the American Revolution*, 71, 100
ACKERMAN, W. K., *Early Illinois Railroads*, 156
ADAMS, Alice D., *The Neglected Period of Anti-Slavery in America*, 201
ADAMS, E. D., *British Interests and Activities in Texas*, 288
ADAMS, H., *History of the United States*, 18, 23
— *The Education of Henry Adams—an Autobiography*, 38
ADAMS, H. B., *The Germanic Origin of New England Towns*, 18
— *Maryland's Influence upon Land Cessions to the United States*, 100
— *Saxon Tithingmen in America*, 18
Herbert B. Adams, Tributes of Friends, 38
ADAMS, J. T., *Henry Adams*, 38
— *New England in the Republic*, 198
— *Provincial Society, 1690-1763*, 64, 102
— *Revolutionary New England*, 64
ADAMS, R. G., *Political Ideas of the American Revolution*, 101
ADAMS, W. F., *Ireland and Irish Emigration to the New World*, 149
ALBION, R. G., *Forests and Sea Power*, 68
ALBRIGHT, G. L., *Official Explorations for Pacific Railroads*, 157
ALDEN, G. H., *New Governments West of the Alleghanies before 1780*,
                                                                [48, 71
ALDEN, J. R., *John Stuart and the Southern Colonial Frontier*, 69
ALVORD, C. W. *The Illinois Country*, 69
— *The Mississippi Valley in British Politics*, 24, 48, 68, 71
— and BIDGOOD, L., *The First Explorations of the Trans-Allegheny
          Region by the Virginians*, 70
— (ed.), *The Centennial History of Illinois*, 157-8
AMBLER, C. H., *A History of Transportation in the Ohio Valley*, 153
— *Sectionalism in Virginia from 1776 to 1861*, 199
AMERICAN COUNCIL OF LEARNED SOCIETIES, *Report of the Committee on
     Linguistic and National Stocks in the Population of the United States*,
ANDERSON, G. L., *General William J. Palmer*, 157   [148
ANDERSON, N., *Desert Saints*, 241
ANDREW, A. P., *Statistics for the United States*, 239
ANDREWS, C. M., *The Boston Merchants and the Non-Importation Move-
          ment*, 101
— *The Colonial Background of the American Revolution*, 64

ANDREWS, C. M.—*continued*
— *The Colonial Period*, 64
— 'These forty years', 37
ANGLE, P. M., *A Shelf of Lincoln Books*, 208
ARMES, Ethel M., *The Story of Coal and Iron in Alabama*, 245
ARNETT, A. M., *The Populist Movement in Georgia*, 242
ASHLEY, W. J., *Surveys, Historic and Economic*, 67
AUCHAMPAUGH, P. G., *James Buchanan and his Cabinet on the Eve of Secession*, 207

BABCOCK, K. C., *The Scandinavian Element in the United States*, 150
BACON-FOSTER, Corra, *Early Chapters in the Development of the Potomac Route to the West*, 152
BAER, W. N., *The Economic Development of the Cigar Industry in the United States*, 244
BAILEY, Edith A., *Influences towards Radicalism in Connecticut*, 65
BAILEY, K. P., *The Ohio Company of Virginia and the Westward Movement*, [71
BAILEY, T. A., *The Policy of the United States towards Neutrals*, 290
— *Theodore Roosevelt and the Japanese-American Crisis*, 289
— *Woodrow Wilson and the Lost Peace*, 290
BAKER, G. P., *The Formation of the New England Railroad Systems*, 155
BAKER, R. S., *Woodrow Wilson, Life and Letters*, 286
— *Woodrow Wilson and World Settlement*, 286, 290
BALDWIN, Alice M., *The New England Clergy and the American Revolution*, 103
BALDWIN, L. D., *The Keelboat Age on Western Waters*, 154
— *Whiskey Rebels; the Story of a Frontier Uprising*, 104
BALLAGH, J. C., *A History of Slavery in Virginia*, 206
BANCROFT, F., *Calhoun and the South Carolina Nullification Movement*,
— *Slave-Trading in the Old South*, 205   [200
BARCK, O. T., jr., *New York City during the War for Independence*, 105
BARCLAY, T. S., *The Liberal Republican Movement in Missouri*, 210
BARGER, H., and LANDSBERG, H. H., *American Agriculture*, 291
BARINGER, W. E., *A House Dividing*, 208
— *Lincoln's Rise to Power*, 208
BARKER, C. A., *The Background of the Revolution in Maryland*, 106
BARNARD, H., '*Eagle Forgotten*', 247
BARNES, G. H., *The Anti-Slavery Impulse*, 201
BARRETT, J. A., *Evolution of the Ordinance of 1787*, 100
BARRS, B., *East Florida in the American Revolution*, 106
BARTLETT, Marguerite G., *The Chief Phases of Pennsylvania Politics in the Jacksonian Period*, 198
BARTLETT, R. J., *The League to Enforce Peace*, 290
BASSETT, J. S., *Anti-Slavery Leaders of North Carolina*, 206

BEVERIDGE, A. J., *Abraham Lincoln*, 208

BIDWELL, P. W., 'Rural Economy in New England at the beginning of the nineteenth century', 199
— *Tariff Policy of the United States*, 292
— and FALCONER, J. I., *History of Agriculture in the Northern United States*, 197

BIESELE, R. L., *The History of the German Settlements in Texas*, 149

BILLINGTON, R. A., *Westward Expansion; a History of the American Frontier*, 149

BINING, A. C., *British Regulation of the Colonial Iron Industry*, 68

BINKLEY, W. C., *The Expansionist Movement in Texas*, 161-2

BINNS, A., *Northwest Gateway*, 246

BISHOP, A. L., *The State Works of Pennsylvania*, 153

BISHOP, C. F., *History of Elections in the American Colonies*, 67

BISSON, T. A., *American Policy in the Far East*, 289

BLAKESLEE, G. H., *The Recent Foreign Policy of the United States*, 290

BLAKEY, R. G., *The United States Beet-Sugar Industry and the Tariff*, 244

BLANDI, J. G., *Maryland Business Corporations*, 199

BLEGEN, T. C., *Norwegian Migration to America*, 150
— *Norwegian Migration to America; the American Transition*, 150

BLINKOFF, M., *The Influence of Charles A. Beard upon American Historiography*, 39

BODLEY, T., *History of Kentucky before the Louisiana Purchase in 1803*,
— *Our First Great West*, 71, 160   [70, 160

BOGART, E. L., *Internal Improvements and State Debt in Ohio*, 153
— *Peacham; the Story of a Vermont Hill Town*, 245-6

BOGEN, J. I., *The Anthracite Railroads*, 155

BOGGESS, A. C., *The Settlement of Illinois*, 150

BOLTON, H. E., *Texas in the Middle Eighteenth Century*, 159
— *Athanase de Mézières and the Louisiana-Texas Frontier*, 159
— (ed.), *Arredondo's Historical Proof of Spain's Title to Georgia*, 69
— and Ross, Mary, *The Debatable Land*, 69

BOND, B. W., jr., *The Civilization of the Old Northwest*, 158
— *The Quit-rent System in the American Colonies*, 67
— *State Government in Maryland*, 106

BOUCHER, C. S., *The Ante-Bellum Attitude of South Carolina towards Manufacturing and Agriculture*, 203
— *The Nullification Controversy in South Carolina*, 200
— *The Secession and Cooperation Movements in South Carolina*, 204
— *South Carolina and the South on the Eve of Secession*, 204

BOWERS, C. G., *Beveridge and the Progressive Era*, 286

BOWYER, C. S., *Waterways of New Jersey*, 153

BOYD, J. P., 'State and local Historical Societies in the United States', 39

BOYD, Minnie C., *Alabama in the Fifties*, 161, 204

BOYD, W. K., *The Federal Period, 1783-1860*.   Vol. ii of the *History of North Carolina*, 199

BRACKETT, J. R., *The Negro in Maryland*, 205

BRADLEE, F. B. C., *The Eastern Railroad*, 155

— *The Boston and Lowell Railroad*, 155

BRAYER, H. O., *William Blackmore*, vol. i, 151, 241; vol. ii, 154

BRAZEAL, B. R., *The Brotherhood of Sleeping Car Porters*, 248

BREBNER, J. B., *New England's Outpost*, 64

BREWTON, W. W., *Life of Thomas E. Watson*, 242

BRIGANCE, W. H., *Jeremiah Sullivan Black*, 207

BRIGGS, H. E., 'An appraisal of historical writings on the Great Plains since 1920', 40

BRISSENDEN, P. F., *The I.W.W.; a Study of American Syndicalism*, 286-7

BROOKS, R. P., *The Agrarian Revolution in Georgia*, 242

BROOKS, Van Wyck, *The Flowering of New England*, 198

BROWN, A. C., *The Old Bay Line*, 156

BROWN, C. K., *A State Movement in Railroad Development*, 156

BROWN, E. S., *The Constitutional History of the Louisiana Purchase*, 160

BROWN, Vera L., *Anglo-Spanish Relations in the Closing Years of the Colonial Era*, 159

BROWN, W. A., jr., *The United States and the Restoration of World Trade*,

BROWNE, H. J., *The Catholic Church and the Knights of Labor*, 240   [292

BROWNE, W. R., *Altgeld of Illinois*, 247

BROWNSON, H. G., *History of the Illinois Central Railroad to 1870*, 156

BRUMMER, S. D., *Political History of New York State during the Period of the Civil War*, 209

BRUNHOUSE, R. L., *The Counter-Revolution in Pennsylvania*, 105

BRYCE, J., *The American Commonwealth*, 248

— *Modern Democracies*, 248

BUCK, P. H., *The Road to Reunion*, 240

BUCK, S. J., 'Clarence Walworth Alvord, historian', 39

— *The Granger Movement*, 242

— and Elizabeth H., *The Planting of Civilization in Western Pennsylvania*, 69

BUCKMASTER, Henrietta, *Let My People Go*, 201

BUCKNAM, W. F., *A History of Boston Division Number Sixty-one Brotherhood of Locomotive Engineers*, 248

BUELL, R. L., *The Washington Conference*, 290

BULLOCK, C. J., *Essays on the Monetary History of the United States*, 72

BUREAU OF THE CENSUS, *A Century of Population Growth*, 68, 148

BURNETT, E. C. (ed.), *Letters of Members of the Continental Congress*, 104

BURNS, J. F., *Controversies between Royal Governors and their Assemblies in the North American Colonies*, 67

CADMAN, J. W., jr., *The Corporation in New Jersey*, 243
CAHILL, Marion C., *Shorter Hours*, 246
CALLAHAN, J. M., *American Relations in the Pacific and the Far East*, 288
— *The Diplomatic History of the Southern Confederacy*, 288
CALLAWAY, J. E., *The Early Settlement of Georgia*, 66
Cambridge Modern History, vol. vii, 63
CAMPBELL, E. G., *The Reorganization of the American Railroad System*,
CAMPBELL, Persia C., *American Agricultural Policy*, 292 [155
CAPERS, G. M., jr., *The Biography of a River Town*, 246
CAPPON, L. J., 'Two decades of historical activity in Virginia', 40
CARMAN, H. J., and LUTHIN, R. H., *Lincoln and the Patronage*, 208
— DAVID, H., and GUTHRIE, P. N. (eds.), *The Path I Trod*, 247
CARPENTER, J. T., *The South as a Conscious Minority*, 203
CARROLL, B. H., *Die Annexion von Texas*, 288
CARROLL, E. M., *Origins of the Whig Party*, 200
CARROLL, J. C., *Slave Insurrections in the United States*, 205
CARSEL, W., *A History of the Chicago Ladies' Garment Workers' Union*,
CARTER, C. E., *Great Britain and the Illinois Country*, 48, 71 [248
CARY, J. W., *Organization and History of the Chicago, Milwaukee and
St. Paul Railway Company*, 156
CASH, W. J., *The Mind of the South*, 203
CASKEY, W. M., *Secession and Restoration of Louisiana*, 204
CATER, H. D. (ed.), *Henry Adams and His Friends*, 38-9
CATLIN, G. B., *The Story of Detroit*, 246
CATTERALL, Helen T., *Judicial Cases concerning American Slavery and
the Negro*, 203, 206
— 'Some antecedents of the Dred Scott case', 203
CAUGHEY, J. W., *Bernado de Galvez in Louisiana*, 159-60
— *McGillivray of the Creeks*, 70, 160
CAUTHEN, C. E., *South Carolina goes to War*, 210
CHADDOCK, R. E., *Ohio before 1850*, 157
CHADSEY, C. E., *The Struggle between President Johnson and Congress
over Reconstruction*, 210
CHADWICK, F. E., *The Relations of the United States and Spain*, 288
CHAFEE, Z., jr., *Freedom of Speech*, 287
— *Free Speech in the United States*, 287
CHAMBERS, H. E., *Mississippi Valley Beginnings*, 69
CHANNING, E., *A History of the United States*, 7, 63, 99
— HART, A. B., and TURNER, F. J., *Guide to the Study and Reading
of American History*, 22
CHASE, E. E., *Maine Railroads*, 155
CHILDS, Frances S., *French Refugee Life in the United States*, 106
CHINARD, G., *Jefferson et les idéologues*, 106
CHUGERMAN, S., *Lester F. Ward*, 239-40

CLARK, Blanche H., *The Tennessee Yeoman*, 161

CLARK, D. E., *The West in American History*, 148-9, 240

CLARK, Dora M., *British Opinion and the American Revolution*, 102

CLARK, J. B., *Populism in Alabama*, 242

CLARK, J. D., *The Federal Trust Policy*, 244

CLARK, J. S., *The Life and Letters of John Fiske*, 38

CLARK, O. B., *The Politics of Iowa during the Civil War*, 209   [156

CLARK, T. D., *A Pioneer Southern Railroad from New Orleans to Cairo*,

CLARK, V .S., *History of Manufactures in the United States*, 67, 197 [243

CLARKE, Mary P., *Parliamentary Privilege in the American Colonies*, 67

CLARKSON, G. B., *Industrial America in the World War*, 287

CLAYTON, P., *The Aftermath of the Civil War in Arkansas*, 211

CLELAND, R. G., *The Cattle on a Thousand Hills*, 241

CLEMEN, R. A., *The American Livestock and Meat Industry*, 244

CLEVELAND, Catharine C., *The Great Revival in the West*, 158

CLEVELAND, F. A., and POWELL, F. W., *Railroad Promotion and Capitalization in the United States*, 154

CLOUGH, S. B., *A Century of American Life Insurance*, 245

COCHRAN, T. C., 'A decade of American histories', 40

— *The Pabst Brewing Company*, 245

— 'Research in American economic history', 40

— and MILLER, W., *The Age of Enterprise*, 243

COFFIN, V., *The Province of Quebec and the Early American Revolution*,

COLE, A. C., *The Era of the Civil War*, 202, 209   [100

— *The Whig Party in the South*, 200-1

COLE, A. H., *The American Wool Manufacture*, 244

COLEMAN, C. H., *The Election of 1868*, 210

COLEMAN, J. W., *Labor Disturbances in Pennsylvania*, 247

COLEMAN, McA., *Eugene V. Debs*, 247

COLLINS, W. H., *The Domestic Slave Trade of the Southern States*, 205

COMAN, Katharine, *Economic Beginnings of the Far West*, 240

COMMAGER, H. S., *The American Mind*, 239

COMMONS, J. R., *History of Labor in the United States*, 197, 246

— *Races and Immigrants in America*, 149

— et al., *A Documentary History of American Industrial Society*, 246

CONNOR, R. D. W., *The Colonial and Revolutionary Periods*, 66

COOLEY, H. S., *A Study of Slavery in New Jersey*, 205

COOLIDGE, A. C., *The United States as a World Power*, 288

COOLIDGE, Mary R., *Chinese Immigration*, 288, 289

COPELAND, M. T., *The Cotton Manufacturing Industry of the United States*, 244

COPPOCK, H. F., 'Herbert Levi Osgood', 39

CORRY, J. P., *Indian Affairs in Georgia*, 70

CORWIN, E. S., *The Doctrine of Judicial Review*, 203

COTTERILL, R. S., *The Old South*, 203
COULTER, E. M., *The Cincinnati Southern Railroad*, 156
— *The Civil War and Readjustment in Kentucky*, 209, 211
— 'What the South has done about its history', 39
COUPLAND, R., *The American Revolution and the British Empire*, 103
— *The Quebec Act*, 100
COX, I. J., *The Early Exploration of Louisiana*, 159
— *The West Florida Controversy*, 160
CRANDALL, A. W., *The Early History of the Republican Party*, 201
CRANE, V. W., *The Southern Frontier*, 69
CRAVEN, A., *The Coming of the Civil War*, 200
— *The Repressible Conflict*, 200
— *Soil Exhaustion as a Factor in the Agricultural History of Virginia and Maryland*, 199
CRENSHAW, O., *The Slave States in the Presidential Election of 1860*, 207
CRIBBS, G. A., *The Frontier Policy of Pennsylvania*, 69
CRITTENDEN, C. C., *The Commerce of North Carolina*, 101
CRITTENDEN, C., and GODARD, Doris, *Historical Societies in the United States and Canada: a Handbook*, 39
CROSS, A. L., *The Anglican Episcopate and the American Colonies*, 67
— *Eighteenth Century Documents relating to the Royal Forest, the Sheriffs and Smuggling*, 68
CROSS, I. B., *A History of the Labor Movement in California*, 247
CROWELL, B., and WILSON, R. F., *How America Went to War*, 287
CROWL, P. A., *Maryland during and after the Revolution*, 106
CRUMP, Helen J., *Colonial Admiralty Jurisdiction in the Seventeenth Century*, 67
CUNZ, D., *The Maryland Germans; a History*, 149
CURTIS, F., *The Republican Party*, 201
CUSHING, H. A., *History of the Transition from Provincial to Commonwealth Government in Massachusetts*, 105

DAGGETT, S., *Chapters on the History of the Southern Pacific*, 157
— *Railroad Reorganization*, 154-5
DALE, E. E., *Cow Country*, 241
— *The Indians of the Southwest*, 161
— *The Range Cattle Industry*, 241
DANIELS, W. M., *American Railroads*, 154
DARLING, A. B., *Our Rising Empire*, 160
— *Political Changes in Massachusetts*, 198
DARLINGTON, Mary C., *History of Colonel Henry Bouquet and the Western Frontiers of Pennsylvania*, 69
DAVENPORT, F. G., *Ante-Bellum Kentucky*, 204
DAVID, H., *The History of the Haymarket Affair*, 247

DAVIDSON, P., *Propaganda and the American Revolution,* 102
DAVIS, C. S., *The Cotton Kingdom in Alabama,* 161, 204
DAVIS, E. A. (ed.), *Plantation Life in the Florida Parishes of Louisiana,*
DAVIS, H. O., *America's Trade Equality Policy,* 292   [205
DAVIS, J. P., *The Union Pacific Railway,* 157
DAVIS, J. S., *Essays in the Earlier History of American Corporations,* 150
— *On Agricultural Policy,* 291-2
— *Wheat and the AAA,* 292
DAVIS, S. L., *Pennsylvania Politics, 1860-1863,* 209
DAVIS, W. W., *The Civil War and Reconstruction in Florida,* 211
DAVITT, L. J., *A Re-Study of the Movement toward American Independence,*
DELAP, S. A., *The Populist Party in North Carolina,* 242   [103
DENMAN, C. P., *The Secession Movement in Alabama,* 204
DENNETT, T., *Americans in Eastern Asia,* 289
— *Roosevelt and the Russo-Japanese War,* 289
DERRICK, S. M., *Centennial History of South Carolina Railroad,* 156
DESTLER, C. McA., *American Radicalism,* 239
DEWEY, D. R., *Financial History of the United States,* 242
DIAMOND, W., *The Economic Thought of Woodrow Wilson,* 286
DICK, E., *The Dixie Frontier,* 70
— *Sod-house Frontier,* 241
— *Vanguards of the Frontier,* 240
DICKERSON, O. M., *American Colonial Government,* 66
DIEBOLD, W., *New Directions in our Trade Policy,* 292
DIETRICH, Ethel B., *Far Eastern Trade of the United States,* 289
DILLA, Harriette M., *The Politics of Michigan,* 158
DIXON, F. H., *Railroads and Government,* 155
— *A Traffic History of the Mississippi River System,* 153
DOBIE, Edith, *The Political Career of Stephen Mallory White,* 249
DODSON, L., *Alexander Spotswood, Governor of Colonial Virginia,* 66
DOMBROWSKI, J., *The Early Days of Christian Socialism in America,* 240
DONDORE, Dorothy A., *The Prairie and the Making of Middle America,*
DONOVAN, H. D. A., *The Barnburners,* 201   [158
DORFMAN, J., *The Economic Mind in American Civilization,* 239
DORMAN, L., *Party Politics in Alabama from 1850 through 1860,* 161
DOSTER, J. F., *Alabama's First Railroad Commission,* 154
DOWNES, R. C., *Frontier Ohio,* 150
DOWNEY, E. H., *History of Labor Legislation in Iowa,* 247
DOYLE, J. A., *The Colonies under the House of Hanover,* 63
— *The English in America,* 7
DOZIER, H. D., *A History of the Atlantic Coast Line Railroad,* 156
DRAKE, T. E., *Quakers and Slavery in America,* 205
DU BOIS, E. W. B., *The Suppression of the African Slave-Trade to the
United States of America,* 205

DULLES, F. R., *Labor in America*, 246

DUMMEIER, E. F., HEFLEBOWER, R. B., and NORMAN, T., *Economics with Application to Agriculture*, 291

DUMOND, D. L., *Anti-Slavery Origins of the Civil War in the United* [States, 201
— *Roosevelt to Roosevelt*, 285
— *The Secession Movement*, 204
— (ed.), *Southern Editorials on Secession*, 204

DUNAWAY, W. F., *The Scotch-Irish of Colonial Pennsylvania*, 68
— *History of the James River and Kanawha Company*, 152

DUNHAM, C. F., *The Attitude of the Northern Clergy toward the South*, 207

DUNLAP, L. W., *American Historical Societies, 1790-1860*, 39-40

DUNN, W. E., *Spanish and French Rivalry in the Gulf Region of the United States*, 159

DUNNING, W. A., *Essays on the Civil War and Reconstruction*, 20, 21, 207
— 'A generation of American historiography', 37-8

DURRENBERGER, J. A., *Turnpikes*, 152

EAST, R. A., *Business Enterprise in the American Revolutionary Era*, 101

EASTERBY, J. H. (ed.), *The South Carolina Rice Plantation*, 205

EATON, C., *A History of the Old South*, 203
— *Freedom of Thought in the Old South*, 203

EAVES, L., *A History of California Labor Legislation*, 247

ECKENRODE, H. J., *The Political History of Virginia during the Re-* [construction, 211
— *The Revolution in Virginia*, 106

EDGINGTON, T. B., *The Monroe Doctrine*, 288

EDWARDS, G. W., *New York as an Eighteenth Century Municipality,* [100
1731-1776, 65

EGERTON, H. E., *The Causes and Character of the American Revolution*, 150-1

EGLESTON, M., *The Land System of the New England Colonies*, 150-1

EISELEN, M. R., *The Rise of Pennsylvania Protectionism*, 198-9

ELLIS, D. M., *Landlords and Farmers in the Hudson-Mohawk Region,* [69, 198

EMERICK, C. F., *The Credit System and the Public Domain*, 151

ERDMAN, C. R., jr., *The New Jersey Constitution of 1776*, 105

ERHORN, Irmgard, *Die deutsche Einwanderung der Dreissiger und Achtundvierziger in die Vereinigten Staaten und ihre Stellung zur nordamerikanischen Politik*, 149

ERNST, R., *Immigrant Life in New York City*, 149

ESAREY, L., *A History of Indiana from its Exploration to 1850*, 157
— *A History of Indiana from 1850 to the Present*, 157

EVANS, C., *History of the United Mine Workers of America*, 248

FARISH, H. D., *The Circuit Rider Dismounts*, 211

FARNAM, H. W., *Chapters in the History of Social Legislation in the United States to 1860*, 197

FARRAND, M., *The Framing of the Constitution of the United States*, 104
— (ed.), *The Records of the Federal Convention of 1787*, 104
FAUST, A. B., *The German Element in the United States*, 68, 149
FAŸ, B., *L'esprit révolutionnaire en France et aux États-Unis à la fin du XVIIIe siècle*, 106
FEE, W. R., *The Transition from Aristocracy to Democracy in New Jersey*,
FERGUSON, R. J., *Early Western Pennsylvania Politics*, 105, 198   [198
FICKLEN, J. R., *History of Reconstruction in Louisiana*, 211
FISH, C. R., *The Civil Service and the Patronage*, 249
— *The Restoration of the Southern Railroads*, 156
FISHER, E. J., *New Jersey as a Royal Province*, 65
FISKE, J., *The Critical Period of American History* (etc.), 7
FITE, E. D., *The Presidential Campaign of 1860*, 207
— *Social and Industrial Conditions in the North during the Civil War*,
FITZGERALD, D. A., *Livestock under the AAA*, 292   [209
FLACK, H. E., *The Adoption of the Fourteenth Amendment*, 211
— *Spanish-American Diplomatic Relations Preceding the War of 1898*,
FLANDERS, R. B., *Plantation Slavery in Georgia*, 206   [288
FLEMING, D. F., *The United States and World Organization*, 290
— *The United States and the League of Nations*, 290
FLEMING, W. L., *Civil War and Reconstruction in Alabama*, 211
FLIPPIN, P. S., 'Royal government in Georgia, 1752-1776', 66
— *The Royal Government in Virginia*, 66
— *The Financial Administration of the Colony of Virginia*, 66
FOLMSBEE, S. J., *Sectionalism and Internal Improvements in Tennessee*, 161
FOLWELL, W. W., *A History of Minnesota*, 158
FONER, P. S., *Business and Slavery*, 207
FORD, Amelia C., *Colonial Precedents of our National Land System*, 150
FORD, W. C., *et al.*, *Journals of the Continental Congress*, 104
FOREMAN, G., *Advancing Frontier*, 161
— *Indians and Pioneers*, 161
FOSSUM, P. R., *The Agrarian Movement in North Dakota*, 242
FOSTER, J. W., *A Century of American Diplomacy*, 287
— *The Practice of Diplomacy*, 287
— *American Diplomacy in the Orient*, 288
FOULKE, W. D., *Fighting the Spoilsmen*, 249
FOX, D. R., *The Decline of Aristocracy in the Politics of New York*, 198
— *Herbert Levi Osgood. An American Scholar*, 39
— 'State history', 39
— (ed.), *A Quarter Century of Learning, 1904-29*, 37
— (ed.), *Sources of Culture in the Middle West*, 158
FOX, E. L., *The American Colonization Society*, 201
FRANKFURTER, F., and GREENE, N., *The Labor Injunction*, 248
FRANKLIN, J. H., *The Free Negro in North Carolina*, 206

FRANZ, A., *Die Kolonisation des Mississippitales bis zum Ausgange der französischen Herrschaft*, 159

FREEMAN, D. S., *R. E. Lee; a Biography*, 207

— *The South to Posterity*, 40

FRIEDENWALD, H., *The Declaration of Independence*, 101

FROTHINGHAM, T. G., *The Naval History of the World War*, vol. iii, 287

FRY, W. H., *New Hampshire as a Royal Province*, 65

FULLER, G. N., *Economic and Social Beginnings of Michigan*, 158

FULLER, H. B., *The Purchase of Florida*, 160, 288

GAINES, F. P., *The Southern Plantation*, 205

GALLOWAY, J. D., *The First Transcontinental Railroad*, 157

GALSTER, Augusta E., *The Labor Movement in the Shoe Industry*, 248

GAMMON, S. R., *The Presidential Campaign of 1832*, 200

GARIS, R. L., *Immigration Restriction*, 287

GARNER, J. W., *American Foreign Policies*, 290

— *International Law and the World War*, 290

— *Reconstruction in Mississippi*, 211

GARWOOD, D., *Crossroads of America*, 246

GATES, P. W., *The Illinois Central Railroad*, 150, 155, 156

GAYARRÉ, C., *History of Louisiana*, 159

GEPHART, W. F., *Transportation and Industrial Development in the Middle*

GEWEHR, W. M., *The Great Awakening in Virginia*, 103   [*West*, 153

GIBB, G. S., *The Saco-Lowell Shops*, 245

— *The Whitesmiths of Taunton*, 245

GIDDENS, P. H., *The Birth of the Oil Industry*, 244

GIESECKE, A. A., *Commercial Legislation before 1789*, 67

GILBERT, E. W., *The Exploration of Western America*, 241

GILPATRICK, D. H., *Jeffersonian Democracy in North Carolina*, 106

GINGER, R., *The Bending Cross*, 247

GITTINGER, R., *The Formation of the State of Oklahoma*, 241

GLASSON, W. H., *History of Military Pension Legislation in the United States*, 249

— *Federal Military Pensions in the United States*, 249

GOLDMAN, E. F., *John Bach McMaster, American Historian*, 38

GOMPERS, S., *Seventy Years of Life and Labor*, 247

GOODWIN, C., *The Trans-Mississippi West*, 241

GORDON, J. H., *Illinois Railway Legislation and Commission Control since 1870*, 154

GOSNELL, H. F., *Boss Platt and his New York Machine*, 249

GOULD, C. P., *The Land System in Maryland*, 65-6

— *Money and Transportation in Maryland*, 66

GRAHAM, G. S., *British Policy and Canada*, 100

GRAY, L. C., *History of Agriculture in the Southern States to 1860*, 197

GRAY, W., *The Hidden Civil War*, 208

GREEN, Constance McL., *Holyoke, Massachusetts*, 245
— *History of Naugatuck, Connecticut*, 245

GREEN, F. M., *Constitutional Development in the South Atlantic States*,
— 'Writing and research in Southern history', 39   [199

GREENE, E. B., *The Foundations of American Nationality*, 103
— 'Our pioneer Historical Societies', 39
— *Provincial America, 1696-1740*, 63
— *The Provincial Governor in the English Colonies of North America*,
— *The Revolutionary Generation*, 102   [41, 66
— and HARRINGTON, Virginia D., *American Population before the
    Federal Census of 1790*, 68

GREENE, L. J., *The Negro in Colonial New England*, 205

GREER, T. H., *American Social Reform Movements*, 240

GRISWOLD, A. W., *The Far Eastern Policy of the United States*, 289

GRODINSKY, J., *The Iowa Pool*, 156

GUTTRIDGE, G. H., *English Whiggism and the American Revolution*, 102
— (ed.), *The American Correspondence of a Bristol Merchant*, 101

HACKER, L. M., *American Problems of Today*, 285
— *A Short History of the New Deal*, 291

HALSEY, F. W., *The Old New York Frontier*, 69

HAMER, P. M., *The Secession Movement in South Carolina*, 204

HAMILTON, J. G. de R., *Party Politics in North Carolina*, 199
— *Reconstruction in North Carolina*, 211
— (ed.), *Truth in History and Other Essays by William A. Dunning*, 39

HAMMOND, M. B., *The Cotton Industry*, 244

HANCOCK, W. K., *Survey of British Commonwealth Affairs*, vol. i, 102

HANDLIN, O., *Boston's Immigrants*, 149
— and Mary F., *Commonwealth; a Study of the Role of Government in
    the American Economy; Massachusetts, 1774-1861*, 198, 243

HANEY, L. H., *A Congressional History of Railways in the United States*,
    vol. i, *to 1850*, 154 ; vol. ii, *1850-1887*, 154

HANNA, C. A., *The Scotch-Irish*, 68
— *The Wilderness Trail*, 69

HANSEN, M. L., *The Atlantic Migration*, 149
— *The Immigrant in American History*, 149

HARBORD, J. G., *America in the World War*, 287
— *The American Expeditionary Forces*, 287
— *The American Army in France*, 287

HARDING, S. B., *The Contest over the Ratification of the Federal Constitution
    in the State of Massachusetts*, 105

HARDING, W. P. G., *The Formative Period of the Federal Reserve System*,

HARGRAVE, F. F., *A Pioneer Indiana Railroad*, 156   [286

HARLOW, A. F., *Steelways of New England*, 155

HARMON, G. D., *Aspects of Slavery and Expansion*, 202

HARRINGTON, Virginia D., *The New York Merchant on the Eve of the Revolution*, 101

HARRIS, N. D., *Negro Servitude in Illinois*, 206

HARRIS, S. E., *Twenty Years of Federal Reserve Policy*, 291

HARRISON, F., *Virginia Land Grants*, 71

HART, A. B., *The Foundations of American Foreign Policy*, 288

— (ed.), *Commonwealth History of Massachusetts*, vol. ii, 65

HART, F. H., *The Valley of Virginia in the American Revolution*, 106

HART, J., *The American Presidency in Action, 1789*, 104

HARTSOUGH, Mildred L., *From Canoe to Steel Barge on the Upper Mississippi*, 154

— *The Twin Cities as Metropolitan Market*, 246

HARTZ, L., *Economic Policy and Democratic Thought; Pennsylvania, 1776-1860*, 198, 243

HARVEY, G., *Henry Clay Frick*, 244

HARVEY, R. H., *Samuel Gompers*, 247

HAWGOOD, J. A., *The Tragedy of German-America*, 149

HAYNES, F. E., *Third Party Movements since the Civil War*, 242

— *James Baird Weaver*, 242

— *Social Politics in the United States*, 239

HAZELTON, J. H., *The Declaration of Independence, its History*, 101

HAZEN, C. D., *Contemporary American Opinion of the French Revolution*, 107

HEATON, H., 'Recent developments in economic history', 40

HEDGES, J. B., *Henry Villard and the Railways of the Northwest*, 157

HEINRICH, P., *La Louisiane sous la Compagnie des Indes*, 159

HENDERSON, G. F. R., *Stonewall Jackson and the American Civil War*, [207

HENDRICK, B. J., *The Life of Andrew Carnegie*, 244

— *Lincoln's War Cabinet*, 208

— *Statesmen of the Lost Cause*, 210

— and SIMS, W. S., *The Victory at Sea*, 287

HENRY, H. M., *The Police Control of Slavery in South Carolina*, 206

HENRY, R. S., *The Story of the Confederacy*, 210

HEPBURN, A. B., *A History of Currency in the United States*, 243

HERTZ, G. B., *The Old Colonial System*, 67

HESSELTINE, W. B., *Lincoln and the War Governors*, 208

HIBBARD, B. H., *A History of Public Land Policies*, 150

HICKOK, C. T., *The Negro in Ohio*, 206

HICKS, F. C. (ed.), *High Finance in the Sixties*, 154

HICKS, J. D., *The Constitutions of the Northwest States*, 158

— *The Populist Revolt*, 242

HIGGINS, Ruth L., *Expansion in New York*, 69

HILL, H. W., *An Historical Review of Waterways and Canal Construction in New York State*, 153

HILL, R. T., *The Public Domain and Democracy*, 151

HILL, W. C., 'Memoir of Albert Bushnell Hart', 38

HINKHOUSE, F. J., *The Preliminaries of the American Revolution as seen in the English Press*, 102

Historical Statistics of the United States, 148, 239

History of the South, 203

HOCKETT, H. C., *Western Influences on Political Parties to 1825*, 197

HODDER, F. H., 'The genesis of the Kansas-Nebraska Act', 202
— 'Railroad background of the Kansas-Nebraska Act', 202
— 'Some aspects of the English bill for the admission of Kansas',
— 'Some phases of the Dred Scott case', 203   [202

HOFSTADTER, R., *Social Darwinism in American Thought, 1860-1915*,

HOLDEN, W. C., *Alkali Trails*, 162, 241   [232-3, 239

HOLLANDER, J. H., *The Cincinnati Southern Railway*, 156

HOLLIS, J. P., *The Early Period of Reconstruction in South Carolina*, 211

HOLT, E. A., *Party Politics in Ohio*, 157

HOON, Elizabeth E., *The Organization of the English Customs System*, 67

HOPKINS, C. H., *The Rise of the Social Gospel in American Protestantism*,
                                                         [240

HOPKINS, J. A., jr., *Economic History of the Production of Beef Cattle in*

HOTBLACK, Kate, *Chatham's Colonial Policy*, 67   [*Iowa*, 241

HOUCK, L., *The Spanish Régime in Missouri*, 160

HOUSTON, D. F., *A Critical Study of Nullification in South Carolina*, 200

HOWARD, C. N., *The British Development of West Florida*, 66

HOWARD, G. E., *Preliminaries of the Revolution*, 99

HOWE, M. A. de W., *James Ford Rhodes*, 38

HOWER, R. M., *History of an Advertising Agency*, 245
— *History of Macy's of New York*, 245

HOWLAND, C. P., *Survey of American Foreign Relations*, 291

HUBBARD, H. A., *A Chapter in Early Arizona Transportation History*, 157

HUBBART, H. C., *The Older Middle West*, 158

HUGH-JONES, E. M., and RADICE, E. A., *An American Experiment*, 291

HULBERT, A. B., *Historic Highways*, 152
— *The Ohio River*, 153
— *Soil: its Influence on the History of the United States*, 149

HUMPHREYS, R. A., *Latin America: a Selective Guide to Publications in English*, 289

HUNGERFORD, E., *A Century of Progress*, 155
— *Men and Iron*, 155
— *The Story of the Baltimore and Ohio Railroad*, 155-6
— *The Story of the Rome, Watertown and Ogdensburgh Railroad*, 155

HUNT, R. L., *A History of the Farmer Movements in the Southwest*, 242

HUNTER, L. C., *Steamboats on the Western Rivers*, 154
HUNTINGTON, C. C., and McCLELLAND, C. P., *History of the Ohio Canals*, 153
HURWITZ, H. L., *Theodore Roosevelt and Labor in New York State*, 248
HUTCHINSON, W. T. (ed.), *The Marcus W. Jernegan Essays in American Historiography*, 37, 38
HUTSON, A. C., jr., *The Coal Miners' Insurrection of 1891 in Anderson County, Tennessee*, 247
HÜTTER, J. P., *La question de la monnaie d'argent aux États-Unis*, 243
— *L'incidence économique de la frappe de monnaie d'argent aux États-*
HYDE, C. C., *International Law*, 290   [*Unis*, 243

ICHIHASHI, Y., *Japanese in the United States*, 289
— *The Washington Conference and After*, 289, 290
IVEY, P. W., *The Père Marquette Railroad Company*, 156

JACK, T. H., *Sectionalism and Party Politics in Alabama*, 161
JACKSON, L. P., *Free Negro Labor and Property Holding in Virginia*, 206
JAMES, J. A., *The Life of George Rogers Clark*, 71
'John Franklin Jameson', 39
JAMESON, J. F., *The American Revolution Considered as a Social Movement*,
— *The History of Historical Writing in America*, 37   [102
— McMASTER, J. B., and CHANNING, E., 'The present state of historical writing in America', 37
JANSON, Florence E., *The Background of Swedish Immigration*, 150
JARCHOW, M. E., *The Earth Brought Forth*, 158
JENKINS, W. S., *Pro-Slavery Thought in the Old South*, 205
JENKS, J. W., and CLARK, W. E., *The Trust Problem*, 243-4
JENSEN, M., *The Articles of Confederation*, 98, 104
— *The New Nation*, 104
JERNEGAN, M. W., *The American Colonies, 1492-1750*, 64
— *Laboring and Dependent Classes in Colonial America*, 68
JOHNSON, A., *Stephen A. Douglas*, 202
JOHNSON, C., *British West Florida*, 66
JOHNSON, E. R., *American Railway Transportation*, 154
— *et al.*, *History of Domestic and Foreign Commerce of the United States*,
JOHNSON, Ida A., *The Michigan Fur Trade*, 71   [67, 243
JOHNSON, J. G., *The Colonial Southeast*, 70
JOHNSON, S. C., *A History of Emigration from the United Kingdom to North America*, 149
JOHNSON, Z. T., *The Political Policies of Howell Cobb*, 207   [153
JONES, C. L., *The Economic History of the Anthracite-Tidewater Canals*,
JONES, E., *The Anthracite Coal Combination in the United States*, 244
JONES, H. M., *America and French Culture*, 106
— *The Life of Moses Coit Tyler*, 38

JONES, J. M., *Tariff Retaliation*, 292
JONES, M. B., *Vermont in the Making*, 65
JORDAN, W. T., *Hugh Davis and his Alabama Plantation*, 205

KAYSEN, J. P., *The Railroads of Wisconsin*, 156
KEASEBEY, L. M., *The Nicaragua Canal and the Monroe Doctrine*, 288
KEGLEY, F. B., *Kegley's Virginia Frontier*, 70   [66, 101-2
KEITH, A. B., *Constitutional History of the First British Empire*,
KELLOGG, Louise P., *The British Régime in Wisconsin and the Northwest*, 71
— *The French Régime in Wisconsin and the Northwest*, 69
— 'The passing of a great teacher—Frederick Jackson Turner', 38
KEMMERER, D. L., *Path to Freedom*, 65
KENDRICK, B. B., *The Journal of the Joint Committee of Fifteen on Reconstruction*, 210-11
— and ARNETT, A. M., *The South looks at its Past*, 245
KENNAN, G., *E. H. Harriman: a Biography*, 157
KERR, J. L., *The Story of a Southern Carrier*, 156   [*Official*, 65
KEYES, Alice M., *Cadwalader Colden, a Representative Eighteenth Century*
KILE, O. M., *The Farm Bureau through Three Decades*, 292
KIMBALL, E., *The Public Life of Joseph Dudley*, 65
KING, W. L., *Melville Weston Fuller*, 240
KIRKLAND, E. C., *Men, Cities and Transportation*, 152, 155
KISTLER, Thelma M., *The Rise of Railroads in the Connecticut River*
KLEIN, P. S., *Pennsylvania Politics*, 198   [*Valley*, 155
KLEIN, T. B., *The Canals of Pennsylvania*, 152-3
KNAPP, C. M., *New Jersey Politics during the Period of the Civil War and Reconstruction*, 209
KNAUTH, O. W., *The Policy of the United States towards Industrial Monopoly*, 244
KNITTLE, W. A., *Early Eighteenth Century Palatine Emigration*, 68, 149
KNOLES, G. H., *The Presidential Campaign of 1892*, 249
KNOWLTON, Evelyn H., *Pepperell's Progress*, 245
KNUST, H., *Montesquieu und die Verfassungen der Vereinigten Staaten von Amerika*, 106
KONKLE, B. A., *George Bryan and the Constitution of Pennsylvania*, 105
KOONTZ, L. K., *Robert Dinwiddie*, 71
— *The Virginia Frontier*, 70
KRAUS, H., *Monroedoktrin in ihren Beziehungen zur amerikanischen Diplomatie und zum Völkerrecht*, 289
KREIDER, C., *The Anglo-American Trade Agreement*, 292
KUHLMANN, C. B., *The Development of the Flour-Milling Industry in the United States*, 244

LABAREE, L. W., 'Charles McLean Andrews, historian', 39
— *Royal Government in America*, 66

LANE, J. R., *A Political History of Connecticut during the Civil War*, 209
LANE, W. J., *From Indian Trail to Iron Horse*, 152
LANG, A. S., *Financial History of the Public Lands in Texas*, 151
LANNING, J. T., *The Diplomatic History of Georgia*, 70
LARKIN, J. D., *The President's Control of the Tariff*, 292
LARSON, Henrietta M., *Guide to Business History*, 245
LASSERAY, A., *Les français sous les treize étoiles*, 106
LATANÉ, J. H., *America as a World Power*, 287-8
LATHROP, B. F., *Migration into East Texas*, 150
LATOURETTE, K. S., *The History of Early Relations between the United States and China*, 289
LAUCK, W. J., *The Causes of the Panic of 1893*, 243
LAUGHLIN, Sceva B., *Missouri Politics during the Civil War*, 209
LAUVRIÈRE, É., *Histoire de la Louisiane française*, 159
LEAKE, J. M., *The Virginia Committee System and the American Revolution*, 106
LECKY, W. E. H., *A History of England in the Eighteenth Century*, 99
LEWINSON, P., *Race, Class and Party*, 211
LEWIS, E. R., *A History of American Political Thought from the Civil War to the World War*, 239
LEWIS, G. E., *The Indiana Company*, 71
LEWIS, O., *Sea Routes to the Gold Fields*, 202
LIBBY, O. G., *The Geographical Distribution of the Vote of the Thirteen States on the Federal Constitution, 1787-8*, 87, 88, 103-4
LINCOLN, C. H., *The Revolutionary Movement in Pennsylvania*, 65
LINDBERG, J. S., *The Background of Swedish Emigration*, 150
LINDSEY, A., *The Pullman Strike*, 247
LINGLEY, C. R., *The Transition in Virginia from Colony to Commonwealth*, 106
LINK, A. S., 'A decade of biographical contributions to recent American history', 40
— *Wilson; the Road to the White House*, 286
LINK, E. P., *Democratic Republican Societies*, 107
LIPPINCOTT, I., *A Century and a Half of Fur Trade at St. Louis*, 71
LIPPMANN, W., SCROGGS, W. O., *et al.*, *The United States in World Affairs*, 291
LIVELY, R. A., *The South in Action*, 154
LIVERMORE, S., *Early American Land Companies*, 71
LIVINGOOD, J. W., *The Philadelphia-Baltimore Trade Rivalry*, 153
LLOYD, A. Y., *The Slavery Controversy*, 201-2
LOCKE, Mary S., *Anti-Slavery in America*, 201
LOCKLIN, D. P., *Railroad Regulation since 1920*, 155
LOKKEN, R. L., *Iowa Public Land Disposal*, 143, 151
LONN, Ella, *Desertion of Alabama Troops from the Confederate Army*, 210

Lonn, Ella—*continued*
— *Desertion during the Civil War*, 207
— *Salt as a factor in the Confederacy*, 210   [*America*, 67-8
Lord, Eleanor L., *Industrial Experiments in the British Colonies of North*
Lorwin, L. L., *The American Federation of Labor*, 247
Lounsbury, R. G., *The British Fishery at Newfoundland*, 68
Lowrey, L. T., *Northern Opinion of Approaching Secession*, 207
Lowrie, S. H., *Culture Conflict in Texas*, 162
Lucas, W. A., *From the Hills to the Hudson*, 155
Ludlum, D. M., *Social Ferment in Vermont*, 198
Lundin, L., *Cockpit of the Revolution*, 105
Luthin, R. H., *The First Lincoln Campaign*, 208
Lynch, W. O., 'The South and its history', 40
Lyon, E. W., *Louisiana in French Diplomacy*, 160
Lyon, L. S., et al., *The National Industrial Recovery Administration*, 291

Macartney, C. E., *Lincoln and his Cabinet*, 208
McCain, J. R., *Georgia as a Proprietary Province*, 66
McCaleb, W. F., *The Aaron Burr Conspiracy*, 160
McClellan, W. S., *Smuggling in the American Colonies at the Outbreak
    of the Revolution*, 101
McClure, W., *A New American Commercial Policy*, 292
McCormac, E. I., *Colonial Opposition to Imperial Authority during the
    French and Indian War*, 67
McCormick, R. P., *Experiment in Independence*, 105
McCrady, E., *The History of South Carolina under the Proprietary
    Government*, 66
— *The History of South Carolina under Royal Government*, 66
Macdonald, D. J., and Lynch, E. A., *Coal and Unionism*, 248
McDougle, I. E., *Slavery in Kentucky*, 206
McGinty, G. W., *Louisiana Redeemed*, 211
McGrane, R. C., *William Allen; a Study in Western Democracy*, 242
McGregor, J. C., *The Disruption of Virginia*, 209
McIlwain, C. H., *The American Revolution*, 101
— (ed.), *An Abridgement of the Indian Affairs*, 69
McKay, G. L., *Early American Currency*, 72
McKee, S., jr., *Labor in Colonial New York*, 68
McKelvey, B., *Rochester, the Water-Power City*, 246
— *Rochester, the Flower City*, 246   [*Colonies*, 67
McKinley, A. E., *The Suffrage Franchise in the Thirteen English*
McKitrick, R., *The Public Land System of Texas*, 151
McLaughlin, A. C., *A Constitutional History of the United States*, 104
— *The Courts, the Constitution and Parties*, 104
— *The Foundations of American Constitutionalism*, 104

McLENDON, S. G., *History of the Public Domain of Georgia*, 151

McMASTER, J. B., *A History of the People of the United States from the Revolution to the Civil War*, 7   [105-6

— and STONE, F. D. (eds.), *Pennsylvania and the Federal Constitution*,

MACMILLAN, Margaret B., *The War Governors in the American Revolution*, 105

McMURRAY, D. L., *Coxey's Army*, 247

MACY, J., *Political Parties*, 200

MAHAN, A. T., *The Interest of America in International Conditions*, 288

MALIN, J. C., *Indian Policy and Westward Expansion*, 202

— *John Brown and the Legend of the Fifty-six*, 202

— *The United States after the World War*, 285

MARK, I., *Agrarian Conflicts in Colonial New York*, 198

MARSHALL, T. M., *A History of the Western Boundary of the Louisiana Purchase*, 160

MARTIN, A. E., *The Anti-Slavery Movement in Kentucky prior to 1850*,

MARTIN, Chester, *Empire and Commonwealth*, 100   [201

MARTIN, Margaret E., *Merchants and Trade of the Connecticut River Valley*, 198

MARTIN, R. C., *The People's Party in Texas*, 242

MARTIN, S. W., *Florida during the Territorial Days*, 161

MARTIN, W. E., *Early History of Internal Improvements in Alabama*, 161

MASON, F. N. (ed.), *John Norton & Sons*, 101

MATHEWS, J. M., *Legislative and Judicial History of the Fifteenth Amendment*, 211

MATHEWS, Lois K., *The Expansion of New England*, 149

MAXSON, C. H., *The Great Awakening in the Middle Colonies*, 103

MAY, H. F., *The Protestant Churches and Industrial America*, 240

MAYBEE, R. H., *Railroad Competition and the Oil Trade*, 154, 244

MENEELY, A. H., *The War Department, 1861*, 207

MERENESS, N. D., *Maryland as a Proprietary Province*, 65

MERIWETHER, R. L., *The Expansion of South Carolina*, 66

MERK, F., *Economic History of Wisconsin during the Civil War Decade*,

MERRIAM, C. E., *American Political Ideas*, 239   [158, 209

MERRICK, G. B., *Old Times on the Upper Mississippi*, 154

MEYER, B. H., *History of Transportation in the United States before 1860*,

MEYER, J. C., *Church and State in Massachusetts*, 198   [151

MEYERS, W. S., *The Self-Reconstruction of Maryland*, 211

MILLER, D. H., *The Drafting of the Covenant*, 290

— *The Peace Pact of Paris*, 290

MILLER, E. I., *The Legislature of the Province of Virginia; its Internal Development*, 66

MILLER, J. M., *The Genesis of Western Culture*, 158

MILLION, J. W., *State Aid to Railways in Missouri*, 156

MILLS, J. C., *Our Inland Seas*, 153
MILTON, G. F., *Abraham Lincoln and the Fifth Column*, 208
— *The Age of Hate*, 210
— *The Eve of Conflict*, 200
MINER, C. E., *The Ratification of the Federal Constitution by the State of New York*, 105
MINNIGERODE, M., *Jefferson Friend of France, 1793; the Career of Edmond Charles Genêt*, 107
MITCHELL, B., *The Rise of the Cotton Mills in the South*, 245
— and G. S., *The Industrial Revolution in the South*, 245
MILLER, J. C., *Origins of the American Revolution*, 103
MOGER, A. W., *The Rebuilding of the Old Dominion*, 211
MOHR, W. H., *Federal Indian Relations*, 100
MONAGHAN, J., *Diplomat in Carpet Slippers*, 209
— *Lincoln Bibliography*, 208
MOOD, F. (ed.), *The Early Writings of Frederick Jackson Turner*, 38, 148
MOODY, V. A., *Slavery on Louisiana Sugar Plantations*, 206
MOORE, A. B., *History of Alabama and her People*, 161
— *Conscription and Conflict in the Confederacy*, 210
MOORE, C. W., *Timing a Century*, 245
MORISON, S. E. 'Edward Channing', 38
— *The Maritime History of Massachusetts*, 198
— *The Ropemakers of Plymouth*, 245
— (ed.), *The Development of Harvard University*, 37
MORRIS, R. B., *Government and Labor in Early America*, 198
— *Studies in the History of American Law*, 67
— (ed.), *The Era of the American Revolution*, 103
MORRISSEY, Alice M., *The American Defence of Neutral Rights*, 290
MORSE, A. E., *The Federalist Party in Massachusetts to the Year 1800*, [105
MORSE, J. M., *A Neglected Period of Connecticut's History*, 198
MOTT, E. H., *Between the Ocean and the Lakes*, 153
MOTTELI, H., *Die schweizerische Auswanderung nach Nord-Amerika*, [149-50
MOWAT, C. L., *East Florida as a British Province*, 66
MOWRY, G. E., *Theodore Roosevelt and the Progressive Movement*, 286
MUELLER, H. R., *The Whig Party in Pennsylvania*, 198
MULLETT, C. F., *Colonial Claims to Home Rule*, 101
— *Fundamental Law and the American Revolution*, 102
MUNFORD, B. B., *Virginia's Attitude towards Slavery and Secession*, 206
MUNRO, W. B., *The Government of American Cities*, 245
MURRAY, P., *The Whig Party in Georgia*, 199
MUSSEY, H. R., *Combination in the Mining Industry*, 244
MYRDAL, G., *An American Dilemma*, 204

NAVIN, T. R., *The Whitin Machine Works since 1831*, 245

NELSON, H., *The Swedes and the Swedish Settlements in North America,*
NELSON, J. P., *Address; the Chesapeake and Ohio Railway,* 156   [150
NETTELS, C. P., *The Money Supply of the American Colonies before
    1720,* 72
— *The Roots of American Civilization,* 64, 72, 103
NEVINS, A., *The American States during and after the Revolution,* 90, 105
— *Grover Cleveland,* 249
— *Hamilton Fish,* 210
— *Henry White,* 290
— *John D. Rockefeller,* 244
— *Ordeal of the Union,* 200
— *The Emergence of Lincoln,* 200   [199
NEWSOME, A. R., *The Presidential Election of 1824 in North Carolina,*
NEWTON, L. W., and GAMBRELL, H. P., *A Social and Political History
    of Texas,* 161
NICHOLS, R. F., *Franklin Pierce,* 201
— *The Democratic Machine,* 201
— *The Disruption of American Democracy,* 201, 203, 207
NICOLAY, J. G., and HAY, J., *Abraham Lincoln,* 207, 209
NOBLIN, S., *Leonidas Lafayette Polk,* 242   [199
NORTON, C. C., *The Democratic Party in Ante-Bellum North Carolina,*
NORWOOD, J. N., *The Schism in the Methodist Episcopal Church, 1844,*
                                                                      [201
NOTTER, H., *The Origins of the Foreign Policy of Woodrow Wilson,* 289
NOURSE, E. C., *et al., Three Years of the Agricultural Adjustment Ad-
    ministration,* 292
NOYES, A. D., *Forty Years of American Finance,* 242-3
— *The War Period of American Finance,* 286
NYE, R. B., *Fettered Freedom,* 201

OBERHOLTZER, E. P., *A History of the United States since the Civil War,*
ODUM, H. W. (ed.), *American Masters of Social Science,* 38   [8, 38
*Official History of the Great Strike of 1886 on the Southwestern Railway
    System,* 247
OGG, F. A., *National Progress,* 285
— *The Opening of the Mississippi,* 160
OLIVER, J. W., *History of Civil War Military Pensions,* 249
D'ORMESSON, W., *La première mission officielle de la France aux États-
    Unis, Conrad-Alexandre Gérard,* 106
OSGOOD, E. S., *The Day of the Cattleman,* 241
OSGOOD, H. L., *The American Colonies in the Seventeenth Century,* 20
— *The American Colonies in the Eighteenth Century,* 20, 64
OSTROGORSKY, M. Y., *La démocratie et l'organisation des partis politiques,*
— *Democracy and the Organization of Political Parties,* 248   [248

PLUMMER, W. C., *The Road Policy of Pennsylvania*, 152
POAGE, G. R., *Henry Clay and the Whig Party*, 200
POOLEY, W. V., *The Settlement of Illinois from 1830 to 1850*, 150
PORTER, G. H., *Ohio Politics during the Civil War*, 157
POSEY, W. B., *The Development of Methodism in the Old Southwest*, 161
POTTER, D. M., *Lincoln and his Party in the Secession Crisis*, 208
— *The Lincoln Theme and American National Historiography*, 208
POTTS, C. S., *Railroad Transportation in Texas*, 157
POUND, A., *Johnson of the Mohawks*, 70
POWDERLEY, T. V., *Thirty Years of Labor*, 247
PRINGLE, H. F., *Theodore Roosevelt*, 286
— *The Life and Times of William Howard Taft*, 286
PURCELL, R. J., *Connecticut in Transition*, 105
PURDY, T. C., 'Report on the canals of the United States', 152
PUTNAM, J. W., *The Illinois and Michigan Canal*, 153
PUTNAM, Mary B., *The Baptists and Slavery*, 201
PYLE, J. G., *The Life of James J. Hill*, 157

QUAIFE, M. M., *Chicago and the Old Northwest*, 158
— *Wisconsin, its History and its People*, 158
— *The Doctrine of Non-intervention with Slavery in the Territories*, 202
QUALEY, C. C., *Norwegian Settlement in the United States*, 150
QUILLIN, F. U., *The Color Line in Ohio*, 206

RAINWATER, P. L., *Mississippi; Storm Center of Secession*, 204
RAMSDELL, C. W., *Behind the Lines in the Southern Confederacy*, 210
— *Reconstruction in Texas*, 211
RANDALL, J. G., *The Civil War and Reconstruction*, 206-7
— *Constitutional Problems under Lincoln*, 208
— *Lincoln the President*, 208
RAPER, C. L., *North Carolina; a Study in English Colonial Government*, 66
RAUCH, B., *The History of the New Deal*, 291
RAY, P. O., *The Repeal of the Missouri Compromise*, 202
— 'The genesis of the Kansas-Nebraska Act', 202
READ, C. (ed.), *The Constitution Reconsidered*, 104
REDDAWAY, W. F., *The Monroe Doctrine*, 288
REED, L. S., *The Labor Philosophy of Samuel Gompers*, 247
REED, Susan M., *Church and State in Massachusetts*, 65
REEVES, J. S., *American Diplomacy under Tyler and Polk*, 288
REIZENSTEIN, M., *The Economic History of the Baltimore and Ohio Rail-
RENAUT, F. P., *La question de la Louisiane*, 160   [road, 156
*Report of the Commission to locate the Sites of the Frontier Forts of Pennsyl-
vania*, 69
RHODES, J. F., *History of the United States from the Compromise of 1850*,
                                                                      [7, 250

RICE, Madeleine H., *American Catholic Opinion in the Slavery Controversy*, 201

RICE, S. A. (ed.), *Methods in Social Science*, 38

RICH, B. M., *The Presidents and Civil Disorder*, 248

RICHARDS, H. I., *Cotton and the AAA*, 292

RICHARDSON, R. N., *The Comanche Barrier to South Plains Settlement*, RICHMAN, I. B., *Ioway to Iowa*, 158 [161

RICKARD, T. A., *A History of American Mining*, 241, 244

RIDDELL, W. R., *Michigan under British Rule*, 71

RIDDLE, D. W., *Lincoln Runs for Congress*, 208

RIEGEL, R. E., *The Story of the Western Railroads*, 157

RIPLEY, W. Z., *Railroads, Rates and Regulation*, 154

— *Railroads, Finance and Organization*, 154

RISTER, C. C., *Land Hunger*, 241

— *Oil! Titan of the Southwest*, 244

— *Southern Plainsmen*, 241

— *The South-Western Frontier*, 241

RIVES, G. L., *The United States and Mexico*, 288

ROBBINS, R. M., *Our Landed Heritage*, 150

ROBERTSON, J. A., *Louisiana under the Rule of Spain, France, and the United States*, 160

ROBINSON, E. E., *The Presidential Vote, 1896-1932*, 286

— *The Presidential Vote, 1936*, 291

ROBINSON, J. S., *The Amalgamated Association of Iron, Steel, and Tin Workers*, 248

ROBINSON, W. A., *Jeffersonian Democracy in New England*, 105

ROBINSON, W. M., jr., *Justice in Grey*, 210

ROBINSON, W. W., *Land in California*, 151

ROBISON, D. M., *Bob Taylor and the Agrarian Revolt in Tennessee*, 242

ROGIN, L., *The Introduction of Farm Machinery*, 291

ROOS, C. F., *NRA Economic Planning*, 291

ROOSEVELT, T. R., *The Winning of the West*, 19

ROOT, W. T., *The Relations of Pennsylvania with the British Government*, 65

ROSENBERGER, J. L., *The Pennsylvania Germans*, 149 [ment, 65

ROSENBERRY, Lois K. M., *Migrations from Connecticut prior to 1800*, 149

ROSS, E. D., 'A generation of prairie historiography', 40

— 'Oberholtzer's *History of the United States since the Civil War*', 38

ROSS, G., *Cleveland; the Making of a City*, 246

ROWE, H. B., *Tobacco under the AAA*, 292

ROYCE, C. C., *Indian Land Cessions in the United States*, 71

RUSK, R. L., *The Literature of the Middle Western Frontier*, 158

RUSSEL, R. R., *Economic Aspects of Southern Sectionalism*, 203

— *Improvement of Communication with the Pacific Coast as an Issue in American Politics*, 202

RUSSELL, E. B., *The Review of American Colonial Legislation by the King in Council*, 67
RUSSELL, N. V., *The British Régime in Michigan*, 71

SALLET, R., *Russlanddeutsche Siedlungen in den Vereinigten Staaten von Amerika*, 149
SANBORN, J. B., *Congressional Grants of Land in Aid of Railways*, 154
SANDERLIN, W. S., *The Great National Project*, 152
SATO, S., *History of the Land Question*, 150   [*War*, 290
SAVAGE, C., *Policy of the United States toward Maritime Commerce in*
SAVAGE, W. S., *The Controversy over the Distribution of Abolition Literature*, 201
SAVELLE, M., *George Morgan, Colony Builder*, 70
SCARBOROUGH, Ruth, *The Opposition to Slavery in Georgia*, 206
Joseph Schafer, Student of Agriculture, 39
SCHAFER, J., 'The author of the "frontier hypothesis" ', 38
— *The Social History of American Agriculture*, 199
— *A History of Agriculture in Wisconsin*, 31, 137, 158
— *Four Wisconsin Counties*, 158
— *The Wisconsin Lead Region*, 158
— *The Winnebago-Horicon Basin*, 158
— *Wisconsin Domesday Book. Town Studies*, 151
SCHAPER, W. A., 'Sectionalism and representation in South Carolina', 66
SCHATTSCHNEIDER, E. E., *Politics, Pressures and the Tariff*, 292
SCHLEGEL, M. W., *Ruler of the Reading*, 155
SCHLESINGER, A. M., *The Colonial Merchants and the American Revolution*, 75, 100-1
— *New Viewpoints in American History*, 103
— (ed.), *Historical Scholarship in America*, 37
SCHLESINGER, A. M., jr., *The Age of Jackson*, 198
SCHOTTER, H. W., *The Growth and Development of the Pennsylvania Railroad Company*, 155
SCHULTZ, H. S., *Nationalism and Sectionalism in South Carolina*, 204
SCHUYLER, R. L., *The Constitution of the United States*, 104
— *Parliament and the British Empire*, 101
— *The Transition in Illinois from British to American Government*,
SCHWAB, J. C., *The Confederate States of America*, 210   [48, 71
SCRUGHAM, Mary, *The Peaceable Americans of 1860-1861*, 207
SELLERS, J. B., *Slavery in Alabama*, 206
SELLERS, Leila, *Charleston Business on the Eve of the American Revolution*,
SELSAM, J. P., *The Pennsylvania Constitution of 1776*, 105   [101
SEMPLE, Ellen C., *American History and its Geographical Conditions*,
SERRANO Y SANZ, M., *El Brigadièr Jaime Wilkinson*, 160 [151-2, 207

SEVERANCE, F. H. (ed.), *Canal Enlargement in New York State*, 153
— *The Holland Land Co. and Canal Construction in Western New York*, 153
SEYMOUR, C., *American Diplomacy during the World War*, 289-90
American Neutrality, 290
SHAMBAUGH, B. F. (ed.), *Constitution and Records of the Claim Association of Johnson County, Iowa*, 151
SHANKS, H. T., *The Secession Movement in Virginia*, 204
SHANNON, F. A., *The Farmers' Last Frontier*, 241
— *The Organization and Administration of the Union Army*, 207
SHARFMAN, I. L., *The Inter-State Commerce Commission*, 154, 240
SHAW, Helen L., *British Administration of the Southern Indians*, 70
SHEARER, A. H., 'State Historical Societies', 39
SHELDON, W. du B., *Populism in the Old Dominion*, 242
SHEPHERD, W. R., *History of Proprietary Government in Pennsylvania*, 65
SHERMAN, C. E., *Original Ohio Land Subdivisions*, 151
SHINN, C. H., *Land Laws of Mining Districts*, 151, 241
— *Mining Camps*, ed. J. H. Jackson, 241
SHLAKMAN, Vera, *Economic History of a Factory Town*, 246
SHOEMAKER, F. C., *Missouri's Struggle for Statehood*, 158, 200   [287
SHOTWELL, J. T. (ed.), *Economic and Social History of the World War*,
SCHOULER, J., *History of the United States of America under the Constitution*, 7
SHRYOCK, R. H., *Georgia and the Union in 1850*, 204
SHUGG, R. W., *Origins of Class Struggle in Louisiana*, 204
SIEBERT, W. H., *The Underground Railroad from Slavery to Freedom*, 201
SIKES, E. W., *The Transition of North Carolina from a Colony*, 106
SIMIAND, F., *Inflation et stabilisation alternées*, 243
SIMKINS, F. B., *The Tillman Movement in South Carolina*, 242
— *Pitchfork Ben Tillman*, 242
— and WOODY, R. H., *South Carolina during Reconstruction*, 211
SIMMS, H. H., *A Decade of Sectional Controversy*, 200
— *The Rise of the Whigs in Virginia*, 199
SIMONDS, F. H., *American Foreign Policy in the Post-War Years*, 290
SITTERSON, J. C., *The Secession Movement in North Carolina*, 204
SLICK, S. E., *William Trent and the West*, 70
SMALLEY, E. V., *History of the Northern Pacific Railroad*, 157
SMITH, A. E., *Colonists in Bondage*, 68
SMITH, C. F., *Charles Kendall Adams*, 38
SMITH, D. H., *The United States Civil Service Commission*, 249
SMITH, E. C., *The Borderland in the Civil War*, 209
SMITH, J. H., *Appeals to the Privy Council from the American Plantations*, 67
SMITH, T. C., *The Liberty and Free Soil Parties in the Northwest*, 201
— *The Wars between England and America*, 103

SMITH, W. R., *South Carolina as a Royal Province*, 66

SPAULDING, E. W., *New York in the Critical Period*, 105

SPECTOR, Margaret M., *The American Department of the British Government*, 67

SPEED, T., *The Union Cause in Kentucky*, 209

SPENCER, C. W., *Phases of Royal Government in New York*, 65

SPENCER, H. R., *Constitutional Conflict in Provincial Massachusetts*, 65

SPERO, S. D., and HARRIS, A. L., *The Black Worker*, 204

SPIEGEL, Käthe, *Kulturgeschichtliche Grundlagen der Amerikanischen Revolution*, 64, 102   [*System*, 243

SPRAGUE, O. M. W., *History of Crises under the National Banking*

STALEY, E., *History of the Illinois State Federation of Labor*, 248

STAMPP, K. M., *Indiana Politics during the Civil War*, 209

STAPLES, T. S., *Reconstruction in Arkansas*, 211

Statistical Atlas, 68, 148, 239

Statistical Review of Immigration, 1820-1910, 148

STEELE, M. F., *American Campaigns*, 207

STEEL-MAITLAND, A., *The New America*, 291

STEPHENS, G. W., *Some Aspects of Inter-sectional Rivalry for the Commerce of the Upper Mississippi Valley*, 153

STEPHENSON, G. M., *A History of American Immigration*, 149
     Political History of the Public Lands, 150   [ship', 39

STEPHENSON, W. H., 'A half century of Southern historical scholar-
— *Alexander Porter, Whig Planter of Old Louisiana*, 205
— 'Herbert B. Adams and southern historical scholarship at the Johns Hopkins University', 39
— 'John Spencer Bassett as a historian of the South', 39
— 'William P. Trent as a historian of the South', 40

STEVENS, F. W., *The Beginnings of the New York Central Railroad*, 155

STEVENS, G. A., *New York Typographical Union No. 6*, 248

STEVENS, W. E., *The Northwest Fur Trade*, 71

STEWART, F. M., *The National Civil Service Reform League*, 249

STILL, B., *Milwaukee*, 246

STILWELL, L. D., *Migration from Vermont*, 149

STIMSON, H. L., *The Far Eastern Crisis*, 289

STOCKTON, T. F., *The International Moulders' Union of North America*,

STONE, A. H., *Studies in the American Race Problem*, 204   [248

STOWELL, C. J., *Studies in Trade Unionism in the Custom Tailoring Trade*, 248

STRAKHOVSKY, L. I., *The Origins of American Intervention in North Russia, 1918*, 290

STREATER, F. B., *Political Parties in Michigan*, 158

STUCKEY, L., *The Iowa Federation of Labor*, 248

SULLIVAN, Kathryn, *Maryland and France*, 106

SUMMERS, F. P., *The Baltimore and Ohio in the Civil War*, 207
SURREY, Nancy M. M., *The Commerce of Louisiana during the French Régime*, 159
SUTHERLAND, Stella H., *Population Distribution in Colonial America*, 68
SWANEY, C. B., *Episcopal Methodism and Slavery*, 201
SWISHER, C. B., *American Constitutional Development*, 240, 286
— *Roger B. Taney*, 203, 240
SYDNOR, C. S., *The Development of Southern Sectionalism*, 203
— *Slavery in Mississippi*, 206
— 'The Southern experiment in writing social history', 40
— (ed.), *A Gentleman of the Old Natchez Region*, 205
SYRETT, H. C., *The City of Brooklyn*, 246

TANNER, E. P., *The Province of New Jersey*, 65
TANSILL, C. C., *America Goes to War*, 290
TARBELL, Ida M., *The History of the Standard Oil Company*, 244
— *The Life of Elbert H. Gary*, 244
TASCA, H. J., *The Reciprocal Trade Policy of the United States*, 292
TAUSSIG, F. W., *The Tariff History of the United States*, 200, 292
TAYLOR, A. A., *The Negro in South Carolina during Reconstruction*, 212
— *The Negro in Tennessee*, 212
TAYLOR, R. H., *Ante-Bellum South Carolina*, 199
— *The Free Negro in North Carolina*, 206
— *Slaveholding in North Carolina*, 206
Theory and Practice in Historical Study: a Report of the Committee on Historiography, 38, 200
THOMAS, H. C., *The Return of the Democratic Party to Power in 1884*,
THOMAS, M. E., *Nativism in the Old Northwest*, 201 [249
THOMPSON, C. Mildred, *Reconstruction in Georgia*, 211
THOMPSON, H., *From the Cottonfield to the Cotton Mill*, 245
THOMPSON, S. B., *Confederate Purchasing Operations Abroad*, 210
THOMPSON, W. S., and WHELPTON, P. K., *Population Trends in the United States*, 239
THORNTON, H. J., *The History of the Quaker Oats Company*, 245
THWAITES, R. G., *France in America, 1497-1763*, 63
TILDEN, A., *The Legislation of the Civil War Period considered as a Basis of the Agricultural Revolution in the United States*, 291
TILLEY, J. S., *Lincoln Takes Command*, 208
TILLEY, Nannie M., *The Bright-Tobacco Industry*, 244
TINKCOM, H. M., *The Republicans and Federalists in Pennsylvania*, 106
TRAVIS, I. D., *The History of the Clayton-Bulwer Treaty*, 288
TREAT, P. J., *Japan and the United States*, 289
— *Diplomatic Relations between the United States and Japan*, 289
— *The National Land System*, 150

22

TRENHOLME, Louise I., *The Ratification of the Federal Constitution in North*
TREVELYAN, G. O., *The American Revolution*, 99   [*Carolina*, 106
— *George III and C. J. Fox*, 99
TREXLER, H. A., *Slavery in Missouri*, 206
TRIMBLE, B. R., *Chief Justice Waite*, 240
TRIMBLE, W. J., *The Mining Advance into the Inland Empire*, 241
TROTTMAN, N., *History of the Union Pacific*, 157
TRUETT, R .B., *Trade and Travel around the Southern Appalachians before*
TURNER, E. R., *The Negro in Pennsylvania*, 205   [*1830*, 70
TURNER, F. J., *The Frontier in American History*, 20, 108, 148
— *The Rise of the New West, 1819-29*, 112, 148
TWISS, B. R., *Lawyers and the Constitution*, 240
TYLER, Alice F., *Freedom's Ferment*, 197
TYLER, M. C., *A History of American Literature*, 11, 102
— *The Literary History of the American Revolution*, 11, 102

U.S. BUREAU OF FOREIGN AND DOMESTIC COMMERCE, *One Hundred Years of American Immigration*, 148
The United States in the World Economy, 37, 291
UNITED STATES TARIFF COMMISSION, *Reciprocity and Commercial Treaties*,
UPTON, R. F., *Revolutionary New Hampshire*, 105   [292

VANDIVER, F. E., *Confederate Blockade running through Bermuda*, 210
VAN DER ZEE, J., *The British in Iowa*, 149
VAN DEUSEN, J. G., *The Ante-Bellum Southern Commercial Conventions*,
— *Economic Bases of Disunion in South Carolina*, 203   [203
VAN HISE, C. R., *Concentration and Control*, 243
— *The Conservation of Natural Resources in the United States*, 242
VAN TYNE, C. H., *England and America, Rivals in the American Revolu-*
— *The American Revolution*, 99   [*tion*, 103
— *The Causes of the War of Independence*, 99
— *The War of Independence. American Phase*, 99
VAN VLECK, G. W., *The Panic of 1857*, 201
VENABLE, W. H., *Beginnings of Literary Culture in the Ohio Valley*, 158
VERHOEFF, Mary, *The Kentucky Mountains*, 152
— *The Kentucky River Navigation*, 153   [*française*, 159
DE VILLIERS DU TERRAGE, M., *Les dernières années de la Louisiane*
VOGT, P. L., *The Sugar Refining Industry in the United States*, 244
VOLWILER, A. T., *George Croghan and the Westward Movement*, 70
VÖSSLER, O., *Die Amerikanischen Revolutionsideale in ihrem Verhältnis zu dem Europäischen*, 106

WABEKE, B. H., *Dutch Emigration to North America*, 150
WAGSTAFF, H. M., *State Rights and Political Parties in North Carolina*, 199
WALLACE, J., *The History of Illinois and Louisiana under French Rule*,
WALLACE, P. A. W., *Conrad Weiser*, 70   [159

WALSH, Correa M., *The Political Science of John Adams*, 101 [69

WALTON, J. S., *Conrad Weiser and the Indian Policy of Colonial Pennsylvania,*

WARD, G. W., *The Early Development of the Chesapeake and Ohio Canal Project*, 152

WARE, Caroline F., *The Early New England Cotton Manufacture*, 198

WARE, Edith E., *Political Opinion in Massachusetts during Civil War and Reconstruction*, 209

WARE, N. J., *The Industrial Worker*, 198
— *The Labor Movement in the United States*, 246

WARREN, C., *The Making of the Constitution*, 104
— *The Supreme Court in United States History*, 203

WASHBURNE, G. A., *Imperial Control of the Administration of Justice in the Thirteen American Colonies*, 67

WAY, W., jr., *The Clinchfield Railroad*, 156

WEBB, W. P., *The Great Plains*, 35, 240

WEBERG, F. P., *The Panic of 1893*, 243

WEBSTER, H. J., *History of the Democratic Party Organisation in the Northwest*, 158

WEBSTER, Laura J., *The Operation of the Freedman's Bureau in South*

WEEDEN, W. B., *Early Rhode Island*, 65 [*Carolina*, 211-12
— *Economic and Social History of New England*, 64-5
— *War Government, Federal and State, in Massachusetts, New York, Pennsylvania, and Indiana, 1861-1865*, 209

WEEKS, S. B., *Southern Quakers and Slavery*, 205

WEINBERG, A. K., *Manifest Destiny*, 240

WELLINGTON, R. G., *The Political and Sectional Influence of the Public*

WENDER, H., *Southern Commercial Conventions*, 203 [*Lands*, 150

WERTENBAKER, T. J., *Father Knickerbocker Rebels*, 105
— *Norfolk; Historic Southern Port*, 246

WESLEY, C. H., *Negro Labor in the United States*, 204

WESLEY, E. B., *Guarding the Frontier*, 161

WEST, R. S., jr., *Gideon Welles; Lincoln's Navy Department*, 208

WESTON, Florence, *The Presidential Election of 1828*, 200

WHARTON, V. L., *The Negro in Mississippi*, 212

WHITAKER, A. P., *The Mississippi Question*, 160
— *The Spanish-American Frontier*, 160

Autobiography of Andrew Dixon White, 38

WHITE, H. K., *History of the Union Pacific Railway*, 157

WHITE, Laura A., *Robert Barnwell Rhett; Father of Secession*, 204

WHITE, L. D., *The Federalists; a Study in Administrative History*, 104

WHITFIELD, T. M., *Slavery in Virginia*, 206

WHITFORD, N. E., *History of the Canal System of the State of New York,*

WHITNEY, J. L., *Justin Winsor*, 38 [153

WILDMAN, M. S., *Money Inflation in the United States*, 243

WILEY, B. I., *Southern Negroes*, 212
WILGUS, W. J., *The Role of Transportation in the Development of Vermont*,
WILLIAMS, B. H., *Economic Foreign Policy of the United States*, 291   [152
WILLIAMS, F. W., *Anson Burlingame and the First Chinese Mission to
     Foreign Powers*, 288
WILLIAMS, K. P., *Lincoln Finds a General*, 208-9
WILLIAMS, S. C., *Dawn of Tennessee Valley and Tennessee History*, 70,
     — *Tennessee during the Revolutionary War*, 160   [160
     — *History of the Lost State of Franklin*, 160-1
     — *The Beginnings of West Tennessee*, 161
WILLIAMS, T. H., *Lincoln and the Radicals*, 208
WILLIAMSON, A. S., *Credit Relations between Colonial and English
     Merchants in the Eighteenth Century*, 72, 101
WILLIAMSON, C., *Vermont in Quandary*, 65, 198
WILLOUGHBY, W. F., *Government Organization in Wartime and After*,
WILSON, H. F., *The Hill Country of Northern New England*, 199   [287
WILSON, Woodrow, *History of the American People*, 8
WINSOR, J., *Narrative and Critical History of America*, 6-7
     — *The Mississippi Basin*, 69
     — *The Westward Movement*, 69
WITTKE, C., *We Who Built America*, 149
     — (ed.), *The History of the State of Ohio*, 157
WOLFBEIN, S. L., *The Decline of a Cotton Textile City*, 246
WOLFE, J. H., *Jeffersonian Democracy in South Carolina*, 106
WOLMAN, L., *The Growth of American Trade Unions*, 246-7
WOOD, G. A., *William Shirley, Governor of Massachusetts*, 65
WOOD, W. B., and EDMONDS, J. E., *The Civil War in the United States*,
WOODBURN, J. A., *Causes of the American Revolution*, 103   [207
WOODSON, C. G., *The Education of the Negro prior to 1861*, 205
WOODWARD, C. Vann, *Tom Watson, Agrarian Rebel*, 242
WOODWORTH, J. V., *American Tool Making and Interchangeable Manu-
WOODY, C. H., *The Growth of Federal Government*, 286   [*facturing*, 244
WOOLLEY, E. C., *The Reconstruction of Georgia*, 211
WRIGHT, B. F., jr., *American Interpretations of Natural Law*, 102
     — *The Contract Clause of the Constitution*, 240
WRIGHT, J. M., *The Free Negro in Maryland*, 205-6

YELLEN, S., *American Labor Struggles*, 247
YOUNG, E., *Special Report on Immigration*, 148   [152
YOUNG, J. S., *A Political and Constitutional Study of the Cumberland Road*,

ZABRISKIE, E. H., *American-Russian Rivalry in the Far East*, 289
ZAHLER, Helene S., *Eastern Working Men and National Land Policy*,
ZEICHNER, O., *Connecticut's Years of Controversy*, 65   [151

INDEX

References in italics are to the Bibliographical Notes

Minnesota, Historical Society, 32
—, University of, 32
— *Minnesota History*, 32
Mississippi, state of, historical work
    on, 33, 145, *161*
— Department of Archives and His-
    tory, 34
— Historical Society, 34
— Historical Society *Publications*, 34
Mississippi valley, area of, 108; popula-
    tion of, 108, *148*
        First white penetration into, 50;
    French occupation of, 50, 51, 53;
    approaches to from mainland
    colonies, 51, 52, 53, 109–10;
    English advance into, 51, 52;
    Anglo-French rivalry in Ohio valley,
    50, 51, in lower Mississippi valley,
    51–2
        Capital investment in develop-
    ment of, 77, 134, 163, 165–6, 263
        Settlement of, 108–48, 220, 222–
    3, *240–2*; by settlers from south-east,
    110–11, 112–13, 123, 138, 142, 146,
    147; effect upon internal economy
    of North Atlantic states, 165–6,
    167–8; effect upon old South, 166–
    7, 168–70; attitude of South to-
    wards, 163, of Northeast, 111, 119–
    20, 163; change in course of, 112,
    119–20, 123–5, 139; effect of, upon
    balance of power, 111, 170–1,
    178, and upon attitude of older
    sections, 125, 129, 131–2, 163,
    164–5, 167, 169
        See also Lower Mississippi Valley;
    Middle Border; Old Northwest
Mississippi Valley Historical Associa-
    tion, 27, 34
Mississippi Valley Historical Review, 27
Missouri, historical activities in, 33;
    German settlements in, 122;
    Scandinavian settlements in, 122;
    situation in, 1854, 174; slavery in,
    187
Missouri Compromise, repeal of, 172–7
Mobile & Chicago Railroad, 134
Mobile & Ohio Railroad, 134
Mohawk river, 109, 118
Mohawk, valley of, 52
Molasses Act, 78–9
Mommsen, Theodore, 13
Monetary system of the United States,
    225–7, 236–7, *242–3*; New Deal
    and, 273; *see also* Currency

Monongahela river, 53, 113, 118
Monroe Doctrine, 258–60, 261, 263
Montana, 219, 220, 225
— State Historical Society, 35
Montreal, 125
Morrill Act, 142
Morris, Gouverneur, 91
Most-favoured-nation clause, 280–1
Munich, 10
Municipal history, *245–6*
Municipal reform, demand for, 236
Munster, emigration from, 121
Muskingum river, 116

Narrative histories, 7–8
Nashville, Tenn., 110
National Industrial Recovery Act, 273,
National Road, 110   [276
Nationalism, growth of, 213, 215–17,
    233–5, 255, 268
Natural resources, exploitation of,
    235–6, *241–2*
Nebraska, historical work on, 32, 142;
    land purchase in, 144–5; railroads
    in, 222
—, Territory of, 172
Negro, the, position of after emancipa-
    tion, 191, *211–12*; enfranchisement
    of, 193
Neutral rights, 192, 266
Nevada, 225
New colonies, plans for erection of, 56
New Deal, the, 234, 235, 272–7, 283,
    284–5, *291*
New England, changes in, 166, 167;
    emigration from, 119 123, 138, 139,
    140, *149*; contribution of to popula-
    tion of up-state New York and
    Pennsylvania, 119; Illinois, 120,
    Indiana, 120, Michigan, 119, 120,
    Ohio, 119, 141, Wisconsin, 119;
    West India trade of, 80
*New England Historical and Genealogical
    Register*, 26
New Hampshire Historical Society, 25
New Mexico, 221
New Orleans, 116, 118, 119, 123, 125,
New River, 110   [219
New York, port of, 110, 125; West
    India trade of, 80
— Historical Society, 25
— state, Scandinavian settlements in,
    122; emigration from, 120, 138;
    New England migration into, 109,
    119, 123, 138

Map 1

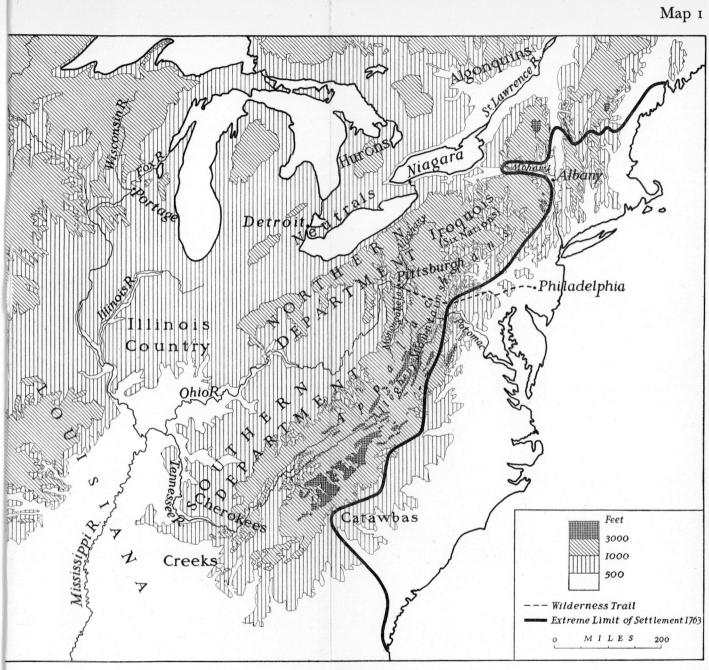

Algonquins

St.Lawrence R.

Wisconsin R.

Fox R.

Portage

Hurons

Niagara

Mohawk

Albany

Detroit

Neutrals

NORTHERN

Illinois R.

Iroquois

[Six Nations]

DEPARTMENT

Pittsburgh

Philadelphia

Illinois
Country

LOUISIANA

Monongahela R.

Potomac

Ohio R.

SOUTHERN

Appalachian Mts.

Tennessee R.

Cherokees

Catawbas

DEPARTMENT

Creeks

Mississippi R.

Feet	
	3000
	1000
	500

– – – Wilderness Trail

━━━ Extreme Limit of Settlement 1763

0   M I L E S   200

The Back Lands in the Eighteenth Century